THE CONSTITUTIONAL CONVENTION OF 1787

Recent Titles in the Guides to Historical Events in America
Randall M. Miller, Series Editor

McCarthyism and the Red Scare: A Reference Guide
William T. Walker

The Underground Railroad: A Reference Guide
Kerry Walters

Lincoln, the Rise of the Republicans, and the Coming of the Civil War: A Reference Guide
Kerry Walters

America in the Cold War: A Reference Guide
William T. Walker

Andrew Jackson and the Rise of the Democrats: A Reference Guide
Mark R. Cheathem

The Progressive Era: A Reference Guide
Francis J. Sicius

Reconstruction: A Reference Guide
Paul E. Teed and Melissa Ladd Teed

The War for American Independence: A Reference Guide
Mark Edward Lender

The Constitutional Convention of 1787

A Reference Guide

Stuart Leibiger

Guides to Historic Events in America
Randall M. Miller, Series Editor

BLOOMSBURY ACADEMIC
NEW YORK • LONDON • OXFORD • NEW DELHI • SYDNEY

BLOOMSBURY ACADEMIC
Bloomsbury Publishing Inc
1385 Broadway, New York, NY 10018, USA
50 Bedford Square, London, WC1B 3DP, UK
29 Earlsfort Terrace, Dublin 2, Ireland

BLOOMSBURY, BLOOMSBURY ACADEMIC and the Diana logo
are trademarks of Bloomsbury Publishing Plc

First published in the United States of America by ABC-CLIO 2019
Paperback edition published by Bloomsbury Academic 2024

Copyright © Bloomsbury Publishing Inc, 2024

Cover photo: The Constitution of the United States. (National Archive)

All rights reserved. No part of this publication may be reproduced or
transmitted in any form or by any means, electronic or mechanical,
including photocopying, recording, or any information storage or retrieval
system, without prior permission in writing from the publishers.

Bloomsbury Publishing Inc does not have any control over, or responsibility for,
any third-party websites referred to or in this book. All internet addresses given
in this book were correct at the time of going to press. The author and publisher
regret any inconvenience caused if addresses have changed or sites have
ceased to exist, but can accept no responsibility for any such changes.

A catalog record for this book is available from the Library of Congress.

ISBN: HB: 978-1-4408-6296-0
      PB: 979-8-7651-2024-8
      ePDF: 978-1-4408-6297-7
      eBook: 979-8-2160-6528-9

Series: Guides to Historic Events in America

To find out more about our authors and books visit www.bloomsbury.com
and sign up for our newsletters.

For My Mother

Gisela W. Leibiger

"The Grand Convention—
may they form a Constitution
for an eternal Republic"

Toast
Society of the Cincinnati Celebration
Trenton, New Jersey
July 4, 1787

Contents

List of Illustrations	xi
Series Foreword	xv
Preface: A System to Last for Ages	xvii
Delegates to the Constitutional Convention	xxv
Speeches, Motions, and Committee Assignments in the Constitutional Convention	xxvii
Chronology	xxxi

Chapter 1.	The Road to Philadelphia	1
Chapter 2.	The Triumph of the Virginia Plan	45
Chapter 3.	The Great Compromise	89
Chapter 4.	Ironing Out the Details	127
Chapter 5.	The Executive, the Judiciary, Postponed Parts, and the Signing	159
Chapter 6.	Ratification of the Constitution and the Bill of Rights	199

Conclusion	237
Biographical Essays	239
John Dickinson (1732–1808)	239
Benjamin Franklin (1706–1790)	240

Elbridge Gerry (1744–1814) — 241

Alexander Hamilton (1757–1804) — 242

Rufus King (1755–1827) — 243

James Madison (1751–1836) — 244

George Mason (1725–1792) — 245

Gouverneur Morris (1752–1816) — 245

Edmund Randolph (1753–1813) — 246

Roger Sherman (1721–1793) — 247

George Washington (1732–1799) — 248

James Wilson (1742–1798) — 249

Primary Documents — **251**

1. Annapolis Convention Report, September 14, 1786 — 251

2. Virginia Appoints Delegates to the Constitutional Convention, November–December, 1786 — 254

3. The Confederation Congress's Resolution Approving the Constitutional Convention, February 21, 1787 — 256

4. James Madison to George Washington, April 16, 1787 — 257

5. The Virginia Plan, May 29, 1787 — 261

6. The New Jersey Plan, June 15, 1787 — 264

7. Alexander Hamilton's Plan of Government, June 18, 1787 — 266

8. Benjamin Franklin's Speech, September 17, 1787 — 268

9. Cover Letter Transmitting the Constitution to the Confederation Congress, September 17, 1787 — 271

10. The Confederation Congress's Resolution Transmitting the Constitution to the State Legislatures, September 28, 1787	272
11. James Wilson's State House Yard Speech, October 6, 1787	273
12. George Mason's Objections to This Constitution of Government, October 7, 1787	279
13. Brutus I, October 18, 1787	281
14. Amendments Recommended by the Massachusetts Ratification Convention, February 6, 1788	292
15. *The Federalist*, Number 51, February 8, 1788	295
Bibliographical Essay	301
Index	307

List of Illustrations

Known as the "Father of the Constitution," James Madison of Virginia drafted the Virginia Plan and took detailed notes of the debates at the Constitutional Convention.   12

George Washington resided at his beloved Mount Vernon plantation on the Potomac River in Virginia, where he practiced scientific farming and landscape design. The Mount Vernon Conference, the precursor to the Annapolis and Philadelphia conventions, met here in March 1785.   17

This statue of "Reluctant Statesman" George Mason of Virginia is part of the George Mason Memorial on the Mall in Washington, D.C. Mason sat on the Grand Committee of Eleven that proposed the Great Compromise. He later refused to sign the completed Constitution because he believed that it would allow the North to dominate the South and that it would lead to monarchy or aristocracy.   19

This broadside offers a reward for the capture of Daniel Shays, namesake of Shays's Rebellion in Massachusetts. Shays had received a sword made of gold from the Marquis de Lafayette in honor of his military service during the Revolutionary War. Shays fled to Vermont, an independent republic, to avoid apprehension and later settled in New York.   29

Engraving by W. Birch of the Pennsylvania State House in Philadelphia as it looked during the Constitutional Convention. The convention met from May 25 to September 17, 1787, in the Assembly Room of the State House. The Pennsylvania ratification convention later met in the same location. Today the building is known as Independence Hall. 47

Engraving of a portrait of George Washington painted by Charles Willson Peale while Washington was in Philadelphia for the Constitutional Convention. Unanimously elected president of the convention, Washington delivered only two short speeches during the gathering. Anticipating that he would be elected the first president under the Constitution, the delegates designed a strong and independent executive branch with him in mind. 61

Edmund Randolph of Virginia presented the Virginia Plan to the Constitutional Convention. He later refused to sign the completed Constitution because he wished to allow the states to propose amendments to be considered by a second constitutional convention. 65

At age eighty-one, Benjamin Franklin of Pennsylvania was the oldest delegate present at the convention. Although he offered undistinguished policy proposals, he played a major role as an advocate for compromise. His speech on the convention's last day urged the delegates to overcome their doubts and sign the Constitution. 81

William Paterson of New Jersey, a chief spokesman for the small states, presented the New Jersey Plan to the convention in June as an alternative to the Virginia Plan. After the passage of the Great Compromise, he advocated a strong federal government. 91

In June, Alexander Hamilton of New York gave a lengthy speech calling for a powerful federal government with a president and senate that served during good behavior. After being outvoted by his antinationalist colleagues from New York in the early weeks of the convention, Hamilton went home. He returned in time to be the lone signer from his state. 96

List of Illustrations

Although Roger Sherman of Connecticut attended the Constitutional Convention as a last-minute substitute, he became one of the most important delegates. Sherman advocated the Great Compromise over representation in Congress that broke the deadlock between the large and small states.	101
Major William Jackson, the secretary of the Constitutional Convention, kept a journal of the delegates' motions and votes. This journal entry for July 16, 1787, records the vote that approved the Great Compromise.	121
James Wilson of Pennsylvania spoke more times at the convention than any other delegate. An advocate of popular sovereignty, he favored election of the president by the people. He served on the Committee of Detail that prepared the first draft of the Constitution.	129
John Rutledge of South Carolina chaired the Committee of Detail that prepared the first draft of the Constitution. This draft enumerated the powers of Congress and included tremendous protections for the institution of slavery.	135
Gouverneur Morris of Pennsylvania spoke eloquently against the institution of slavery at the Constitutional Convention. A member of the Committee of Style, he drafted the final version of the Constitution, as well as the accompanying cover letter to the Confederation Congress.	141
John Dickinson of Delaware became the first delegate to propose what eventually became the Great Compromise, which based representation in the House of Representatives on population and granted the states equal representation in the Senate. Dickinson also served on the Committee on Postponed Parts that redesigned the presidency in September.	163
Elbridge Gerry of Massachusetts chaired the Grand Committee of Eleven that proposed the Great Compromise. He later refused to sign the completed Constitution because he thought the federal government had been given too much power, especially to create a permanent military establishment.	175

This 1788 political cartoon captures the drama of ratification by depicting the hand of God reaching out of the clouds to erect the Massachusetts pillar in the "Grand Federal Edifice." Each time another state ratified the Constitution, newspapers issued an updated version of this cartoon.   201

The title page of *The Federalist*, a series of essays written by Alexander Hamilton, James Madison, and John Jay to promote the ratification of the Constitution in New York. Prepared in response to the Antifederalist "Brutus" essays probably written by Melancton Smith, *The Federalist* is perhaps the best exposition of the Constitution ever written.   210

A procession celebrating New York's 1788 ratification of the Constitution. The banner on the "Ship of State" float honors Alexander Hamilton's efforts in the Constitutional Convention and at the state ratification convention.   222

Series Foreword

Perhaps no people have been more difficult to comprehend than the Americans. As J. Hector St. Jean de Crèvecoeur asked during the American Revolution, countless others have echoed ever after—"What then is this American, this new man?" What, indeed? Americans then and after have been, and remain, a people in the process of becoming. They have been, and are, a people in motion, whether coming from a distant shore, crossing the mighty Mississippi, or packing off to the suburbs, and all the while following the promise of an American dream of realizing life, liberty, and happiness. The directions of such movement have changed, and sometimes the trajectory has taken a downward arc in terms of civil war and economic depression, but always the process has continued.

Making sense of that American experience demands attention to critical moments—events—that reflected and affected American ideas and identities. Although Americans have constructed an almost linear narrative of progress from the days of George Washington to today in relating their common history, they also have marked that history by recognizing particular events as pivotal in explaining who and why they believed and acted as they did at particular times and over time. Such events have forced Americans to consider closely their true interests. They also have challenged their commitment to professed beliefs of freedom and liberty, equality and opportunity, tolerance and generosity. Whether fighting for independence or empire, drafting and implementing a frame of government, reconstructing a nation divided by civil war, struggling for basic rights and the franchise, creating a mass-mediated culture, standing up for capitalism and democracy and against communism, to name several critical developments, Americans have understood that historic events are more than just moments. They are processes of change made clear through particular events but not bound to a single moment or instance. Such thinking about the character and consequence of American history informs this new series of *Guides to Historic Events in America*.

Drawing on the latest and best literature, and bringing together narrative overviews and critical chapters of important historic events, the books in the series function as both reference guides and informed analyses to critical events that have shaped American life, culture, society, economy, and politics and fixed America's place in the world. The books do not promise a comprehensive reading and rendering of American history. Such is not yet, if ever, possible for any single work or series. Nor do they chart a single interpretive line, though they share common concerns and methods of inquiry. Each book stands alone, resting on the expertise of the author and the strength of the evidence. At the same time, taken together the books in this new series will provide a dynamic portrait of that ongoing work in progress, America itself.

Each book follows a common format, with a chronology, historical overview, topical chapters on aspects of the historical event under examination, a set of biographies of key figures, selected essential primary documents, and an annotated bibliography. As such, each book holds many uses for students, teachers, and the general public wanting and needing to know the principal issues and the pertinent arguments and evidence on significant events in American history. The combination of historical description and analysis, biographies, and primary documents also moves readers to approach each critical event from multiple perspectives and with a critical eye. Each book in its structure and content invites students and teachers, in and out of the classroom, to consider and debate the character and consequence(s) of the historic event in question. Such debate invariably will bring readers back to that most critical and never-ending question of what was/is "the American" and what does, and must, "America" mean.

Randall M. Miller
Saint Joseph's University, Philadelphia

PREFACE
A SYSTEM TO LAST FOR AGES

The fifty-five men who gathered at the Pennsylvania State House in Philadelphia during the spring and summer of 1787 wrote a new constitution for the United States of America. Their motive was to revise or replace the failing Confederation with a more effective republican government capable of keeping the thirteen states united in a single Union for decades, if not centuries, to come. As James Madison put it, they hoped to design "a system" of government "to last for ages." The key to success would be devising a framework that allowed the majority to rule but that protected the rights of minorities. It would be a challenge to create a stronger central government so soon after overthrowing the strong central government of Great Britain.[1]

The convention participants expressed admiration for one another. Eighty-one-year-old Benjamin Franklin described the gathering as *une assemble des notables.* George Mason, the author of Virginia's 1776 Declaration of Rights, pronounced his fellow attendees "men of fine republican principles. America has certainly, upon this occasion, drawn forth her first characters; there are upon this Convention many gentlemen of the most respectable abilities, and so far as I can discover, of the purest intentions." James Madison, too, characterized the delegates as "the most respectable characters," while William Samuel Johnson of Connecticut declared them as "the most able men in America." From Paris, Thomas Jefferson agreed with this consensus, glowingly proclaiming the convention "an assembly of demigods." Ezra Stiles, the president of Yale College, judged the delegates to be "some of the most sensible and great characters in America."[2]

The convention featured some of the most brilliant men in America, including James Madison, Alexander Hamilton, George Washington, Benjamin Franklin, James Wilson, and Gouverneur Morris. But many (perhaps most) of the delegates possessed more ordinary abilities, as evidenced by the fact that only about one-third of them actively participated in the debates. It is also true that many of the nation's most brilliant minds did not attend: Thomas Jefferson, John Adams, Patrick Henry, John Jay, Richard Henry Lee, and George Clinton. It would have been difficult, if not impossible, however, to bring more talent together in one room at one time in eighteenth-century America than those who assembled in the Pennsylvania State House during the spring and summer of 1787. In James Madison's opinion, the convention "may be said to be the best contribution of talents the States could make," while Franklin considered it "the most august and respectable Assembly he ever was in his life."[3]

"The eyes and hopes of all are turned towards this new assembly," to save "the cause of republican liberty," explained Madison. Mason agreed that "the eyes of the United States are turned upon this assembly, and their expectations raised to a very anxious degree" in hopes that the convention would establish "a wise and just government." Did anything besides a desire to preserve republicanism motivate these men to travel great distances and give up their summer to participate in a convention for which they received only modest compensation from their states?[4]

The delegates (mostly middle aged, college-educated lawyers, planters, merchants, and former army officers) were all wealthy white men who harbored attitudes typical of their class. They were deeply troubled by the passage of state laws creating inflationary paper currencies and other measures that provided relief to debtors but that also made it harder for creditors to collect debts. Viewing such enactments as examples of majority tyranny against the wealthy, they hoped to shift power to a stronger federal government that would prevent the states from passing pro-debtor legislation of this sort.

But to argue, as historian Charles Beard did in the early twentieth century, that the delegates acted as a monolithic group exclusively to protect the economic interests of the rich is an oversimplification. The participants certainly safeguarded property rights, but they aimed to benefit all free Americans, not just the wealthy. While affluent, the delegates came from a variety of professions and geographic regions of the country whose economic interests often clashed with one another. Northern merchants and southern planters, for example, disagreed over a variety of economic issues, such as duties on both imports and exports.[5]

The positions of the delegates were shaped not only by their desire to preserve republicanism and protect their class interests, but also by their individual temperaments and life experiences. Former Continental Army officers like Washington and Hamilton, who had witnessed how a weak central government had hampered the war effort, became strong nationalists. Madison, who as a member of the Virginia legislature deplored how popular majorities trampled the rights of religious and propertied minorities, wanted Congress to be able to veto state laws. Those like Elbridge Gerry of Massachusetts, who experienced Shays's Rebellion firsthand, distrusted placing too much power directly in the hands of the people. Wilson of Pennsylvania, in contrast, who grew up in an egalitarian community in Scotland and who read Scottish Common Sense Philosophy, favored popular sovereignty.

The delegates pursued the interests not only of their nation and their class, but also of their specific states. These men had to secure benefits for their constituents to ensure that their states would ratify the new constitution. The Lower South, for example, sought to protect the institution of slavery, while delegates from northern states pursued favorable commercial policies. The result was a summer filled with disagreements, clashes, compromises, and accommodations. None of the delegates came away from the convention completely happy with the final constitution, but all but three of them emerged satisfied enough to support its ratification. They knew they had not designed a perfect constitution but believed that their creation was a vast improvement on the existing Articles of Confederation. They felt confident that they had drawn up a government that would help both their country and their states grow and prosper. Interestingly, the convention's eclectic handiwork did not contain a single provision that had not already appeared in the state constitutions, the state bills of rights, and the Articles of Confederation. But the mixture was new.

In writing this book, I have aimed for a relatively short (about 250 pages, excluding the Biographical Essays and Primary Documents), scholarly history of the 1787 Constitutional Convention. Many books on the convention use a topical approach, analyzing in turn the struggles such as those between the North and the South and between the large states and small states. When lecturing on the convention to undergraduates, I use the topical approach myself, because it is well organized and tidy. The problem with the topical approach is that it is too neat and tidy, thereby obscuring the complexity and messiness that characterized the convention. The Constitution's various provisions were not reached in isolation. Instead they were debated simultaneously and influenced each other. In this volume, I have for the most part used a chronological narrative format to capture that complexity, messiness, and unfolding daily drama behind the writing of the U.S. Constitution, as well as the role of contingency in that process. Based largely on primary sources, my account of the convention weighs in on some of the historiographical debates, large and small, that have taken place among scholars about the convention. It also seeks to be more factually accurate than many of the other histories of the convention.[6]

Chapter 1 examines the national and state issues that led to the calling of the Constitutional Convention. It also traces the events leading up to the convention, including the Annapolis convention and Shays's Rebellion. I tell the story of the Mount Vernon Conference, an early link in the chain of events that resulted in the Philadelphia convention, an episode that most other studies neglect.[7] This chapter argues that the Confederation's inability to solve pressing problems at both the national and state levels produced a consensus on the need for political reform that led to the convention. The fifty-five delegates who met in Philadelphia believed that the convention offered the last chance to save both a republican government and the Union of the states.

Chapter 2 chronicles events from the opening of the convention on May 25, 1787, to mid-June. During this interval the delegates appointed a president and secretary, adopted rules, and began debating the Virginia Plan. This proposal called for an entirely new national government with executive, legislative, and judicial branches that operated on the people directly without the states as intermediaries. After three weeks the Virginia Plan emerged triumphant thanks to a coalition consisting of big states (who favored basing legislative representation on state population) and Lower South states (who favored counting slaves as three-fifths of free people toward representation in both houses of congress).

Chapter 3 looks at the New Jersey Plan, the small-state counterattack against the Virginia Plan. This proposal, consisting of amendments to strengthen the existing Confederation, suffered defeat but produced a long deadlock that threatened to break up the convention. Eventually, the small states forced the large states to accept the Great Compromise of July 16, 1787, that provided for a lower legislative house based on population and an upper legislative house in which each state had two senators. Even though the New Jersey Plan failed, the small states got what they wanted: state equality in one house of a bicameral legislature.

Chapter 4 analyzes the first draft of the Constitution prepared by the Committee of Detail, presented to the convention in early August. This version for the first time enumerated the powers of congress. It also included dramatic new protections for the institution of slavery. For the remainder of the month, the delegates hammered out the details of the new framework. They accepted an enumeration of legislative powers but scaled back the protections of slavery, for example by allowing congress to close the African slave trade after twenty years.

Chapter 5 narrates the creation of the executive and judicial branches. While this chapter is topical in that it discusses the entire evolution of these two branches, it presents each of these stories in chronological narrative format. The creation of the presidency, more than any other issue, illustrates the complexity and messiness of the convention. The debates over the presidency went in circles, because a change in one aspect of the office (such as whether congress or the people would elect the president) necessitated changes in other areas (such as how long of a term the president would serve). The convention eventually adopted a strong, independent executive indirectly elected by the people through an electoral college. This chapter also covers the drafting of the final version of the Constitution by the Committee of Style, and the signing of the completed document on September 17. The states represented in Philadelphia unanimously supported the Constitution, but three delegates refused to sign it.

Chapter 6 covers the ratification of the Constitution and the adoption of the Bill of Rights. Ratification, a sophisticated national, state, and local debate, was decided by thirteen separate contests in thirteen separate states. In each state, the specific issues differed, but the essential question in each state remained whether the Constitution would improve or worsen the lives of its citizens. The Antifederalist opponents of the

Constitution warned that eventually power would consolidate in the federal government, resulting in a tyranny. The Federalist supporters of the Constitution secured ratification not only based on the strength of their arguments, but also through skillful politicking. In addition, they possessed significant advantages, such as the backing of most of the nation's newspapers and the support of George Washington and Benjamin Franklin, America's most influential men. Turning point moments included Massachusetts's ratification with recommendatory amendments, and New York's ratification after the approvals of ten other states convinced the Antifederalists there to give in. In 1789, James Madison authored the Bill of Rights and pushed it through the First Federal Congress. Madison acted to reassure Antifederalists, to preclude structural amendments that would have weakened the powers of federal government, and to improve the Constitution by better protecting rights. The ratification of the Bill of Rights by the states in 1791 diminished opposition to the Constitution and solidified its political legitimacy.

I have included minimal biographical information about the convention delegates in the main text, although I have quoted firsthand descriptions of many of them. Brief sketches of the lives of twelve of the most prominent delegates may be found in the Biographical Essays section. The Primary Documents section does not include the Articles of Confederation, the U.S. Constitution, or the Bill of Rights because these documents are readily available in print or digital form. Instead, the Primary Documents section contains fifteen instructive but less well-known sources on the framing and ratification of the Constitution.

In quoting from primary sources, I have not modernized spelling or punctuation. Nor have I capitalized the words *constitution*, *senate*, *house of representatives*, and *congress* until late in the book, when the Constitutional Convention completed drafting the U.S. Constitution.

This book, two years in the making, would not have been possible without the assistance of many people. I would like to recognize those who helped me the most. Randall M. Miller, the editor of the *Guides to Historic Events in America* series, who recruited me to write this volume, provided encouragement and valuable feedback on both my proposal and manuscript. Michael Millman, my editor at ABC-CLIO Publishers, arranged a convenient timetable for me to complete the book; Erin

Ryan of ABC-CLIO researched and located the illustrations; and Sivakumar Vijayaraghavan, copy editor, carefully read and improved the manuscript. John P. Kaminski, director of the Center for the Study of the American Constitution at the University of Wisconsin (CSAC), read the manuscript. John caught numerous errors, provided suggestions on what to include and what to leave out, and improved my writing in countless ways. Timothy D. Moore, deputy director of CSAC, also read the manuscript, offered many valuable comments for revision, and pointed out useful primary sources. It has been my pleasure to teach with John and Tim in CSAC's Summer Teacher Institutes in Madison, Wisconsin, for the past five years. I gained many insights on the framing and ratification of the Constitution from teaching with them. La Salle University generously awarded me a sabbatical during the 2017–2018 academic year, followed by a leave during the Fall 2018 semester, so that I could research and write this book. Graduate student assistant Juliana Mastrangelo tabulated attendance statistics on the delegates to the Constitutional Convention.

I would like to thank my wife, Jennifer T. Leibiger, and my children, Ethan and Laura, for providing love, diversion, and respite. This book is dedicated to my mother, Gisela W. Leibiger, who turned ninety years old in 2019, for her love, encouragement, and support throughout my life.

NOTES

1. Adrienne Koch, ed., *Notes of Debates in the Federal Convention of 1787 Reported by James Madison* (Athens: Ohio University Press, 1966), hereafter cited as *NDFC*, 194. The delegates, many of whom were slaveholders, did not include African Americans in their definition of minorities. To them minorities meant free whites whose religious or property interests were in jeopardy.

2. Max Farrand, ed., *The Records of the Federal Convention of 1787*. 1937 rev. ed. in four vols., reprint (New Haven, CT: Yale University Press, 1974), hereafter cited as *RFC*, 3:21, 32, 36, 49, 76; Mark David Hall, *Roger Sherman and the Creation of the American Republic* (New York: Oxford University Press, 2013), 118.

3. *RFC*, 33, 37.

4. Ibid., 32, 37.

5. Charles Beard, *An Economic Interpretation of the Constitution of the United States* (New York: Macmillan, 1913).

6. Michael Klarman, *The Framers' Coup: The Making of the United States Constitution* (New York: Oxford University Press, 2016), and Christopher Collier and James Lincoln Collier, *Decision in Philadelphia: The Constitutional Convention of 1787* (New York: Ballantine Books, 1987), use a topical format to analyze the convention.

7. For example, Klarman's *The Framers' Coup*, an 865-page book, does not discuss the Mount Vernon Conference.

Delegates to the Constitutional Convention

Connecticut
Oliver Ellsworth
William Samuel Johnson
Roger Sherman

Delaware
Richard Bassett
Gunning Bedford
Jacob Broom
John Dickinson
George Read

Georgia
Abraham Baldwin
William Few
William Houstoun
William Pierce

Maryland
Daniel Carroll
Daniel of St. Thomas Jenifer
Luther Martin
James McHenry
John Francis Mercer

Massachusetts
Elbridge Gerry
Nathaniel Gorham
Rufus King
Caleb Strong

New York
Alexander Hamilton
John Lansing
Robert Yates

New Jersey
David Brearley
Jonathan Dayton
William Churchill Houston
William Livingston
William Paterson

North Carolina
William Blount
William R. Davie
Alexander Martin
Richard Dobbs Spaight
Hugh Williamson

Pennsylvania
George Clymer
Thomas Fitzsimons
Benjamin Franklin
Jared Ingersoll
Thomas Mifflin
Gouverneur Morris
Robert Morris
James Wilson

New Hampshire
Nicholas Gilman
John Langdon

Virginia
John Blair
James McClurg
James Madison
George Mason
Edmund Randolph
George Washington
George Wythe

South Carolina
Pierce Butler
Charles Pinckney
Charles Cotesworth Pinckney
John Rutledge

Speeches, Motions, and Committee Assignments in the Constitutional Convention

(Compiled by John P. Kaminski and Michael E. Stevens, Printed by Permission)

Delegate, State	Speeches	Motions	Committees
1. James Wilson, Pennsylvania	172	49	2
2. Gouverneur Morris, Pennsylvania	171	78	4
3. James Madison, Virginia	167	72	4
4. Roger Sherman, Connecticut	131	46	4
5. George Mason, Virginia	127	36	4
6. Elbridge Gerry, Massachusetts	113	55	1
7. Edmund Randolph, Virginia	79	44	3
8. Rufus King, Massachusetts	78	22	6
9. Hugh Williamson, North Carolina	77	35	5
10. Charles Pinckney, South Carolina	74	58	1
11. Oliver Ellsworth, Connecticut	72	28	2
12. Nathaniel Gorham, Massachusetts	69	12	4
13. John Rutledge, South Carolina	52	38	5

14. Pierce Butler, South Carolina	52	23	2
15. John Dickinson, Delaware	47	21	4
16. Luther Martin, Maryland	38	23	2
17. Charles Cotesworth Pinckney, South Carolina	34	20	2
18. Benjamin Franklin, Pennsylvania	27	13	2
19. George Read, Delaware	26	12	2
20. Alexander Hamilton, New York	25	11	2
21. John Langdon, New Hampshire	25	4	3
22. Daniel Carroll, Maryland	23	17	3
23. John Francis Mercer, Maryland	20	4	0
24. William Samuel Johnson, Connecticut	16	7	4
25. William Paterson, New Jersey	12	5	1
26. Jonathan Dayton, New Jersey	12	7	1
27. Gunning Bedford, Jr., Delaware	10	3	1
28. Caleb Strong, Massachusetts	9	3	0
29. Abraham Baldwin, Georgia	8	2	4
30. George Clymer, Pennsylvania	7	2	2
31. David Brearley, New Jersey	6	4	2
32. Jacob Broom, Delaware	5	11	0
33. William R. Davie, North Carolina	5	2	1
34. James McHenry, Maryland	5	7	1
35. Thomas FitzSimons, Pennsylvania	5	2	1
36. Richard Dobbs Spaight, North Carolina	4	13	0
37. John Lansing, Jr., New York	4	3	0
38. Daniel of St. Thomas Jenifer, Maryland	4	2	0
39. George Wythe, Virginia	4	0	1
40. William Houstoun, Georgia	3	6	1
41. James McClurg, Virginia	3	2	0
42. William Pierce, Georgia	3	1	0
43. George Washington, Virginia	2	0	0

44. Jared Ingersoll, Pennsylvania	2	0	0
45. William Livingston, New Jersey	2	0	3
46. Robert Morris, Pennsylvania	1	2	0
47. William Blount, North Carolina	1	0	0
48. William Few, Georgia	0	0	1
49. Nicholas Gilman, New Hampshire	0	0	1
50. Alexander Martin, North Carolina	0	3	0
51. Thomas Mifflin, Pennsylvania	0	1	0
52. Robert Yates, New York	0	0	2
53. Richard Bassett, Delaware	0	0	0
54. William Churchill Houston, New Jersey	0	0	0
55. John Blair, Virginia	0	0	0

Total number of speeches, 1,832.

Chronology

1777

November 15 — Articles of Confederation is approved by the Continental Congress.

1781

March 1 — Articles of Confederation is ratified.

1785

March 24–28 — Mount Vernon conference meets.

1786

January 21 — Virginia calls a meeting of states to consider granting Congress power to regulate commerce.

September 11–14 — Annapolis convention meets.

November 23 — Virginia becomes the first state to authorize the election of delegates to the Constitutional Convention.

1787

February 21 — Confederation Congress approves Constitutional Convention.

May 14 — Constitutional Convention meets but quorum not present.

May 25 — Constitutional Convention opens and elects George Washington convention president.

May 29 — Edmund Randolph introduces the Virginia Plan.

June 15	William Paterson introduces the New Jersey Plan.
June 19	New Jersey Plan is defeated.
July 2	Constitutional Convention appoints Grand Committee of Eleven to address conflict over legislative representation.
July 6	Grand Committee of Eleven reports to the convention.
July 13	Confederation Congress adopts the Northwest Ordinance.
July 16	Constitutional Convention approves the Great Compromise.
July 17	Constitutional Convention rejects congressional veto of state laws that conflict with the constitution or federal treaties.
July 23	Constitutional Convention appoints Committee of Detail.
August 6	Committee of Detail presents a draft constitution to the convention.
August 25	Constitutional Convention allows slave trade to remain open at least until 1808.
August 29	Constitutional Convention agrees to fugitive slave clause and to allow a bare majority of congress to pass commercial laws.
August 31	Constitutional Convention appoints Committee on Postponed Parts.
September 4	Committee on Postponed Parts proposes changes to the executive branch.
September 6	Constitutional Convention approves changes to the executive branch.
September 8	Constitutional Convention appoints Committee of Style.
September 12	Committee of Style presents the final draft of the constitution to the convention.
September 17	Constitutional Convention signs the Constitution and adjourns.
September 28	Confederation Congress transmits Constitution to the states.
December 7	Delaware convention ratifies the Constitution.

Chronology

December 12	Pennsylvania convention ratifies the Constitution.
December 18	New Jersey convention ratifies the Constitution.
December 31	Georgia convention ratifies the Constitution.

1788

January 9	Connecticut convention ratifies the Constitution.
February 6	Massachusetts convention ratifies the Constitution.
February 22	First session of New Hampshire convention adjourns.
March 24	Rhode Island referendum rejects Constitution.
April 26	Maryland convention ratifies the Constitution.
May 23	South Carolina convention ratifies the Constitution.
June 21	Second session of New Hampshire convention ratifies the Constitution.
June 25	Virginia convention ratifies the Constitution.
July 26	New York convention ratifies the Constitution.
August 2	First North Carolina convention rejects the Constitution.
September 13	Confederation Congress sets dates and procedures for the First Federal Elections and the meeting of the First Federal Congress.

1789

April 6	First Federal Congress attains quorum.
April 30	George Washington is inaugurated president.
June 8	James Madison delivers a speech in Congress calling for a Bill of Rights.
September 28	Congress approves twelve amendment proposals.
November 21	Second North Carolina convention ratifies the Constitution.

1790

May 29	Rhode Island convention ratifies the Constitution.

1791

December 15	Bill of Rights is ratified.

CHAPTER 1

THE ROAD TO PHILADELPHIA

When Americans declared their independence in 1776, they had to decide what kind of government should replace the British monarchy. Reacting against the executive tyranny of King George III, Americans not surprisingly adopted a confederation, with a weak central government consisting of a Congress unable to tax or regulate commerce, and state governments that possessed all authority not expressly delegated to Congress. The state governments, unlike the central government, generally consisted of executive, legislative, and judicial branches, but they were not co-equal. Instead excessively powerful assemblies dominated most state governments. These unchecked legislatures, much to Americans' surprise, engaged in tyranny of the majority. Meanwhile, the feeble Confederation Congress proved unable to solve pressing national problems, including paying the Revolutionary War debt, opening the Mississippi River to American navigation, and evicting British troops from the Northwest Territory by the Great Lakes.

These dual state and national problems convinced men like George Washington, Alexander Hamilton, and James Madison that the Confederation needed to be scrapped in favor of a stronger federal government that operated directly on the people without the states as intermediaries. Madison hoped to solve the dilemma of majority tyranny in the states by creating a national government of co-equal branches that could check and balance one another, and by arming that government with the power to strike down unjust state laws.

A conference at George Washington's Mount Vernon plantation to coordinate commercial policies between Virginia and Maryland formed an early link in the chain of events leading to the 1787 Constitutional

Convention. A desire to bring more states into the commercial talks led to the 1786 Annapolis convention, which in turn called the 1787 convention. Shays's Rebellion in Massachusetts alarmed the country, helping to convince all the states except Rhode Island to attend the convention. By forging a consensus in favor of reforming the Confederation, the events of late 1786 and early 1787 set the stage set for the establishment of a strong national government with taxation and commercial powers.

Shortly after declaring independence, the Continental Congress began drafting a national constitution. The resulting document, the "Articles of Confederation and Perpetual Union," was written by Congress, not by a specially elected constitutional convention. Not until 1781 did all the state legislatures ratify the Articles of Confederation. The delay occurred because states lacking claims to western lands (especially Maryland) refused to approve the Articles until states possessing such claims (especially Virginia) ceded their western lands to Congress. The Articles remained the nation's constitution from 1781 through 1789, when it was replaced by the U.S. Constitution written by the 1787 Philadelphia convention and ratified by the states.[1]

Unlike the British system, which placed sovereignty in the King-in-Parliament, Revolutionary Americans evolved the idea that sovereignty rests with the people, who then delegate powers to the branches and levels of government. The Articles of Confederation embodied this concept. The Confederation featured both national and state governments. The states possessed all powers except those expressly delegated to Congress by the Articles. The Confederation was essentially a group of states leagued together for certain limited common purposes, such as defense and foreign policy. Having just separated themselves from a distant and oppressive centralized government in England, Americans refused to create a similar regime, instead decentralizing most power to the state level. Conventional wisdom associated with the French political theorist Baron de Montesquieu held that liberty would be most secure with government close to the people and limited in geographical size. In America, moreover, there had never been any form of central government among the colonies prior to 1774. Thirteen separate colonial assemblies had always been the traditional governing bodies in America. In 1754, the colonies had overwhelmingly rejected the Albany Plan, an attempt to unite them under a single government.

Like the Continental Congress that preceded it, the Confederation Congress consisted of a single house. Instead of having separate, co-equal branches, the Confederation Congress exercised executive, legislative, and judicial functions.

State legislatures determined how delegates would be appointed. In every state except Connecticut and Rhode Island, the legislature elected delegates to Congress. In those two states, the legislatures allowed the delegates to be chosen by the people. Each state delegation, consisting of at least two but no more than seven men, had one vote in Congress no matter the size of the state population. States with small populations benefitted from this one-state, one-vote system because it made them just as powerful as their more populous counterparts. Delaware, for example, possessed just as much voting strength as Virginia, which had over twelve times as many people.[2]

Because most political power rested with the states, greater opportunity existed there for political creativity than in the Confederation Congress. After independence, the most talented men opted to serve at the state level, where they could participate in the unique task of drafting state constitutions from scratch. Thomas Jefferson provides a case in point. When Jefferson arrived in Philadelphia in the spring of 1776 to take his seat in the Continental Congress, he accepted appointment to the Declaration of Independence drafting committee and then received the task of writing the document. Instead of feeling excited to be at the center of action, Jefferson expressed frustration that he was not back home in Virginia helping to draft the state's constitution. Jefferson jealously watched his friend, colleague, and former law instructor, George Wythe, head home to participate in the Virginia convention. Jefferson even prepared a draft constitution, which he asked Wythe to present to the convention. Jefferson's attitude is both typical and revealing about the national government during the 1770s and 1780s.[3]

Jefferson soon left Congress, serving in Virginia's House of Delegates before becoming the state's governor in 1779. Patrick Henry, John Dickinson, and Samuel Adams also took posts back home. Some congressmen, like George Washington, entered the army, while others, including Benjamin Franklin and John Adams, accepted foreign appointments. These departures caused the level of talent in Congress to slip over time.

The method of voting in Congress encouraged delegates to be absent from that body. Two or three delegates could cast their state's lone ballot just as well as six or seven could, so there was no need for everyone to attend. If a state delegation slipped below two members, the state lost its right to vote. This rule did not ensure the presence of at least two delegates from each state, however. Some states entirely lost their vote due to absenteeism. The Articles required a majority of seven states for Congress to act and required a supermajority of nine states to undertake certain critical measures involving war and peace. These rules in a sense encouraged states to be absent from Congress. If a state lost its vote due to absent delegates, it did not have to worry that anything important would be done while it was gone, because its absence simply made a supermajority virtually impossible to achieve. And when absenteeism halted the governing process, even more delegates went home, further exacerbating the situation.

Under these circumstances, states often could find only mediocre men willing to serve in Congress. Delegates faced strenuous journeys to the capital, long stretches away from home, little financial compensation, and limited prestige and power. Consider the evolution of the Virginia delegation. In 1775 and 1776, Virginia sent truly great men to Congress, including George Washington, Patrick Henry, George Wythe, and Thomas Jefferson. By 1780, with the Revolutionary War in its darkest days and political talent more in demand than ever, those luminaries had left Congress, only to be replaced by much less noteworthy men like Meriwether Smith, Cyrus Griffin, and William Fleming. And then, just when it looked as if things could not get any worse, two of the three Virginians went home, and the state entirely lost its vote!

At army headquarters, General Washington cried out in despair. How could his state, the largest and most prestigious one, have sunk so low as to lose its vote in Congress? As he always did at bleak moments, Washington wrote letters of appeal to the states. He begged the Virginia Assembly to restore men of talent to Philadelphia. The state legislature responded by electing an entirely new delegation to Congress that included the brilliant young James Madison, only twenty-nine years old. Other states simultaneously sent higher-caliber men to Congress, temporarily reviving it until the end of the war in 1783.[4]

A few able delegates, like Madison, eagerly served in Congress. But they were sent home after three years. The Articles of Confederation had a term-limit provision preventing any delegate from serving more than

The Road to Philadelphia

three years out of six. After three years in Congress, a delegate had to sit out three years before returning. This provision removed the most experienced and well-informed members. After serving in Congress from 1780 to 1783, Madison had to leave until 1787, when he became eligible to be reappointed.[5]

Since neither the Continental nor the Confederation governments had a separate executive branch, everything had to be done by committee. Hardly the most efficient method, government by committee left the delegates overworked and exhausted most of the time. Simultaneously acting as legislators, executives, and judges stretched congressmen too thin. John Adams could not write the Declaration of Independence because he served on so many committees. When Madison and other newcomers joined Congress in 1780, they abandoned government by committee and created executive departments administered by secretaries appointed by Congress—a superintendent of finance, a secretary of foreign affairs, and a secretary at war—in addition to the already-existing postmaster general. They also created an appellate court for prizes and captures and appointed a commission to settle a land dispute between Connecticut and Pennsylvania.

Congress's resurgence lasted until the war ended, when it reverted to "imbecility," even losing the stability of a permanent capital. In 1783, drunk and unruly Pennsylvania soldiers, upset at not getting paid, fired guns outside the State House (Independence Hall) in Philadelphia. The disgruntled troops targeted not Congress but the Pennsylvania Assembly that met in the same building. Feeling nervous and unsafe, Congress fled to Princeton, then migrated to Annapolis, and eventually took residence in New York City.[6]

The Confederation proved unable to resolve several challenges that faced the United States in the aftermath of the Revolutionary War. By late 1784, the new nation entered perhaps the worst recession in American history prior to the Great Depression. With the imposition of British and French restrictions on American trade to the West Indies, postwar exports fell by 25 percent. Congress could not alleviate the nation's economic distress because the states controlled commerce. Each state had its own trade regulations and its own currency. Without power to regulate commerce, Congress could not negotiate trade agreements with foreign nations. Nor could individual states take effective action. When Massachusetts tried to wring commercial concession from Great Britain through trade restrictions, other states simply took advantage, stepping up their trade with the British. Yet the states still rejected special grants of power to Congress to regulate commerce because they feared centralized tyranny.[7]

Congress faced foreign and domestic war debts that had to be paid to establish national credit. Attempts to raise revenue yielded disappointing results, whether by requisitioning funds from the states, granting taxation power to the Confederation, selling western lands and loan-office securities, or turning the debt over to the states. This requisition system encouraged states to become free riders, enjoying the benefits of the Confederation without paying for them. As a result, Congress received only one-third of the money due to it from the states. Despite receiving loans from France and Spain, Congress had little choice but to print paper money, leading to inflation. By 1779, the Continental dollar was only worth a penny of hard currency, inspiring the expression "Not worth a Continental." James Madison concluded that "the radical defect of the old confederation lay in the power of the States . . . to disregard . . . the authorisd requisitions & regulations of Congress."[8]

All attempts to grant Congress the authority to tax failed. A 1781 proposal for Congress to levy and collect a 5 percent duty on imports suffered defeat when Rhode Island, fearing centralized despotism, rejected it, followed by Virginia's rescinding of its adoption. In 1783, Congress again sought an independent revenue, this time through a 5 percent impost coupled with a mandatory requisition. Although all the states eventually approved the impost, they placed restrictions upon it, some of which Congress rejected. Only five states agreed to pay the accompanying requisition.[9]

A primary reason that amendments to the Confederation failed is that the Articles required every state legislature to approve them. This exceedingly high threshold allowed a single small state, representing as few as 1/33 of the American people, to kill an amendment. Even worse, all it took to stop an amendment was the opposition of 51 percent of the people of a small state, representing less than 2 percent of the American people. This standard could never be met.

Congress faced intractable problems in the West. Because the states refused to honor provisions of the 1783 peace treaty requiring American debtors to pay prewar debts to British creditors, Great Britain refused to evacuate military posts in the Northwest Territory. Instead, the British incited the Indians to attack frontier settlements. Congress found itself powerless either to make the states adhere to the treaty or to evict the British by force. In 1784, when Spain closed the Mississippi River to American traffic, trans-Appalachian settlers, for whom that waterway provided the only access to a port, threatened secession. These congressional failures tempted frontiersmen, many of them recent migrants from Europe lacking a strong attachment to the United States or republicanism, to consider breaking away to join Great Britain or Spain. Rumors circulated along the frontier of conspiracies to annex portions of the West to one or the other of these empires.[10]

In July 1776, the Declaration of Independence transformed the thirteen British colonies into thirteen American states. Even before independence, however, the provincial congresses in four colonies wrote and approved constitutions. New Hampshire adopted a new governmental charter in January 1776. South Carolina and Virginia did so in March and June, respectively, and New Jersey followed suit at the beginning of July. In response to a May 1776 resolution of the Continental Congress authored by John Adams, seven additional states also began drawing up new charters to replace the colonial ones that would soon be terminated. Instead of drafting new constitutions, Connecticut and Rhode Island updated their existing charters to make them republican instead of monarchical. The late 1770s marked an exciting time in which the thirteen states launched thirteen different republican governments. Each state became a separate laboratory for political experiments. Ideas that worked in one state were sometimes later copied by other states.[11]

Pennsylvania adopted perhaps the most radical and innovative constitution of all. The state created a unicameral legislature and an executive council administered by a president. This arrangement seemed to make sense for an American state. Great Britain needed a bicameral legislature, with the House of Lords representing the hereditary aristocracy, and the House of Commons representing the rest of the population. But America lacked an aristocracy, so there was no need for a second legislative house. And since King George III had demonstrated that a one-man executive was prone to tyranny, it made sense to divide executive power among a group of men who could check one other.[12]

Envisioning the legislature as the most powerful governmental branch, all the states except Pennsylvania and Georgia created bicameral legislatures with the idea that the upper house (or senate) would check the lower house. But if both houses were elected by the same constituents, why would the senate act any differently from the house? The state constitutions tried to insulate the upper houses from short-term public pressure by giving their members longer terms in office. Higher age limits to serve as senators, it was hoped, would also add maturity and wisdom to their deliberations.[13]

Each state began by writing a republican constitution that established the fundamental guidelines by which the government would operate. (In a republic—as opposed to a democracy—people elect representatives who govern for them.) A constitution need not be written in a single document. The British Constitution, for example, consists of all the laws enacted by Parliament as well as judicial rulings. A unique contribution of Revolutionary America to political science is the idea of a written constitution. Americans became the first people to write their political charters in a single document. Having just escaped tyranny, Americans wanted to prevent future despotism by spelling out the government's powers as clearly as possible in a single document.

A constitution is law, but it is a supreme form of law that takes precedence over legislation passed by a legislature. To differentiate a constitution from ordinary statutes in the hierarchy of law, a constitution should not be written by a legislature. Revolutionary Americans came up with a new method of creating a constitution: a special body known as constitutional convention elected by the people for the sole and express purpose of writing the document. Before it could go into effect, the constitution would then be ratified by the sovereign people in special election. Ordinary laws passed by the legislature then had to conform to the constitution. Constitutional conventions are a second unique American contribution to political science. In 1779, Massachusetts held the first-ever constitutional convention solely elected to draw up a new state charter, which was ratified by the people of the state the following year. Previously adopted state constitutions were not ratified by the people in referendums. Instead, the legislatures that drafted them declared them in force by fiat. James Madison considered Virginia's 1776 constitution as lacking political legitimacy because it was never ratified by the people of the state.

Nor was the Articles of Confederation, which was drafted by Congress and approved by the state legislatures.[14]

Instead of enumerating the powers of the legislatures, the state constitutions issued blanket grants of power. To protect the personal rights of the people against these blanket grants of power, several state constitutions were prefaced with bills of rights safeguarding freedom of speech, the press, religion, assembly, and so on. Including bills of rights as part of written constitutions is a third unique American contribution to political science. Virginia's Declaration of Rights, written by George Mason and adopted on June 12, 1776, became a model for the other states that later wrote bills of rights. The Articles of Confederation did not include a bill of rights because Congress possessed no authority to act directly on the American people. Instead, the state governments served as intermediaries between Congress and the people.[15]

Writing constitutions was not easy, because it had never really been done before. The provincial congresses that framed the first state constitutions had to envision the political problems that might arise over time and design mechanisms to address them. Just like any invention, these constitutions, once put into operation, revealed design flaws and bugs that eventually forced their framers back to the drawing board. These constitutional glitches eventually had to be fixed, either through amendments or by adopting entirely new constitutions.

One problem particularly characterized the first state constitutions: they did not adequately balance political power among three co-equal branches of government. Instead, these constitutions placed (to varying degrees) too much political power in the legislative branch, and not enough in the executive and judicial branches. Virginia's governor, for example, was elected by the state legislature, served only a one-year term, possessed no veto, and could act only with the consent of a council appointed by the legislature. Historical context explains this imbalance in the state constitutions. During the colonial period, the colony assemblies had used their control of the purse gradually to wrest political power from the royal governors. This process mirrored what Parliament had done to the king in England. The framers of the state constitutions, moreover, overreacted to the executive tyranny of King George III by going too far in the opposite direction, creating muscular legislatures and weak governors.

But what if a state legislature passed an unconstitutional law? What if an assembly engaged in majority tyranny, trampling the rights of a minority group? Popularly backed legislative majorities in several states did just that, enacting statutes that violated the rights of religious or propertied minorities. Connecticut's "Act for Securing the Rights of Conscience" required church attendance, supported established religion with tax revenue, upheld the Sabbath, required families to own Bibles, and demanded that officeholders take Christian oaths. In Rhode Island and North Carolina, many men of modest wealth and education got elected to the legislatures, filling a political vacuum left by the departure of more privileged Loyalists who had occupied the colonial assembles. These new arrivals adopted extremely pro-debtor inflationary paper currencies that many saw as majority tyranny against creditors forced to accept repayment in depreciated currency. Under the first state constitutions, there was no way to overturn unjust laws that violated minority rights. The governors often lacked the means to strike such laws down by veto, and state judiciaries in most cases failed to exercise judicial review. What good were the state bills of rights if the political system rarely enforced them?[16]

In 1776, Americans simply did not yet understand that a popularly elected legislature could be as tyrannical as a king. In the past, having experienced minority tyranny only in the form of a despot, they had trouble grasping majority tyranny in the form of a popularly backed legislature. In the Hollywood film *The Patriot*, fictional protagonist Benjamin Martin confounds the South Carolina Assembly by asking, "Why should I trade one tyrant 3,000 miles away for 3,000 tyrants one mile away?" That fictitious line is reminiscent of what Thomas Jefferson wrote about Virginia's legislature: "173 despots would surely be as oppressive as one." Whether tyranny sprang from a single individual or many individuals mattered little. The shocking realization that rule by people could be oppressive caused many Americans to rethink their political assumptions. A constitution needed truly co-equal branches equipped with checks and balances to protect the rights of minorities.[17]

No one thought more deeply about the problem of majority tyranny than James Madison. As a Virginia delegate to the Continental and Confederation congresses, he tried but failed to obtain for the national government the power to collect revenue through an impost. Forced from Congress in 1783 by the Articles' term-limit provision, Madison won election to the Virginia House of Delegates. Assuming his duties in Richmond, Madison immediately felt unease over the "multiplicity" and "mutability" of state laws drafted by inexperienced, amateurish state legislators. That is, Virginia's legislature passed and repealed so many contradictory statutes that the public could hardly keep track of what the laws were. Much of the legislation violated the sovereignty of other states or invaded the prerogatives of Congress. Madison hypothesized that this governmental shortcoming could be addressed by ensuring that the upper house (or senate) contained more experienced lawmakers skilled in drafting legislation, and through a council of revision staffed by members of the executive and judicial branches to review bills before passage into law.[18]

By 1785, Madison also became increasingly disturbed by the "injustice" of state laws, as he witnessed an all-powerful legislature engaging in majority tyranny. Virginia's constitution lacked checks and balances to keep the legislature in line and to protect the rights of religious and propertied minorities. Years later, Madison explained that the misdeeds of the state legislatures played as great a role in bringing about the new U.S. Constitution as did the failures of the Confederation Congress: "The abuses committed within the individual States previous to the present Constitution, by interested or misguided majorities, were among the prominent causes of its adoption," he wrote. "The evils issuing from these sources contributed more to that uneasiness which produced the Convention, and prepared the public mind for a general reform, than those which accrued to our national character and interest from the inadequacy of the Confederation to its immediate objects." Turning conventional wisdom on its head, Madison argued that in a large republic the size of the United States, self-interested majorities would have a harder time forging a tyrannical majority than in a small republic the size of a single state. "Those who framed and ratified the Constitution," he explained, "inferred . . . that by dividing the power of Govt." between federal and state levels "and thereby enlarging the practicable sphere of government, unjust majorities would be" less likely.[19]

"Never have I seen *so much mind in so little matter!*" observed one contemporary about the physically small and frail Madison. "From a spirit of industry and application which he possesses in a most eminent degree, he always comes forward the best informed Man of any point in debate," wrote Constitutional Convention colleague William Pierce. "Mr. Madison is about 37 years of age, a Gentleman of great modesty,—with a remarkable sweet temper. He is easy and unreserved among his acquaintances, and has a most agreeable style of conversation." William Jackson, the secretary of the Constitutional Convention, succinctly pronounced Madison "by far the most efficient member" of that body.[20]

Today Madison is known at the "Father of the Constitution," but his biggest contribution came before the Constitutional Convention even met. In the spring of 1787, Madison prepared the "Virginia Plan," which became the starting point for the Philadelphia convention. Madison based this blueprint on a combination of his own practical political experience, and on his extensive study of the history of "Ancient and Modern Confederacies." Aiming to replace the confederation form of government

Known as the "Father of the Constitution," James Madison of Virginia drafted the Virginia Plan and took detailed notes of the debates at the Constitutional Convention. (National Gallery of Art)

with a national government that operated directly on the people, the Virginia Plan called for a bicameral legislature, with representation in both houses based on each state's free population or taxes paid. Congressional districts in each state would elect the lower house, and the lower house would in turn elect the upper house. The Virginia Plan proposed giving more power to congress, especially the power to tax and regulate commerce. It also included strong executive and judicial branches to balance the legislature. To protect against majority tyranny, Madison proposed granting congress a veto power over state legislation. If a state passed a law that violated the rights of the minority, congress could strike it down. Madison thus wanted to use the federal government (a big republic) to solve the problem of majority tyranny within the states (little republics). In Philadelphia, the Virginia delegation scaled back Madison's absolute congressional veto, restricting the proposal to state laws that violated the federal constitution. Finally, an executive-judicial council of revision would approve laws before they went into effect. It could even overturn congressional vetoes of state laws.[21]

Fortunately, Madison acquired a powerful ally to help him promote his proposed reforms. George Washington thoroughly agreed with Madison's diagnosis of the role the states played in the Confederation's failure. "The primary cause of all our disorders lies in the different State Governments, and in the tenacity of that power which pervades the whole of their systems," Washington declared. "Whilst independent sovereignty is so ardently contended for, whilst the local views of each State and separate interests by which they are too much govern'd will not yield to a more enlarged scale of politicks; incompatibility in the laws of different States, and disrespect to those of the general government must render the situation of this great Country weak, inefficient and disgraceful. It has already done so,—almost to the final dessolution of it—weak at home and disregarded abroad is our present condition, and contemptible enough it is."[22]

With a large and athletic frame, Washington cut a commanding and majestic figure. "His person," wrote Thomas Jefferson, "was fine, his stature exactly what one would wish, his deportment easy, erect, and noble . . . the most graceful figure that could be seen on horseback." His handsome facial features included high cheekbones, a prominent nose, and blue-gray eyes. Abigail Adams noted that Washington "has a dignity which forbids Familiarity mixed with an easy affability which created Love and Reverence." At a ball celebrating Washington's retirement from the army, one observer recorded that "the General danced every set, that all the ladies might have the pleasure of dancing with him, or as it has since been handsomely expressed, *get a touch of him.*" Washington treated people with generosity, respect, and politeness, but he could also be demanding and unforgiving. He possessed the self-discipline to keep his explosive temper in check. He reached decisions deliberately but carried them out resolutely. Washington loved domesticity and farming, but demonstrated political skill, financial shrewdness, and material acquisitiveness. In public, he veiled his personal views and feelings behind an inscrutable veneer.[23]

James Madison contrasted his public and private personalities: "Washington was not fluent or ready in conversation, and was inclined to be taciturn in general society. In the company of two or three intimate friends, however, he was talkative, and when a little excited was sometimes fluent and even eloquent. The story so often repeated of his never laughing . . . is wholly untrue." Although he enjoyed listening to friends banter, "he took little part in it himself. He was particularly pleased with the jokes, good humor, and hilarity of his companions." Above all, Washington exhibited duty and honor, and prized his carefully cultivated image and reputation. Historian W. W. Abbot writes that he possessed "an uncommon awareness of self." He understood "that what he did, and how others perceived his decisions and deeds, always mattered."[24]

Washington's wartime efforts to subordinate local interests to national interests left him, of all the Founders, with perhaps the clearest vision of a continental American republic. He recognized that a strong Union would lead to national security and prosperity. Washington's 1783 "Circular to the States," announcing his permanent retirement from public life, called for a stronger federal government.

It is a myth that after leaving the army in 1783, George Washington spent three quiet years in retirement at Mount Vernon until summoned to the 1787 Federal Convention. Retirement implies relaxation and focusing entirely on private affairs. This term does not apply to Washington because his involvement in public affairs continued. In the postwar period, he endeavored to bind the states together into a strong national Union. If nothing were done, he feared, states might break away from the Confederation to become separate nations. Some might even ally with rival European powers or go to war among themselves. For their own protection, states then would have to militarize, leading to despotism. America might become like Europe, periodically devastated by warfare and permanently subject to tyranny.[25]

Washington recognized that the trans-Appalachian frontier might break away and join the Spanish or British empires. "The Western settlers," he wrote, "stand as it were upon a pivot—the touch of a feather, would turn them any way." To avert the crisis, and to complete the Revolution, Washington wanted to cement together the nation's vast geographical regions. The primary theme of Washington's entire political career, including his postwar years at Mount Vernon, is his quest to unite the states. He saw a strong Union of the states under an effective constitution as the key to liberty.[26]

Washington got the ball rolling toward political reform by successfully lobbying Virginia and Maryland to join forces to improve the navigation of the Potomac River. In 1785, the two states jointly chartered a private venture called the Potomac River Company. The brainchild of Washington, the Potomac Company planned to make the river navigable deep into the Ohio Country. It would then build portage roads to navigable waters running into the Ohio River. Rather than a canal company that builds a continuous still water canal alongside a waterway, this venture endeavored to make the river itself navigable by dredging the riverbed to remove obstructions. While the Potomac Company did build canals, especially one around the Great Falls west of present-day Washington, D.C., its primary goal was to make the Potomac River itself navigable.[27]

Washington had several motives for backing the Potomac River Company, of which he became the president in 1785. His biggest goal was to cement East and West into an insoluble Union by developing a commercial highway to the Ohio Country. "The consequences to the Union" of opening the Potomac to the West "are immense—& and more so in a political, than in a Commercial point," he wrote, "for unless we can connect the New States, which are rising to our view in the Regions back of us, with those on the Atlantic by interest . . . they will be quite a distinct People, and ultimately may be very troublesome neighbors to us."[28]

Before the Potomac Company could begin its work, however, Virginia and Maryland had to figure out how to share the river. In the 1780s, the

Potomac already had a long history of overlapping and conflicting claims. In 1609, King James I of England granted the Potomac to the colony of Virginia. But in 1632 King Charles I awarded Maryland jurisdiction over the river. Virginia's 1776 Constitution refused to relinquish "the free navigation and use of" the river. Maryland's 1776 Constitution upheld its own absolute control over the waterway. There things stood for nearly a decade, with the two state constitutions in conflict over navigation rights on the Potomac. Now in 1785, this issue needed to be sorted out because of the creation of the Potomac River Company.[29]

A year earlier, the Virginia legislature had appointed four commissioners—George Mason, Edmund Randolph, James Madison, and Alexander Henderson—to confer with Maryland to establish joint jurisdiction over the river. In empowering its commissioners to negotiate with Maryland, however, Virginia drew up flawed instructions. The state's instructions failed to cover many critical issues, including jurisdiction over the Chesapeake Bay and the Pocomoke River (which runs into the Chesapeake Bay).[30]

Somehow, Virginia governor Patrick Henry then neglected to notify Virginia's commissioners of their appointment. Historian Norman Risjord argues that Henry's failure to inform the delegates amounted to willful obstruction. "The governor," Risjord writes, "who had little interest in trade regulations and even less in secret conclaves of like-minded nationalists, was trying to scuttle the whole project." While Henry certainly was no nationalist, and while some (like Madison and Washington) hoped the conference would be a first step toward a reform of the Articles of Confederation, this interpretation is too conspiratorial. It reads Henry's later Antifederalism backward to 1785. Instead of threatening Virginia's sovereignty, the Mount Vernon Conference aimed to strengthen the state. The governor's failure to spread the word amounted not to obstruction, but bureaucratic incompetence. Henry may have been a spellbinding orator, but he had trouble carrying out routine executive functions. And so, the four Virginia commissioners remained in the dark about their assignment.[31]

Maryland was much more on the ball. It named four prominent commissioners—Thomas Johnson, Daniel of St. Thomas Jenifer, Thomas Stone, and Samuel Chase—and empowered them to negotiate all the issues involved. The Maryland delegates were prominent men. Thomas Johnson, who ended up not participating in the conference, had served in the First and Second Continental Congresses before being elected the first governor of Maryland. Two of the three who attended, Thomas Stone and Samuel Chase, signed the Declaration of Independence, and the third, Jenifer, attended the 1787 Constitutional Convention.

The Marylanders decided that the meeting would begin in Alexandria on March 21, 1785. But when they sent word to Virginia, Governor Henry dropped the ball again, this time failing to notify the commissioners when the meeting would take place. Edmund Randolph later ascribed the oversight "to the forgetfulness of our friend Henry." When Randolph subsequently confronted Henry about what went wrong, the governor lamely claimed that "he could not recollect," meekly suggesting that he had sent the instructions to Madison "with several other public papers." He had not. Not receiving word to the contrary, the Marylanders assumed the meeting was all set.[32]

When Jenifer stopped at Mount Vernon on his way to Alexandria, Washington checked whether his neighbor, George Mason of Gunston

George Washington resided at his beloved Mount Vernon plantation on the Potomac River in Virginia, where he practiced scientific farming and landscape design. The Mount Vernon Conference, the precursor to the Annapolis and Philadelphia conventions, met here in March 1785. (Courtesy of Stuart Leibiger)

Hall plantation, one of Virginia's commissioners, had received an invitation to the meeting. Mason replied that he had just found out about it by chance a day or two earlier in a letter from the Maryland commissioners. Washington immediately sent his carriage to pick up Mason and take him to Alexandria to attend the conference.[33]

Mason posed a sharp contrast to his famous neighbor, with whom he shared a long friendship. Whereas Washington grew his hair long and tied it in a queue, Mason shaved his head and wore a wig. Whereas Washington was healthy, athletic, and active, Mason lived a sedentary life because he suffered from gout. A type of arthritis, gout hit Mason in his thirties. For the rest of his life he experienced periodic debilitating attacks that left him either hobbling on crutches or completely immobile for weeks at a time. The pain shaped his personality, leaving him grouchy, irritable, impatient, short tempered, acid tongued, and self-absorbed. Although they were friends, Washington found Mason kind of an oddball—too reclusive, too quarrelsome with neighbors and colleagues, too stingy with money, and too unwilling to serve the public. Contemporaries praised Mason despite his quirks. Thomas Jefferson pronounced him "a man of the first order of wisdom" and "one of our really great men." Madison described him as "a powerful reasoner, a profound statesman, and a devoted Republican."[34]

On March 21, 1785, Jenifer left Mount Vernon to join the other Marylanders assembled in Alexandria. Mason was the only Virginia commissioner present. The participants quickly located another Old Dominion appointee, local merchant Alexander Henderson. But Madison and Randolph were nowhere to be found. The five commissioners agreed to wait a couple of days for the missing Virginians. When Mason received a letter from Randolph that did not even mention the conference, it became clear that the two missing Virginians had not been notified and would not appear. The meeting thus began with only Mason and Henderson representing Virginia. Madison and Randolph did not attend the conference because Governor Henry never informed them about it. Indeed, Madison did not even find out about the gathering until three months later. Although Mason and Henderson lacked instructions from their state, they nevertheless negotiated rather "than to disappoint the Maryd. Commissioners" who had come a long way in bad weather and were eager to reach an agreement.[35]

The Road to Philadelphia

This statue of "Reluctant Statesman" George Mason of Virginia is part of the George Mason Memorial on the Mall in Washington, D.C. Mason sat on the Grand Committee of Eleven that proposed the Great Compromise. He later refused to sign the completed Constitution because he believed that it would allow the North to dominate the South and that it would lead to monarchy or aristocracy. (Courtesy of Stuart Leibiger)

Washington himself went to Alexandria on March 22 to see what was going on, and while there he invited the delegates—all his friends and acquaintances—to adjourn to Mount Vernon. They accepted the invitation but waited another two days in Alexandria to give the missing commissioners a chance to arrive before relocating the conference. "Upon the particular Invitation of the General," Mason wrote, the meeting adjourned "to Mount Vernon, and finished the Business there."[36]

On March 24, Washington sent his carriage to Alexandria to bring Mason to Mount Vernon. That evening, the two Virginians discussed the agenda for the next day. The following afternoon, Henderson and the three Marylanders arrived. The conference resumed after dinner that day and lasted until the 28th. The commissioners worked hard on Saturday,

March 26. On Sunday, they took a break, with Stone and Henderson each leaving Mount Vernon to run personal errands. On Monday, with everyone back, the commissioners wrapped up their business.[37]

Washington hosted the conference but was not officially a commissioner and did not sign the final agreement. It is uncertain whether he participated in the formal sessions, though he very well may have. Clearly, he played a large unofficial role in the conference. At the very least, Washington conferred and socialized with the five commissioners extensively between sessions and during meals. As the future president of the Potomac Company (he accepted that post two months later), he provided an invaluable resource for the participants. More than hospitality motivated Washington to host the conference. With the meeting under his roof, he could keep tabs on what was going on, and even influence the proceedings. Settling the two states' jurisdictional dispute over the Potomac was vital to his river improvement project. But he also wanted to strategize about how to achieve larger nationalistic reforms. And so, while Washington was not an official participant, he might as well have been one.[38]

The attendees enthusiastically shared Washington's dream of getting Maryland and Virginia to cooperate in opening a commercial highway to the West. They also sympathized with Washington's larger goal of strengthening the Confederation. At the 1787 Constitutional Convention, Jennifer would be the most nationalistic member of the Maryland delegation. Stone turned down appointment to the 1787 convention only because his wife faced a terminal illness.

Anyone searching Washington's diaries for intimate details of the conference will be disappointed. Mainly a weather journal and a guest log, the diary is not introspective. It records simple facts, not deep thoughts or personal impressions. The entry for Sunday, March 27th, the third day of the conference, reads, "Wind Southerly all day but not much of it. Morning cloudy & more or less so all day." The only information the diary provides about the conference is the date and time the various commissioners arrived at and departed from Mount Vernon.[39]

While terribly frustrating, the diary's silence nevertheless points to one significant conclusion: Washington found the gathering important enough to stay home while it took place. In March 1785, Washington oversaw a huge landscape gardening project at Mount Vernon. Every day he busily supervised the planting and pruning of trees and shrubs on the west front of the mansion. This endeavor was part of his larger plan to replace formal, geometric gardens with a naturalistic setting that featured carefully prepared and cultivated views (or vistas) to the surrounding lands beyond.[40]

During the four days of the conference, Washington set aside this landscape gardening project to stay inside the mansion, and even broke his routine of making daily rides to inspect his farms. Usually Washington did not vary his schedule for visitors, but these guests were important enough to keep him at home. The conference was a top priority for him, and so he spent as much time as possible with his company. Further evidence that the commissioners monopolized Washington's attention comes from Washington's papers. His personal correspondence dropped off dramatically during the four days of the conference. He dashed off only one short letter from March 25 to March 28.[41]

During the conference, Virginia commissioners Mason and Henderson did their best despite lacking formal instructions from their state. They unknowingly violated the missing instructions, which required three of the state's delegates to be present before conducting official business. Unaware that they were not authorized to deliberate over the Chesapeake Bay and the Pocomoke River, they also made agreements respecting those waters. Mason later regarded it as a blessing in disguise that he and Henderson did not know the limits of their authority, because they were able to negotiate on equal terms with the Marylanders. Had they possessed their official instructions, then conflicts with the Maryland instructions would have prevented any negotiations from taking place at all.[42]

During the four days of talks, the commissioners reached an agreement drafted by Mason known as the Mount Vernon Compact. Article Six provided that "the River Potomack shall be considered as a common High Way, for the purpose of Navigation and Commerce to the Citizens of Virginia and Maryland and of the United States and to all other Persons in amity with the said States trading to or from Virginia or Maryland." This declaration established the important principle that river commerce was a matter of national as well as state concern.[43]

The compact exempted from duties ships sailing on the Chesapeake Bay from one state to the other and protected the fishing rights of both states' citizens. The two states agreed to split the cost of building and maintaining "light Houses, Beacons, Bouys, or other necessary Signals" on Chesapeake Bay and in the Potomac River. They also pledged to coordinate their law enforcement statutes on these waterways and to assist one another in the collection of debts and the punishment of smugglers. The compact avoided the controversial border between the two states. That issue remained unresolved for nearly a century, until an arbitration ruling in 1877 set the state line at the low water mark on the Virginia shore.[44]

The commissioners also drafted a letter inviting Pennsylvania to participate in building a road within that state from the Potomac River to navigable waters flowing into the Ohio River. In a cover letter addressed to the Virginia House of Delegates, Mason and Henderson suggested that the two states should meet annually to discuss commerce. Perhaps the most significant outcome of the conference, this letter helped lead to the Annapolis and Philadelphia conventions.[45]

In calling for future meetings, in contacting Pennsylvania, and in opening the river to all U.S. citizens, the Mount Vernon Conference went beyond its intended purpose, taking a huge, early step on the road to the 1787 Philadelphia convention. For the first time, two states attempted to coordinate commercial policies including currency, debts, and tariffs. These same issues needed to be made uniform among all the states. It also requested the calling of additional meetings to be attended by more states. Although strictly a state initiative, the conference went a long way toward comprehensively addressing these issues at the federal level.

The fall session of Maryland's General Assembly promptly ratified the compact and suggested that Delaware also be invited to participate in future conferences. The correspondence with Pennsylvania and Delaware would help convince those states to take part in the Annapolis convention. When an attack of gout prevented Mason from attending the Virginia legislature, Madison took charge of getting the Mount Vernon Compact ratified. At Madison's urging, Virginia accepted the agreement even though it did not conform to the state's original instructions.[46]

Madison also tried, but failed, to convince the legislature to submit the agreement to Congress for approval in accordance with Article VI of the Confederation: "No two or more States shall enter into any treaty, confederation or alliance whatever between them, without the consent of the United States in Congress assembled." Madison privately questioned the legality of the Mount Vernon Compact because Congress never approved it, and even considered it an example of states trespassing on the authority of Congress. In his 1787 memorandum "Vices of the Political System of the United States," Madison listed the "unlicensed" compact under the heading "Encroachments by the States on the federal authority." Although Madison believed the compact violated the Articles of Confederation, the U.S. Supreme Court in 1894 determined that it did not conflict with the U.S. Constitution. In *Wharton vs. Wise* the Court upheld the compact as a legal agreement because it was ratified by both states and ruled that it does not conflict with Article VI of the Constitution regulating agreements among states.[47]

The Mount Vernon Conference led to the 1786 Annapolis convention, although that was not Madison's original plan to achieve national political reform. Madison initially preferred an amendment to the Articles over the calling of a convention because he was afraid a convention might weaken Congress without achieving anything positive. Madison hoped to convince the fall 1785 session of the Virginia legislature to initiate an amendment to the Articles of Confederation granting Congress the power to regulate commerce for twenty-five years. Antinationalist state legislators reduced the duration of the measure to thirteen years. Madison and his nationalist supporters let this watered-down proposal die. With his efforts to amend the Articles having failed, and the Virginia legislative session drawing to a close, Madison now risked a convention as a last resort.[48]

In January 1786, on the last day of Virginia's legislative session, Madison's ally John Tyler (father of the future president) offered a resolution calling an interstate conference. Tyler rather than Madison made this suggestion because Madison's nationalism was getting on the nerves of some localists in the Virginia legislature. Years later, Madison explained to Noah Webster "that the [Annapolis] proposition, tho' probably growing out of efforts made by myself to convince the Legislature of the necessity of investing Congress with" commercial power "was introduced by another member, more likely to have the ear of the Legislature on the occasion, than one whose long & late service in Congs., might subject him to the suspicion of a bias in favor of that body." Tyler was a wolf in sheep's clothing, as it were.[49]

Building on the Mount Vernon Compact's call for interstate talks, Tyler's resolution requested Virginia to appoint commissioners to a conference of all the states to discuss allowing Congress to regulate commerce. This convention would "take into consideration the trade of the United States" and "consider how far a uniform system in their commercial regulations may be necessary to their common interest and their permanent harmony." In short, Madison and his allies failed with plan A, and so they quickly improvised plan B. Plan A was an amendment giving Congress commercial power. Plan B fell back on the Mount Vernon Conference's call for a follow-up convention of states. The legislature appointed Madison, Edmund Randolph, St. George Tucker, Walter Jones, Meriwether Smith, George Mason, and David Ross as commissioners, any three of whom could act for the state. Those appointees in turn invited all the states to meet at Annapolis in September 1786.[50]

The call for the Annapolis convention was based on the Mount Vernon Conference's proposal for further talks among the states. Madison explained to Washington that the meeting "seems naturally to grow out of the proposed appointment of Commssrs for Virga. & Maryd, concerted at Mount Vernon for keeping up harmony in the commercial regulations of the two States. Maryd has ratified the Report, but has invited into the plan Delaware and Penna. who will naturally pay the same compliment to their neighbours &c. &c." At some point in the early 1830s, while writing a preface to his *Notes of Debates in the Federal Convention of 1787*, Madison again narrated the chain of events that led to the Annapolis convention: the Mount Vernon Conference had "recommended a uniformity in the regulations" of Virginia and Maryland "on several subjects & particularly on those having relation to foreign trade." Maryland then invited Delaware and Pennsylvania to participate in future talks, and they in turn invited other states. This "illustration of the necessity of a uniformity throughout all the States" naturally led to "the passage of a Resolution which proposed a Convention" at Annapolis.[51]

Even though it led to the Annapolis convention, some historians argue that the Mount Vernon Conference was more antinationalistic than nationalistic in nature, "an overt flaunting of the Congress," because the two states tried to solve their commercial problems on their own, without input from Congress. This theory does not fit the thinking of Madison and Washington. They believed that if two states took the reform initiative, then others would quickly join in, eventually leading to the formation of a stronger national government. Madison, it will be recalled, had tried to get Virginia to submit the Mount Vernon Compact to Congress for approval.[52]

Years later, Edward Coles, Madison's White House secretary, recorded the following: "I remember hearing Mr. Madison speak of what passed during a visit he made to Mt. Vernon, about the time of the embarrassments experienced from conflicting commercial regulations of Va. & Maryland; & his having said he had long conversations with Genl: Washington on the subject," wrote Coles. "In those conversations reference was made . . . to other difficulties growing out of the articles of Confederation, of which Mr. Madison . . . urge[d] that advantage should be taken of the" Mount Vernon Compact "to urge on the Legislatures the adoption of measures of relief to a greater extent than was generally contemplated: In fine to remedy this, as well as other grievances, the Country was subjected to, under the articles of Confederation—in which views & wishes, I understood Mr. Madison to say, Genl: Washington concurred."[53]

Privately still doubting a convention instead of amendments as the best means to strengthen Congress, Madison warned that too much should not be attempted at Annapolis. If the delegates merely demonstrated their good intentions, then the states might sponsor a subsequent convention. Madison hoped that a follow-up meeting would enact national reform, but he doubted even a second convention could achieve that much. "The efforts for bringing about" political reform through amendments to the Articles "have miscarried," Madison mused. "Let a Convention then be tried. If it succeeds in the first instance, it can be repeated as other defects force themselves on the public attention. . . . The option . . . lay between doing what was done and doing nothing. Whether a right choice was made time only can prove. I am not in general an advocate for temporizing or partial remedies. But a rigor in this respect, if pushed too far may hazard every thing." It is remarkable that even as he worked so hard for political reform, Madison remained pessimistic about the chances for success. He did not harbor illusions that change would be easy. He knew it would be a struggle.[54]

In the spring and summer of 1786, an issue that threatened to sabotage the Annapolis convention arose. Congress's Secretary for Foreign Affairs John Jay, negotiating with Spanish envoy Don Diego de Gardoqui, asked Congress to change instructions prohibiting him from relinquishing America's right to navigate the Mississippi River that was critical to southern and western farmers. Spain required this concession in return for a commercial treaty that would primarily benefit the Northeast. Sectional debate raged in Congress until August, when the seven northernmost states voted in favor of Jay's request. The measure nevertheless failed because the Articles of Confederation required a supermajority of nine states to ratify treaties. So desperate were southerners for Mississippi navigation and so desperate were northerners for commercial concessions that each section vowed to form its own confederacy if it did not get its way.[55]

In September 1786 the Annapolis convention met at a time of confusion and sectional distrust generated by Jay's negotiations, eliminating any chance of giving Congress power over commerce. The northern states, believing that the South was not serious about reform, either did not send commissioners or did not send them on time. Nobody was there from Connecticut, Massachusetts, Rhode Island, and New Hampshire. Most southern states suspected northerners of favoring either an allmighty federal government or even a dissolution of the Union. Nobody was there from Georgia, South Carolina, and North Carolina. Even the host state, Maryland, absented itself, leaving only five states in attendance—Virginia, Delaware, Pennsylvania, New Jersey, and New York. Nor did the city of Annapolis roll out the red carpet. Since the state did not officially participate, the commissioners could not meet in the State House. Instead, they met in Mann's Tavern, the boardinghouse where they lodged.[56]

Only three commissioners attended on Monday, September 4, the scheduled date for the convention to begin. A week later, twelve delegates had arrived, and the meeting finally began with the election of John Dickinson of Delaware as chairman. In the end, only twelve participants showed up in Annapolis, three from Virginia, three from Delaware, one from Pennsylvania, three from New Jersey, and two from New York. But those twelve men changed history.[57]

Twenty-nine-year-old Alexander Hamilton represented New York. Expressing skepticism about the viability of republicanism, he unabashedly admired the British monarchical system as the ideal form of government. An immigrant from the West Indies, he also lacked a deep attachment to his state. In 1780, he became the first vocal advocate of a constitutional convention to enact political reform. Two years later, he backed a successful resolution in the New York legislature for Congress to call a national convention. Long before the Virginians turned to the convention strategy, in short, Hamilton called for such a meeting.[58]

Friends, foes, and even Hamilton himself commented on his boundless ambition. "That he is ambitious I shall readily grant," wrote Washington, "but it is of that laudable kind which prompts a man to excel in whatever he takes in hand." John Adams less charitably later described Hamilton as "a bastard brat of a Scottish pedlar," with "no more gratitude than a Cat," whose "fornications, adulteries, and his incests—were propagated far and wide." Fellow Constitutional Convention delegate William Pierce noted that the small, fair-skinned, red-headed Hamilton had "something too feeble in his voice to be equal to the strains of oratory . . . he is rather a convincing Speaker, than a blazing Orator."[59]

The Annapolis convention provided Hamilton the opportunity to push his nationalistic agenda. The convention met from September 11 to 14. But what was it to do? Given the disappointing turnout, the commissioners simply could not proceed with their assigned task of advocating congressional regulation of commerce. Some preferred to give up and go home, while others favored action. New Jersey's instructions, authorizing a full reform of the Articles, offered a ray of hope. The activists included Madison of Virginia, Abraham Clark of New Jersey, Tench Coxe of Pennsylvania, and, especially, Hamilton of New York. Rather than to undermine the reform movement by adjourning without doing anything constructive, the commissioners took an audacious step. In a unanimous report drafted by Hamilton, the convention pronounced the situation of the Confederacy "delicate and critical." Hamilton's Annapolis convention report is the origin of the famous term "the critical period" that has come to describe affairs under the Confederation.[60]

The Annapolis convention report, issued on September 14, 1786, invited all the states to meet in Philadelphia the following May to discuss something much larger than commerce. The commissioners called on the next convention to examine all the Confederation's defects and to create an effective national government. The report invited the states to appoint delegates "to meet at Philadelphia on the second Monday in May next, to take into consideration the situation of the United States, to devise such further provisions as shall appear to them necessary to render the Constitution of the Federal Government adequate to the exigencies of the Union." The commissioners sent their report to all the states and to Congress.[61]

The Annapolis convention report by itself was not enough to ensure attendance at the Philadelphia convention. It also took a crisis in Massachusetts to help convince the states to appoint delegates, and to convince those delegates to participate. That crisis was Shays's Rebellion, an uprising of western Massachusetts farmers against their own state government.

Shays's Rebellion, a widely misunderstood event, is an interesting study in history, memory, and historiography. An old cliché states that history is written by the winners, who put their own spin on events, sometimes distorting the historical record. Shays's Rebellion is a good example. In Shays's Rebellion, eastern Massachusetts elites shaped the historical interpretation of the uprising. The "winners'" version misrepresents the rebellion in some ways, making the rebels who ended up on the losing side look bad. Students are often taught that Shays's Rebellion was an uprising of impoverished debtors exclusively from the western half of the state. The Shaysites are often presented as a lawless mob from the dregs of society who were fortunately suppressed by the forces of law and order and justice.

This interpretation presents a caricature of the rebels—a stereotype originally pinned on them by their foes. This misrepresentation found its way into history when it was adopted by an eastern Massachusetts elite named George Richards Minot, who wrote the first history of the insurgency in 1788. Minot blamed Shaysites for the rebellion, not state officials, an interpretation that prevailed for decades thereafter. The historical record has been corrected by modern scholarship, especially by Leonard L. Richards, who has demonstrated that the eastern Massachusetts elite who subdued the uprising intentionally created a false picture of the insurgents to discredit them. Later historians then perpetuated the myth until it became entrenched in the historical record.[62]

One myth associated with the rebellion is that the Shaysites were Loyalists during the Revolutionary War. The reality is that most of the rebels fought on the American side, both in the Continental Army and in the militia, as officers and enlisted men. Daniel Shays, the Rebellion's titular leader, served for five years, rising to the rank of captain. Shays even received a sword with a golden handle as a gift from the Marquis de Lafayette in recognition of his military record.

> PENNSYLVANIA, ff.
>
> By the *President* and the *Supreme Executive Council* of the Commonwealth of *Pennsylvania*,
>
> A PROCLAMATION.
>
> WHEREAS the General Affembly of this Commonwealth, by a law entituled 'An act for co-operating with "the ftate of Maffachufetts bay, agreeable to the articles of "confederation, in the apprehending of the proclaimed rebels "DANIEL SHAYS, LUKE DAY, ADAM WHEELER "and ELI PARSONS," have enacted, "that rewards additional to thofe offered and promifed to be paid by the ftate "of Maffachufetts Bay, for the apprehending the aforefaid "rebels, be offered by this ftate;" WE do hereby offer the following rewards to any perfon or perfons who fhall, within the limits of this ftate, apprehend the rebels aforefaid, and fecure them in the gaol of the city and county of Philadelphia, viz For the apprehending of the faid Daniel Shays, and fecuring him as aforefaid, the reward of *One hundred and Fifty Pounds* lawful money of the ftate of Maffachufetts Bay, and *One Hundred Pounds* lawful money of this ftate; and for the apprehending the faid Luke Day, Adam Wheeler and Eli Parfons, and fecuring them as aforefaid, the reward (refpectively) of *One Hundred Pounds* lawful money of Maffachufetts Bay and *Fifty Pounds* lawful money of this ftate: And all judges, juftices, fheriffs and conftables are hereby ftrictly enjoined and required to make diligent fearch and enquiry after, and to ufe their utmoft endeavours to apprehend and fecure the faid Daniel Shays, Luke Day, Adam Wheeler and Eli Parfons, their aiders, abettors and comforters, and every of them, fo that they may be dealt with according to law.
>
> GIVEN in Council, under the hand of the Prefident, and the Seal of the State, at Philadelphia, this tenth day of March, in the year of our Lord one thoufand feven hundred and eighty-feven.
>
> BENJAMIN FRANKLIN.
>
> ATTEST
>
> JOHN ARMSTRONG, jun. Secretary.

This broadside offers a reward for the capture of Daniel Shays, namesake of Shays's Rebellion in Massachusetts. Shays had received a sword made of gold from the Marquis de Lafayette in honor of his military service during the Revolutionary War. Shays fled to Vermont, an independent republic, to avoid apprehension and later settled in New York. (Library of Congress)

As former Revolutionary War soldiers, the Shaysites faced a fundamental injustice. Because the Massachusetts and Confederation governments could not raise much revenue, they never paid these troops their back wages. These veterans, in short, were public creditors. Some were so bereft of cash that they sold their government debt certificates to speculators for pennies on the dollar. Now these veterans were being taxed by the state government to raise revenue that would ultimately pay the face value of the certificates, in some cases to the very speculators to whom they had sold them!

Another inaccuracy is that the Shaysites were lower-class debtors. Far from being the dregs of society, they were in fact middle-class farmers who owned large tracts of land and nice houses. With over 100 acres of land, Daniel Shays was one of the wealthiest men in his town. Shaysites were not debtors in the sense of owing more than they possessed. They were only debtors in the sense that they were dragged into debtor's court for small sums of money that they could not pay in hard cash during the postwar recession that hit subsistence-surplus farmers of western Massachusetts especially hard. To satisfy these debts, they frequently had to sell their lands or homes, often at undervalued prices. Those who failed to dispose of their property in fire sales faced foreclosure by the courts. Shays's Rebellion raises interesting questions about the social acceptability of debt at different periods in history. Today, debt is the American way. People buy houses and cars on credit without being looked down upon as debtors. Shaysites owned their own houses. They were cash-poor farmers who could not at the moment pay relatively small debts in specie.

In the fall of 1786, mobs forcibly closed half a dozen state civil courts to protest high state taxes and a lack of debtor relief. Massachusetts's refusal to provide debt or tax relief to struggling farmers led to this protest. The state imposed high property taxes that fell heavily on land-rich, cash-poor farmers. In the 1780s, Massachusetts taxes were higher than British taxes had ever been, and they fell most heavily on the western half of the state. Unlike other states, Massachusetts refused to grant any relief to westerners in the form of an inflationary paper currency or stay laws. Westerners also lacked easy access to the state government located far away in Boston. Many towns could not even afford to send representatives such a great distance.[63]

Shaysites also wanted to reform Massachusetts's 1780 constitution, which they felt was too aristocratic. This first charter drafted by a constitutional convention and ratified by the people is often seen as a farsighted document because it balanced power among three co-equal branches of government. But it was also more unfair to westerners than the constitutions in other states, and all attempts to reform it failed. Westerners wanted a more democratic constitution that did not favor rich over poor, and east over west. First, westerners wanted the state legislature, in which eastern Massachusetts was overrepresented and western Massachusetts was underrepresented, to be reapportioned. Second, Shaysites wanted the constitution to be made more democratic. They sought more elective offices, more frequent elections, and lower property qualifications for voting and for holding office. Third, western farmers wanted a unicameral legislature instead of a bicameral legislature, which they saw as undemocratic and expensive. Westerners felt that just like Great Britain before the Revolution, the Massachusetts government ignored those on the periphery, or treated them like second-class citizens. They saw themselves carrying on the Revolution by resisting a distant, oppressive government, this time in Boston instead of London.[64]

Another myth involves the so-called head of the rebellion, Daniel Shays. Easterners inflated him into the leader of the insurgents, portraying him as a would-be tyrant or perhaps even a British agent. In fact, Shays merely led the largest single contingent of protestors, and his original goal was debt relief and constitutional reform, not revolution. This grassroots bottom-up movement had no overall chief.[65]

At first westerners protested peacefully, within the democratic process, holding county conventions and submitting petitions to the state legislature, but to no avail. Peaceful protest having failed, the "Regulators" (as they styled themselves) turned militant, closing local civil courts (not criminal ones) by force to halt foreclosure proceedings. Most of the court closures were in central or western Massachusetts, but one took place in Concord, the very cradle of the Revolution, in September 1786, only a few miles from Boston. At another encounter the same month in Springfield, located in south-central Massachusetts, state forces led by General William Shepard seized weapons from the town's federal arsenal to protect the court against the Regulators. In the end, the court postponed its session and no violence occurred.[66]

Massachusetts authorities saw these activities not as a constitutional reform movement, but as a lawless challenge to republican government. To Governor James Bowdoin, this movement had nothing to do with the Revolution, a protest that had resisted taxation without representation, not taxation with representation. Viewing the situation as a simple case of right versus wrong and good versus evil, Bowdoin summoned the local militia to restore order. Instead of turning out in the state's defense, many of the militia joined the protest. The governor next turned to the federal government for help. After receiving alarmed reports from prominent Massachusetts men, the Confederation requisitioned the states for funds to raise troops to suppress the uprising. Congress nervously masked its purpose, claiming the troops would subdue hostile Indians. Virginia alone responded with funding for troops.

With the attempt to recruit federal forces having failed, Massachusetts now faced the unrest on its own. Bowdoin suppressed the rebellion with mercenaries raised by wealthy Bostonians. Funded by private subscription, the governor's 3,000-man army consisted entirely of easterners hired exclusively for a single campaign. Former Revolutionary War general Benjamin Lincoln commanded the force.

The establishment of a standing army, a traditional warning sign of tyranny, only radicalized the protesters. Before the raising of Lincoln's army, the insurgents' goal was economic relief and constitutional reform. But once easterners raised an army against them, the Shaysites changed their goal from constitutional reform to overthrow of the state government, now truly becoming rebels. Prophesies of state officials became self-fulfilling: by raising an army they created a true rebellion. Lincoln's mercenaries ultimately routed the Shaysites in a surprise attack at the Battle of Petersham, fought in a blinding snowstorm in February 1787. Thereafter the rebellion quickly died out, with most of the leaders, including Daniel Shays, fleeing to Vermont, an independent republic. Despite its military defeat, the rebellion in some ways succeeded politically. In 1787 Bowdoin lost his bid for reelection as governor in a landslide to John Hancock, who granted indemnity to most of the rebels. Once Bowdoin suffered defeat, the legislature cut taxes.[67]

As eastern elites lost their political grip on the state, they turned their attention to empowering the federal government. Before Shays's Rebellion, Massachusetts was not highly responsive to calls for streng-thening the Confederation and had even missed the Annapolis convention. But after the uprising, the state's elite, including Bowdoin, Henry Knox, Nathaniel Gorham, and Rufus King, supported the reform movement. At least one member of that group, Nathaniel Gorham, openly favored a return to monarchy. Gorham went so far as to write a letter to Prince Henry of Prussia, inviting him to become the monarch of America! Even men like Elbridge Gerry, who feared centralized power, now agreed that the time had come to strengthen the Confederation.

Massachusetts elites intentionally manipulated Shays's Rebellion to promote the idea that the United States faced an imminent crisis that only the upcoming Federal Convention could avert. Henry Knox, Washington's trusted artillery commander during the Revolutionary War, wrote wildly exaggerated reports of the uprising to correspondents around the country, including his former commander in chief. Accusing the rebels of having a radical agenda, Knox declared that the Shaysite "creed is, 'That the property of the United States has been protected from the confiscations of Britain by the joint exertions of all, and therefore ought to be the common property of all.'" That is, Knox broadcast the false claim that the rebels were levelers who wanted to redistribute the land of the wealthy to the poor. In urging New Hampshire to attend the convention, Knox wrote with similar hyperbole, "We are verging fast to anarchy . . . the present convention is the only means to avoid the most flagitious evils that ever afflicted three millions of freemen."[68]

Outside Massachusetts, the rebellion reinforced the preexisting views of leaders like Madison and Washington of the need for nationalistic reform. Knox's reports helped convince the latter to support the upcoming convention. After all, Washington did not want to see Mount Vernon carved up and distributed to the have-nots. Reading Knox's propaganda, Washington began to wonder whether the predictions of America's enemies were coming true. Was mankind truly incapable of governing himself? Would Americans have to give up on republican government and go back to monarchy? But Washington also expressed deep concern over the conservative Massachusetts elite who welcomed absolutism. "I am told that even respectable characters speak of a monarchical form of government without horror," he exclaimed. "But how irrevocable & tremendous! What a triumph for the advocates of despotism to find that we are incapable of governing ourselves, and that systems founded on the basis of equal liberty are merely ideal & fallacious!" Washington did not want to see reactionary forces use Shays's Rebellion as an excuse to move the nation back toward rule by a king. Washington believed that lawlessness must be suppressed, but also that the Shaysites' legitimate grievances must be addressed.[69]

Shays's Rebellion convinced Washington, Madison, and others that it was not just anarchy from below that threatened the republic. Rather, the nation faced a double threat—anarchy from below, and monarchy from above. For many leaders, this double threat marked the crisis of the American union. They became convinced that if dramatic measures were not taken, it could spell the end of republican government for all people, for all time.

In deciding whether to accept appointment to the Philadelphia convention, Washington faced perhaps the most difficult decision of his entire public life. He knew that his attendance could bring tremendous prestige to the convention. But what if only a few delegates showed up, as had happened at Annapolis? He might end up wasting his prestige on a failed convention. He knew that he had to spend his precious prestige at precisely the right moment to have maximum impact in promoting political reform. He simply wasn't sure that moment had arrived. Without Washington's knowledge, Madison, as a member of the Virginia legislature, nominated him as a delegate to the convention. When Washington insisted that his name be removed from the Virginia delegation, Madison convinced him to leave it there. Even if Washington did not attend, Madison argued, the expectation that he would participate ensured that other states would send their best men. Ultimately, the resultant full turnout persuaded Washington that he should participate after all—an outcome that would never have happened without Madison's shrewd tactics.

Other factors made Washington reluctant to attend the convention. In 1783, when he resigned from the army, his "Circular to the States" called for a stronger federal government, but at the same time announced his permanent departure from public life. Washington worried that to attend the convention would break his 1783 pledge never more to hold public office. Another issue that bothered Washington was the Federal Convention's lack of political legitimacy. The convention, which had not been endorsed by Congress, was an extralegal or perhaps even an unconstitutional gathering. If Washington attended and the convention further undermined Congress without achieving reform, then he might go down in history not as Cincinnatus, but as Caesar. Some historians have criticized Washington for his reluctance to attend the convention, but his caution was justified.

Congress's endorsement of the convention in February 1787, along with Washington's belief that the gathering offered the last chance to save the American republic, ultimately convinced him to attend. Washington always obsessed over his reputation, and how his actions would look. After initially inclining Washington to stay home, this concern instead helped convince him to attend. With the republic crumbling, he now decided that he would appear worse if he stayed home than if he participated in the convention. If he did not step forward in this moment of crisis, it might appear as if he did not support republicanism. He pondered, "Whether my non-attendance in this Convention will not be considered as a dereliction to republicanism—nay more—whether other motives may not (however injuriously) be ascribed to me for not exerting myself on this occasion in support of it."[70]

Shays's Rebellion did not cause the Constitutional Convention. Instead, it helped ensure attendance at a gathering that had already been scheduled. The insurgency sent shock waves across the country precisely when the states were deciding whether to appoint delegates to the convention. The significance of Shays's Rebellion is that it helped to convince all the states—except Rhode Island—to send delegates to Philadelphia. Perhaps the best way to understand the significance of Shays's Rebellion is by asking a counterfactual question: what if that uprising had never taken place? Without that disturbance, the 1787 convention might have failed because of low turnout. Shays's Rebellion was a timely event, a contingency that changed American history. By protesting an unfair state constitution, the Shaysites unwittingly helped to usher in a new federal constitution.

Rather than waiting for Congress to act, seven states approved the Philadelphia convention based on the Annapolis call alone: Virginia, New Jersey, Pennsylvania, North Carolina, New Hampshire, Delaware, and Georgia. Virginia's legislature acted first, voting in November 1787 to attend the convention and then appointing its delegates in December. Virginia wisely named George Washington, Patrick Henry, and other luminaries to the delegation, and then circulated those names to the other states to encourage their participation.

Five states (New York, South Carolina, Massachusetts, Connecticut, and Maryland) did not appoint delegates until after Congress endorsed the convention on February 21, 1787, "for the sole and express purpose of revising the Articles of Confederation." Massachusetts and Connecticut cited Congress's action in their resolutions. Maryland did not appoint delegates until May 26, the day after the convention began. Rhode Island refused to attend. Unlike other states, its legislature was dominated by middle-class men like the Shaysites in Massachusetts.

Content that power had been decentralized to the state level, they had no desire to create another distant centralized government. Rhode Island's dominant Country party opposed the convention because it correctly anticipated that that body would ban the states from issuing paper money. The state's mercantile interests carried too little weight to buck the anti-convention tide.[71]

The convention could hardly have succeeded without the sanction of the Confederation Congress. But could Congress approve a gathering that might overthrow the Articles or that might not follow the Articles' amendment procedure? Congress's ultimate endorsement of the convention illustrates the emerging consensus that the Confederation verged on collapse. Congress's resolution of February 21, 1787, attempted to reconcile the call issued by the Annapolis convention with the amendment provision of the Articles of Confederation. It authorized a convention "for the sole and express purpose of revising the Articles" to make them "adequate to the exigencies of Government & the preservation of the Union." Any recommendations the convention made would then have to be approved by Congress and all the state legislatures as prescribed by the Articles.[72]

The Annapolis report thus outlined a broader agenda than did Congress's resolution. The former called for rendering the Constitution "adequate to the exigencies of the Union," whereas Congress advocated merely "revising" the Articles. The Annapolis report already anticipated a true political revolution that would entirely replace the Articles of Confederation. For Congress to go that far would be to advocate its own overthrow. Seven of the twelve states that appointed delegates empowered them to act under the broader call of the Annapolis report rather than under the narrower call of Congress.

A perfect storm of factors came together late in 1786 and early in 1787 to create a virtual consensus among American leaders in general and particularly among the delegates appointed to attend the convention that the Confederation—and republican government—was collapsing. "Our affairs are considered on all hands as at a most serious crisis," wrote Madison, for "the cause of republican liberty." Having calmed down somewhat since his call for monarchy, Massachusetts delegate Nathaniel Gorham believed that "the business of the Convention is of the last importance for if the meeting or its doings should prove abortive the present phantom of a Government must soon expire." Washington warned "that something is necessary, none will deny; for the situation of the general government, if it can be called a government, is shaken to its foundation. . . . In a word, it is at an end; and, unless a remedy is soon applied, anarchy and confusion will inevitably ensue."[73]

The solution required a strengthening of the central government. Delaware delegate Jacob Broom asserted, "It is universally agreed that something ought to be done to establish the Government of the United States upon a more respectable footing than the present system." By forging an overwhelming majority in favor of reform of the Confederation, the events of 1786 and early 1787 set the stage for the Constitutional Convention to create a national government with taxation and commercial power. According to Gouverneur Morris, "Never, in the flow of time, was there a moment so propitious, as that in which the Convention assembled. The States had been convinced, by melancholy experience, how inadequate they were to the management of our national concerns."[74]

Altogether, the states appointed seventy-four delegates to the convention, but only fifty-five of them attended at one time or another. Those who went sympathized with nationalistic reform. Many of those who declined to participate, while conceding the need for change, hesitated to shift taxation power to Congress. Patrick Henry of Virginia famously turned down his invitation, supposedly observing that "he smelt a rat." Thus, a self-selection process took place in which those who might have obstructed the convention from adopting dramatic constitutional alterations absented themselves from the proceedings.[75]

The assessment that the United States faced a crisis brought on by the Confederation's utter inability to resolve pressing issues, generate revenue, or inspire public confidence appears in retrospect to have been an accurate one. Henry Knox exaggerated the imminent catastrophic consequences Americans faced, but the country truly suffered from political paralysis. With the Confederation unable to solve pressing problems, men of influence acted to prevent disunion and to save republican government, not to protect the class interests of the wealthy. This interpretation rejects the claims of historians like Charles Beard that selfish economic interests motivated the Founders. It also disputes Merrill Jensen's thesis that the nation did not really face a "critical period," and that the Confederation could have been salvaged. True, the Confederation government had achieved many successes, including winning the Revolutionary War and passing the Northwest Ordinance to regulate western land settlement, but accomplishments had given way to stalemate.[76]

As May brought leaves to Pennsylvania's trees, delegates trickled into Philadelphia. With a population of almost 40,000 people in 1787, America's largest city contained many boarding houses, such as the Indian Queen Tavern and the City Tavern, where the delegates could reside, caucus, and dine. A visitor noted that the former establishment "is kept in an elegant style, and consists of a large pile of buildings, with many spacious halls, and numerous small apartments, appropriated for lodging rooms." George Mason wrote that he and his son "are at the old *Indian Queen* in Fourth Street, where we are very well accommodated, have a good room to ourselves, and are charged only twenty-five Pennsylvania currency per day, including our servants [slaves] and horses." In addition to shops, theaters, and other cosmopolitan amenities, Philadelphia offered a religiously and ethnically diverse and tolerant atmosphere, where men of varying cultures and faiths felt comfortable. Many of the delegates found Philadelphia, the former national capital, a familiar place. Southerners, however, considered the antislavery views of many city residents unsettling. Numerous guests crowded into town that spring. In addition to the Constitutional Convention, three other conventions met in Philadelphia—the Baptists, the Presbyterians, and an organization of Revolutionary War officers known as the Society of the Cincinnati.[77]

James Madison arrived in Philadelphia on May 5 and took up lodgings at Mary House's boardinghouse at Fifth and High (later renamed Market) streets, where he had stayed many times before. When Washington arrived on May 13, according to Madison, he received "the acclamations of the people, as well as more sober marks of the affection and veneration which continue to be felt for his character." Even after being in the city for several weeks, Washington's appearance in the streets still drew a crowd. "The Number of People that followed him, on all Sides, was astonishing," wrote Philadelphian Jacob Hiltzheimer. Robert Morris, a Revolutionary War financier and Pennsylvania delegate to the convention, prevailed on Washington to stay as a guest in his mansion located at Sixth and High streets. (Martha Washington had remained at Mount Vernon.) As his first order of business, Washington paid his respects to the city's most famous resident, Benjamin Franklin. Virginia and Pennsylvania were officially present in time for the scheduled opening of the convention on May 14, but none of the other delegations had enough members present yet to participate. Eager to get to work on a political revolution, Madison had to cool his heels until less-punctual delegates arrived.[78]

NOTES

1. Richard B. Morris, *The Forging of the Union, 1781–1789* (New York: Harper & Row, 1987), 80–91.

2. See Jack N. Rakove, *The Beginnings of National Politics: An Interpretive History of the Continental Congress* (New York: Alfred A. Knopf, 1979).

3. Norman J. Risjord, *Thomas Jefferson* (Madison, WI: Madison House, 1994), 32–34.

4. Stuart Leibiger, *Founding Friendship: George Washington, James Madison, and the Creation of the American Republic* (Charlottesville: University of Virginia Press, 1999), 16–17.

5. Stuart Leibiger, "James Madison," in Stephen L. Schechter et al., eds., *American Governance* (New York: Macmillan Reference, 2016), 3:225–29.

6. Kenneth R. Bowling, *The Creation of Washington, D.C.: The Idea and Location of the American Capital* (Fairfax, VA: George Mason University Press, 1991), 30–42.

7. George William Van Cleve, *We Have Not a Government: The Articles of Confederation and the Road to the Constitutional Convention* (Chicago, IL: University of Chicago Press, 2017), 17–47, 102–29.

8. Ibid., 48–101; Max Farrand, ed., *The Records of the Federal Convention of 1787.* 1937 rev. ed. in four vols., reprint (New Haven, CT: Yale University Press, 1974), hereafter cited as *RFC*, 3:523.

9. Van Cleve, *We Have Not a Government*, 48–101.

10. Ibid., 133–85.

11. Willi Paul Adams, *The First American Constitutions: Republican Ideology and the Making of the State Constitutions in the Revolutionary Era* (Chapel Hill: University of North Carolina Press, 1980), 5–6; Danielle Allen, *Our Declaration: A Reading of the Declaration of Independence in Defense of Equality* (New York: Liveright, 2014), 59–64.

12. Adams, *The First American Constitutions*, 76–80. See also Gordon Wood, *The Creation of the American Republic, 1776–1787* (Chapel Hill: University of North Carolina Press, 1969).

13. Ibid., 262–66.

14. Ibid., 86–93.

15. Ibid., 146–47.

16. Hall, *Roger Sherman*, 86–87; Van Cleve, *We Have Not a Government*, 189–213.

17. Merrill Peterson, ed., *Jefferson: Writings* (New York: Library of America, 1984), 245.

18. Leibiger, "James Madison," 225. The definitive biography is Ralph Ketcham, *James Madison: A Biography* (New York: Macmillan, 1971).

19. Jack N. Rakove, *A Politician Thinking: The Creative Mind of James Madison* (Norman: University of Oklahoma Press, 2017), 54–95; Jack N. Rakove, *James Madison and the Creation of the American Republic* (Glenview, IL: Scott, Foresman, 1990), 30–52; James H. Hutson, ed., *Supplement to Max Farrand's* The Records of the Federal Convention of 1787 (New Haven, CT: Yale University Press, 1987), hereafter cited as *RFC Supplement*, 319; William T. Hutchinson et al., eds., *The Papers of James Madison, Congressional Series*, 17 vols. (Chicago, IL, and Charlottesville: University of Chicago Press and University of Virginia Press, 1962–1991), hereafter cited as *PJM*, 10:212.

20. John P. Kaminski and Timothy D. Moore, eds., *An Assembly of Demigods: Word Portraits of the Delegates to the Constitutional Convention by Their Contemporaries* (Madison, WI: Parallel Press, 2012), hereafter cited as *Demigods*, 173; Drew R. McCoy, *The Last of the Fathers: James Madison and the Republican Legacy* (Cambridge, MA: Cambridge University Press, 1989), xiii; *RFC*, 3:426.

21. *PJM*, 10:12–18.

22. *RFC*, 3:51.

23. *Demigods*, 205, 216, 228; Leibiger, *Founding Friendship*, 5–6.

24. Leibiger, *Founding Friendship*, 6.

25. Edward L. Larson, *The Return of George Washington* (New York: HarperCollins, 2014), 33–66.

26. W. W. Abbot et al., eds., *The Papers of George Washington, Confederation Series*, 6 vols. (Charlottesville: University of Virginia Press, 1992–1997), hereafter cited as *PGW-CS*, 2:89–96, quoted at 92.

27. Leibiger, *Founding Friendship*, 33–57.

28. *PGW-CS*, 3:300.

29. Constitution of Virginia, 1776, http://nhinet.org/ccs/docs/va-1776.htm; Constitution of Maryland, 1776, http://avalon.law.yale.edu/17th_century/ma02.asp.

30. *Journal of the House of Delegates of Virginia*, Spring 1784 Sess., 84.

31. Norman J. Risjord, *Chesapeake Politics, 1781–1800* (New York: Columbia University Press, 1978), 258; Robert A. Rutland, ed., *The Papers of George Mason*, 3 vols. (Chapel Hill: University of North Carolina Press, 1970), hereafter cited as *PGM*, 2:826; *PJM*, 8:324.

32. *PGM*, 2:826–27; *PJM*, 8:324.

The Road to Philadelphia

33. Ibid., 2:826–27; Donald Jackson and Dorothy Twohig, eds., *The Diaries of George Washington*, 6 vols. (Charlottesville: University of Virginia Press, 1976–1979), hereafter cited as *DGW*, 4:105.

34. Jeff Broadwater, *George Mason: Forgotten Founder* (Chapel Hill: University of North Carolina Press, 2006), quoted at 136; *Demigods*, 189.

35. *DGW*, 4:106–7; *PJM*, 8:337–38 & n1.

36. *PJM*, 8:337–38 & n1.

37. *DGW*, 4:107–9.

38. *PGW-CS*, 2:562.

39. *DGW*, 4:107–9.

40. Ibid.; Joseph Manca, *George Washington's Eye: Landscape, Architecture, and Design at Mount Vernon* (Baltimore, MD: Johns Hopkins University Press, 2012), 83–118.

41. *DGW*, 4:107–9; *PGW-CS*, 2:460–68. It is not clear where in the mansion the conference met, but the commissioners probably gathered in the West Parlor, a room adjoining the main hallway of the house. Washington described the West Parlor, used for family entertainments, as "the best place in my House," so this is likely where he invited his important guests to transact their business. Furnished with a sofa, several chairs, and small tables, the room was the right size for a meeting of only five men. The West Parlor provided the perfect setting to hold friendly talks and to reach a consensus over the issues separating the two states.

The conference most certainly did not meet in the large dining room on the north end of the house. The "New Room," as Washington called it, was much too spacious for such a small group of men. Still under construction in 1785, the room was not plastered until the following year. Nor did the room have heat, because Washington had not yet installed the fireplace that he received as a gift from merchant Samuel Vaughn. Thus, the New Room would have been much too drafty for the talks to be held there. *PGW-CS*, 3:155. *Official Guidebook: George Washington's Mount Vernon* (Mount Vernon, VA: Mount Vernon Ladies Association, no publication date), 51–55; *DGW*, 4:96–111, 114, 291–92.

42. *PGM*, 2:826–27.

43. Ibid., 818.

44. Ibid., 816–21; 54 U.S. 2 (2003).

45. *PGM*, 2:816, 822–23.

46. *Votes and Proceedings of the House of Delegates of the State of Maryland*, Nov. 1785 Sess., 7, 10, 19; *Votes and Proceedings of the Senate of Maryland*, Nov. 1785 Sess., 3, 7.

47. *PJM*, 8:457–61, 9:348–49; *PGM*, 2:835–38; *Journal of the House of Delegates of Virginia*, 1785 Sess., 119; 153 U.S. 155.

48. *PJM*, 8:409–10; 413–15, 431–32, 476–77.

49. *Journal of the House of Delegates of Virginia*, 1785 Sess., 153; *PJM*, 8:476–77. Madison's March 10, 1826, letter to Webster corrected a mistake in his Oct. 12, 1804, letter to Webster taking credit for the resolution that led to the Annapolis convention. That letter stated, "In 1785, I [Madison] made a proposition with success in the [Virginia] Legislature . . . for the appt. of Commissrs. to meet at Annapolis such Commissrs. as might be appointed by the other States, in order to form some plan for investing Congress with the regulation & taxation of Commerce." James Madison Papers, Library of Congress.

50. *Journal of the House of Delegates of Virginia*, 1785 Sess., 153; *PJM*, 8:470–71, 476–77, 483.

51. *PJM*, 8:439; Adrienne Koch, ed., *Notes of Debates in the Federal Convention of 1787 Reported by James Madison* (Athens: Ohio University Press, 1966), hereafter cited as *NDFC*, 9–10.

52. Forrest McDonald, *E Pluribus Unum: The Formation of the American Republic, 1776–1790*, 2nd ed. (Indianapolis, IN: Liberty Press, 1979), 236; Irving Brant, *James Madison*, 6 vols. (Indianapolis, IN: Bobbs-Merrill, 1941–1961), 2:375–78; 51.

53. Edward Coles, "Letters of Edward Coles," 3rd installment, *William & Mary Quarterly*, 2nd ser., 7 (1927), 171.

54. *PJM*, 8:505.

55. Leibiger, *Founding Friendship*, 59–61.

56. Ibid.; Morris, *Forging the Union*, 252–57.

57. Morris, *Forging the Union*, 252–57.

58. Rakove, *Politician Thinking*, 32–33; *RFC*, 3:14, 418.

59. *Demigods*, 67, 70, 79, 82, 85–86.

60. Harold C. Syrett et al., eds., *The Papers of Alexander Hamilton*, 27 vols. (New York: Columbia University Press, 1961–1987), 3:686–90.

61. Ibid.

62. Leonard L. Richards, *Shays's Rebellion: The American Revolution's Final Battle* (Philadelphia: University of Pennsylvania Press, 2002), ix–x, 1–3, 159–62.

63. Ibid., 4–27.

64. Ibid., 7–11, 71–74.

65. Ibid., 26–27.

66. Ibid., 43–62; Sean Condon, *Shays's Rebellion: Authority and Distress in Post-Revolutionary America* (Baltimore, MD: Johns Hopkins University Press, 2015), 58–61.

67. Richards, *Shays's Rebellion*, 23–42.

68. Ibid., 117–38; *RFC Supplement*, 13; *PGW-CS*, 4:300.

69. *PGW-CS*, 4:213, 477–84.

70. Ibid., 5:74–75; Leibiger, *Founding Friendship*, 58–70.

71. *RFC*, 3:13–14, 559–86; John P. Kaminski et al., eds., "Introduction to the Ratification of the Constitution in Rhode Island," in *Documentary History of the Ratification of the Constitution Digital Edition* (Charlottesville: University of Virginia Press, 2009), hereafter cited as *DHRCDE*, 7–8.

72. *RFC*, 3:13–14.

73. *RFC*, 3:31, 37; *RFC Supplement*, 14.

74. *RFC*, 3:391; *RFC Supplement*, 16.

75. Lance Banning, *Founding Visions: The Ideas, Individuals, and Intersections That Created America* (Lexington: University Press of Kentucky, 2014), 111.

76. Beard, *An Economic Interpretation of the Constitution*; Merrill Jensen, *The New Nation: A History of the United States during the Confederation, 1774–1781* (New York: Random House, 1950); *RFC*, 3:31. My interpretation agrees with Van Cleve, *We Have Not a Government*, 7–13.

77. *RFC*, 3:24, 58; Stuart Leibiger, "Constitutional Convention of 1787," *The Encyclopedia of Greater Philadelphia*, https://philadelphiaencyclopedia.org/archive/constitutional-convention/.

78. *PJM*, 9:415; Leibiger, *Founding Friendship*, 70; *RFC Supplement*, 52.

CHAPTER 2

THE TRIUMPH OF THE VIRGINIA PLAN

After convening on May 25, 1787, the Constitutional Convention unanimously elected George Washington its president and adopted rules to govern its proceedings. Of his own volition, James Madison began recording the daily debates to preserve them, he later claimed, for posterity. On May 29, the first substantive day of debate, Virginia governor Edmund Randolph presented the Virginia Plan, a series of resolutions outlining not a modest revision of the Articles of Confederation, but an entirely new national government with executive, legislative, and judicial branches that operated on the people directly without the states as intermediaries. Representation in congress would be based on each state's free population or taxes paid, not state equality. Over the next three weeks the delegates, sitting as the committee of the whole, debated the resolutions one by one. The Virginia Plan survived this process largely intact thanks to the emergence of an alliance between the large, populous states of Virginia, Pennsylvania, and Massachusetts, and the Lower South states of Georgia, South Carolina, and North Carolina. Especially pleasing to these three slave states was a provision counting slaves as three-fifths of free people toward representation in both houses of congress, which would help safeguard their slave property and enhance their political power. The small-population states of Connecticut, Delaware, Maryland, and New Jersey increasingly fearful of being swallowed up by the large states, announced on June 14 that they would present an alternative to the Virginia Plan. New York, a mid-sized state that opposed a powerful federal government, also sided with the small states.

On Monday, May 14, the scheduled date for the convention to open, "a small number only," according to Madison, gathered in the Assembly

Room of the Pennsylvania State House. The forty-by-forty-foot ground floor chamber to the east of the main hallway was normally used by the Pennsylvania Assembly. It had three large windows to the north facing Chestnut Street, and three large windows to the South facing the State House Yard. The presiding officer sat against the paneled eastern wall adorned with carved pilasters. The furnishings included separate tables and chairs to accommodate each state delegation. One delegate aptly described the chamber as "neat but not elegant."[1]

The room already had a rich history, having witnessed George Washington's appointment as commander in chief of the Continental Army and the adoption and signing of the Declaration of Independence. The Pennsylvania State House, today known as Independence Hall, was constructed in the 1750s. By the 1780s, the original steeple had been taken down and replaced with a lower three-story structure featuring "a hipped roof capped by a finial." The much taller bell tower that stands there now was built in 1828. Manasseh Cutler, who visited Philadelphia in July 1787, described "a noble building" whose "architecture is in a richer and grander style than any public building I have before seen."[2]

The delays occasioned by tardy delegates, Washington complained, "greatly impede public measures, and serve to sour the temper of the punctual members, who do not like to idle away their time." On May 16, Franklin hosted those present for a dinner featuring a "cask of porter" that won "universal approbation." George Mason, who arrived on May 17, wrote that "the Virginia Deputies (who are all here) meet and confer together two or three hours every day in order to form a proper correspondence of sentiments." Madison used these informal pre-convention discussions to gain the support of colleagues like Mason, who had not yet formed "any opinion upon the great subject of our mission," for his Virginia Plan. All the delegates present gathered at the State House every day at 3 p.m. to determine whether a quorum had been achieved yet. Conversations also took place at these meetings. Joining the Virginians were the delegates from Pennsylvania, the only other state with enough participants present to be officially represented. Mason wrote that these talks, attended by a handful of delegates from the other states, allowed the men "to grow into some acquaintance with each other."[3]

Pennsylvania's eight-man delegation, the largest of any state, consisted entirely of Philadelphians. One of them, Gouverneur Morris, a powerful

Engraving by W. Birch of the Pennsylvania State House in Philadelphia as it looked during the Constitutional Convention. The convention met from May 25 to September 17, 1787, in the Assembly Room of the State House. The Pennsylvania ratification convention later met in the same location. Today the building is known as Independence Hall. (Library of Congress)

nationalist, earned a reputation as an eloquent writer while a member of the Continental Congress. "I have drawn and expect to draw almost if not all the Publications of Congress of any Importance," he boasted in 1778. By all accounts charming and sociable—especially among women—Morris also possessed a reputation for rakishness and arrogance. "No Man has more wit," commented Georgia delegate William Pierce, "nor can anyone engage the attention more than Mr. Morris." Another contemporary described him as "refined as a European, free as an American, he . . . is welcomed with pleasure in Philadelphia society." George Washington captured Morris's darker side: "His Manners . . . are oftentimes disgusting" and his "immoral & loose expressions had created opinions of himself that were not favorable to him." A severe carriage accident in 1780 resulted in the amputation of his leg below the knee. With Morris's womanizing reputation in mind, John Jay wrote, "I am almost tempted to wish he had lost something else."⁴

Gouverneur Morris fully supported Madison's nationalist agenda, but he and Robert Morris, also of Pennsylvania, wanted the states big in population (hereafter called "large states") to insist that voting in the convention not be based on the traditional one-state, one-vote rule used under the Articles of Confederation. To grant the states an equal vote in the convention, they warned, would allow the states small in population (hereafter called "small states") "to negative every good system of Government." The Virginia delegates agreed on strategy but disagreed on tactics. They concurred that a final constitution must not be based on state equality but warned that to try to abandon voting by state delegations in the convention itself would immediately "beget fatal altercations" that would doom the gathering from the outset. The Virginians argued that "it would be easier to prevail on" the small states "in the course of the deliberations, to give up their equality for the sake of an effective Government" rather than immediately to "throw them on the mercy of the large States." The Virginians won this tactical debate. The large states agreed to the one-state, one-vote rule during the convention. In so doing, they saved the convention from a premature break up but also gave the small states a significant advantage of which they made the most. The divisive large state-small state split over representation had already reared its head.⁵

George Read of Delaware grew alarmed over the conversation between the Virginians and the Pennsylvanians. "Of a low stature, and a weak constitution," Read, wrote William Pierce, tried the patience of his listeners because "his voice is feeble, and his articulation so bad that few can have patience to attend to him." Despite having been appointed Delaware's attorney general by King George III, Read joined the colonial resistance movement against Great Britain. A member of the Second Continental Congress, Read had signed the Declaration of Independence despite having voted against the break with Great Britain. A powerful force in Delaware politics, Read had represented the state at the Annapolis convention.⁶

Recognizing the threat the Virginia Plan posed to the less-populous states, Read urged his colleague John Dickinson to make haste for Philadelphia. "The small States," he warned, "should keep a strict watch upon the movements and propositions from the larger States, who will probably combine to swallow up the smaller ones." Of all the states, Delaware alone had instructed its delegates not to change the Confederation's equal state voting system. Read himself had engineered this directive.[7]

Each state's instructions to its delegates specified how many of them needed to be present officially to represent the state and to cast votes. Maryland and Connecticut required only one delegate to be in attendance; North Carolina, New Hampshire, Georgia, and South Carolina required two; Virginia, New Jersey, Delaware, and Massachusetts required three; and Pennsylvania required four. New York was the one and only state that did not set a threshold in its instructions. The convention decided that two of New York's three delegates had to be present for the state to cast a vote.[8]

The convention formally began on Friday, May 25, with seven states (a majority) now officially represented: New York, New Jersey, Pennsylvania, Delaware, Virginia, North Carolina, and South Carolina. Only Rufus King of Massachusetts had arrived from New England. Several others from that region encountered travel delays because of rainy weather. The following Monday, additional arrivals from Connecticut and Massachusetts raised the number of states officially represented to nine. Georgia and Maryland became official on May 31 and June 2, respectively. New Hampshire appointed delegates but because the state neglected to appropriate money to pay for their travel, those men stayed home. Rather than to allow the state to continue entirely unrepresented, wealthy merchant John Langdon eventually agreed to cover his own expenses and those of his colleague Nicholas Gillman. Not until July 21, with the convention already two months under way, did these two men arrive to represent New Hampshire. Rhode Island never attended.[9]

Robert Morris of Pennsylvania stood to begin the proceedings. After immigrating to America from England in 1747 at age thirteen, Morris apprenticed as a Philadelphia merchant and later emerged as one of the richest businessmen in the United States. As a member of the Second Continental Congress, he voted against independence because he thought it premature, but nevertheless signed the Declaration. He earned the title "Financier of the Revolution" by raising funds to procure weapons and supplies for American forces during the war with Great Britain. As the Confederation's superintendent of finance from 1781 to 1784, he pushed for a strong national government that could repay the foreign and domestic war debt. Americans who feared centralized power, and who associated sophisticated economic policies with the tyranny and corruption of Great Britain, distrusted Morris's fiscal dealings. Many believed that Morris lined his pockets by mixing personal and public business. In 1786, he had attended the Annapolis convention.[10]

Speaking for the Pennsylvania delegation, Morris nominated George Washington to be the convention's president. Only Benjamin Franklin possessed the prestige to rival Washington for the position. By making the nomination, Morris signaled that Pennsylvania stood aside, allowing Washington to be the only nominee. Madison noted that Franklin himself had hoped to make the nomination but stayed home that day because of poor weather. Seconding the nomination, John Rutledge of South Carolina voiced "confidence that the choice would be unanimous." Washington's presence in the room kept Rutledge from heaping praise on him. After unanimous election "by ballot" of the state delegations, Washington assumed the presiding officer's chair on a raised platform at the front of the Assembly Room. The Chippendale-style chair had a half sun carved into its backrest. Washington "in a very emphatic manner thanked the Convention for the honor they had conferred on him." He "reminded" his associates "of the novelty of the scene of business in which he was to act," apologized for not being better qualified for the task of presiding, and begged "indulgence" for any "involuntary errors which his inexperience might occasion." Privately, Washington wrote that he was "much against my wish, unanimously placed in the Chair."[11]

Aside his short acceptance statement, Washington did not deliver any remarks lengthy enough to be considered a speech until the last day of the convention. How do we account for Washington's silence in debate during the convention? Those who see Washington as a figurehead rather than a thoughtful, contemplative man might argue that he did not speak because he had little to say about the issues before the convention. Nothing could be further from the truth. Washington held deep convictions about the type of government he wished to see created. His strong nationalism was heavily shaped by his often-frustrating experiences as commander in chief of the Continental Army during the Revolutionary War, when he had been hampered by the weakness, inefficiency, and impoverishment of the Confederation. A large-state man, he firmly supported the Virginia Plan and wished for a muscular but republican government with a powerful and effective executive branch. Washington always voted within the Virginia delegation, sometimes tipping the balance one way or the other.

Washington remained silent during the convention for three reasons. First, as the convention president and the most prestigious man in attendance, he felt obligated to remain above the fray. It simply would not do for a man of such decorum to be besting his colleagues in debate over minor points, or worse yet, being bested by them. As Washington put it on the convention's last day, "His situation had hitherto restrained him from offering his sentiments on questions" on the floor. Second, although Washington at times had addressed his troops with eloquence, he was not an orator in the parliamentary sense of the word. Besides, there were plenty of skilled speakers who could articulate his views with much greater cogency, especially his friend James Madison, with whom he saw eye-to-eye on the political reforms that ought to take place. Finally, just as Washington had been the presumptive convention president, he would also be the nation's presumptive chief executive should one be created. The delegates spent much of the spring and summer of 1787 designing the presidency. It was seemingly inappropriate for the man who might someday hold that office to take the lead in designing it.[12]

Despite his silence in debate, Washington found other ways to shape the proceedings. When dining and socializing with various delegates after hours, he doubtless made his views and wishes known. Jonathan Dayton of New Jersey reminisced that a stern glance from Washington on the convention floor could make an errant delegate regret an ill-advised statement. William Pierce of Georgia recorded a story that nicely captures Washington's influence over his colleagues. In August, each delegate received a printed version of a draft constitution prepared by the Committee of Detail. According to the convention's rules of secrecy, this document was to be kept strictly confidential. "One Morning," wrote Pierce,

> by accident, one of the Members dropt his copy of the propositions, which being luckily picked up by General [Thomas] Mifflin was presented to General Washington, our President, who put it in his Pocket.—After the debates of the Day were over . . . the General arose from his seat, and . . . addressed the Convention in the following manner,—
>
> "Gentlemen
>
> "I am sorry to find that some one Member of this Body, has been so neglectful of the secrets of the Convention as to drop in the State House a

copy of their proceedings, which by accident was picked up and delivered to me this Morning.—I must entreat Gentlemen to be more careful, least our transactions get into the News Papers, and disturb the public repose by premature speculations.—I know not whose Paper it is, but there it is (throwing it down on the Table,)—let him who owns it take it."—At the same time he bowed, picked up his Hat, and quitted the room with a dignity so severe that every Person seemed alarmed. . . . It is something remarkable that no Person ever owned the Paper.

Upon reaching into his own pocket and failing to locate his copy of the document, Pierce became panic-stricken that he was the careless individual who had endangered the convention's confidentiality. "But advancing up to the Table, my fears soon dissipated,—I found it to be in the hand writing of another Person.—When I went to my lodgings at the Indian Queen, I found my copy in a Coat Pocket which I had pulled off that Morning."[13]

The convention appointed William Jackson as convention secretary and charged him with recording the convention's votes and resolutions in a journal. A former major in the Continental Army, Jackson had served as an aide to General Washington and as assistant secretary at war under the Confederation. He had escorted his former commander in chief into the city and had lobbied him and other delegates for the job of convention secretary. Jackson won the position over rival candidates John Beckley, the clerk of Virginia's House of Delegates, who had accompanied Virginia governor Edmund Randolph to Philadelphia in hopes of obtaining the appointment, and William Temple Franklin, who lacked qualifications but possessed the support of his famous grandfather. Philadelphian William Shippen found "Old Dr. F. much mortified that he had not Interest enough to procure the place for his Grandson." Jackson's record-keeping left much to be desired. When in 1818 Secretary of State John Quincy Adams prepared the convention journal for publication, he found it disorganized and slovenly. "So imperfect, and in such disorder" appeared the journal, wrote Adams, "that to have published" it as it was "would have given to the public a book useless and in many respects inexplicable." Jackson's duties did not include recording the speeches and debates at the convention. James Madison took it upon himself to perform that task.[14]

In an essay that became the preface to his *Notes of Debates in the Federal Convention of 1787,* Madison late in life explained what motived him to record the convention's proceedings. As a student of "the History of the most distinguished Confederacies, particularly those of antiquity," he often found himself frustrated by the lack of contemporary accounts chronicling "the process, the principles, the reasons, & the anticipations, which prevailed in the formation of them." He hoped that by taking notes on the formation of the constitution, he would spare future generations the same frustration.

"In pursuance of the task I had assumed I chose a seat in front of the presiding member, with the other members on my right & left hands," explained Madison. "In this favorable position for hearing all that passed, I noted in terms legible & in abbreviations & marks intelligible to myself what was read from the Chair or spoken by the members; and losing not a moment unnecessarily between the adjournment & reassembling of the Convention I was enabled to write out my daily notes . . . during the session or within a few finishing days after its close." Since he did not miss a single day all summer, "nor more than a casual fraction of an hour in any day," he "could not have lost a single speech, unless a very short one." Madison condensed each five-hour day into about five to ten printed pages. It was not easy work. In July, he informed Jefferson, "I have taken lengthy notes of every thing that has yet passed, and mean to go on with the drudgery, if no indisposition obliges me to discontinue it."[15]

The speeches Madison recorded "were neither furnished, nor revised, nor sanctioned, by the speakers, but written out from my notes, aided by the freshness of my recollections." The only exceptions were one speech each by Edmund Randolph, Alexander Hamilton, and Gouverneur Morris, and several speeches prepared by Benjamin Franklin, all of which were either approved by or supplied in writing by the speaker himself.[16]

Of ten delegates who took notes of one sort or another, Madison clearly did the best job. Madison took about 75 percent of the surviving notes taken at the convention. The other nine notetakers combined took only 25 percent of the notes. He alone recorded the entire convention every day from start to finish. Each of the other notetakers missed at least a month of the convention. Only Madison took notes for the first half of July, when the convention adopted the Great Compromise over representation.[17]

How credible of a primary source is Madison's Notes? Madison went through his Notes several times during the remainder of his life, trying—he claimed—to make them more complete and accurate. In 1789, he borrowed Secretary Jackson's convention journal from George Washington to make corrections to the motions and votes recorded in his Notes. After Secretary of State John Quincy Adams published the convention journal for the U.S. government in 1819, Madison again used it to corroborate his Notes. Madison also mined the convention notes of New York delegate Robert Yates when they appeared in print in 1821, further enhancing his Notes.

After the posthumous publication of Madison's Notes in 1840, supporters of Alexander Hamilton questioned their veracity. Throughout the nineteenth and twentieth centuries, a handful of other scholars did as well. They suggested that Madison altered his Notes for partisan political purposes, exaggerating the nationalism and anti-republicanism of some delegates (especially Hamilton), and minimizing that of others, including himself. Perhaps the most famous debunker of Madison's Notes was William W. Crosskey, professor of law at the University of Chicago, who developed an elaborate theory that Madison forged the convention speeches of various delegates and inserted them in his Notes. Crosskey never provided evidence to back up his stunning charges.

In 1987, James H. Hutson, the director of the Manuscript Division of the Library of Congress, defended the veracity of Madison's Notes. After comparing a 1790s transcript of Madison's Notes with the 1840 version, and after verifying that the paper that Madison used to write the Notes did not come from a later era, Hutson concluded that Madison's motive in revising his Notes "was the laudable one of giving the American people as thorough a record as he could of a seminal event in their history." Hutson added that "a heavy burden of proof rests upon those who would contend that Madison, as editor, progressively corrupted his notes after 1787."[18]

In her 2015 book *Madison's Hand*, Mary Sarah Bilder takes on that weighty burden. Bilder accuses Madison of revising his Notes with 20/20 hindsight. By 1790, Madison, a Virginia member of the U.S. House of Representatives, was now certain that Treasury Secretary Alexander Hamilton aimed to restore a British-style monarchy in America. Bilder claims that Madison then went back and rewrote his own convention addresses

The Triumph of the Virginia Plan

to distance himself from the nationalism of Hamilton's June 18, 1787, speech advocating a president and senate for life and a drastic reduction in the powers of the states. For example, Madison supposedly minimized his criticisms of the state governments and downplayed his support of a congressional power to veto state laws, a strong executive, and an aristocratic senate that would protect the property interests of the wealthy. Bilder even suggests that the replacement speeches included attacks on slavery that Madison never delivered at the convention.[19]

Bilder's Madison is obsessed with removing inconsistencies in his political record and making sure that his Notes did not conflict with the accounts of other convention delegates. Is Bilder right that Madison later doctored the record? Or is Hutson right that Madison made only minor corrections in the name of historical accuracy? Given Madison's longstanding frustration with those who willfully or inadvertently distorted his views, it is likely that he revised his Notes to clarify his positions at the 1787 convention rather than to change them.

Up until the publication of *Madison's Hand*, most historians agreed with Hutson, accepting the Notes, by and large, as a faithful account of the convention. Even after the publication of *Madison's Hand*, there is still much to be said for this interpretation. If, as Gordon Lloyd has argued, Madison doctored his notes late in life to make himself look better, he was a poor doctor. Madison recorded the remarks of delegates who sharply disagreed with him, in clear, forceful, cogent terms. In the Notes, moreover, Madison faithfully presents himself as having been an inflexible and stubborn partisan who suffered many defeats during the convention.[20]

Madison's Notes are unquestionably the best historical source available for the convention, and so historians rely heavily upon them. We should remember, however, that the Notes are not an infallible gospel, but rather a primary source that must be mined carefully and skeptically, just like other evidence. Material gleaned from the Notes must be read critically and weighed against other primary sources. Madison's biases and state of mind must always be factored into the equation. In short, Madison's Notes challenge historians to engage in the rigorous process of informed speculation that is a hallmark of their profession.

The convention rounded out its first day by appointing George Wythe, Alexander Hamilton, and Charles Pinckney to a committee to propose rules to govern the convention's proceedings. After spending a weekend preparing recommendations, the Rules Committee reported to the full convention on Monday, May 28. A floor debate resulted in several additions to the committee's suggestions. The delegates agreed that voting would be by state, that seven states had to be present to conduct business, and that a majority of the states present would carry a vote. Those recognized by the president to speak were to be listened to with respect. No side conversations or reading was permitted when a delegate took the floor. Committees would be appointed by a vote of the delegates. No decisions of the convention were final; any vote could be reconsidered and changed provided one day's notice be given. This key rule allowed a bold proposal like Madison's Virginia Plan, intended to replace the Confederation with a much more powerful national government, to become the focus of debate. The delegates knew that they could experiment with controversial ideas because any decisions they made could be overturned later.[21]

The convention wisely adopted rules of secrecy that Madison later pronounced a key to the convention's ultimate success. The most important secrecy rule decreed "that nothing spoken in the House be printed, or otherwise published or communicated without leave." Mason reported to his son that "all communications of the proceedings are forbidden during the sitting of the Convention." Secrecy served numerous purposes. First, it allowed the delegates to speak their minds freely. Madison explained that it would "secure unbiased discussions within doors." Second, confidentiality ensured that the delegates spoke to one another, instead of grandstanding for the media or for their constituents back home. Virginia's chancellor, Edmund Pendleton, believed that confidentiality caused "the Ebulitions of fire, fancy & Party amongst the Members to evaporate." Third, secrecy prevented outside interests from exerting pressure on the convention until the entire package was complete. Hamilton insisted, "Had the deliberations been open . . . the clamours of faction would have prevented any satisfactory result." Fourth, confidentiality helped prevent false rumors from agitating the public mind. Without secrecy, wrote Alexander Martin of North Carolina, "unfavourable Representations might be made by imprudent printers of the many crude matters & things daily uttered & produced in this Body, which . . . might make an undue impression on the too credulous and unthinking Mobility." Madison wrote that secrecy would save "the Community from a thousand erroneous and perhaps mischievous reports." Fifth, secrecy made it possible for individual delegates to reconsider their positions and change their votes over time without having to worry about charges of inconsistency. "No man felt himself obliged," wrote Madison, "to retain his opinions any longer than he was satisfied of their propriety and truth, and was open to the force of argument." To further encourage open-mindedness, the votes of individual members were not recorded in the convention journal.[22]

The secrecy rules provoked little public controversy during the time that the convention sat because legislative bodies usually met in secret. The Continental and Confederation congresses met behind closed doors, as did many of the conventions that drafted state constitutions. Madison did not perceive "any discontent . . . at the concealment." From Paris, however, Minister to France Thomas Jefferson complained that the delegates "began their deliberations by so abominable a precedent as that of tying up the tongues of their members," a mistake caused by "ignorance of the value of public discussions." Luther Martin of Maryland, not yet present when the convention opened, later complained that secrecy prevented participants "from corresponding" with statesmen outside the convention "upon the subjects under our discussion."[23]

Most of the participants honored the secrecy rules in good faith. William Pierce wrote to his friend St. George Tucker, "I wish it was in my power to give you some information respecting the proceedings of the Convention, but we are enjoined to secrecy. I dare not say any thing." Richard Dobbs Spaight informed North Carolina governor Richard Caswell, "not being at Liberty to Communicate anything that passes in the Convention, I have nothing to write about." Before joining the delegates in Philadelphia, William Blount of North Carolina noted, "The Members of the Convention observe such inviolable Secrecy that it is altogether unknown out of doors what they are doing." Washington adhered to the rules so literally that he included no details of the convention in his private diary. On June 1 he wrote, "Attending in Convention and nothing being suffered to transpire no minutes of the proceedings has been, or will be inserted in this diary."[24]

The secrecy rules did not prevent clever delegates from quieting public concerns about what the convention was up to. In August, for example, the *Pennsylvania Journal* quoted convention members as saying "tho' we cannot, affirmatively, tell you what we are doing, we can, negatively, tell you what we are not doing—we never once thought of a king."[25]

A few delegates proved unwilling or unable to maintain confidentiality, especially those who left the convention early. To justify divulging information, Nicholas Gilman wrote, "Secrecy is not otherwise enjoined than as prudence may dictate to each individual." Upon returning home for good in July, Robert Yates and John Lansing told New York governor George Clinton what the convention was up to. Another early departure, James McClurg, shared convention details with a fellow member of Virginia's council of state. Even Pierce (despite his declaration as mentioned earlier) briefed fellow legislators when he resumed attendance in the Confederation Congress in New York, causing one legislator to wonder whether he "fully understood the true meaning, full and just extent of the order not to communicate." Those who stayed to the end of the convention could not always keep quiet. Rufus King filled in Congressman Nathan Dane on the convention's progress, and William Blount reported to Richard Caswell. Some members updated absent members on what they missed. From Virginia, McClurg thanked Madison "for your communication of the proceedings of the Convention, since I left them."[26]

During a social gathering at his home, Benjamin Franklin nearly revealed convention secrets to the Reverend Manasseh Cutler. Showing Cutler an exceedingly rare two-headed snake preserved in a jar, Franklin pondered what would happen if one head of the snake went one way around the stem of a plant and the other head went the other way, and neither "would consent to come back or give way to the other." According to Cutler, the situation reminded Franklin of "a humorous matter that had that day taken place in Convention." As Franklin spoke, "He seemed to forget that everything in the Convention was to be kept a profound secret; but the secrecy of Convention matters was suggested to him, which stopped him and deprived me of the story he was going to tell."[27]

The blackout did not keep newspapers from running stories on the convention's progress, but their reports were not accurate. One rather wild account had Rhode Island being dismissed from the Union. As the summer progressed, anticipation grew. "The public mind is very impatient for the event," wrote Madison, "and various reports are circulating which tend to inflame Curiosity."[28]

The secrecy rule applied only while the convention sat. On its last day, September 17, the convention lifted the ban. In June, Yates wrote that one of the rules "strictly prohibits the communication of . . . business until the final close" of the convention. The following month, Randolph informed a correspondent, "we are not yet discharged from the obligation of secrecy." In September, Madison assured his father that "as soon as the tie of secresy shall be dissolved I will forward the proceedings of the Convention." Once the convention ended, Pierce wrote that "the veil of secrecy . . . is now taken off." Interestingly, however, Madison ultimately decided to publish his convention notes posthumously in part because he believed the secrecy rule to some degree still held. "Delicacy also seemed to require some respect to the" secrecy rule, he wrote, "so long as the policy of that rule could be regarded as in any degree unexpired."[29]

To keep their proceedings confidential, the convention kept the doors and windows of the Assembly Room sealed shut and posted "two doorkeepers" inside and outside the building to keep curious passersby from hearing what was going on. The stifling atmosphere must have made the delegates' heavy, layered woolen clothing exceedingly uncomfortable. After the convention complained to the city about street noise from passing carriages, the street commissioners resolved that "a Quantity of Gravell now haulling out of the Sewer in Fourth Street, be laid on Chestnut Street, in front of the State House."[30]

The hot, humid weather in Philadelphia during the summer of 1787 has become the stuff of legend. Not only did the delegates have to overcome the differences among themselves, but they also had to endure sweltering heat in the closed Assembly Room. Contrary to the popular view, however, the temperature in the city that summer was below normal. Weather historian David M. Ludlum concludes that "Philadelphia enjoyed a cool summer in 1787," with temperatures in July, August, and September beneath the average. "This 9th of June is the first day of this Spring that a Fire would be disagreeable," wrote local resident William Shippen, "so cold and wet has been the Season." On June 3, Massachusetts delegate Rufus King wrote, "The weather has been, and continues, very cold for the season; we have now a Fire in our Chamber and find it extremely pleasant." Of course, even a cool summer in Philadelphia can be uncomfortably warm, especially if it is humid. Meeting in a sealed room without ventilation cannot be pleasant even in coolest of summers. To the New England delegates, moreover, the city would still have felt hot. And even cool summers have hot stretches. "The Heat here is and has been intense," complained William Paterson in July. "Philada. is, I think, the warmest place I have been in." The following month, Elbridge Gerry observed that "this City is now and has been for several Days excessive hot."[31]

The delegates convened each day at 10 a.m. until early June, when they began convening an hour later at 11 a.m. Typically, they deliberated for about five hours each day before adjourning at around 3 or 4 p.m. On some days, however, their sessions lasted only an hour; on other days they lasted up to seven. They met Monday through Saturday and took Sunday off for rest. In mid-August, John Rutledge, increasingly frustrated by the convention's slow pace, attempted to speed up things. Emphasizing the "extreme anxiety of many members . . . to bring the business to an end," he moved that the convention extend its sessions from 10 a.m. through 4 p.m. The delegates overwhelmingly approved the suggestion. Their ardor did not hold up for even a week. Six days later they unanimously agreed to resume adjourning at 3 p.m.[32]

John Langdon facetiously conjured the scene for an acquaintance:

> Figure to yourself the Great Washington, with a Dignity peculiar to himself, taking the Chair. The Notables are seated . . . the Business of the day is open'd with great Solemnity and good Order. The Importance of the Business, the Dignified Character of Many . . . the Eloquence of Some and the Regularity of the whole gives a Ton[e] to the proceedings which is extreamly pleasing. Your old Friend takes his Seat. Conscious of his upright Intentions, and as far as his poor Abilities will go keep his eye single to what is righteous and of good Report.[33]

The full schedule by no means meant all work and no play for the delegates, however. During the 127 days of the convention, George Washington enjoyed an unbelievably active social life. He went out to dinner 106 times, went out to tea 72 times, took 13 day trips to visit gardens, vineyards, bee houses, fishing holes and other sites, and attended a concert or the theater 6 times. He also sat for the artist Charles Willson Peale three times, and for artist Robert Edge Pine once. He went to church twice. On Saturdays, Washington usually dined with a group of delegates, known as a "club," either at the City Tavern or at an estate outside Philadelphia known as Springsbury. July 9 was a busy day, even for Washington. According to his diary, he "sat in the Morning for Mr. Peale. Attended Convention. Dined at Mr. Morris's & accompanied Mrs. Morris to Doctr. Redmans 3 Miles in the Country where we drank tea and returned." Washington's crowded calendar did not keep him from writing lengthy letters each week with instructions to the manager of his farms at Mount Vernon.[34]

The Triumph of the Virginia Plan

Engraving of a portrait of George Washington painted by Charles Willson Peale while Washington was in Philadelphia for the Constitutional Convention. Unanimously elected president of the convention, Washington delivered only two short speeches during the gathering. Anticipating that he would be elected the first president under the Constitution, the delegates designed a strong and independent executive branch with him in mind. (Library of Congress)

Washington spent quite a bit of time socializing with the Powells and the Binghams. Forty-four-year-old Elizabeth Powell and her husband, merchant and former Philadelphia mayor Samuel Powell, regularly hosted groups of delegates at their mansion on Third Street. Washington, who respected Elizabeth's intellect and who held political discussions with her, often joined the Powells for tea. Washington also enjoyed the company of Philadelphia businessman William Bingham and his beautiful twenty-four-year-old wife, Anne. The niece of Elizabeth Powell, Anne entertained Washington at her palatial home adjacent to the Powell residence half a dozen times that summer.[35]

Other conventioneers also pursued numerous social and cultural events, although none appears to have been as assiduous as their president. On Sunday, May 21, the Virginia delegation (minus Washington) attended a Catholic Mass, according to George Mason, mainly, "out of Curiosity." Although impressed "with the Solemnity of" the service, Mason felt "somewhat disgusted with the frequent Tinkling of a little Bell," that reminded him "of the drawing up [of] the Curtain for a Puppet-Shew." In July, Oliver Ellsworth went to see the arm of an Egyptian mummy. "My curiosity was highly gratified the other day by clasping the hand of a woman who died many hundred years ago," he wrote to his wife. "The flesh, which I tried with my knife, cuts and looks much like smoked beef." In August, Ellsworth's Connecticut colleague, William Samuel Johnson, observed a demonstration in the Delaware River of inventor John Fitch's prototype steamboat.[36]

But other delegates did not enjoy Philadelphia's social life as much as Washington did. "I mix with company without enjoying it and am perfectly tired with flattery and forms," Ellsworth wrote. "To be very fashionable we must be very trifling and make and receive a thousand professions which everybody knows there is no truth in." Gerry disparagingly described Philadelphians as being like "Monks and Nuns cloistered in a monastery." Only two days into the convention, George Mason declared, "I begin to grow heartily tired of the etiquette and nonsense so fashionable in this city." In a similar vein, John Langdon complained that "notwithstanding the Riches and Splendor of this City the fatiguing sameness makes me sick." Even Washington himself, despite his booked calendar, had, by September, become "quite homesick."[37]

A recurrent theme in the delegates' letters home is their need for cash to pay their room and board. The financially strapped, notoriously parsimonious state governments did not appropriate much travel money for the convention participants, often leaving them short of funds. Since no one expected the convention to last three-and-one-half months, moreover, many of the delegates ran low on money. In September, Richard Dobbs Spaight wrote, "My situation here is extremely distressing as I expected . . . to stay only six weeks or two months at farthest." Those who came up short wrote to state officials pleading for financial relief, and in the meantime begged cash from fellow delegates, local residents, or members of the Confederation Congress in New York. Spaight worried that he would not be able to leave the city unless he could "get money to pay off my accounts here and bear my expenses home" which he could do only "by borrowing" or by getting "some friend" to cosign a loan. William Blount, Rufus King, John Francis Mercer, Caleb Strong, Hugh Williamson, and Luther Martin expressed similar worries.[38]

All of a state's delegates rarely attended the convention at the same time. Pressing personal matters often called individuals home. George Wythe of Virginia rushed home early in June to attend to his terminally ill wife, and soon after resigned his appointment. William Churchill Houston of New Jersey, suffering from tuberculosis, resigned his seat less than two weeks into the convention, having attended a total of three days. Some of those who also sat in the Confederation Congress in New York shuttled back and forth between the two bodies. Delegates from nearby states often rotated in and out of Philadelphia to make sure that enough of them remained present so that their state would not lose its vote. Jonathan Dayton of New Jersey, which required three delegates to be present, informed his colleague David Brearly in June that he would remain at home "until I am informed . . . that my attendance in Philadelphia is necessary to keep up the representation."[39]

How many of the fifty-five delegates attended each day's deliberations? A record of definite and probable daily attendance compiled by Gordon Lloyd shows that from June 1 to July 10, the number of delegates present each day was in the low forties. From July 11 to August 7, daily attendance dropped into the high thirties. From August 8 to August 23, the number climbed back up to the low forties. From August 24 to September 15, the number slipped back into the high thirties. On the last day, September 17, forty-one delegates attended. The maximum number of delegates present on any day was as high as forty-five (on three dates in late June), and the minimum present on any day was twenty-nine on May 25, the convention's first day. The number of state delegations officially present ranged between seven and eleven.[40]

On May 29, Governor Randolph of Virginia "opened the main business" by presenting the Virginia Plan to the convention. Randolph explained that "as the convention had originated from Virginia . . . his colleagues supposed that some proposition was expected from them." The Virginia Plan, an ambitious set of resolutions for replacing the Confederation, was mostly the work of James Madison. Drafted during the spring of 1787, Madison had already begun selling his plan to other delegates from his state before leaving the Old Dominion. Once in Philadelphia, he convinced the Virginia delegation that it should be proposed to the entire convention. Although all the Virginians supported Madison's plan, they remained free to oppose aspects of it in debate.[41]

Randolph rather than Madison presented the plan on the convention floor because, as governor, he officially led Virginia's delegation. The thirty-three-year-old Randolph came from a prominent Virginia family and boasted impressive oratorical skills. "A young Gentleman in whom unite all the accomplishments of the Scholar, and the Statesman," wrote William Pierce, Randolph "came forward with the postulata, or first principles, on which the Convention acted,—and he supported them with a force of eloquence and reasoning that did him great honor.—He has a most harmonious voice, a fine person and striking manners." But others described Randolph in less flattering terms. Many found him indecisive and wishy-washy. Cyrus Griffin called him "timid and undecided," while Virginia legislator Francis Corbin described his "doublings and turnings" as "*too Machiavellian and not Machiavellian Enough.*" Thomas Jefferson pronounced Randolph "the poorest Cameleon I ever saw having no colour of his own, & reflecting that nearest him."[42]

Randolph, "in a long and elaborate speech," described the Confederation as "totally inadequate to the peace, safety and security" of the country. Indeed, "the confederation fulfilled *none* of the objects for which it was framed." Randolph admonished the delegates not to allow "the defects of the confederation" to cause "the fulfillment of the prophesies of American downfall." To avoid this fate, they needed to form a government that would prevent foreign invasion, maintain order between and within the states, secure commercial advantages that the states could not obtain individually, defend itself against "incroachment" by the states, secure revenue from the states, be supreme to the state constitutions, and "be based on the republican principle." In short, "the Articles of Confederation ought to be so corrected & enlarged as to accomplish the objects proposed by their institution; namely, 'common defense, security of liberty, and general welfare.'" Randolph diagnosed poorly designed state constitutions as the root of the Confederation's problems. "Our chief danger arises from the democratic parts of our constitutions," he declared. "None of the constitutions have provided sufficient checks against the democracy," leading to majority tyranny within states and state violations of Congress's jurisdiction.[43]

The Triumph of the Virginia Plan

Edmund Randolph of Virginia presented the Virginia Plan to the Constitutional Convention. He later refused to sign the completed Constitution because he wished to allow the states to propose amendments to be considered by a second constitutional convention. (Library of Congress)

Randolph then introduced a series of specific resolutions designed to realize these overarching goals. The resolutions proposed a bicameral legislature in which representation in both houses would be based either on "the number of free inhabitants" or on "Quotas of contribution." Quotas of contribution referred to the amount of federal taxes each state paid. The lower house would be elected by the people of the states, while the upper house would be chosen by the lower house from nominees proposed by the state legislatures. This bicameral body would possess not only the powers "vested in Congress by the Confederation," but would also "legislate in all cases to which the separate States are incompetent." In a dramatic departure from the Articles, the Virginia Plan would empower

Congress "to negative all laws passed by the several States, contravening in the opinion of the National Legislature the articles of Union." This measure was not the unlimited veto of state laws that Madison wanted, which would have enabled the central government to strike down unjust state laws that violated minority rights. It was nevertheless a huge departure from the Articles of Confederation, under which states retained all powers not expressly delegated to Congress.

Under the Virginia Plan, congress could "call forth the force of the Union agst. any member of the Union failing to fulfill its duty under the articles thereof." Although the Virginians sought a national government that would interact directly with the people and could thus implement its laws without assistance, here they continued to think in terms of a confederation that would depend on the states to enforce its decrees. Old ways of thinking died slowly.

The Virginia Plan proposed an executive to be elected by congress who could serve for only one term, and the establishment of a "National Judiciary." Another unusual feature proposed by the Virginia Plan was an executive-judicial "Council of revision" to review bills passed by congress, and to overturn inappropriate congressional vetoes of state laws. Finally, the Virginia Plan called for the convention's proposals to be ratified by state conventions elected by the sovereign people. The Articles had been approved by the state legislatures but had never been ratified by popularly elected state conventions. Ratification by state legislatures suggested that state laws reigned supreme over federal law. Ratification by conventions would establish the new constitution as the supreme law of the land.[44]

Less nationalistic delegates reacted to the Virginia Plan with varying degrees of alarm because Randolph had proposed not a revision of the existing Confederation, but the introduction of a brand-new, energetic national government that went far beyond Congress's charge to the convention. Robert Yates of New York disapprovingly noted that Randolph unabashedly aimed for "a strong *consolidated* union, in which the idea of states should be nearly annihilated." Yates and his colleague John Lansing, allies of New York governor George Clinton, opposed a strong central government. Most small state men, however, were less troubled by the proposed power of the central government than how legislative representation would be apportioned. With representation based on state population or taxes paid instead of state equality, this new, more powerful government would be dominated by the populous states.[45]

After Randolph presented the Virginia Plan, Charles Pinckney of South Carolina also presented to the convention a "draught of a federal Government which he had prepared." Pinckney, a lawyer from a prominent and affluent planter family, served in the Continental Congress from 1778 to 1779. He had, as a lieutenant during the Revolutionary War, been incarcerated by the British following the fall of Charleston in 1780. After his parole, he entered the Confederation Congress. The Virginians were not fond of Pinckney. Washington and Madison found the twenty-nine-year-old preoccupied with self-promotion. Mason wholeheartedly agreed and called him a "C—b," meaning "coxcomb" (a self-important person).[46]

No contemporary copy of Pinckney's Plan survives. Madison, who claimed he never received a promised copy from the author, omitted it from his Notes. Robert Yates, James McHenry of Maryland, and William Paterson, the three other delegates who took notes that day, also failed to include Pinckney's Plan, perhaps because Pinckney himself "confessed that it was grounded on the same principles as" the Virginia Plan. Although not debated by the convention, the Pinckney Plan circulated among the delegates before the convention opened. Later it was referred to the Committee of Detail that met late in July to prepare a draft constitution.[47]

In 1818, when Secretary of State John Quincy Adams prepared the Convention Journal for publication, he failed to locate a copy of Pinckney's Plan. At Adams's request, Pinckney sent what he claimed to be the original plan. According to Adams, Pinckney insisted that "the whole plan of the Constitution was his, and that the Convention had done nothing more than to deteriorate his work by altering some of his favorite provisions." The document that Pinckney provided and that Adams published, however, was clearly not the original Pinckney Plan. The writing and ink suggest that it was written in 1818, and the watermark on the paper reads 1797. The plan included features that Pinckney opposed in debate during the convention, as well as provisions that only emerged much later that summer. Rather than being his original plan, the document appears to be a modified version of a draft constitution prepared late in July by the Committee of Detail. A month after the convention ended, Pinckney published a pamphlet entitled "Observations on the Plan of Government Submitted to the Federal Convention." This publication—a speech introducing his plan that was never actually delivered to the delegates and that may have been altered by Pinckney before going to press—also differs from the document he sent to Adams.

Although Pinckney's original plan no longer exists, much of its contents can be gleaned from excerpts that James Wilson, a member of the Committee of Detail, copied from it. The Pinckney Plan called for three "separate and distinct" branches of government. Representation in a bicameral "Congress," consisting of a "House of Delegates" and a "Senate," would be based on population, counting slaves as three-fifths of free people. The state legislatures would elect the house, which would in turn elect the senate. Congress's enumerated powers included raising armies, waging war, regulating commerce, requisitioning revenue from the states, and making appointments. No state law could take effect until approved by congress. A "P[residen]t U. S." elected annually by the legislature would govern with the assistance of a council consisting of heads of the executive departments. Pinckney's Plan protected freedom of speech, freedom of the press, trial by jury, and the writ of habeas corpus. Several features of the U.S. Constitution can be traced back to the Pinckney Plan, including the names "House," "Senate," and "President," the Three-Fifths Compromise, and an enumeration of congress's powers.

It is a mystery why Pinckney presented a separate plan, especially since he arrived in Philadelphia early enough to join the pre-convention deliberations and he even resided in the same boarding house as Madison and other Virginians. The main differences between the two proposals are that Pinckney's plan called for the state legislatures (not the voters) to choose congressmen, it counted three-fifths of slaves toward representation in congress, it would requisition funds from the state governments, and it enumerated the powers of congress. In the 1830s, Madison and Rufus King refuted Pinckney's assertion that his "Plan was substantially adopted" by the convention, and that he played the principal role in drafting the U.S. Constitution. Pinckney's false claim that he was the youngest convention delegate further undermined his credibility. Although he was twenty-nine in 1787, Pinckney later maintained that he was two years younger than twenty-six-year-old Jonathan Dayton![48]

The Triumph of the Virginia Plan

On May 30, the convention went into a committee of the whole to debate the Virginia Plan. The committee of the whole is a parliamentary procedure that allowed the convention to follow relaxed rules conducive to debate. Essentially, the convention declared itself a committee consisting of its entire membership. The committee of the whole debated the Virginia Plan, and later the New Jersey Plan, through June 19. Upon completion of debate in the committee of the whole, the agreed-upon resolutions were referred to the full convention for approval. When the convention first went into the committee of the whole, the delegates elected an experienced parliamentarian, Nathaniel Gorham of Massachusetts, to preside, enabling Washington to step down to resume his seat with the Virginia delegation. A former speaker of the Massachusetts House of Representatives and former president of the Confederation Congress, Gorham presided over the convention whenever it went into a committee of the whole. William Pierce described Gorham as "a Merchant in Boston, high in reputation, and much in the esteem of his Country-men."[49]

Over the next three weeks, the committee of the whole debated the Virginia Plan resolution-by-resolution, considering, in turn, the legislative, executive, and judicial powers of the government. The Virginia Plan, which essentially aimed to replace the Articles of Confederation with a new national government that operated directly on the people with legislative representation based on either each state's free population or taxes paid, for the most part survived this process intact. The Virginia Plan won support from the big states (Virginia, Pennsylvania, and Massachusetts) as well as from the Lower South (North Carolina, South Carolina, and Georgia). South Carolina and Georgia allied with the large states in return for protection of the institution of slavery. As both a populous state and a slave state, North Carolina possessed a double reason to support this alliance. Table 2.1 shows the population of the thirteen states according to the 1790 census.

On May 30, Randolph moved and Gouverneur Morris seconded an amended version of Resolution 1 of the Virginia Plan that only a national government of people "consisting of a *supreme* Legislative, Executive and Judiciary," not a federal system, could "accomplish the objects proposed by the articles of Confederation, namely common defense, security of liberty, & genl. welfare." A discussion ensued of the meaning of the terms *national* and *federal*. Gouverneur Morris equated a federal government

Table 2.1 U.S. Population According to the 1790 Census

	Total Population	Free Population	Enslaved Population
New Hampshire	141,899	141,742	157
Massachusetts	378,566	378,566	0
Rhode Island	69,112	68,154	958
Connecticut	237,655	235,007	2,648
New York	340,241	319,048	21,193
New Jersey	184,139	172,716	11,423
Pennsylvania	443,611	439,094	3,707
Delaware	59,096	50,209	8,887
Maryland	319,728	216,692	103,036
Virginia	747,550	454,923	292,627
North Carolina	395,005	294,222	100,783
South Carolina	249,073	141,979	107,094
Georgia	82,548	53,284	29,264
Total	1,926,677	1,272,558	654,121

Source: https://userpages.umbc.edu/~bouton/History407/SlaveStats.htm.

with a confederation, or "a mere compact resting on the good faith of the parties." He defined a national government, in contrast, as having "compleat and *compulsive*" supremacy over the states. George Mason clarified that in a confederation, the central government interacted with the state governments, which in turn interacted with the people. But in a national regime the central government interacted directly with the people, without the states serving as intermediaries. Years later, Madison elaborated on the meaning of these terms. "With respect to the term 'National' as contradistinguished from the term 'federal,'" he explained, "it was not meant to express the *extent* of power, but the *mode* of *its operation*." Charles Cotesworth Pinckney of South Carolina and Elbridge Gerry expressed doubt whether the convention was authorized to adopt any form of government other than a confederation. Despite this concern, the convention easily approved the resolution authorizing a national government with only Connecticut opposed and New York divided. This vote demonstrates that many of the small state men, especially those from New Jersey

The Triumph of the Virginia Plan

and Delaware, did not oppose a strong national government provided their states were well represented in it.[50]

The convention next waded into the thorny question of legislative representation. Resolution 2 of the Virginia Plan would base each state's representation on taxes paid or the number of free inhabitants. Seeking first to eliminate the one-vote-per-state formula, Madison proposed "that an equitable ratio of representation ought to be substituted" in place of "the equality of suffrage established by the articles of Confederation." Madison's resolution to base representation on either state population or taxes paid was derailed by Read, who pointed out that Delaware's instructions to its delegates forbade them to "change . . . the rule of suffrage" from one-state, one-vote. "In case such a change should be fixed on," Read warned, "it might become their duty to retire from the Convention." Madison responded in vain that while state equality made sense in a confederation, which relied on the states to enforce its decisions, it could not be justified in a national government in which "the acts of the Genl. Govt. would take effect without the intervention of the State legislatures." The convention postponed Madison's resolution out of deference to Delaware, the only state that seriously objected to proportional representation.[51]

The convention on May 31 approved without controversy Resolution 3 of the Virginia Plan "that the national Legislature ought to consist of two branches," or houses. The delegates then considered Resolution 4 that "members of the first branch of the National Legislature ought to be elected by the people of the several States." Roger Sherman and Elbridge Gerry both rejected popular election in favor of election by the state legislatures, suggesting that the people, lacking knowledge of public affairs, would fall victim to demagogues and make poor choices. "The evils we experience," declared Gerry, "flow from the excess of democracy."[52]

A Massachusetts merchant and Harvard graduate, Gerry signed both the Declaration of Independence and the Articles of Confederation. Although he lived to be seventy-two, he described himself as having a weak constitution and did "not expect a long life." Gerry in 1786 married a much younger woman who joined him with their baby daughter in Philadelphia for the first half of the convention, but spent August and September in New York, deemed a healthier location. The delegates joked about the mismatch in appearance between the wispy forty-three-year-old Gerry and his attractive twenty-four-year-old wife. Gerry's separation from her contributed to his increasingly sour mood as the summer progressed that culminated in his refusal to sign the Constitution. By late August, Gerry pronounced himself "sick of being here." A month after the convention, a Philadelphian pronounced Gerry "a man of sense, but a Grumbletonian." Pierce described Gerry, who had a stutter or speech impediment, as a "hesitating and laborious speaker" who nevertheless possessed "a great degree of confidence." Secretary of Congress Charles Thomson noted that Gerry possessed a "feeble voice and uncouth delivery broken and interrupted with many a heck & hem & repetition of ofs & ands," but that he nevertheless "assumed . . . superiority over" his colleagues. Philadelphian Dr. Benjamin Rush, too, mentioned "stammering in his speech." Ellsworth described "a profusion of those hems, that never fail to lengthen out and enliven his oratory." Despite his speech impediment, Madison found Gerry "an active, an able, and interesting delegate."[53]

Gerry had become distrustful of popular sovereignty after witnessing Shays's Rebellion in his state. He warned that New Englanders had "at this time the wildest ideas of Government in the world." Gerry, a so-called Old Republican, also harbored an intense suspicion that a centralized national government would produce despotism. He especially feared that a permanent peacetime military establishment, known in the eighteenth century as a "standing army," would lead to tyranny. Only Massachusetts's inability to suppress Shays's Rebellion had convinced him that the crumbling Confederation needed to be replaced with something stronger.[54]

James Wilson, the convention's most passionate advocate of popular sovereignty, rose to speak. The oldest son of a yeoman farmer, Wilson grew up in Fife in the lowlands of Scotland. Despite his modest origins, he studied at the universities of St. Andrews, Glasgow, and Edinburgh, where he became well versed in Scottish Common Sense philosophy. This egalitarian school of thought taught that anyone could comprehend the word of God, even those lacking extensive education. When applied to politics, this line of reasoning suggested that suffrage could be extended from the few to the many. A Philadelphia attorney, Wilson during the Revolutionary War gained a reputation as an elitist who sympathized with the British during the occupation of Philadelphia.

Helping to write the Articles of Confederation and the Pennsylvania Constitution made him a veteran lawgiver. "Government seems to have been his particular study, all the political institutions of the World he knows in detail," wrote Pierce about the forty-four-year-old Wilson. "No Man is more clear, copious and comprehensive than Mr. Wilson," who "draws the attention not by the charm of his eloquence, but by the force of his reasoning." Former New Jersey congressman Francis Hopkinson insisted that "the Powers of Demosthenes and Cicero seemed to be united in this able Orator." Benjamin Rush concurred that "his eloquence was of the most commanding kind . . . his mind, while he spoke, was one blaze of light." Wearing pewter-rimmed glasses and speaking with a Scottish accent, Wilson often came off as arrogant and haughty.

With no local attachments to hold him back, Wilson became one of the convention's leading nationalists. He also emerged as the convention's most outspoken proponent of popular election of federal officeholders. He disliked Pennsylvania's 1776 constitution not because the legislature was popularly elected, but because it lacked a second house and strong executive and judicial branches to check and balance it. Wilson wanted the people to elect the branches and levels of government, provided that those branches and levels checked and balanced each other.[55]

Wilson advocated "raising the federal pyramid to a considerable altitude, and for that reason wished to give it as broad a basis as possible." That is, for a powerful national government to be compatible with liberty, it needed wide public support. Republican government simply could not succeed without "the confidence of the people." A true nationalist, Wilson also advocated the concept of dual citizenship. As citizens of a state, people interacted with the state government. But instead of state governments interacting with the central government, Wilson favored having citizens also interact directly with the national government. Hence, he wanted the people of the states, rather than the state legislatures, to elect the national congress. For Wilson, sovereignty rested with the people, who then delegated political power to the branches and levels of the government. He therefore believed that the people should elect the legislative and executive branches in as direct a manner as possible.[56]

Unlike Wilson, most of the delegates wanted only the lower house to be popularly elected. George Mason proclaimed that the lower house, "the grand depository of the democratic principle," must mirror not only the states but the different districts of each state as well. Only popular election could protect the interests of poor areas as well as rich ones, enabling the government to be responsive to the people and to gain their affection.

The convention agreed with popular election of the lower house, six states to two, with New Jersey and South Carolina opposed and New York split.[57]

If the people chose the lower house, then who should elect the upper house? Resolution 5 of the Virginia Plan called for election of the senate by the lower house out of nominees chosen by the state legislatures. This concept did not garner much support. Despite having voted for a national government, some delegates still wished to see the states play a role in it. Pierce Butler of South Carolina argued that to deprive the states of the selection of at least one house of the legislature would completely rob them of a voice in the central government. Rufus King of Massachusetts answered that for the upper house to exercise a check on the lower house, it must be smaller and more deliberative. This end could not be accomplished if the state legislatures elected it based on proportional representation. Even if tiny Delaware received only one seat, the number of senators would approach triple digits, a cumbersome size. Unable to agree on a method of choosing the upper house, the delegates postponed it, leaving, recorded Madison, "a chasm . . . in this part of the plan."[58]

What powers should congress have? All agreed that the legislature must possess all of the powers enjoyed by the Confederation Congress, but what additional authority should be added? Resolution 6 of the Virginia Plan would give congress "legislative power in all cases to which the State Legislatures were individually incompetent." South Carolinians Charles Pinckney, John Rutledge, and Butler, ever mindful of any potential threat to slavery, considered this blanket grant of power much too vague. They preferred that congress's powers be clearly enumerated. Madison worried whether an enumeration would provide enough flexibility to solve the problems of the Confederation. With some preferring a blanket grant and some preferring an enumeration at a later time, the delegates approved the resolution 9–0. An indication of how much power the delegates were willing to grant the central government came when the convention expanded without "debate or dissent" the Virginia Plan's proposed congressional veto of state laws that conflicted with the constitution to include state laws that violated federal treaties.

As his thinking evolved, Madison himself spoke up against the Virginia Plan's resolution to allow the general government to coerce states that did not meet their federal obligations, arguing that such punishment would not be necessary in a national government operating directly on the people, as opposed to a confederation, where the states acted as intermediaries between the two. The convention accordingly postponed consideration of that provision in the Virginia Plan. Madison, who now grasped the full implications of a national government, here abandoned a confederal aspect of his blueprint.[59]

John Dickinson of Delaware took the floor to advocate that "considerable powers . . . be left in the hands of the States." William Pierce described the fifty-five-year-old lawyer as "an indifferent Speaker.—With an affected air of wisdom he labors to produce a trifle,—his language is irregular and incorrect." Dickinson, like Mason and Franklin, suffered from gout. "He is a Shadow—tall, but slender as a Reed—pale as ashes," wrote John Adams. "One would think at first Sight that he could not live a Month. Yet upon a more attentive Inspection, he looks as if the Springs of Life were strong enough to last many Years." A small-state nationalist, Dickinson favored a strong central government provided Delaware retained a powerful voice in it.[60]

Addressing the larger question of the role of the large versus the small states, Dickinson "hoped that each state would retain an equal voice at least in one branch of the National Legislature." Dickinson here suggested what—six weeks later—became the Great Compromise over representation in congress. One legislative house should be based on population, and the other should have equal state representation. Had the convention adopted Dickinson's suggestion at the beginning of June, it would have saved weeks of wrangling. But the large-state, pro-national government men were not ready to concede any ground. It took six weeks of contentious debate before these delegates made concessions. In particular, Madison and Wilson did not want to bend to the small-state forces led by Delaware and New Jersey. Always seeking to deny the state legislatures any voice in what they hoped would be a strictly national government, Madison and Wilson simply could not tolerate having an element of confederal government woven into the constitution.[61]

On June 6, the delegates revisited their decision to have the people of the states elect the lower house. Both Pinckneys moved "that the first branch of the national Legislature be elected by the State Legislatures, and not by the people," because the state legislatures would choose more wisely. Ever suspicious of democracy, Gerry once again asserted that popular election in Massachusetts brought "the worst men . . . into the Legislature." He thought it would be fine for the people to nominate congressmen, but the state legislatures should choose them. Sherman, who favored at most only a modest increase in the powers of the Confederation, also preferred to keep elections in the hands of the state legislatures.

Mason responded that since the new government ought to be a national government that operated directly on the people rather than on the states, the people (not the state legislatures) must choose congressmen. Wilson concurred that popular election would ensure that the lower house would mirror the population. "The Legislature ought to be the most exact transcript of the whole Society" and should "possess not only 1st. the *force*, but 2dly. the *mind or sense* of the people at large," he insisted. Wilson maintained that both the national government and the states could concurrently operate directly on the people as long as their jurisdictions were separate and distinct. Popular election, Wilson suggested, would also win public support and legitimacy for the national government. "The people will love and respect the Genl. Govt. if it is immediately founded in their consent," allowing it to "take rank over the State Governments."

Madison, too, insisted that popular election of the lower house would secure "better representatives" and avoid "too great an agency of the State Governments in the General one." He laid out the argument that he later made famous in *The Federalist* 10: in the large, extended republic of the entire United States, the self-interested factions that formed tyrannical majorities in the states would cancel each other out, resulting in the protection of minority rights. "The only remedy" for majority tyranny, he argued, "is to enlarge the sphere, & thereby divide the community into so great a number of interests & parties, that in the 1st. place a majority will not be likely at the same moment to have a common interest separate from that of the whole or of the minority; and in the 2d. place, that in case they shd. have such an interest, they may not be apt to unite in the pursuit of it."

Dickinson again called for the lower house of congress to be elected by the people and the upper to be elected by the state legislatures. "We cannot form a national Govt.," he declared, "unless we draw a Br[anch] from the people, & a Br[anch] from the legislature[s]." He suggested that the domination of the upper house by the state legislatures could be avoided by giving the members of that body long terms in office. Pierce insightfully added that the popular election of the lower house and election of the upper house by the state legislatures would allow "the Citizens of the States" to "be represented both *individually & collectively*." The convention rejected the Pinckneys' resolution for election of the lower house by the state legislatures, eight states to three with only the small states Connecticut and New Jersey joining South Carolina in supporting it. The people would elect the lower house.[62]

On June 7, the convention resumed efforts to fill in the "chasm" (as Madison had described it) in the Virginia Plan by deciding who would elect the upper house. Dickinson again moved that "members of the 2d. branch ought to be chosen by the individual Legislatures." He believed that the legislatures would choose more distinguished senators than the people would, and that "the sense of the States would be better collected through their governments." The state and national governments moreover would then be positioned to check and balance each other. Mason concurred that "the State Legislatures . . . ought to have some means of defending themselves agst. encroachments of the Natl. Govt.," which would be armed with a congressional veto over state laws that conflicted with the constitution. Sherman agreed "that the particular States would thus become interested in supporting the national Governmt. and that a due harmony between the two Governments would be maintained." He agreed with Dickinson that the legislatures would elect the ablest men.

"If we are to establish a national Government, that Government ought to flow from the people at large," Wilson countered. If the people elected the upper house in large districts, "men of intelligence & uprightness" would be chosen. "He did not see the danger of the States being devoured by the Nationl. Govt. On the contrary, he wished to keep them from devouring the national Govt." Wilson "hoped that the national government would be independent of state governments, in order to make it vigorous." History had proven that powerful states were the Achilles heel of confederations.

Charles Pinckney warned that a senate elected by the state legislatures and based on population would be so large as to become unwieldy. Madison chimed in that an upper house elected by the state legislatures would contain too many members to fulfill its intended purpose of checking sudden impulses of the popularly elected lower house. "Enlarge their number and you communicate to them the vices which they are meant to correct," he explained. Allowing the state legislatures to choose the upper house, moreover, would introduce the same shortsighted unwillingness to place national interests over state interests that the convention was trying to fix. Despite these objections, the convention voted 10–0 for election of the upper house by the state legislatures. The "chasm" had finally been filled, but not to Wilson's or Madison's liking![63]

On June 8, Charles Pinckney moved to expand the congressional veto of state laws from extending only to statutes "contrary to the articles of Union, or Treaties with foreign nations" to include "all laws" that congress deemed "improper." Pinckney had included a similar requirement in the plan of government he submitted to the convention in May. Making the congressional veto unlimited, he argued, alone could keep the states "in due subordination to the nation." Astonishingly, Pinckney here favored a provision that potentially would have empowered the federal government to abolish slavery in a state. Madison "seconded the motion . . . as absolutely necessary to a perfect system." It would not only allow the national government to protect itself against encroachments by the states, but it would also allow the national government to strike down state laws that violated the rights of other states and of minorities within their borders. How else would it be possible, he asked, to curb "a constant tendency in the States to encroach on the federal authority; to violate national Treaties; to infringe the rights & interests of each other; [and] to oppress the weaker party within their respective jurisdictions"? Wilson and Dickinson also favored the unlimited veto because they considered it essential to protect the national government against the states.

A congressional veto of state laws amounted to Gerry's worst nightmare: centralized power run amok. It would never be ratified, Gerry insisted, because "the Natl. Legislature with such a power may enslave the States." Gunning Bedford, Jr., of Delaware opposed the unlimited veto because it would be impractical for congress to attempt to review all state laws. He also feared that in a government with representation based on population, the large states of Virginia and Pennsylvania would have one-third of the legislative seats. Those two states combined could almost exercise the veto by themselves, and thus nearly govern the internal affairs of the smaller states. In response, Madison ominously asked Bedford whether the small states would be better off with no union or with one dominated by the large states. The convention defeated the enlarged congressional veto with only the big states of Virginia, Pennsylvania, and Massachusetts voting yes. The large state-small state divide was becoming more visible among the delegates.[64]

On June 9, the small states, increasingly hostile to the Virginia Plan that based representation entirely on population, finally found their voice. David Brearly of New Jersey introduced an idea to the convention that became known as "hotchpot." A sixteenth-century legal term, hotchpot meant "combining of properties into a common lot to ensure equality of division among heirs." The only way proportional representation could be made fair, Brearly explained, would be to "extinguish the present boundary lines of the respective state jurisdictions, and make a new division so that each state is equal." Hotchpot, meaning the redrawing of state lines to give each state the same population, was not a serious proposal. It was instead a rhetorical device designed to make proportional representation seem ridiculously unfair and utterly unworkable.

William Paterson of New Jersey reminded the delegates that the convention had been authorized only to amend the existing Confederation, not to scrap it in favor of a new national government. The convention thus lacked the authority to form a national government in which representation would be based on population. Paterson denounced proportional representation as "striking at the existence of the lesser States." He warned, "N. Jersey will never confederate on the plan before the Committee. She would be swallowed up. He had rather submit to a monarch, to a despot, than to such a fate." Proportional representation, Brearly agreed, meant that "the large States" of Pennsylvania, Virginia, and Massachusetts "will carry every thing before them."

Wilson jumped to his feet to reply. "If the small States will not confederate on this plan, Pena. & he presumed some other States, would not confederate on any other." Since "all authority was derived from the people, equal numbers of people ought to have an equal no. of representatives," he declared. "Are not the Citizens of Pena. equal to those of N. Jersey? Does it require 150 of the former to balance 50 of the latter?" This heated dialogue for the first time created real tension in the room. Fortunately, adjournment from Saturday through Monday allowed tempers to cool. That weekend, an agitated Brearly urged absent fellow New Jersey delegate Jonathan Dayton to "join us immediately," because "the importance of the business really demands it."[65]

On June 11, Franklin rose to speak. John Adams believed that Franklin craved "Reputation and Fame . . . and to set Tongues and Pens male and female, to celebrating him." Adams rather harshly described Franklin as a man "equally selfish and interested, equally vain and ambitious, more jealous and envious, and more false and deceitful," whose "whole Life has been one continued Insult to good Manners and to Decency." William Pierce more charitably wrote that "Dr. Franklin is well known to be the greatest philosopher of the present age," and who "tells a story in a style more engaging than anything I ever heard." Traveler and businessman Elkanah Watson similarly wrote that Franklin regaled his guests "with pleasant anecdote and interesting stories." "His conversation was always a feast to me," recalled Madison. "I never passed half an hour in his company without hearing some observation or anecdote worth remembering."

The president of Pennsylvania's Supreme Executive Council, Franklin, at age eighty-one, suffered chronic pain from gout and kidney stones, for which he took opium. Manasseh Cutler described him as "a short, fat, trunched old man, in a plain Quaker dress, bald pate, and short white locks." Initially left off the Pennsylvania delegation, the state legislature added him once he signified his willingness to serve. Too feeble to walk, he was picked up every morning at home and carried two blocks to the State House in an enclosed sedan chair by convicts from the Walnut Street Prison. Declining health had not, however, impaired his mental faculties. John Jay found "his mind more vigorous than that of any man of his age," and Madison regarded his "vigor of intellect . . . astonishing." Although Franklin offered undistinguished policy proposals, he played a key role in the convention as an advocate of compromise and unity. He frequently entertained groups of delegates at his nearby home, often under the mulberry tree in his yard. Benjamin Rush noted that "Dr. Franklin exhibits daily a spectacle of transcendent benevolence by attending the Convention punctually, and even taking part in its business and deliberations."[66]

The first time Franklin addressed the convention, he begged indulgence for reading prepared remarks rather than to speak from memory, lest he lose his train of thought and omit key points. When Wilson offered to read the speech for him, Franklin accepted. Wilson continued to read Franklin's speeches throughout the convention. On June 11, Franklin reminded the delegates that "we are sent here *to consult*, and not to *contend*, with each other." Franklin called for a restoration of "coolness &

At age eighty-one, Benjamin Franklin of Pennsylvania was the oldest delegate present at the convention. Although he offered undistinguished policy proposals, he played a major role as an advocate for compromise. His speech on the convention's last day urged the delegates to overcome their doubts and sign the Constitution. (Library of Congress)

temper" to the deliberations. He believed "the number of Representatives should bear some proportion to the number of the Represented; and that the decisions shd. be by the majority of members, not the majority of States." Just as the small states feared being swallowed up in a legislature based on population, he explained, so the large states feared being swallowed up in a legislature based on state equality. Dismissing hotchpot as impractical, Franklin offered another, equally unworkable solution: have each state contribute an equivalent, minimal sum of tax revenue to a congress in which each state had an equal number of representatives who voted individually. If more money were needed, the large states could be requisitioned to furnish it. As so often happened after a Franklin proposal, no one either defended or attacked his remarks. The delegates simply moved on. "It is certain that he does not shine much in public Council," wrote Pierce.[67]

The convention approved a motion by King and Wilson that representation in the lower house ought to be based on "some equitable ratio of representation," such as population or wealth. Wilson then moved and Charles Pinckney seconded that representation be based on the number of free people plus three-fifths of slaves. That is, enslaved people would count as three-fifths of free people when calculating representation in the lower house. Wilson and Pinckney, it seems, had cut a deal: South Carolina supported proportional representation in the lower house. In return, Pennsylvania supported counting three-fifths of slaves toward representation in Congress.[68]

Pinckney had included the three-fifths ratio in his plan of government, but it did not originate there. This concept went back to a proposal made in April 1783 by Madison in the Confederation Congress for an amendment to the Articles of Confederation allowing Congress to apportion federal expenses (i.e., taxes) among the states according to population. Only eleven states ratified this amendment (New Hampshire and Rhode Island did not). Although the three-fifths clause (referred to as the "federal ratio") was thus never added to the Articles, Congress nevertheless used it in determining each state's quota of the 1786 federal requisition. With taxes being the issue, southerners preferred to count slaves as zero-fifths of free people, while northerners preferred to count them as five-fifths. Now that the convention was applying the three-fifths ratio to a desirable thing (representation) rather than an undesirable thing (taxation), southerners favored counting slaves as five-fifths of people, and northerners favored counting them as zero-fifths.[69]

An alliance of primarily large states and slave states passed the Wilson-Pinckney resolution 9–2, with New Jersey and Delaware opposed. This resolution solidified the large state-Lower South alliance. Big states Pennsylvania and Massachusetts wanted representation based on population. To secure this outcome, they traded the three-fifths clause to the Lower South. South Carolina and Georgia would have preferred counting slaves as five-fifths of free people, but they were happy to include the federal ratio in the constitution. As large states and slave states, Virginia and North Carolina doubly benefitted from this arrangement. Only Elbridge Gerry questioned, "Why then shd. the blacks, who were property in the South, be in the rule of representation more than the Cattle & horses of the North"[70]

The large state-Lower South alliance was not done yet. Sherman moved that "each State shall have one vote in the 2d. branch" to protect the sovereignty of the states. He warned that "the smaller States would never agree to the plan on any other principle than an equality of suffrage in this branch." Despite Sherman's warning that "every thing . . . depended on this," the large state-Lower South alliance defeated the motion, 6–5, with Connecticut, New York, New Jersey, Delaware, and Maryland opposed. Carrying all before it, the same alliance then approved a Wilson-Hamilton resolution to elect the upper house using the same method as the lower house. Now representation in both houses of congress would be based on free population plus three-fifths of slaves. The small states had been thoroughly beaten on the representation issue.[71]

Having completed its discussion of the Virginia Plan, the committee of the whole reported the agreed-upon resolutions back to the full convention for approval. The revised Virginia Plan provided for a national government with executive, legislative, and judicial branches. The lower legislative house would be elected by the people of the states for three-year terms. The upper house would be elected by the state legislatures for seven-year terms. Congress would have the power to legislate wherever "the separate States are incompetent," and could veto state laws that violated the constitution or treaties. Representation in both houses would be based on each state's free population, plus three-fifths of slaves. The executive (discussed in Chapter 5), a single person chosen by congress for one seven-year term, would have a veto that could be overridden by two-thirds of each house of congress. Supreme Court justices, appointed by the senate, would hold their appointments for life. (The judicial branch is covered in Chapter 6.) Once the proposed constitution was approved by the Confederation Congress, state conventions chosen by the people would ratify the document.[72]

The most populous states of Virginia, Pennsylvania, Massachusetts, and North Carolina had good reason to be pleased with the convention thus far. They had gotten their way on every issue save one: state legislatures rather than the lower house of congress would choose the senate. Lower South states Georgia and South Carolina were equally content. They had secured protection for their slave property by having three-fifths of the slave population count toward representation in both houses of the legislature. The small states, in contrast, had lost on almost all key issues. Thoroughly disgusted with the Virginia Plan because it shifted power from the states to a powerful national government in which they had little voice, the small states of Connecticut, Delaware, Maryland, and New Jersey, along with their mid-sized ally New York, determined to fight back with an alternative plan.

NOTES

1. Adrienne Koch, ed., *Notes of Debates in the Federal Convention of 1787 Reported by James Madison* (Athens: Ohio University Press, 1966), 23, hereafter cited as *NDFC*; Richard B. Morris, *The Framing of the Federal Constitution* (Washington: National Park Service, 1986), 10.

2. Morris, *Framing*, 6; Max Farrand, ed., *The Records of the Federal Convention of 1787*. 1937 rev. ed. in four vols., reprint (New Haven, CT: Yale University Press, 1974), 3:58, hereafter cited as *RFC*.

3. *RFC*, 3:21–23.

4. John P. Kaminski and Michael E. Stevens, "Delegates' Speeches, Motions, and Committee Assignments in the Constitutional Convention," https://csac.history.wisc.edu/document-collections/the-constitutional-convention/delegates-speeches-motions-and-committee-assignments-in-the-constitutional-convention/; *Demigods*, 134–37.

5. *NDFC*, 25.

6. John P. Kaminski and Timothy D. Moore, eds., *An Assembly of Demigods: Word Portraits of the Delegates to the Constitutional Convention by Their Contemporaries* (Madison, WI: Parallel Press, 2012), hereafter cited as *Demigods*, 16, 250.

7. *RFC*, 3:25–28, 575.

8. Ibid., 33, 559–86.

9. Ibid., 28, 35, 61; *NDFC*, 23, 25, 347.

10. *Demigods*, 147, 248.

11. *NDFC*, 23–24; James H. Hutson, ed., *Supplement to Max Farrand's The Records of the Federal Convention of 1787* (New Haven, CT: Yale University Press, 1987), hereafter cited as *RFC Supplement*, 39.

12. *NDFC*, 655.

13. Richard Leffler et al., eds., *William Pierce on the Constitutional Convention and the Constitution* (Dallas, TX: Harlan Crow Library, 2011), 27–28; RFC, 3:471–72.

14. *NDFC*, 24; *RFC*, 3:18, 24, 65, 431; *RFC Supplement*, 1, 20.

15. *NDFC*, 18; *RFC*, 3:60.

16. *NDFC*, 18.

17. Stuart Leibiger, "Where Would We Be without Madison's Notes," unpublished paper, New Horizons in Madison Scholarship Conference, Montpelier, Virginia, Dec. 9, 2017.

18. *RFC Supplement*, xx–xxvi.

19. Bilder's 2015 book makes such bold assertions, and has received so much attention, that it deserves analysis. Whereas Madison insisted that he recorded his famous Notes to preserve for posterity the process of drafting the U.S. Constitution, Bilder argues instead that Madison began recording his Notes as "legislative diaries" for himself and for Thomas Jefferson. Early in the convention, insists Bilder, Madison selectively recorded in a gossipy style from memory only those events that interested him. Not until day four of the convention did he begin taking rough notes during the sessions and then transcribing them soon afterward. During the last seven weeks of the convention, as the delegates fine-tuned the constitution, Madison became so engrossed in the proceedings that his note-taking deteriorated. His rough notes increasingly consisted of brief summaries, incomplete sentences, and abbreviations. After August 21, writes Bilder, the Notes collapsed entirely, because Madison lacked the time to record his rough notes in longhand after hours.

Not until 1789 did Madison transcribe the rough notes from August 21 to the end of the convention. At that time, Bilder hypothesizes, Madison replaced some of his own speeches with new ones written on new pages in place of the original pages. Bilder insists that Madison also began to change the gossipy tone of the Notes to one of detachment, thereby altering his Notes from a legislative diary into a legislative record.

Bilder even claims that Madison did not formulate his famous theory that a geographically extended republic could stifle majority tyranny until after the convention ended. Madison's extended republic argument appears in section eleven of his April 1787 memorandum entitled "Vices of the Political System of the U.S.," and in speeches delivered at the convention. Bilder contends that Madison later rewrote section eleven of his "Vices" essay, as well as his June speeches, to include the extended republic argument, which she believes Madison did not devise until the writing of *The Federalist* 10 late in 1787. In retirement, Bilder insists, Madison further tinkered with his Notes to make them consistent with the notes left behind by other convention delegates.

Bilder is correct that Madison did not transcribe the rough notes taken after August 21 until two years later, but her claim that Madison later substituted sanitized speeches for supposedly embarrassing ones is based on little or no evidence. Bilder invariably—and perversely—attributes the worst possible motives to Madison, especially that he falsified the historical record. She meanwhile accepts the notes left behind by other delegates including Robert Yates and John Lansing at face value even though those notes are much more defective and unreliable. Yates's notes, for example, were altered by Edmond Charles Genet before publication in order to discredit Madison, a political competitor against Genet's father-in-law, George Clinton. Mary Sarah Bilder, *Madison's Hand: Revising the Constitutional Convention* (Cambridge, MA: Harvard University Press, 2015). Stuart Leibiger, "James Madison: Constitutional Convention Spin Doctor?" *Common-Place: The Journal of Early American Life*, 16 (2016), No. 4, http://common-place.org/article/james-madison-constitutional-convention-spin-doctor/.

20. Gordon Lloyd, "Scrawling 'Opportunist' All over Madison's *Notes*," *Law and Liberty*, Nov. 30, 2015, www.libertylawsite.org/book-review/scrawling-opportunist-all-over-madisons-notes/. See also Lynn Uzell, *Redeeming Madison's Notes*, forthcoming.

21. NDFC, 24–27.

22. NDFC, 28; RFC, 3:28, 33, 35, 64, 368, 479; RFC Supplement, 67; PJM, 10:518–19.

23. John P. Kaminski, *Secrecy and the Constitutional Convention* (Madison, WI: Center for the Study of the American Constitution, 2005), 8; RFC, 3:60, 76, 173, 191.

24. Kaminski, *Secrecy*, 8; RFC, 3:46; RFC Supplement, 70, 123; Donald Jackson and Dorothy Twohig, eds., *The Diaries of George Washington*, 6 vols. (Charlottesville: University of Virginia Press, 1976–1979), hereafter cited as DGW, 5:164.

25. RFC, 3:74.

26. Ibid., 48–49, 66; RFC Supplement, 76, 205; William H. Masterson, *William Bount* (Baton Rouge: Louisiana State University Press), 126; Stuart Leibiger, *Founding Friendship: George Washington, James Madison, and the Creation of the American Republic* (Charlottesville: University of Virginia Press, 1999), 80–81.

27. RFC, 3:59.

28. Kaminski, *Secrecy*, 17; RFC, 3:60.

29. RFC Supplement, 42, 182; RFC, 3:76, 100, 447.

30. RFC, 3:74; RFC Supplement, 108.

31. RFC Supplement, 46–47, 163, 223, 325–26.

32. NDFC, 27, 29, 38, 73, 480–81, 528; DGW, 5:185, RFC, 3:71, 73, 81.

33. RFC Supplement, 201.

34. DGW, 5:156–86.

35. Ibid.; Richard Beeman, *Plain Honest Men: The Making of the American Constitution* (New York: Random House, 2009), 193–99. Samuel Powell served as mayor of Philadelphia from 1775 to 1776 and from 1789 to 1790. www.phila.gov/phils/Mayorlst.htm.
36. PGM, 3:881; *RFC Supplement*, 177, 237.
37. *RFC Supplement*, 33, 121, 201, 265; RFC, 3:28.
38. *RFC Supplement*, 34, 107, 111, 130, 141, 144, 174, 199, 256.
39. Ibid., 8, 14, 59, 80; RFC, 3:35, 57.
40. Gordon Lloyd, Constitutional Convention Attendance Record, http://teachingamericanhistory.org/convention/attendance/.
41. NDFC, 28; RFC, 3:473, 525.
42. *Demigods*, 191–92, 250; RFC, 3:525.
43. NDFC, 28–30; RFC, 1:23–24, 26–27.
44. NDFC, 30–33.
45. RFC, 1:24–27.
46. Ibid., 3:131; NDFC, 33; *Demigods*, 159.
47. NDFC, 33; RFC, 1:24, 3:427–28, 478–82.
48. RFC, 3:106–23, 595–609, 427–28, 478–82, 514–15, 531, 536; Beeman, *Plain Honest Men*, 93–98.
49. NDFC, 34; *Demigods*, 49, 242.
50. NDFC, 34–35; RFC, 3:474.
51. NDFC, 37–38.
52. Ibid., 38–40.
53. *RFC Supplement*, 216, 219–20, 233–34, 241–42, 247; RFC, 3:104, 272, 518; Leffler et al., eds. *Pierce*, 40; *Demigods*, 39–40, 47, 242.
54. NDFC, 39, 70.
55. Ibid., 75; *Demigods*, 150–53, 252; Christopher Collier and James Lincoln Collier, *Decision in Philadelphia: The Constitutional Convention of 1787* (New York: Ballantine Books, 1987), 278–88.
56. NDFC, 40; RFC, 1:56–57.
57. NDFC, 39–41.
58. NDFC, 43; RFC, 1:58.
59. NDFC, 43–45.
60. Ibid., 55; *Demigods*, 11–14, 240.
61. NDFC, 55–57.
62. Ibid., 73–79; RFC, 1:142–43.
63. NDFC, 81–87; RFC, 1:157.
64. NDFC, 88–93.
65. Ibid., 93–98; RFC, 1:182, 3:37; *Webster's Ninth New Collegiate Dictionary* (Springfield, MA: Merriam-Webster, 1984).

66. *Demigods*, 105–25, 241–42; *RFC*, 3:33; H. W. Brands, *The First American: The Life and Times of Benjamin Franklin* (New York: Doubleday, 2000), 683.

67. *NDFC*, 51–52, 99–100; *Demigods*, 119.

68. Ibid., 99–103.

69. Garry Wills, *Negro President: Jefferson and the Slave Power* (Boston: Houghton Mifflin, 2003), 50–61.

70. *NDFC*, 103.

71. Ibid., 103–4.

72. Ibid., 115–17.

CHAPTER 3

THE GREAT COMPROMISE

To counter the Virginia Plan, William Paterson, on behalf of the small states, presented the New Jersey Plan on June 15. This proposal, which conformed with Congress's February 21, 1787, resolution, would add executive and judicial branches to the existing Confederation and give it the power to tax imports and regulate commerce. Although the one-state, one-vote system would remain, requisitions on the states for additional money would be based on population, requiring the big states to pay more taxes than the small ones. A serious proposal that would strengthen the Confederation without violating Congress's charge to the convention, the New Jersey Plan nevertheless quickly suffered defeat, but not before making clear that the small states would settle for nothing less than state equality in one house of the legislature. The impasse over representation lasted until mid-July, when the convention passed the troublesome representation issue to a Grand Committee of a delegate from each state. Stacked with compromisers from the large states and hard liners from the small states, this committee—not surprisingly—proposed a settlement that granted the small states what they wanted. The lower house would be based on population, and the upper house would be based on state equality. The small states managed to overcome the large state-Lower South coalition and pass this Great Compromise on July 16 by a 5–4–1 vote because the Massachusetts delegation deadlocked, and the North Carolina delegation switched sides and joined the small states.

The Great Compromise not only protected the interests of the small states, but it also safeguarded the states as states. Congress could pass no law without being approved by both the House of Representatives, elected by the people, and by the Senate, elected by the state legislatures.

William Paterson's parents brought him from Ireland to America at age two. He grew up in Princeton, New Jersey, where his merchant father operated a store. After graduating from his home town's elite college in 1763, he earned a master's degree from the same institution three years later. In college, Paterson became friends with fellow Princetonians Luther Martin and Oliver Ellsworth, both later small-state allies at the convention. Paterson did not share the wealth and aristocratic background of most of his classmates. Pierce described Paterson as "a man of great modesty, with looks that bespeak talents of no great extent." But Pierce believed that Paterson knew exactly when and how to engage in a debate. An example of this skill came on June 15.[1]

Paterson arrived in the Assembly Room that Friday bearing an alternative to the Virginia Plan. Known as the New Jersey Plan, this proposal was drafted by delegates from the small states of Connecticut, Delaware, New Jersey, and Maryland, as well as by Robert Yates and John Lansing of New York. New York, a mid-sized state, sided with the small states because neighboring New Jersey and Connecticut, lacking major port cities, imported and exported through New York City. This trade generated tremendous impost revenue that New York State did not want to lose to a federal government empowered to regulate commerce.[2]

Instead of the adoption of a brand-new national government, the New Jersey Plan recommended "that the articles of Confederation ought to be so revised, corrected & enlarged, as to render the federal Constitution adequate to the exigencies of Government." This language almost matched the wording of the Confederation Congress's instructions to the convention. To the authority of the existing congress, Paterson proposed adding the power to tax imports and to regulate commerce with foreign nations. Should additional revenue be necessary, congress could requisition from the states additional funds based on the free population-plus-three-fifths-of-enslaved-people ratio. (The Confederation Congress at the time used this formula when requisitioning funds from the states.) States that failed to meet their requisitions could be coerced by congress. The New Jersey Plan would also add to the Confederation judicial and executive branches appointed by congress. The president would serve one term and be removable by a majority of the state governors.

Under the New Jersey Plan each state would retain one vote in congress, but the amount of requisitions states paid to the central government would be apportioned based on population, so that large states would pay

William Paterson of New Jersey, a chief spokesman for the small states, presented the New Jersey Plan to the convention in June as an alternative to the Virginia Plan. After the passage of the Great Compromise, he advocated a strong federal government. (Collection of the Supreme Court of the United States)

more than small ones. Although it would significantly strengthen the existing Confederation and comported with the Confederation Congress's February 1787 resolution endorsing the convention, the New Jersey Plan favored the small states to such an extent that the large states would never accept it. The small states may have offered it hoping that the convention would adopt a compromise between it and the Virginia Plan. "The New Jersey Plan was," writes Michael Klarman, "mostly a bargaining ploy by small-state delegations to extract equal state representation in at least one house of the national legislature."[3]

The New Jersey Plan not only protected the interests of the small states, but it also protected the interests of the states themselves, whether large or small. The state legislatures would elect congress, which in turn appointed the executive and judicial branches. The retention of the confederal form of government meant that the states would serve as intermediaries between the central government and the people.

To give the New Jersey Plan "fair deliberation," the convention placed it alongside the Virginia Plan before the committee of the whole for debate. A sharp challenge to the Virginia Plan, the New Jersey Plan, according to Madison, caused "serious anxiety for the result of the Convention." Dickinson, an advocate of a strong national government but one who had also called for a compromise over legislative representation, reprimanded Madison for resisting accommodation: "You see the consequence of pushing things too far." Dickinson pointed out that "some of the members from the small States wish for two branches in the General Legislature and are friends to a good National Government." But by not budging an inch on proportional representation, Madison and his large-state, nationalist allies had driven these small-state nationalists (including Dickinson himself) into the arms of the small-state advocates of confederation. Dickinson and other Delaware and New Jersey delegates wanted a strong national government but not representation based on population. To avoid the latter, they had abandoned the former. Delaware and New Jersey had thus joined forces with New York and Connecticut, who wanted to retain the confederal form of government. The Virginia Plan had indeed fallen into jeopardy.[4]

Debate by the committee of the whole on the two plans did not begin until the next day so that everyone could digest the New Jersey Plan. Delegates from the large states (Virginia, Pennsylvania, and Massachusetts) and the Lower South (Georgia, North Carolina, and South Carolina) supported the Virginia Plan. Delegates from the small states (Connecticut, Delaware, New Jersey) plus mid-sized New York favored the New Jersey Plan. Maryland was divided.

John Lansing of New York, the mayor of Albany and ally of the state's antinationalist governor, George Clinton, opened the debate with an attack on the Virginia Plan. During the Revolutionary War, Lansing served as an aide to General Philip Schuyler before becoming speaker of New York's Assembly and a member of the Confederation Congress. Lansing and other Clintonians worried that if congress took control of commerce, it would cost New York the import revenue it collected from neighboring Connecticut and New Jersey, who lacked major ports. Hamilton described his colleague as "a good young fellow and a good practitioner of the law," but noted that "his friends mistook his talents when they made him a statesman." More than one contemporary commented on Lansing's "slender talents." Pierce observed "a hesitation in his speech, that will prevent his being an Orator." Lansing argued that the Virginia Plan went far beyond the convention's charge to revise the Articles, and that the states would not approve shifting so much power to a national government. New York's legislature, he insisted, would never have sent delegates if it knew the convention would replace the Confederation with a regime that would "destroy or annihilate" the states.[5]

Paterson agreed that the Virginia Plan far exceeded the convention's authority. "If the subsisting confederation is so radically defective as not to admit of amendment," Paterson pleaded, "let us say so and report its insufficiency, and wait for enlarged powers." But the one-state, one-vote system could not be abandoned without the unanimous concurrence of the states. Paterson rejected a bicameral congress as both unnecessary and expensive. The various state delegations were perfectly capable of checking one another in the existing unicameral legislature. "Let us therefore fairly try whether the confederation cannot be mended, and if it can, we shall do our duty, and I believe the people will be satisfied," he concluded.[6]

Wilson contrasted the two plans. One created a new national government of people, the other revised the existing Confederation of states. One had a popularly elected bicameral legislature with representation based on population, the other had a unicameral legislature elected by states that were equally represented. He dismissed the suggestion that the Virginia Plan exceeded the convention's instructions because "he conceived himself authorized to *conclude nothing*, but to be at liberty to *propose any thing*." Wilson did not believe that a national government would be unpopular with the people because national citizenship would not interfere with state citizenship. "Will a Citizen of *Delaware* be degraded by becoming a Citizen of the *United States*?" he asked. Wilson thus argued for dual citizenship, where state and national governments concurrently interacted directly with the people in different spheres of policy. Wilson did not support a continuation of the Confederation because it was not elected by the sovereign people, and because congress lacked a second legislative chamber to check it. A single-house congress amounted to "Legislative despotism," he declared. Most important, "where the principle of unequal Represtn. prevails, there exists a poison wh. eventually will destroy . . . the Government."[7]

Randolph agreed that the convention must be free to propose a suitable remedy, especially given "the imbecility of the existing Confederacy, & the danger of delaying a substantial reform." The alternatives before them were a national plan and a confederal plan. He preferred the former because it operated directly on the people, and so coercion of recalcitrant states would never be necessary to enforce its decrees. A national government would also possess enough strength and independence to maintain itself. The Confederation Congress, in contrast, would always be "obsequious to the views of the States, who are always encroaching on the authority of the U. States." Randolph closed, "I am certain that a national government must be established, and this is the only moment when it can be done."[8]

Monday, June 18 belonged to Alexander Hamilton. After having been "hitherto silent," he spoke for just about the whole session that day. He had, he explained, held his tongue so long in deference to statesmen whose views were so different from his own, especially his two colleagues from New York, Yates and Lansing, who time and again had outvoted him within the delegation. The convention had been called, Hamilton pointed out, to do two mutually exclusive things: to revise the Articles and "to provide for the exigencies of the Union." Given that the latter could not be accomplished under the shackles of the former, the delegates "owed it to our Country" in "this emergency" to do "whatever we should deem essential to its happiness." Hamilton expressed his strong opposition to both plans before the committee. Of the two, however, he judged the New Jersey Plan far worse, because "no amendment of the Confederation leaving the States in possession of their Sovereignty could possibly answer the purpose."

The biggest problem facing the United States, Hamilton argued, was that the interest and loyalty of the people lay with the state governments instead of with the central government, which enabled the states always to "pursue internal interests adverse to those of the whole." This problem could never be solved under the New Jersey Plan's confederal form of government. The dilemma could be solved only by vesting "such a compleat sovereignty in the general Governmt. as will turn all the strong principles & passions . . . on its side." Hamilton further found the New Jersey Plan objectionable because the large states would never agree to the "equality of suffrage . . . so much desired by the small States." But, in Hamilton's opinion, the Virginia Plan was not much better, consisting of *"pork still, with a little change of the sauce."*[9]

Hamilton stunned the convention by declaring that "in his private opinion . . . the British Govt. was the best in the world: and that he doubted much whether anything short of it would do in America." Only the British Constitution had proven successful in simultaneously protecting the interests of rich and poor. Having praised monarchy, Hamilton questioned the viability of republican government. "The voice of the people has been said to be the voice of God," he proclaimed. "However generally this maxim has been quoted and believed, it is not true in fact. The people are turbulent and changing; they seldom judge or determine right." He expressed "despair that a Republican Govt. could be established over so great an extent." Conventional wisdom suggested that "no good" executive "could be established on Republican principles." Hamilton understood that for the moment at least, the American people would only accept a republican government. But he wished to approach as close to monarchy as possible. "We ought to go as far," he insisted, "to attain stability and permanency, as republican principles will admit." He recognized that a constitutional monarchy would not at the moment be acceptable in the United States, but he guessed that public opinion was shifting. As the shortcomings of republicanism emerged, more and more people would recognize the benefits of a monarchy.[10]

Hamilton described his preferred form of government. The legislature would consist of two houses chosen directly or indirectly by the people, with the upper chamber serving during good behavior to check the popular excesses of the lower house. The senate would approve treaties and confirm appointments below the cabinet level. The popularly elected president would also serve during good behavior. "An executive is less dangerous to the liberties of the people when in office during life, than for seven years," he asserted, because he would not resort to corruption to win reelection. That officer would have an absolute veto, make appointments, direct the armed forces, and make treaties. In addition to strengthening the national government, Hamilton aimed to weaken the states. State governors, appointed by the national government, would have an

In June, Alexander Hamilton of New York gave a lengthy speech calling for a powerful federal government with a president and senate that served during good behavior. After being outvoted by his antinationalist colleagues from New York in the early weeks of the convention, Hamilton went home. He returned in time to be the lone signer from his state. (Library of Congress)

absolute veto over state laws. The state militias would be "under the sole and exclusive direction of the United States, the officers of which to be appointed and commissioned by them."

Historians have debated whether Hamilton called for an excessively strong national government simply to make the Virginia Plan seem like sensible middle ground between his proposal and the New Jersey Plan. That is, his speech was not a serious statement of his beliefs, but a caricature of them designed to move the delegates to the right politically. According to this theory, Hamilton secretly hoped that they would end up with the Virginia Plan, in which he genuinely believed.[11]

Madison recorded Hamilton's own explanation of his motives: "He did not mean to offer" his plan "as a proposition to the Committee. It was meant only to give a more correct view of his ideas, and to suggest the amendments which he should probably propose" to the Virginia Plan. Hamilton thus knew that his plan was too extreme to be taken seriously, but he hoped it would promote adoption of an invigorated Virginia Plan. That said, Hamilton fully believed in the merit of his proposals, doubted the viability of republicanism, and genuinely admired monarchy. He himself stated as much, and the other delegates understood that he meant what he said. Indeed, this speech, the gist of which became publicly known after the rule of secrecy was lifted, caused Hamilton considerable trouble years later when he became Treasury secretary under President Washington. It convinced many Americans of Hamilton's monarchism and of his desire to minimize the powers of the states. In the 1790s, opponents of a powerful federal government pointed to Hamilton's June 18 remarks as having let the cat out of the bag about his ultimate goal for America.

When Hamilton's day-long tour de force ended, the Assembly Room fell silent. No one rose to agree or disagree. The delegates adjourned for the day. Having left the Assembly Room, they found their voices. Three days later, Johnson commented that Hamilton "has been praised by every body" but "has been supported by none." Having made his point and finding himself consistently outvoted by his New York colleagues Yates and Lansing, Hamilton went home in late June. He returned to Philadelphia later in the summer, once Yates and Lansing quit the convention for good. Shortly after leaving, Hamilton wrote to Washington that he felt "deeply distressed" over the convention. "I fear that we shall let slip the golden opportunity of rescuing the American empire from disunion anarchy and misery."[12]

On June 19, Madison delivered a mortal blow to the New Jersey Plan. That proposal, he declared, could neither "preserve the Union," nor resolve the problems that faced the states individually and collectively. Madison itemized the issues that the small-state plan would not solve. It would not prevent states from violating U.S. treaties, or from infringing on the authority of the central government. An analysis of the history of confederacies, he explained, demonstrated a "tendency of the parts to encroach on the authority of the whole." The New Jersey Plan, Madison continued, would not prevent the states from trespassing against each other and would not protect the rights of minorities within their borders.

He declared that individual states would still suffer from the "multiplicity," "mutability," and "injustice" of their laws.

"The great difficulty" facing the convention, Madison asserted, "lies in the affair of Representation; and if this could be adjusted, all others would be surmountable." He dismissed hotchpot as a chimerical notion and warned the small states that insisting on the one-vote-per-state formula could only wreck the convention, because the large states would never submit to it. He again asked the small states whether they would be better off with a Union based on proportional representation, or with no Union at all. Finally, Madison refuted the claim that the Confederation could be dissolved only by the unanimous consent of the states. Breach of contract by member states also constituted grounds for termination. Madison summarized the many instances in which individual states had broken federal treaties or otherwise violated the Articles. Madison's speech, coming on the heels of Hamilton's address, vanquished the New Jersey Plan. The committee voted it down seven states to three, with the small state of Connecticut even voting against it. Only New York, New Jersey, and Delaware voted aye.[13]

Why did Connecticut favor the Virginia Plan over the New Jersey Plan? For Connecticut to have voted as it did, at least two of the state's three delegates sided with the large states. Clues can be found the next day. On June 20, that state's delegates began maneuvering the convention toward a compromise that eventually became known as the Great Compromise, or the Connecticut Compromise. According to this deal, the Virginia Plan would be amended so that the states would have an equal number of members in the upper legislative house.

Ellsworth took the first step toward compromise. Educated at Yale College (later renamed Yale University) and at the College of New Jersey (later renamed Princeton University), Ellsworth became an attorney and later served in the Continental Congress. John Adams described Ellsworth as having "the Stiffness of Connecticut . . . His Air and Gilt are not elegant . . . yet his Understanding is as sound, his Information as good and his heart as steady as any Man can boast." Ellsworth moved that the word *national* be dropped from the committee of the whole's report on the Virginia Plan. The resolution would then read, "That the Government of the United States ought to consist of a supreme legislative, Executive and Judiciary." Ellsworth's suggestion, adopted unanimously without debate, opened the door for the creation of a partly national, partly confederal hybrid government instead of a strictly national one. That is, the motion opened the door for a federal government that represented the people and the states simultaneously.[14]

Another Connecticut delegate, Roger Sherman, swung into action next. A member of the committee that drafted the Articles of Confederation, Sherman by 1787 concluded that Congress needed the power to tax and regulate commerce. An exporting state without a major port, Connecticut lost significant revenue from import duties to neighboring New York. If Congress taxed imports, that money would instead go to the national government, allowing Connecticut to get some of it back again through national spending. Wanting the federal regime to resemble Connecticut's government, he favored keeping the Confederation but adding an executive branch that would be chosen and controlled by Congress.[15]

Connecticut originally selected Erastus Wolcott as one of its delegates. But Wolcott, who had never contracted smallpox and who lacked immunity to the illness, turned down the appointment fearing that he would succumb to the disease in Philadelphia. Connecticut sent Sherman in Wolcott's place. Despite being a last-minute replacement and, at age sixty-seven, being the second-oldest man present, Sherman spoke more times than all but three of the delegates.[16]

Thomas Jefferson described Sherman as a man "who never said a foolish thing in his life." "No Man has a better Heart or clearer Head," wrote Pierce. "He is an able politician, and extremely artful in accomplishing any particular object;—it is remarked that he seldom fails." Congressman Jeremiah Wadsworth attested that "he is as cunning as the Devil, and if you attack him, you ought to know him well; he is not easily managed, but if he suspects you are trying to take him in, you may as well catch an Eel by the tail." Yet he was anything but graceful or eloquent. "Mr. Sherman exhibits the oddest shaped character I ever . . . met with," wrote Pierce. "He is awkward . . . and unaccountably strange in his manner. But in his train of thinking there is something regular, deep and comprehensive; yet the oddity of his address, the vulgarisms that accompany his public speaking, and that strange new England cant which runs through his . . . speaking make everything that is connected with him grotesque and laughable." John Adams commented that "Shermans Air is the Reverse of Grace. . . . It is Stiffness, and Awkwardness itself."[17]

Sherman echoed John Dickinson, who had earlier advocated compromise when the large-state delegates insisted on basing representation in both houses on population. "The disparity of the States in point of size," Sherman recognized, "was the main difficulty." He advocated accommodation: "If the difficulty on the subject of representation can not be otherwise got over, he would agree to have two branches, and a proportional representation in one of them; provided each State had an equal voice in the other." Only this solution would protect the interests of both the large and small states. Ellsworth and Sherman had planted the seed of compromise.[18]

Having rejected the New Jersey Plan, the committee of the whole began reconsidering the various provisions of the Virginia Plan. The delegates reaffirmed having a bicameral legislature with the lower house elected by the people. When the committee debated whether the states or the national government should pay the salaries of members of the lower house, a familiar division emerged. The nationalist delegates wanted the general government to pay to keep the lower chamber independent of the state legislatures. The pro-confederation delegates wanted the states to pay for precisely the opposite reason: to keep the lower house responsive to the state legislatures. The former group won, with Connecticut again voting with the majority.[19]

The committee of the whole turned its attention to the election of the upper house, which, according to the revised Virginia Plan, would be elected by the state legislatures based on population. James Wilson called instead for election of the senate by the people of the states. The people hold dual citizenship, he said, state and national. As citizens of the states, they elect the state government. As citizens of the United States, they should also elect the national government. "The Genl. Govt. is not an assemblage of States, but of individuals for certain political purposes," he reasoned. "It is not meant for the States, but for the individuals composing them; the *individuals* therefore not the *States*, ought to be represented in it." To allow the state legislatures to elect the upper chamber "will introduce & cherish local interests & local prejudices." In other words, if the state legislatures chose the upper house, it would become a carbon copy of the defective Confederation Congress.[20]

Ellsworth, Johnson, Williamson, and Mason all instead favored the election of the senate by the state legislatures to protect the states against the central government. The committee of the whole upheld election by the state legislatures 9–2, with only Pennsylvania and Virginia opposed.[21]

The Great Compromise

Although Roger Sherman of Connecticut attended the Constitutional Convention as a last-minute substitute, he became one of the most important delegates. Sherman advocated the Great Compromise over representation in Congress that broke the deadlock between the large and small states. (New York Public Library)

On June 27, Luther Martin of Maryland rose to speak. Educated at the College of New Jersey in Princeton, Martin then moved to Maryland, studied law, became skilled in the courtroom, and earned appointment as the state's attorney general. Martin "often appeared in Court evidently intoxicated," wrote nineteenth-century Supreme Court chief justice Roger B. Taney, who knew him well. Martin "seemed to take pleasure in showing his utter disregard of good taste and refinement in his dress and language and his mode of argument. He was coarse and unseemly at the dinner-table, in his manner of eating, as he was in everything." Christopher Collier suggests that the small states, hoping for a tour de force, had selected Martin to make their case to the convention.[22]

Martin's speech proclaimed that to base representation in both houses of congress on population would allow Virginia, Pennsylvania, and Massachusetts to enslave the rest of the states. Not only would those three states control the national legislature, but they would also control the executive and judiciary because congress would choose the president and appoint justices. He suggested that only carving up the large states into smaller ones would make proportional representation acceptable. "The States are equal & must have equal Influence and equal votes," he proclaimed. He preferred only a modest increase in the powers of the Confederation, suggesting that additional powers could always be added later if necessary. But excessive power once granted "can never be reclaimed."

Martin droned on for three hours before exhaustion forced him to cease for the afternoon. The next day, he resumed his rant where he had left off. An exasperated Madison found it challenging to record the speech, "which was delivered with much diffuseness & considerable vehemence." In corroboration, Pierce wrote that Martin "has a very bad delivery, and [is] so extremely prolix, that he never speaks without tiring the patience of all who hear him." Even Yates, Martin's small-state ally, found him "too diffuse . . . to trace him through the whole, or to methodize his ideas into a systematic . . . arrangement." After the convention ended, Ellsworth condemned Martin for an address that "might have continued two months, but for those marks of fatigue and disgust you saw strongly expressed on whichever side of the house you turned your mortified eyes." Ellsworth added that Martin "exhausted the politeness of the Convention, which . . . prepared to slumber when you rose to speak." If Martin had been selected to make the small-state case, then he proved a disastrous choice.[23]

Madison insisted that small states had nothing to fear from proportional representation because no issue would ever unite the economically- and geographically diverse large states against the small ones. He once again asked whether the less-populous states would be more vulnerable to the large as part of a national Union, or with no Union at all. Wilson supported Madison, comparing the small states under the Confederation to the infamous "rotten boroughs" in England, which had nearly as much representation in Parliament as London even though few people lived in them.[24]

Franklin cited the convention's slow progress and the diverse views of the delegates as "a melancholy proof of the imperfection of the Human Understanding." With "this Assembly, groping as it were in the dark to find political truth," he asked why it had neglected to seek guidance from God. He moved that a clergyman be invited in to lead "prayers imploring the assistance of Heaven." The outlook had become so bleak that America's best-known spokesman for science and Enlightenment sought divine intervention!

Many, especially Hamilton, expressed concern that bringing in a minister at this point would make the public think that the convention was failing. Years later Jonathan Dayton, according to a second-hand account, claimed that in opposing prayers for providential assistance, Hamilton joked that "he did not see the necessity of calling in *foreign aid!*" Washington, according to this anecdote, glared at Hamilton for his impertinence. Religious delegates like Sherman supported Franklin's suggestion. Unable to resolve the disagreement over prayer, itself designed to resolve the impasse over representation, the convention finally quit for the day. Adjournment, wrote Madison, "was at length carried" but only "after several unsuccessful attempts." The delegates could barely agree on anything.[25]

As Franklin's motion revealed, many of the delegates, including Sherman and Johnson of Connecticut, were deeply religious men who believed that government should promote morality and the Christian faith. Those at the other end of the spectrum, like Mason and Madison of Virginia, advocated freedom of conscience and the separation of church and state. Despite these differences, a strong consensus that the central government should stay out of religion emerged at the convention. On August 30, at Charles Pinckney's urging, the convention agreed that the constitution should not require religious qualifications for officeholding. Because the delegates agreed that any government involvement in matters of faith should be handled by the states, religion did not become a contentious issue that summer.[26]

The next morning, June 29, Connecticut resumed its quest for compromise when William Samuel Johnson rose to speak. Educated at Yale and Harvard colleges, Johnson received an honorary doctorate from Oxford University. His efforts to reconcile the colonies and Great Britain led in 1779 to his detention by Connecticut's patriots. According to fellow Yale graduate Enoch Perkins, Johnson's "eloquence" as an orator "was music to the ear." Johnson pointed out that the national and confederal concepts, "instead of being opposed to each other, ought to be combined; that in *one* branch the *people*, ought to be represented; in the *other* the *States*."[27]

Wilson answered that state equality amounted to tyranny by the minority because it would allow seven states, representing only one-third of the American people, to enact legislation against the opposition of six states, representing two-thirds of the people. "Can we forget for whom we are forming a Government?" he asked. "Is it for *men*, or for the imaginary beings called *States?*" State equality, Wilson declared, meant "the establishment of an aristocracy, which is government of the few over the many." Government by states, moreover, would re-create the Confederation Congress, leaving the United States "in the same situation and as much fettered as ever we were."[28]

Building on Wilson's logic, Madison added that state equality would prevent the upper house from exercising key powers requiring stability and calm deliberation, such as the veto over state laws. Madison again warned the Virginia Plan's opponents that the only alternative to proportional representation was disunion. The delegates saw a breakup of the states as a nightmare scenario that would cause individual states to militarize for self-defense, inexorably leading to despotism. Hamilton predicted that disunion would invite European domination or even recolonization of the continent, as the weaker states formed alliances with foreign powers for their own protection.[29]

Gerry reminded the delegates that the one-vote-per-state system was a temporary necessary evil that had been adopted during the crisis of the Revolutionary War. Since then, the states had become "intoxicated with the idea of their *sovereignty*." With the Confederation disintegrating, Gerry lamented that the delegates acted more like partisans than like a "band of brothers, belonging to the same family."

The committee of the whole rejected a motion for representation to be based on state equality in the lower house. Searching for "a ground of compromise," Ellsworth immediately moved that each state have an equal vote in the upper house. "We were partly national; partly federal," he iterated. "The proportional representation in the first branch was conformable to the national principle & would secure the large States agst. the small. An equality of voices was conformable to the federal principle and was necessary to secure the Small States agst. the large." It was the only basis for accommodation, he insisted. "And if no compromise should take place, our meeting would not only be in vain but worse than in vain."[30]

The small states desperately searched for an advantage. On June 30, Brearly of New Jersey moved that the convention implore New Hampshire, the only absent state besides Rhode Island to send delegates forthwith. New Hampshire's attendance would give the small states one additional vote. Rufus King of Massachusetts blocked that move by announcing that New Hampshire would soon arrive. The convention let the matter drop.[31]

A series of large-state delegates including Madison, Wilson, Franklin, and Gouverneur Morris desperately threw out alternative proposals to avoid state equality in the upper house. Madison spoke first. No issue would ever divide the large states against the little ones, he iterated. The real division among the states was not big versus small, but slaveholding versus non-slaveholding. Why not, therefore, base the lower house on free population, and base the upper house on the entire population, including enslaved people? "By this arrangement," he reasoned, "the Southern Scale would have the advantage in one House, and the Northern in the other." Recognizing that this suggestion, doubly advantageous to Virginia as both a large state and a slave state, would draw little support, Madison did not formally introduce it.[32]

Wilson next offered a proposal that at least drew support from the large states. One objection against an upper house based on proportional representation, he conceded, was that it would be too large a body for the calm deliberation required for the responsibilities that would be assigned to it. To keep that body from becoming too large, Wilson suggested granting one member per 100,000 people, but allowing states with fewer than that amount still to have at least one. Wilson regarded this idea as a concession to the small states, but the delegates from those states were not impressed.[33]

Franklin recommended yet another compromise: let each state be equal in the upper chamber, but on appropriations bills, their votes would be weighted based on state population. Unlike many large-state men, Franklin advocated compromise, using an analogy to make his point: "When a broad table is to be made, and the edges of planks do not fit," he explained, "the artist takes a little from both, and makes a good joint." Franklin's proposal met the same fate as Madison's and Wilson's.[34]

Gouverneur Morris offered a fourth plan of representation. He thought the upper and lower houses should represent different orders, or classes, in society. Just as the British House of Lords represented aristocracy, so the upper house should represent wealth. Isolating the wealthy in one chamber, Morris reasoned, would prevent them from dominating the entire congress, indeed the entire government. If the two legislative houses represented rich and poor, then they could check one another. By "setting apart, the aristocratic interest, the popular interest will be combined agst. it," he explained. "He fears the influence of the rich. They will have the same effect here as elsewhere if we do not . . . keep them within their proper sphere." Morris wanted the wealth-based upper house to be appointed by the president and to serve for life. Morris's suggestion received the same dismal response as the previous three.[35]

After these four proposals, all from large-state delegates, fell flat, King on June 30 threw down the gauntlet, announcing that he would never support state equality even in one legislative branch. Gunning Bedford of Delaware responded with equal intransigence. A graduate of the College of New Jersey in Princeton, Bedford served in the Continental Congress and later as Delaware's attorney general. Pierce described him as "a bold and nervous Speaker" with "a very commanding and striking manner" but who was "warm and impetuous in his temper, and precipitate in his judgment." Bedford answered King and the other large-state men with a dire ultimatum. "*I do not, gentlemen, trust you*" not to tyrannize over the small states. "The Large States dare not dissolve the Confederation," he cried. "If they do, the small ones will find some foreign ally . . . who will take them by the hand and do them justice." If individual states allied with foreign powers as Bedford threatened, America would fall victim to periodic wars just like Europe. King shot back that "he was grieved that such a thought had entered" Bedford's heart. "He was more grieved that such an expression had dropped from his lips."[36]

Monday July 2 opened with a 5–5 split vote on whether the states should be equally represented in the upper house. Maryland, which had hitherto been divided, now sided with the small states. Georgia, which had previously voted with the large state-Lower South coalition, this time divided, canceling the delegation's vote. Two of Georgia's delegates, William Pierce and William Few, had left to go to New York to attend the Confederation Congress, of which they were also members. That left Abraham Baldwin and William Houstoun in Philadelphia. Whereas Houstoun continued to vote with the large states, Baldwin switched sides to join the small states. The tie cost Georgia its vote.[37]

How do we explain Baldwin's shift? Previously, he had advocated that "the second branch ought to be the representation of property." This statement clearly places him in the large-state camp, because under the original Virginia Plan, representation in the upper house would be based on either population or taxes paid. So what changed? Baldwin, a native of Connecticut, had only three years earlier relocated to Georgia to advance his economic fortunes as a lawyer on the southwestern frontier. A graduate of Yale College, Baldwin exchanged his original profession as a minister and chaplain for a career in politics, representing his adopted state in the Confederation Congress. Christopher Collier suggests that Connecticut's delegates successfully lobbied Baldwin to join their pro-compromise effort. Or maybe he simply recognized that saving the convention (and the Union) required a concession to the small states. Luther Martin believed that Baldwin acted "from a conviction" that the small states "would go home, and thereby dissolve the convention" if they did not obtain state equality in one house of congress. Pierce noted that the thirty-two-year-old Baldwin "has an accommodating turn of mind."[38]

Maryland's delegation had previously been divided, with its two delegates in attendance canceling each other out. Daniel of St. Thomas Jenifer voted with the large states, and Luther Martin sided with the small states. Maryland's July 2 switch occurred because Jenifer's absence that day allowed Martin alone to cast the state's vote. Maryland was one of only two states that allowed a single delegate to cast its ballot. Richard Beeman hypothesizes that Jenifer, who leaned toward the nationalist position, intentionally did not appear that Monday to enable the state's vote to change. The only evidence supporting this interpretation is Martin's unverifiable post-convention claim that Jenifer entered the Assembly Room immediately after the 5–5 vote was taken. King, according to Martin, hoping the Maryland delegation would now deadlock, asked for a re-vote. But Washington, the presiding officer, allegedly ruled against him. David Stewart, who accepts Martin's version of events, suggests that Washington ruled against King to help break the deadlock over representation. But there is no evidence that Washington had abandoned the large-state position in favor of compromise at this moment in time.[39]

At any rate, the large state-Lower South coalition had finally cracked, revealing its vulnerability. With the convention deadlocked, South Carolinian Charles Cotesworth Pinckney, a planter, lawyer, breveted Revolutionary War general, and the cousin of Charles Pinckney, suggested a new way forward. Why not form "a Committee consisting of a member from each State . . . to devise & report some compromise?" Several delegates supported the committee concept. "It seems we have got to a point that we cannot move one way or another," observed Sherman. "Such a committee is necessary to set us right." Large-state advocates Madison and Wilson, fearing the wind was blowing against them, vociferously opposed it. The former complained that a committee would resolve nothing, because whatever it recommended would still have to be agreed to by the full convention.[40]

Despite these objections, the delegates turned over the matter of representation to a committee on July 2. "Elected by ballot" the Grand Committee of Eleven consisted of Gerry from Massachusetts, Ellsworth from Connecticut, Yates from New York, Paterson from New Jersey, Franklin from Pennsylvania, Bedford from Delaware, Martin from Maryland, Mason from Virginia, William R. Davie from North Carolina, Rutledge from South Carolina, and Baldwin from Georgia. Conspicuously absent were Madison and Wilson. This committee was clearly stacked with compromisers from the large states and the Lower South states, and hardliners from the small states.[41]

Mason, Franklin, and Gerry, representing the large states, had all recently advocated a compromise over representation. Similarly, Davie, Rutledge, and Baldwin, the Lower South members, had also spoken out for accommodation. Indeed, Baldwin had just voted with the small states, deadlocking Georgia. Small-state committee members Ellsworth, Paterson, Bedford, and Martin, in contrast, had demanded state equality in at least one house. Sherman, who took Connecticut's place on the committee when Ellsworth fell sick, adhered to the same position. Yates, who had not spoken in debate, described himself as favoring a *"national government"* based *"on federal principles,"* that is, representation based on state equality. The committee, in short, did not bode well for the large-state nationalists like Madison and Wilson, who wanted representation in both legislative houses to stay based on population.[42]

Exactly how the convention elected committees is unclear. According to the convention rules, "Committees shall be appointed by ballot; and the members who have the greatest number of ballots, altho' not a majority of the votes present, shall be the committee." Was the balloting done by state, with each state voting for one committee member from each state? Or was the balloting done by all the delegates, with each delegate voting for one committee member from each state? David Stewart argues, based on the practices of the Continental and Confederation congresses, that each state delegation selected its member of grand committees of eleven, but that smaller committees were chosen by the delegates voting individually. If Stewart is correct, then the large-state delegations chose to represent them men sympathetic to the small-state position.[43]

Having appointed the Grand Committee of Eleven on July 2, the convention adjourned to celebrate Independence Day. The delegates observed July 4 by joining a procession from the State House to Race Street Church, where they listened to prayer, a musical performance, and an oration on the anniversary of the Declaration of Independence delivered by a local law student identified by Washington as a "Mr. Mitchell."[44]

When the convention resumed business on July 5, Gerry, the Committee of Eleven chair, came forth with a compromise proposal: the lower house would be based on free population plus three-fifths of enslaved people. There would be one representative per 40,000 people, with each state having at least one member. "All bills for raising or appropriating money" would originate in the lower house and could not be amended in the upper house. The states would be equally represented in the upper house. Predictably, the compromise proposal was a victory for the small states. It had been suggested in committee by Franklin and acquiesced in by the large-state committee members, all of whom advocated compromise.[45]

After it was presented to the full convention, Madison attacked the Grand Committee report. State equality, he warned, would enable the minority to rule the majority and the North (with many small states) to rule the South in the upper house. He urged the large states to hold firm. "With justice & the majority of the people on their side," they must inevitably prevail. "With injustice and the minority on their side," the small states must inevitably fail. Madison expressed confidence that none of the latter would seek "her fortunes apart from the other States." The small states would never be so foolish as to "obstinately refuse to accede to a Govt. founded on just principles and promising them substantial protection." The large states simply needed to call the small-state bluff on disunion.[46]

Pronouncing the states the "bane of this Country," Gouverneur Morris, another large-state nationalist, urged the convention to "take out the teeth of the serpents." He had come to the convention "as a Representative of America" and "a Representative of the whole human race," not "to truck and bargain for our particular States." He ominously warned that "this Country must be united. If persuasion does not unite it, the sword will. . . . The stronger party will then make traytors of the weaker; and the Gallows & Halter will finish the work of the sword. How far foreign powers would be ready to take part in the confusions he would not say."[47]

Bedford, Gerry, and Mason, all members of the Committee of Eleven, defended their compromise proposal, arguing that a deal must take place for the Union to be preserved. Mason announced that he "would bury his bones in this City rather than expose his County to the Consequences of a dissolution of the Convention."[48]

Having money bills originate in the lower house was the one benefit offered to the large states in return for state equality in the senate. But Madison did "not regard the exclusive privilege of originating money bills as any concession on the side of the small States," since the upper house still had to agree before any legislation could pass. Wilson and Gouverneur Morris concurred that the proposal provided no advantage to the large states, and that it shut the smaller and abler upper chamber out of the taxing and spending process. Mason and Franklin answered that the representatives of the people must control the purse strings. The delegates then approved the money bills provision of the Committee of Eleven report 9–2, with the large states of Massachusetts and Pennsylvania voting yes. The large-state solidarity had cracked.[49]

On July 7, the convention returned to the bigger question of "allowing each State one vote in the 2d. branch" suggested by the Committee of Eleven report. Sherman expressed confidence that the proposal would give "decision and efficacy" to the government by providing a double check against unwise legislation. "If they vote by States in the 2d. branch, and each state has an equal vote," in that body, he explained, "there must be always a majority of States" in the senate "as well as a majority of the people" in the house of representatives "on the side of public measures." The convention approved this provision of the Grand Committee report 7–2, with Virginia and Pennsylvania voting no, and Massachusetts split. But the real large state-small state showdown would come over the entire Committee of Eleven report. Paterson reminded everyone that "the small States would never be able to defend themselves without an equality of votes in the 2d. branch.... His resolution was fixt. He would meet the large States on that Ground and no other."[50]

Sensing the tide turning against the large states, Randolph prepared a plan "for conciliating the small states" that he hoped would stave off state equality in the upper house. His proposal allowed one vote per state in the senate on several matters including regulating commerce, declaring war, raising troops, and electing the executive. On all other matters the upper house would vote based on state population. The small states, recognizing that they now had the upper hand, apparently rejected the proposal outside the convention, and so Randolph never formally raised it on the Assembly Room floor.[51]

While Randolph groped in vain to avoid state equality in the upper house, Washington perceived that the large states had already lost the senate. "I *almost* despair of seeing a favourable issue to the proceedings of the Convention, and do therefore repent having had any agency in the business," he lamented to Hamilton. "The Men who oppose a strong & energetic government are, in my opinion, narrow minded politicians, or are under the influence of local views."[52]

The convention turned to the Grand Committee recommendation that congressional districts consist of 40,000 people. Gouverneur Morris demanded that representation be based on wealth rather than population since "property was the main object of Society." To base representation on population, Morris feared, would allow growing numbers of poor and ignorant western frontiersmen to decide the fate of the nation without having to pay the government's bills. Gerry and King agreed that representation in the lower house must take property into account. Eager to enhance their representation in congress for their slave property, Rutledge and Butler of South Carolina enthusiastically concurred. The convention committed the matter of each state's representation to a committee composed of Gouverneur Morris, Gorham, Randolph, Rutledge, and King. All but Rutledge came from the three large states. All five came from the large state-Lower South alliance.[53]

On July 9, Gouverneur Morris, chair of the Committee of Five to which the matter of apportionment had been referred, reported back to the full convention. The committee recommended that the first congress have a fifty-six-member lower house, with the number of representatives ranging from one (Delaware) to nine (Virginia). Congress could in the future alter the number of representatives assigned to each state based on its wealth and population. Gorham explained that in determining these numbers, the committee sought to keep the size of the lower chamber manageable, and to account for both the wealth and the population of the states. Apparently, the committee relied on guesswork rather than a quantitative formula of state wealth and population to arrive at these numbers.[54]

Paterson condemned the idea of granting representation to the southern states for their slave property. Southern states did not allow slaveholders extra representation in their legislatures, so why should the general government do so? Representation, Paterson explained, "is an expedient by which an assembly of certain individls. chosen by the people is substituted in place of the inconvenient meeting of the people themselves." Paterson's remarks left him exposed to a counterattack. Madison fired back that Paterson's "doctrine of Representation . . . must for ever silence the pretentions of the small States to an equality of votes with the large ones," in the senate. "They ought to vote in the same proportion in which their citizens would do, if the people of all the States were collectively met."[55]

Unsatisfied with the quantitatively imprecise report of the Morris Committee, the convention handed the matter of legislative apportionment to a new committee of a delegate from each state. Chaired by King, this committee reported back on July 10. Instead of a fifty-six-member lower house, it proposed a sixty-five-member body, with the number of representatives per state varying from one (Delaware) to ten (Virginia). The committee appears to have based these numbers on estimates of each state's population (since no formal census had ever been taken), counting slaves as three-fifths of free people. Questioning whether these numbers accurately accounted for the populations of the various states, delegates haggled over the number of representatives assigned to each state. Should New Hampshire have two or three? Should Georgia be increased from three to four? Madison suggested that for congress faithfully to represent the American people, its size should be doubled from 65 members to 130. Mason agreed, pointing out that with sixty-five members, thirty-eight would form a quorum, and twenty would form a majority of that. Twenty representatives "was certainly too small a number to make laws for America." After Madison's suggestion lost, the convention approved a sixty-five-member lower chamber by a 9–2 vote. South Carolina and Georgia voted no because each believed it deserved an additional representative.[56]

The South Carolinians moved that slaves be counted the same as whites (as five-fifths of free persons) toward representation in the lower house. The motion, easily defeated, opened a larger discussion of whether population alone formed a suitable basis for representation, and whether slaves should be counted as part of the population. Or should representation be based only on free inhabitants? If slave property counted toward representation, then should other property count as well? Wilson summarized the theoretical difficulty. "Are they [slaves] admitted as Citizens?" he asked. If yes, "then why are they not admitted on an equality with White Citizens? are they admitted as property? then why is not other property admitted into the computation?" Having stated the conundrum, Wilson admitted that "these were difficulties however which he thought must be overruled by the necessity of compromise." Wilson had, after all, earlier in the convention, suggested the Three-Fifths Compromise to get the Lower South states to support representation based on population. Gouverneur Morris was not so accommodating. "Reduced to the dilemma of doing injustice to the Southern States or to human nature," he declared, "he must . . . do it to the former."[57]

On July 11, the convention voted down the three-fifths ratio, six states to four, with only Connecticut, Virginia, North Carolina, and Georgia in favor. This vote is often portrayed as a devastating blow to the slaveholding states that quickly forced them to make a concession to the North to get the Three-Fifths Compromise restored. According to this interpretation, the South the next day agreed to a motion by Gouverneur Morris that taxes on the states would be apportioned the same way as population. True, Morris a few days later hinted that his motion had indeed been designed to help restore the Three-Fifths Compromise. The problem with this interpretation is that the defeat of the Three-Fifths Compromise was not inflicted by the North on the South. Instead, it was inflicted by the South on itself. South Carolina and Maryland voted against the Three-Fifths Compromise, the former because it wanted slaves to count as five-fifths of free people, and Maryland because of a technicality over the wording of the resolution. The South thus did not need to make concessions to the North to overturn the vote, but it simply needed to vote in unison to restore the Three-Fifths Compromise. The Morris resolution, moreover, only got one northern state, Pennsylvania, to change its vote, and that ended up being a vote the South did not ultimately even need to restore the Three-Fifths Compromise.[58]

The Lower South delegates, however, vociferously demanded representation in the lower house for their enslaved population. "It was high time now to speak out," proclaimed Davie. "It was meant by some gentlemen to deprive the Southern States of any share of Representation for their blacks." North Carolina would accept nothing less than counting enslaved people as three-fifths of free people. Butler explained that "the security the Southn. States want is that their negroes may not be taken from them, which some gentlemen . . . have a very good mind to do."

Agreeing that "it is high time to speak out," Gouverneur Morris asserted that Pennsylvania would never allow representatives to be awarded for enslaved people. If balancing the interests of the northern and southern states proved elusive, then "instead of attempting to blend incompatible things, let us at once take a friendly leave of each another."[59]

On July 12, the convention approved basing both representation in the lower house and direct taxation on free population plus three-fifths of enslaved people, thereby overturning the previous day's vote. Legislative reapportionment would take place every ten years based on a census. The South had quickly and easily restored the Three-Fifths Compromise, and even did so without South Carolina's support. The vote was 6–2–2, with New Jersey and Delaware, who categorically opposed basing representation in either house on population, voting no. The Massachusetts and South Carolina delegations split, with the former divided over whether slaves should count zero-fifths or three-fifths, and the latter divided over whether slaves should count three-fifths or five-fifths. This time Maryland voted with the slave states. So also did Pennsylvania, presumably because of Morris's resolution on taxation. The fight over the Three-Fifths Compromise had little to do with the justice or injustice of slavery. Instead, it was a battle among the delegates to protect the voting strength of their states in the legislature.[60]

On July 14, Luther Martin confidently called for a final vote on the Great Compromise proposed by the Grand Committee of Eleven, whereby the lower house would be based on population, with slaves counting as three-fifths of free people, and the upper house would be based on state equality. Money bills would originate in the lower house and could not be altered by the senate. Sherman offered as a rationale for the compromise that it would protect the states as states. He "urged the equality of votes not so much as a security for the small States; as for the State Govts. which could not be preserved unless they were represented & had a negative in the Genl. Government." Unwilling to bend on state equality, King argued that a national government that legislated directly for the people had to be based entirely on proportional representation. He "was sure that no Govt. could last that was not founded on just principles. He prefer'd the doing of nothing, to an allowance of an equal vote to all the States" in the upper house.[61]

Wilson once again complained that two-thirds of the American people opposed state equality in the senate. He argued the folly of introducing state agency, the very defect that plagued the Confederation, into the new government. Since the states were the problem, they needed to be removed entirely from the new government. A political remedy simply could not be achieved without eliminating the cause. "Shall we effect the cure by establishing an equality of votes as proposed?" he asked. "No: this very equality carries us directly to [the Confederation] Congress: to the system which it is our duty to rectify."[62]

Echoing Wilson, Madison warned that state equality would make the upper house into another Confederation Congress, a body that was powerless to achieve its objectives. And why was the Confederation powerless? Because the states "joined immediately in mutilating & fettering the Governmt. in such a manner that it has disappointed every hope placed on it." Instead of receiving its instructions from the people, the Confederation received them from the state governments, which themselves suffered from faulty design, because unchecked legislatures pursued short-sighted measures instead of serving the public good. Madison accordingly proposed a whole new compromise: "In all cases where the Genl. Governmt. is to act on the people, let the people be represented and the votes be proportional. In all cases where the Governt. is to act on the States as such, in like manner as Congs. now act on them, let the States be represented & the votes be equal." Madison, of course, knew that since the central government would almost always operate on the people, and not the states, his proposal was tantamount to proportional representation and a complete victory for the large states. Not surprisingly, Madison's proposal won no support.[63]

Charles Pinckney in desperation proposed an alternative compromise favorable to the large states: allow the states to have between one and five members in the upper house depending on population. This measure would still base representation on population but would allow the small states to be overrepresented. Wilson and Madison eagerly backed the motion "as a reasonable compromise," but it went nowhere.[64]

As the first order of business on Monday, July 16, the delegates approved the Great Compromise proposed by the Grand Committee of Eleven. The deal also became known as the Connecticut Compromise because of the indispensable role the state's three delegates, Sherman, Ellsworth, and Johnson, had played since mid-June in brokering it. The small states got their way: the states would be equal in the upper house of a bicameral congress. What had changed that allowed the small states to defeat the previously unconquerable large state-Lower South alliance? Previously, the large states (Virginia, Pennsylvania, and Massachusetts) and the Lower South States (North Carolina, South Carolina, and Georgia) had defeated the small states (Connecticut, New Jersey, Delaware, and Maryland—joined by mid-sized New York) by a vote of 6–5. New York's remaining delegates Robert Yates and John Lansing had gone home a few days before, dropping the small states to only four votes. Fed up with the convention's nationalist course, Yates and Lansing left Philadelphia permanently after the July 10 session.[65]

On July 16, the large state-Lower South alliance lost two states: Massachusetts and North Carolina. The Massachusetts delegates deadlocked evenly, and so the state lost its vote. North Carolina, meanwhile, switched its vote to join the small states. These developments allowed the small states to carry the Great Compromise by a 5–4 vote. Interestingly, Baldwin, who by voting with the small states on July 2 had opened the door to the Grand Committee that proposed the Great Compromise, now once again supported the large states, placing Georgia back in that column. Richard Beeman hypothesizes that had Georgia's vote been needed to pass the Great Compromise, Baldwin would have again voted with the small states.[66]

Within the Massachusetts delegation, Gerry and Strong voted for the compromise, while Gorham and King voted against it, producing a deadlock. Gerry, who had chaired the Grand Committee and delivered its report, explained that "an accommodation must take place," and it could take place on no other ground. The alternative of disunion was not an option. Strong agreed that "if no Accommodation takes place, the Union itself must soon be dissolved." Mutual concession was the only alternative. Strong later iterated the same theme during the Massachusetts ratification debate. "The Convention would have broken up if it had not been agreed to allow an equal representation in the Senate."[67]

Within the North Carolina delegation, Davie and Williamson voted for the compromise while Spaight remained steadfast against it. Blount had, a few days before, left the convention to attend the Confederation Congress in New York, of which he was also a member. The recent attacks on slavery and the three-fifths clause may have influenced Davie and Williamson to support the Great Compromise. Davie had become particularly agitated over this matter, but Williamson, too, defended the South on the issue. A national government that could veto state laws potentially had the power to eliminate slavery. Converting the proposed national government into a national-federal hybrid would give the state legislatures a check on the central government through the upper house. This change could help the southern states protect slavery. Congress could then pass no legislation without the support of both a majority of the people and a majority of the states. This arrangement added a layer of protection for the South's "peculiar institution."

When the new government went into operation, the North outnumbered the South 35–30 in the lower house. Expected southwestern population growth would even the number eventually, it was believed, but for the time being slavery would be vulnerable in a congress with both houses based on population. But weren't Davie and Williamson equally concerned that the North, with seven states to the South's six, would also control an upper house based on state equality? Perhaps not, because the South would catch up to the North more quickly in the number of states than it would in population. Events vindicated this logic. Less than a decade later, with the admission of Tennessee in 1796, the South achieved equality in the Senate, enabling it to block bills harmful to its interests. As it turned out, the South never caught up with the North in the House of Representatives. Had representation in both houses of congress been based on population, the South would always have been a minority in both chambers.

Like Gerry and Strong, Davie and Williamson also worried that if there were no compromise, disunion would be the result. This outcome would also threaten slavery, because southerners would have no guarantee from the North that slave rebellions would be suppressed and that their fugitive slaves would be returned to them.

In August, Williamson hinted to North Carolina governor Richard Caswell the critical role that he and Davie had played in the passage of the Great Compromise, but carefully avoided violating the secrecy rule. Regretting that Davie would soon leave the convention to return home, Williamson explained that "his conduct here has induced me to think highly of his abilities and political principles." No doubt with the Great Compromise in mind, Williamson continued, "We shall on some future occasion be at liberty to explain to your Excellency how difficult a part has fallen to the share of our State in the course of this business and I flatter myself greatly if we have not sustained it with a Principle & firmness that will entitle us to what we will never ask for, the thanks of the public. It will be sufficient for us if we have the satisfaction of believing that we have contributed to the happiness of Millions."[68]

Historian Staughton Lynd hypothesizes that a North-South deal over slavery took place between the Constitutional Convention in Philadelphia and the Confederation Congress meeting simultaneously in New York City. In this alleged bargain, the Confederation Congress on July 13, 1787, passed the Northwest Ordinance forever banning slavery in the Northwest Territory. In return, the Constitutional Convention on July 16 once and for all approved the Great Compromise over representation in congress, including the compromise in which slaves would be counted as three-fifths of free people when determining representation in the lower legislative house.[69]

Three bits of evidence point to this bargain: First, the two bodies in mid-July almost simultaneously reached monumental agreements on slavery, one favorable to the North, and the other favorable to the South. Second, a dozen delegates to the convention also served in Congress, and several of them traveled back and forth between the two bodies. Southerners Blount, Few, and Pierce left Philadelphia for New York so that Congress could achieve a quorum to pass the Northwest Ordinance. Third, Manasseh Cutler, president and chief lobbyist for an organization of New England land speculators called the Ohio Company, made a

The Great Compromise

lightning trip from New York to Philadelphia and back again just before each agreement was consummated. Cutler would have supported a deal over slavery to help pass the Northwest Ordinance favorable to the Ohio Company's land interests. While these three bits of evidence suggest that perhaps a bargain took place, they could also be mere coincidences that prove nothing at all.[70]

There is also evidence suggesting that no such deal took place. None of the delegates who journeyed to Congress in New York ever hinted that a secret pact took place. Moreover, the convention did not suddenly insert the Three-Fifths Compromise into the emerging constitution in mid-July 1787. It had been part of the revised Virginia Plan since June, and, despite being voted down on July 11, never really faced serious jeopardy. Perhaps most important, the South did not need to receive the Three-Fifths Compromise as a concession from the North in return for the Northwest Ordinance ban on slavery because the South favored the ban for economic reasons. Virginia congressman William Grayson explained to James Monroe that "the clause respecting slavery was agreed to by the Southern members for the purpose of preventing Tobacco & Indigo from being made on the N.W. side of the Ohio [River]." In the absence of more concrete and conclusive evidence, the Philadelphia-New York bargain should be viewed as a tantalizing hypothesis and nothing more.[71]

A less comprehensive slavery-related agreement may, however, have taken place: the fugitive slave provisions in the Northwest Ordinance and in the Constitution (discussed in Chapter 4) may have been synchronized. In 1856, Edward Coles, President Madison's White House secretary and later governor of Illinois, recorded his "recollection what I was told" by his former boss: "Conferences and intercommunications" between the members of the convention and Congress led to "a compromise by which the northern or anti-slavery portion of the country agreed to incorporate into the Ordinance and Constitution the provision to restore fugitive slaves; and this mutual and concurrent action was the cause of the similarity of the provision contained in both, and had its influence in creating the great unanimity by which the Ordinance passed, and also making the constitution the more acceptable to slaveholders." A comparison of the fugitive slave provisions in Article IV, Section 2 of the Constitution (added in August) with Article VI of the Northwest Ordinance reveals the similar but not identical language Coles described.[72]

The passage of the Great Compromise left the large-state delegates in disarray. After dominating the proceedings for nearly two months, they had been outmaneuvered and defeated by their small-state adversaries. Randolph pointed out that the morning's vote "had embarrassed the business extremely" because every provision that the delegates had agreed upon thus far was premised upon proportional representation in both legislative houses. Madison, Wilson, and their allies needed to regroup. Randolph accordingly requested that "the Convention might adjourn, that the large States might consider the steps proper to be taken in the present solemn crisis of the business." Still not quite able to fathom that the large states had lost, he added that the small states might also use the time to "deliberate on the means of conciliation."

Randolph meant that the convention should adjourn for the day, but some delegates wondered whether he meant a permanent adjournment, presumably to allow the large states to form their own separate republic. Paterson shot back that "it was high time for the Convention to adjourn," and that if Randolph's motion was "for an adjournment sine die, he would second it with all his heart." But Paterson would offer no conciliation "on any other ground than that of an equality of votes in the 2d. branch."

Randolph clarified that he meant an adjournment merely for the day "in order that some conciliatory experiment might if possible be devised." If concessions to the large states failed to materialize, however, they "might then take such measures . . . as might be necessary." Gerry and Rutledge observed that since the small states would not budge, the large states stood at a crossroads. They could either accept the Great Compromise, or they could break up the convention. On that note, the delegates adjourned for the day.[73]

The next morning, the large states caucused before the opening of formal proceedings but could not agree on a way forward. Some delegates favored acquiescing in the Great Compromise, reasoning that preserving the Union was more important than devising a perfect government. Others maintained "that as a division of the Convention into two opinions was unavoidable," the large states, representing a majority of the American people, should offer their own superior plan to the states. Madison noted in disgust that "time was wasted in vague conversation . . . without any specific proposition or agreement." Several small-state delegates also attended. The scene they witnessed convinced them that they had

Major William Jackson, the secretary of the Constitutional Convention, kept a journal of the delegates' motions and votes. This journal entry for July 16, 1787, records the vote that approved the Great Compromise. (National Archives)

nothing to fear from the large states. Far from turning the tables, this caucus sealed the small-state victory.[74]

Having achieved their goal of state equality in the senate, the small-state nationalists like Dickinson, Ellsworth, and Paterson now found themselves once again free to support a strong central government as they had at the outset of the convention before the adoption of proportional representation in both houses of congress. In 1883, historian George Bancroft learned "from the lips of Madison" that "from the day when every doubt of the right of the smaller states to an equal vote in the senate was quieted, they . . . exceeded all others in zeal for granting powers to the general government." Indeed, Paterson in particular "was for the rest of his life a federalist of federalists." In 1836, Madison himself wrote, "as soon as the smaller States had secured more than a proportional share in the proposed Government, they became favourable to augmentations of its powers."[75]

If the Great Compromise impacted the course of the small-state nationalists, it also affected the behavior of the large-state nationalists like Madison, Wilson, and Gouverneur Morris. Dubious of a senate that would now be under the influence of the states, the large-state nationalists now favored shifting some of that body's power over matters such as appointments and foreign policy to the executive and judicial branches. "It is well known," Madison later wrote, "that the large States . . . regarded the aggregate powers of the Senate as the most objectionable feature of the Constitution." Consequently, he explained, "after the compromise which allowed an equality of votes in the Senate, that consideration . . . will account for the abridgment of its powers by associating the Executive in the exercise of them."[76]

After July 16, the delegates realized for the first time that the convention would successfully agree on a constitution. It was just a question of how long it would take to iron out the details. "The Convention goes on well, and . . . there is hope of great Good to result from their Counsels," observed Franklin after the adoption of the Great Compromise. "The Convention have nearly agreed on the principles and outlines of a system," wrote Williamson on the exact same day. Two weeks later, Davie explained that he had decided to return home to North Carolina because "the great outlines are now marked . . . the residue of the work will rather be tedious than difficult." It would not only be tedious, but time consuming as well. "The business is difficult and unavoidably takes up much time," Paterson wrote the day after the adoption of the Great Compromise. "But I think we shall eventually agree upon and adopt a system that will give strength and harmony to the Union and render us a great and happy people."[77]

NOTES

1. Christopher Collier and James Lincoln Collier, *Decision in Philadelphia: The Constitutional Convention of 1787* (New York: Ballantine Books, 1987), 136–42;

The Great Compromise

John P. Kaminski and Timothy D. Moore, eds., *An Assembly of Demigods: Word Portraits of the Delegates to the Constitutional Convention by Their Contemporaries* (Madison, WI: Parallel Press, 2012), hereafter cited as *Demigods*, 65, 248–49.

2. Adrienne Koch, ed., *Notes of Debates in the Federal Convention of 1787 Reported by James Madison* (Athens: Ohio University Press, 1966), hereafter cited as *NDFC*, 118; Max Farrand, ed., *The Records of the Federal Convention of 1787*. 1937 rev. ed. in four vols., reprint (New Haven, CT: Yale University Press, 1974), hereafter cited as *RFC*, 3:179.

3. *NDFC*, 118; Michael Klarman, *The Framers' Coup: The Making of the United States Constitution* (New York: Oxford University Press, 2016). Klarman adds that the New Jersey Plan "was mainly a bid by small-state delegations to preserve the principle of equal state representation in at least one branch of the national legislature, not an embrace of unicameralism on its merits," 169.

4. *NDFC*, 118.
5. Ibid., 121–22; *Demigods*, 87–88, 245; *RFC*, 1:257.
6. *NDFC*, 121–22; *RFC*, 1:258–60.
7. *RFC*, 1:266; *NDFC*, 124–27.
8. *RFC*, 1:263; *NDFC*, 127–29.
9. *RFC*, 1:301; *NDFC*, 129–33.
10. *RFC*, 1:299; *NDFC*, 134–36.
11. *NDFC*, 136–39; Collier, *Decision*, 86; *RFC*, 1:300.
12. *NDFC*, 137–39; *RFC*, 1:363, 3:54, 367.
13. *NDFC*, 142–48.
14. Ibid., 154–55; *Demigods*, 2–3, 240–41.
15. Stuart Leibiger, "Reformed Christianity and the Founding," *Review of Politics*, 75 (2013), 1–3.
16. James H. Hutson, ed., *Supplement to Max Farrand's* The Records of the Federal Convention of 1787 (New Haven, CT: Yale University Press, 1987), hereafter cited as *RFC Supplement*, 3–4.
17. *Demigods*, 5–6; Collier, *Decision*, 128.
18. *NDFC*, 160–62.
19. Ibid., 170–72.
20. Ibid., 188–89.
21. Ibid., 189–91.
22. Collier, *Decision*, 159; *Demigods*, 28.
23. *NDFC*, 201–4; *RFC*, 1:439–42, 3:272; *Demigods*, 26.
24. *NDFC*, 206–8.
25. Ibid., 209–11; *RFC*, 3:472.
26. *NDFC*, 561.
27. Ibid., 211; *Demigods*, 4, 244.

28. NDFC, 220–22; RFC, 1:495.
29. NDFC, 211–12, 220–23.
30. Ibid., 214–18.
31. Ibid., 219–20.
32. Ibid., 223–25.
33. Ibid., 226.
34. Ibid., 226–27.
35. Ibid., 233–35.
36. Ibid., 227–31; *Demigods*, 9, 237; RFC, 1:500–501.
37. NDFC, 231–32.
38. Ibid., 219; Collier, *Decision*, 170–72; RFC, 3:188; *Demigods*, 18; See also David O. Stewart, *The Summer of 1787: The Men Who Wrote the Constitution* (New York: Simon & Schuster, 2007), 108–9.
39. Richard Beeman, *Plain Honest Men: The Making of the American Constitution* (New York: Random House, 2009), 187; RFC, 3:188; Stewart, *Summer of 1787*, 109–10.
40. NDFC, 232–36; RFC, 1:517.
41. NDFC, 237.
42. RFC, 1:522.
43. NDFC, 26; David O. Stewart, "Who Picked Committees at the Constitutional Convention," *Journal of the American Revolution*, Sept. 13, 2018, https://allthingsliberty.com/2018/09/who-picked-the-committees-at-the-constitutional-convention/.
44. *RFC Supplement*, 145; DGW, 5:174.
45. NDFC, 237–38.
46. Ibid., 238–40.
47. Ibid., 240–41.
48. Ibid., 242–44.
49. Ibid., 238, 249–52.
50. Ibid., 253–54.
51. RFC, 3:55–56.
52. Ibid., 56.
53. NDFC, 244–48.
54. Ibid., 256–58.
55. Ibid., 259.
56. Ibid., 260–65.
57. Ibid., 268–76.
58. Ibid., 265–78, 362.
59. Ibid., 278, 286.
60. Ibid., 278–82.

61. Ibid., 291–92.
62. Ibid., 295–97.
63. Ibid., 293–95.
64. Ibid., 290–91.
65. Ibid., 297; RFC, 3:247.
66. Beeman, *Plain Honest Men*, 222.
67. NDFC, 291, 293; RFC, 3:261–62.
68. RFC, 3:70–71.
69. Staughton Lynd, "The Compromise of 1787," *Political Science Quarterly*, 81 (1966), 225–50. See also Lynd, *Class Conflict, Slavery, and the United States Constitution* (Indianapolis, IN: Bobbs-Merrill, 1967).
70. Collier, *Decision*, 215–22; Stewart, *Summer of 1787*, 137–49.
71. Paul H. Smith et al., eds. *Letters of Delegates to Congress, 1774–1789*, 25 vols. (Washington: Library of Congress, 1976–2000), 24:394. George William Van Cleve speculates that the concession that the South received in return for the Northwest Ordinance ban on slavery came from the Confederation Congress, not the Constitutional Convention: northerners in Congress agreed to give up attempts to abandon to Spain Mississippi River navigation rights so vital to Southerners. A problem with this theory is that a treaty that gave up the right to navigate the Mississippi could not be ratified in Congress. Thus, northerners didn't give up anything. Van Cleve, *A Slaveholder's Union: Slavery, Politics and the Constitution in the Early Republic* (Chicago, IL: University of Chicago Press, 2010).
72. RFC Supplement, 321.
73. NDFC, 299–301.
74. Ibid., 301–2.
75. RFC Supplement, 322; RFC, 3:538.
76. RFC, 3: 503, 534.
77. Ibid., 61, 68; RFC Supplement, 172.

CHAPTER 4

IRONING OUT THE DETAILS

After the adoption of the Great Compromise, the committee of the whole completed its consideration of the Virginia Plan. During this process, much to James Madison's dismay, the delegates struck out the congressional veto of state laws. The delegates then appointed a five-man Committee of Detail to shape the resolutions already adopted into a draft constitution. Committee members Edmund Randolph and James Wilson wrote successive drafts that John Rutledge subsequently edited. After a ten-day adjournment from July 26 to August 6, Rutledge presented the committee's work to the convention. The draft contained two especially noteworthy new features: First, instead of a blanket grant of power, it specifically enumerated the powers of congress, but also included a "necessary and proper" clause. Second, it included several protections for the Lower South and the institution of slavery. The African slave trade would remain open indefinitely, neither slave imports nor exports of any kind could be taxed, and commercial laws could be passed only by a two-thirds supermajority in each house of congress.

Throughout August, the convention debated provisions of the draft constitution dealing with money bills, qualifications for voting and officeholding, congress's enumerated powers, congressional pay, bill of rights provisions, and the regulation of state militias. The most contentious debates, however, revolved around slavery, with the North rolling back some of the draft constitution's protections of slavery. Gorham on August 15 complained that he "saw no end to these difficulties and postponements" because "some could not agree to the form of Government before the powers were defined. Others could not agree to the powers till it was seen how the Government was to be formed." Despite Gorham's frustration, the convention in fact sluggishly but steadily proceeded toward a final constitution. "By *slow* . . . movements," wrote Washington four days later, "the business of the Convention progresses."[1]

The passage of the Great Compromise had been a stunning defeat for Madison. But more bad news was yet to come: the congressional veto of state laws that violated the constitution or federal treaties became the delegates' next target. That provision came up on July 17 as the convention continued to discuss the Virginia Plan as revised by the committee of the whole. Madison defended the veto "as essential to the efficacy & security of the Genl. Govt." He argued that the state judiciaries lacked the independence to overturn state laws that favored "particular interests" of a state "in opposition to the general interest" of the United States. Madison concluded that "a power of negativing the improper laws of the States is at once the most mild & certain means of preserving the harmony of the system." Surprisingly, the veto faced opposition from Madison's fellow nationalist, Gouverneur Morris, who maintained that the proper remedy for bad state laws would be judicial review by the federal supreme court. Besides, Morris added, the proposal "would disgust all the States," preventing ratification of any constitution proposed by the convention. The delegates rejected the congressional veto seven states to three.[2]

In place of the veto, Luther Martin suggested a supremacy clause, which the convention agreed to. National laws and treaties would be "the supreme law of the respective States" to which the state judiciaries would have to submit "anything in the respective laws of the individual States to the contrary notwithstanding." This resolution, which Martin borrowed from the New Jersey Plan, would make federal law supreme to state law. But would it make federal law supreme to state constitutions? That answer remained unclear, which may explain why the resolution passed unanimously. The final Constitution resolved this ambiguity by declaring the Constitution the supreme law of the land, "anything *in the Constitution* or laws of any State to the contrary notwithstanding" (italics added).[3]

Once more before the convention ended, on August 23, Charles Pinckney endeavored to revive Madison's idea of a congressional veto of state laws conflicting "with the general interests and harmony of the Union." Pinckney proposed requiring a two-thirds supermajority of both houses to overturn a state law. Wilson pronounced the veto "the key-stone wanted to compleat the wide arch of Government, we are raising. The power of self-defense had been urged as necessary for the State Governments. It was equally necessary for the General Government." Federal judges by themselves, Wilson warned, would lack the force to strike down state laws by judicial review. Sherman countered that the supremacy clause would sufficiently protect the federal government against the states. A congressional veto "would damn and ought to damn, the Constitution," Rutledge declared. "Will any State ever agree to be bound hand & foot in this manner?" Once again, the congressional veto went down to defeat. Perhaps with slavery in mind, the Lower South states voted "no" even though the

James Wilson of Pennsylvania spoke more times at the convention than any other delegate. An advocate of popular sovereignty, he favored election of the president by the people. He served on the Committee of Detail that prepared the first draft of the Constitution. (Collection of the Supreme Court of the United States)

supermajority requirement for legislation would have allowed the region to block any attack on their peculiar institution.[4]

The delegates took up the revised Virginia Plan's call for the constitution to be ratified by conventions of the people in each of the states. Ellsworth, Paterson, and Gerry wanted the state legislatures to make the ratification decision. Gerry predicted that "great confusion . . . would result from a recurrence to the people." Ellsworth agreed that "more was to be expected from the Legislatures than from the people." Neither man explained, however, why a popularly elected legislature would make wiser choices than a convention elected by the people.

Mason pronounced ratification by state conventions rather than by the state legislatures "one of the most important and essential" features of the constitution. If the state legislatures approved the national constitution, it would make states supreme to the federal government. Morris added that since the constitution would create a national government of people, not a confederation of states, the sovereign people of the states had to decide ratification through specially elected conventions. King and Madison agreed that ratification by the sovereign people would give political legitimacy to the new constitution and would distinguish it from a mere league of states.

The proponents of ratification by conventions offered practical reasons as well as theoretical ones. Mason warned that state legislatures could later rescind their ratifications. With legislative ratification, he explained, "the National Govt. would stand in each State on the weak and tottering foundation of an Act of Assembly." But ratification by conventions would be permanent because those bodies would adjourn *sine die* after completing their business. Gorham gave three more practical reasons in favor of conventions: First, the legislatures would be reluctant to vote for a constitution that would give some of their power to the central government. Second, state legislative ratification would double the hurdles for the constitution, because both the lower and upper houses would have to approve. Third, many of the constitution's most eloquent proponents (some of whom sat before him) did not sit in the legislatures, but they could get elected to state conventions. The delegates voted overwhelmingly in favor of ratification by state conventions. They did not, however, finalize how many states would have to ratify for the constitution to go into effect.[5]

Ironing Out the Details

The delegates debated the size of the senate. When Gouverneur Morris advocated three members per state, Gorham and Mason objected that the chamber would then become too large to achieve the stability and calm deliberation necessary to check any unwise impulses of the popularly elected lower chamber. The convention agreed on two senators per state, who would cast their votes individually rather than by state. Per capita voting somewhat offset the powers of the states in the upper house. Unless a given state's members voted together, the votes would cancel each other out.[6]

Gerry moved that a committee be appointed to incorporate everything that had been agreed upon thus far into a draft constitution. On July 24, the convention accordingly named Rutledge of South Carolina, Randolph of Virginia, Wilson of Pennsylvania, Ellsworth of Connecticut, and Gorham of Massachusetts to serve on the Committee of Detail. These five men had played significant roles in convention debate, and each represented a geographic region of the country, from the Lower South to northern New England. In addition to the revised Virginia Plan, both the defeated New Jersey Plan and the never-debated Pinckney Plan were referred to the committee for reference.

Before the convention adjourned for the Committee of Detail to perform its task, several delegates voiced concerns and made requests. Charles Cotesworth Pinckney of South Carolina "reminded the Convention that if the Committee should fail to insert some security to the Southern States agst. an emancipation of slaves, and taxes on exports," he would vote against its draft. Daniel Carroll of Maryland hoped that direct taxation would not be apportioned according to population until an accurate census had been completed. Gouverneur Morris hinted that the direct taxation provision had been approved merely to get more northern states to accept the Three-Fifths Compromise and could now be safely omitted.[7]

On July 26, the convention adjourned for ten days to allow the Committee of Detail to complete its work. The revised Virginia Plan referred to the committee provided for supreme executive, legislative, and judicial branches. A bicameral legislature would exercise the powers held by the Confederation Congress, and also act in all other areas of collective concern to the states. Laws and treaties made by central government would be supreme to state laws.

The lower house would be elected by the people of the states for two-year terms. At the outset, it would consist of sixty-five members, with each state initially assigned between one and ten representatives. Both representation and direct taxation would be based on free population plus three-fifths of enslaved people. Congress would be empowered to reapportion this body based on a decennial census. All money bills would originate in the lower house and could not be altered by the upper house. The senate would be chosen by the state legislatures for six-year terms. There would be two members per state who would vote individually.

A single executive, elected by congress for one seven-year term, would execute the laws and exercise a limited veto. He would be impeachable for "malpractice or neglect of duty." The judiciary would consist of a supreme court appointed by the upper house to serve during good behavior. Its jurisdiction would include national laws and national issues. Congress could create lower national courts if necessary. (The evolution of the executive and judicial branches is discussed in Chapter 5.) The agreed-upon resolutions also guaranteed each state a republican form of government and protection against foreign or domestic violence. The constitution would be ratified by state conventions elected by the people. National officeholders had to be property-holding citizens.[8]

Although deeply disappointed by state equality in the upper house, the election of that body by the state legislatures, and the elimination of the congressional veto, Madison nevertheless still had reason to be pleased with the overall course of events. His original Virginia Plan had survived largely intact, but with significant alterations that benefited the states, especially the small states and the slave states. The provision allowing state legislatures to elect the upper house, and the elimination of the proposed congressional veto of state law, aided the states. State equality in the upper chamber advantaged the small states. The Three-Fifths Compromise, which partially counted enslaved people for purposes of congressional representation, served the slave states.

In committee, Randolph prepared a crude first draft of the constitution in outline form, which Rutledge marked up with changes. "The draft of a fundamental constitution," Randolph's draft observed, ought to use "simple and precise language" to minimize conflicting interpretations of intent, and "to insert essential principles only," rather than to become mired in minute details of government operation. He suggested a preamble to explain that the federal government would achieve the "general happiness" that the Confederation had failed to attain. But he argued that the natural rights of man proclaimed in the Declaration of Independence did not need to be repeated. Wilson turned Randolph's outline into a prose draft, which Rutledge again edited. Wilson began his draft with the words "We the People of the States," and then listed all thirteen of them by name.[9]

The committee's final draft included the provisions of the revised Virginia Plan, but also incorporated new features. The draft borrowed from Charles Pinckney's plan of government the names "United States of America," "Congress," "House," "Speaker of the House," "Senate," "President of the Senate," "President of the United States," and "Supreme Court." Randolph and Wilson used the name "Governor" for the chief executive, but Rutledge changed it to "President." Qualifications in each state to vote for the House of Representatives would be the same as the qualification to vote for the lower house of the state legislature. There would be one congressional district per 40,000 people. Congress could decide whether to impose property qualifications on its members. The states, not the central government, would pay congressmen.[10]

Randolph's draft specifically enumerated the powers of congress. This decision made the draft constitution very different from the state constitutions, which included blanket grants of powers to the legislatures and then forbade them from doing certain things through the inclusion of bills of rights. Rather than a blanket grant of authority, the draft constitution itemized congress's powers, which included imposing import duties, regulating commerce, and coining money. Congress could also raise troops, make war, and call out the state militias. The senate would have the power to make treaties and to settle territorial disputes between states. The draft constitution also forbade the states from doing certain activities, such as coining money, collecting import duties, and making treaties. These restrictions—along with the supremacy clause—took the place of the failed congressional veto of state laws.[11]

Most of the delegates probably assumed all along that an enumeration of congressional powers would be included in the constitution at some point in the drafting process. For them, the previous vague language "that the national legislature ought to possess the legislative rights vested in

Congress by the confederation; and moreover, to legislate in all cases for the general interests of the union, and also in those to which the states are separately incompetent, or in which the harmony of the United States may be interrupted by the exercise of individual legislation" was meant to be temporary. Others had not yet made up their minds on the matter. Southerners must have worried that a blanket grant of power would allow congress to abolish slavery.[12]

One of Wilson's revisions to Randolph's draft empowered congress "to make all laws that shall be necessary and proper for carrying into execution the foregoing powers, and all other powers vested by this Constitution in the government of the United States." This "necessary and proper" clause granted congress some leeway in executing its enumerated powers. That this critical alteration unfettered congress from the letter of its enumerated powers became abundantly clear over the following two centuries. Ironically, Wilson's necessary and proper clause, added to enable congress to carry out its enumerated powers, eventually became so broadly interpreted that it made the federal government nearly as powerful as a blanket grant would have.[13]

Committee chair John Rutledge, a South Carolinian, resolved to protect the interests of his region and its "peculiar institution." After receiving a legal education at Middle Temple, London, Rutledge entered politics. He served in the Continental Congress, became governor of South Carolina from 1776 to 1782, and then entered the Confederation Congress. A Charleston planter, Rutledge lost most of his property to British confiscation after the capture of the city in 1780.[14]

At Rutledge's insistence, the Committee of Detail draft included tremendous new protections for the South and slavery. Congress could neither prohibit nor tax the African slave trade. Furthermore, duties on exports were banned, thus ensuring that congress could not tax the agricultural staples of the South (mainly tobacco, rice, and indigo) as a means to discourage or eliminate slavery. Nor could congress enact commercial laws without the support of a two-thirds supermajority in each house. This feature enabled southerners to block any legislation that they believed undermined its slave economy. For example, the South could reject a law requiring southern products to be exported in American shipping (owned mostly by Northerners). British laws of this sort, known as "Navigation Acts," had, before the Revolution, mandated that British ships carry imports and exports to and from the colonies. These acts angered the colonists, helping to drive them toward independence.[15]

John Rutledge of South Carolina chaired the Committee of Detail that prepared the first draft of the Constitution. This draft enumerated the powers of Congress and included tremendous protections for the institution of slavery. (Collection of the Supreme Court of the United States)

These proslavery provisions addressed C. C. Pinckney's warning to the Committee of Detail that the South and slavery had to be protected. The composition of the committee certainly favored that region. Committee chair Rutledge of South Carolina, described by German-born French diplomat Louis-Guillaume Otto as "the proudest and most imperious man in the United States," forcefully defended the interests of the Lower South. Randolph of Virginia always acted with great deference to his slaveholding constituents. Wilson of Pennsylvania had proposed the Three-Fifths Compromise in return for the Lower South's support of proportional representation in congress. Ellsworth, like the other Connecticut delegates, had steadily appeased the South in the name of compromise. That left Gorham of Massachusetts alone to resist proslavery provisions, not enough to make a difference regardless of his views.[16]

"The President of the United States" would have as his title "His Excellency," the same title that had been used to address George Washington as commander in chief of the Continental Army during the Revolutionary War. The draft included a presidential oath of office and called for periodic state of the union addresses. The president could be impeached for "treason, bribery, or corruption," but not for maladministration, as specified in the revised Virginia Plan. The president's pardon power did not provide protection against impeachments. The Supreme Court would try impeachments and would have original jurisdiction in cases arising on the high seas and in cases between different states or citizens of different states.[17]

While the Committee of Detail labored, the rest of the delegates enjoyed a respite from their sessions at the State House. Washington took two short trips over the break. Accompanied by Gouverneur Morris, he went on July 30 to Valley Forge. The next day, while Morris fished for trout, Washington toured the remains of the Continental Army's 1777–1778 encampment site. As he "visited all the Works, wch. were in Ruins," he must have reflected on the uncertain days he had spent there, and perhaps compared them with the uncertain days the convention faced. En route to his lodgings for the evening, he encountered "some Farmers at Work, and entering into Conversation with them," obtained "information with respect to the mode of cultivating Buck Wheat." This excursion caused Washington to turn down an invitation from Elizabeth Powell to attend a performance of Richard Sheridan's *The School for Scandal*. His tongue-in-cheek note of apology regretted having to miss the show "after waiting so long to receive a lesson on the School for Scandal." On August 3, Washington joined Gouverneur Morris, and Robert Morris and his wife, for a trip to Trenton, where he spent two days fishing for perch.[18]

Many of the delegates took advantage of the recess to travel home. Sherman and Johnson journeyed back to Connecticut. Several current and former members of the Confederation Congress, including Butler, Gerry, Few, Pierce, and Blount, headed for New York, which they regarded as a healthier location than Philadelphia. Charles Cotesworth Pinckney and his wife visited Bethlehem, Pennsylvania, to gratify their curiosity about the faith of the Moravians who lived there. McClurg returned to

Virginia never to return to the convention again. Paterson, who went home to New Jersey, only came back in mid-September to add his name to the finished constitution.[19]

On Monday, August 6, Rutledge, chair of the Committee of Detail, presented the draft constitution to the convention. After each delegate received a copy confidentially printed by John Dunlap and David Claypoole of the *Pennsylvania Packet*, the delegates adjourned for the day to digest the plan.[20]

That afternoon, the five Maryland delegates—Daniel Carroll, Daniel of St. Thomas Jenifer, James McHenry, Luther Martin, and recently arrived John Francis Mercer—met to coordinate the state's response to the Committee of Detail draft. When Mercer asked whether the people of Maryland "would embrace such a system," Martin insisted they would not. Hoping to unite the delegation, McHenry suggested that they offer a motion to scrap the committee report in favor of strengthening the existing Confederation. Martin liked the idea, but Carroll, Jenifer, and Mercer rejected it, declaring the current governmental structure inadequate.

The Marylanders met again the next day, this time without Martin, who had gone to New York for the week. They agreed that the right to originate money bills ought not to rest exclusively with the house of representatives, that they should insist on retaining the supermajority requirement in congress to pass commercial legislation, and that the federal power to tax had to be curbed. "We almost shuddered at the fate of the commerce of Maryland should we be unable to make any change in this extraordinary power" over taxation, McHenry wrote. Jenifer seemed less adamant on these points than Carroll and McHenry, while Mercer expressed his willingness to "go with the stream."[21]

On August 7, the convention took up the Committee of Detail draft. This slow- but-steady process lasted for over a month, until the appointment of the Committee of Style on September 9 to draft the final Constitution. The convention considered the provision of the Great Compromise that forbade the senate from originating or amending money bills. Charles Pinckney argued that the smaller and presumably more talented upper chamber should not be denied the right to propose money bills. Large-state delegates Gouverneur Morris, Wilson, and Madison, who viewed the provision as a meaningless concession to the big states, also wanted to get rid of it.

Mason defended the provision that he, as a member of the Grand Committee of Eleven, had helped devise. He believed the senate's small size and long term of office would make it an aristocratic body. Giving it the "purse strings" on top of its other powers would only make it more powerful. Mason announced that unless the house alone could introduce money bills, he would withdraw his support for the Great Compromise. Morris accused Mason of bluffing and insisted that state equality in the senate was a done deal regardless of what happened with the origination of money bills. Williamson declared that North Carolina had supported the Great Compromise only because of this provision. He might have added that his vote, which had flipped North Carolina from opposition to support of the deal, had been decisive in the passage of the Great Compromise. The convention on August 9 nevertheless struck out the provision requiring money bills to originate in the house of representatives.[22]

Randolph would not abandon the money bills issue. He demanded that the small states honor the one concession given to the large states by the Great Compromise. The constitution would not win public support if the power to tax and spend did not belong to the popularly elected branch. "When the people behold in the Senate, the countenance of an aristocracy; and in the president, the form at least of a little monarch," he warned, "will not their alarms be sufficiently raised without taking from their immediate representatives, a right which has been so long appropriated to them." On August 13, Randolph moved that only bills for raising revenue—as opposed to all money bills—must originate in the lower house and could not be amended by the senate.[23]

Mason again insisted that since the people would pay taxes, the people's representatives in the house of representatives should levy taxes. Because the states would not pay taxes, the senate should not levy taxes. "The purse strings," in short, "should be in the hands of the Representatives of the people." Gerry agreed that "taxation & representation are strongly associated in the minds of the people, and they will not agree that any but their immediate representatives should meddle with their purses." Dickinson also predicted that the people would demand that money bills originate in the house. After all, eight state constitutions featured similar provisions requiring money bills to originate in the lower legislative chamber.

Wilson challenged this logic. If both houses had to approve revenue bills, what difference did it make whether they originated in the house or senate? If "the purse was to have two strings," he asked, "both houses must concur in untying, and of what importance could it be which untied first and which last." Madison predicted that however good Randolph's distinction between revenue and money bills was in theory, it would never work in practice, because disputes would arise over the definition of a revenue bill. For example, was a tariff a revenue bill or a regulation of commerce? Madison bitterly noted that Virginia, Pennsylvania, and South Carolina, three of the five states that had opposed state equality in the senate, also opposed the money bills provision that had been offered "as a compensation for the sacrifice extorted from them." Rutledge, Carroll, and McHenry, who hailed from states whose constitutions specified that money bills originate in the lower house, all attested that the requirement created legislative chaos. The Marylanders, it will be recalled, had, in their meetings a couple of days before, targeted this provision. The convention again voted against having money bills begin exclusively in the house. Williamson, furious over this decision, complained, "We have now got a House of Lords which is to originate money bills."[24]

Williamson's anger suggested that the fight over money bills was not yet done. On August 15, Strong moved that bills for revenue, appropriations, and federal salaries must originate in the house. Mason and Gorham argued that without this provision, the senate would become too powerful. Williamson warned that if the upper house could propose money bills, the delegates would not arm it with other important powers, lest that body become too energetic. The convention postponed the issue until those other senate powers could be established. On September 8, the convention accepted a committee recommendation that "bills for raising revenue shall originate in the House of Representatives." The senate could, however, amend such bills. The British House of Lords, in contrast, could only accept or reject money bills passed by the House of Commons.[25]

The Committee of Detail report specified that those qualified to vote for the legislature in each state could also vote for congressmen. Gouverneur Morris moved instead that only landholders be allowed to vote for congress, arguing that those without real estate lack economic independence. Instead of being financially independent, landless people are dependent on employers or landlords, who would influence their votes. "Give the votes to people who have no property, and they will sell them to the rich" leading to aristocracy, Morris predicted. "Will such men be the secure & faithful Guardians of liberty?" he asked. "Will they be the impregnable barrier agst. aristocracy? Dickinson agreed with Morris that freeholders were "the best guardians of liberty" forming "a necessary defense agst. the dangerous influence of those multitudes without property." Madison, who expected the numbers of property-less people to rise over time, also feared that they would either threaten "the rights of property & the public liberty" or they would "become the tools of opulence & ambition."

Wilson and Butler answered that to disenfranchise in national elections people who could vote in state elections would not be popular. Rutledge thought that restricting suffrage to freeholders "would create division among the people & make enemies of all those who should be excluded." Ellsworth thought that anybody who pays taxes ought to have a say in how the money is spent. Mason argued that all types of property holders possessed a stake in society and "ought to share in all its rights & privileges." Franklin added that the "virtue & public spirit" displayed by many "common people . . . during the war" entitled them to a vote in national elections. Take away a man's right to vote, in sum, and you take away his allegiance to his country. Every state except Delaware voted against a landholding requirement to vote.[26]

Having failed to impose a property requirement to vote for congress, Gouverneur Morris tried to restrict legislative officeholding. Advocating limits on "the privileges which emigrants [from overseas] would enjoy among us," he moved to require fourteen years' citizenship instead of four to become a senator. Morris explained that he did not wish to mimic Indians, who often "carried their hospitality so far as to offer to strangers their wives and daughters." He would provide guests to his home with food and lodging, "but would not carry the complaisance so far as, to bed them with his wife." He did not trust "those philosophical gentlemen, those Citizens of the World as they call themselves," who readily shifted allegiance from country to country. Realists, Morris admonished, must view immigrants as a threat to national security. Pinckney agreed, pointing out that it would be unwise for recent immigrants to serve in the senate and vote on treaties with their native countries. Butler also favored the motion, admitting that as an immigrant from Ireland, it had taken him years to shake off the attachments of his birth.

Gouverneur Morris of Pennsylvania spoke eloquently against the institution of slavery at the Constitutional Convention. A member of the Committee of Style, he drafted the final version of the Constitution, as well as the accompanying cover letter to the Confederation Congress. (Library of Congress)

Madison thought such a lengthy citizenship requirement for officeholding would discourage immigration to America and would give an unflattering "tincture of illiberality to the Constitution." Franklin warned against equating length of citizenship with patriotism. He reminded the delegates that during the Revolution, many immigrants had sacrificed for their adopted country, while many native-born Americans sided with Britain. Wilson wondered whether Morris's motion would require fourteen years of citizenship in a single state to become a senator. Exhibiting great emotion, Wilson, who had in the late 1770s resided in Maryland, decried a restriction that would ban him from serving in the senate. After rejecting fourteen, thirteen, and ten years of U.S. citizenship to become a senator, the convention approved nine years. After a similar debate over the House, the convention kept the U.S. citizenship requirement at seven years. Every congressman also had to "be an inhabitant of that state in which he shall be chosen."[27]

Late in July, the convention debated whether legislators would be required to own property. Mason moved to require members of congress to possess "landed property," and to prohibit those with "unsettled" accounts or debts to the government from serving in that body. These prerequisites, he argued, would prevent the corrupt, self-serving schemes that had often emerged in the state legislatures. Gerry warned that without such a requirement, "we might have a legislature composed of public debtors, pensioners, placemen & contractors." Madison successfully moved that the word "landed" be struck out so as not to discriminate against those employed in commerce and manufacturing.

Several delegates pointed out that men often had unsettled accounts with the government through no fault of their own. Ellsworth questioned the exclusion of debtors. "Is the smallest as well as largest debtor to be excluded?" he asked. And how would the public even know the financial status of candidates? The convention struck from Mason's motion both the unsettled accounts and debtor provisions, leaving in place the property requirement to sit in congress.[28]

Charles Pinckney moved that not only legislators, but also that "the Executive, and the Judges, should be possessed of competent property to make them independent & respectable." He suggested a net worth of $100,000 for the president, and $50,000 for judges and congressmen. Rutledge and Ellsworth supported property requirements in theory but were not sure how to account for variations in wealth from region to region and over time. Franklin thought that property requirements "tended to debase the spirit of the common people," discouraged immigration, and would damage the reputation of the United States among "the most liberal and enlightened men" in Europe. Pinckney's motion suffered a decisive defeat. The final constitution eliminated all property requirements for officeholding.[29]

On August 14, Charles Pinckney challenged an article of the draft constitution that forbade members of congress from holding other federal appointments while in office, and in the case of senators, for one year afterward. Why should the government be deprived of the services of the most capable men, he asked? He hoped the senate would "become a School of public Ministers, a nursery of Statesmen." He moved instead that congressmen should resign their seats before assuming another national office. Not a single state constitution, Pinckney pointed out, had a proviso forbidding members of the legislature from holding other offices.

Wilson supported Pinckney, arguing that to deprive congressmen of the ability to hold other offices would "prostrate the Natl. Legislature" by removing "its power of attracting those talents which were necessary to give weight to the Governt. and to render it useful to the people." Gouverneur Morris reminded the delegates that in 1775, the fittest man to lead the Continental Army had been a delegate to Congress. Such a rule would have prevented the appointment of George Washington as commander in chief.

Mercer of Maryland also wanted to get rid of the article, but on very different grounds. He declared the American government already an aristocracy, where a few officeholders "can & will draw emoluments for themselves from the many." Mercer insisted that "Governmts. can only be maintained by *force* or *influence*." Since the proposed president lacked force, he needed to be armed with influence in the form of patronage appointments for members of congress with which he could buy legislative support for his policies. Mercer advocated a British-style system, where the king and prime minister built a majority in Parliament by handing out government jobs and political favors.

Mason sarcastically agreed that they should get rid of the article forbidding dual officeholding to open the floodgates of corruption and aristocracy. He was all for "inviting into the Legislative Service, those generous & benevolent characters who will" spend their time "carving out offices & rewards" for themselves. Gerry, too, opposed incentivizing the senate to create lucrative offices to fill with its own members. And Williamson condemned having "a whole Legislature at liberty to cut out offices for one another." The delegates postponed a decision until they determined the senate's powers. The final constitution forbade congressmen from simultaneously serving in other federal offices.[30]

The draft constitution called for congressmen to be paid by the state legislatures. Ellsworth, afraid of making congress too dependent on the states, moved instead that the national government provide compensation. Gouverneur Morris added that payment by the legislatures would place an unfair burden on states distant from the seat of government, because their congressmen would face higher transportation costs. Langdon, who footed his own and Gilman's convention expenses because of New Hampshire's parsimony, heartily agreed. Sherman wondered whether the stingy state legislatures might pay so little that only rich men could serve in congress.

Carroll asserted that allowing the state legislatures to compensate congressmen undermined the whole purpose of the convention, which was to replace a confederal government with a national one. It would make "the dependence of both Houses on the State Legislatures" complete, he complained. "The States can now say: if you do not comply with our wishes, we will starve you; if you do we will reward you. The new Govt. in this form was nothing more than a second edition of Congress in two volumes, instead of one." Dickinson concurred on "the necessity of making the Genl. Govt. independent of the prejudices, passions, and improper views of the State Legislatures."

Ellsworth warned that payment by the national government instead of the states would allow congressmen to set their own compensation, a dangerous conflict of interest. Butler and Luther Martin emphasized that payment by the states ensured that congressmen, especially senators elected by the state legislatures, would answer to the states. Mason rejoined that the House of Representatives was not meant to be answerable to the state legislatures. The convention agreed by a 9–2 vote that the national government would compensate congressmen.[31]

The convention without controversy or debate approved both the Committee of Detail's decision to enumerate the powers of congress, and the insertion of the "necessary and proper" clause. This acceptance suggests that the delegates anticipated that these provisions would be inserted as the constitution took shape. The convention worked its way through the enumerated powers of congress. After a short discussion the delegates decided not to require a state legislature's request before the national government could "subdue a rebellion in any State." The power to "make war" was narrowed to "declare war."[32]

Several delegates suggested adding additional enumerated powers to the draft constitution. Madison proposed granting the power to create territorial governments, to govern a capital city, and to establish a national university. Charles Pinckney wanted to empower congress to issue patents and "charters of incorporation." Pinckney also hoped to limit congress's powers by including bill of rights protections for the freedom of the press and the writ of habeas corpus (to ensure that the government provide judicial due process to those arrested and to bring them to a speedy trial). He also hoped to forbid the quartering of troops in private homes and religious tests for officeholding. The Committee of Detail rejected Madison's additional enumerated powers and Pinckney's bill of rights provisions.[33]

In debate on August 22, the convention added to the draft constitution two rights-related measures not suggested by Pinckney, one prohibiting ex post facto laws (retroactive punishment for offenses that were not crimes at the time committed), and the other prohibiting bills of attainder (legislative charges and punishment for crimes without judicial due process of law or a conviction). After debating whether these protections already existed without being expressly written in the constitution, and whether their inclusion implied that congress could exceed its enumerated powers, the delegates inserted them.[34]

On August 28, Pinckney again tried to protect habeas corpus by moving that the writ should "not be suspended but on the most urgent occasions," and not for more than a year. Wilson and Rutledge thought the suspension of the writ should be entirely forbidden. The delegates adopted a sentence suggested by Gouverneur Morris: "The privilege of the writ of Habeas Corpus shall not be suspended; unless where in cases of Rebellion or invasion the public safety may require it." The use of the passive voice instead of the words "congress shall have the power" may be owing to the fact that when the delegates approved this provision, they had no idea where in the Constitution it would be placed. Although the convention placed this sentence in Article I on the legislative branch, the fact that it is written in the passive voice later raised questions about whether the president can also suspend the writ. During the Civil War, Abraham Lincoln made the clever argument that the Framers used the passive voice because they intended to allow the executive to suspend the writ if a national emergency arose when congress was not in session.[35]

Mason wanted congress to regulate the state militias so that they could serve as a substitute for a peacetime standing army so feared by Revolutionary era Americans as a precursor of tyranny. Gerry of Massachusetts, which had experienced occupation by British regular forces before the Revolution, pronounced "an army dangerous in time of peace." He moved to limit the number of troops congress could raise in peacetime, suggesting no more than 3,000. Charles Pinckney and Dayton warned that such a clause would prevent the nation from preparing for invasion and war. According to tradition, Washington sarcastically "suggested a countermotion that 'no foreign enemy should invade the United States at any time, with more than 3,000 troops.'" The convention overwhelmingly rejected Gerry's motion.[36]

The discussion turned back to Mason's original motion for the federal government to regulate the state militias. Delegates debated how to achieve enough uniformity for the various state militias to cooperate for common defense without depriving the states of their autonomy in the matter. Views ranged from giving the national government limited control over the state militias to granting it complete control. At the far end of the spectrum stood Charles Pinckney, who argued the need for a true national military establishment in the form of a standing army. The convention voted to submit this issue to a grand committee of a delegate from each state. William Livingston of New Jersey, chair of the Grand Committee of Eleven charged with determining militia issues, recommended on August 21 that the federal government "make laws for organizing arming and disciplining" the state militias, but that the states would be responsible for officering and training them.[37]

The convention approved the committee's militia recommendation after a short debate. Gerry, ever distrustful of a strong central government, and Luther Martin, a state sovereignty advocate, both opposed granting the federal government power over the military. Madison rebutted that "the Discipline of the Militia is evidently a *National* concern, and ought to be provided for in the *National* Constitution." He argued that federal control of the militia would be the only way to avoid a peacetime standing army that Gerry so dreaded. When Madison suggested that the federal government appoint some militia officers, Gerry exploded, "As the States are not to be abolished, he wondered at the attempts that were made to give" the federal government "powers inconsistent with their existence. He warned the Convention agst. pushing the experiment too far."[38]

On August 8, Rufus King of Massachusetts took aim at the pro-South, proslavery portions of the draft constitution. Pennsylvania congressman John Bayard described the thirty-two-year-old King as having "a graceful Attitude—a fine flow of Words & . . . a thorough acquaintance of the Subject on which He speaks. This gives him an unrival'd Influence."

Pierce detected a "rudeness of manner" in King's speech, but nevertheless pronounced him "among the Luminaries of the present Age."[39]

King launched an attack on the three-fifths clause. Counting slaves toward representation in congress "was a most grating circumstance to his mind, & and he believed would be so to a great part of the people of America." King announced that he had acquiesced in that compromise thus far because he expected the South to reciprocate. Indeed, King had even chaired the Committee of Five that on July 10 recommended restoring the three-fifths ratio for determining representation in congress. "He had hoped that this concession would have produced a readiness which had not been manifested, to strengthen the Genl. Govt. and to mark a full confidence in it." Instead the Committee of Detail's draft constitution had provided the South additional sectional benefits. King particularly deplored that congress could neither prohibit the African slave trade nor tax exports. The constitution required all the states collectively to suppress slave rebellions but allowed the southern states to continue to import slaves, increasing the danger of unrest. The document also barred the national government from taxing southern exports to raise revenue that might be needed to suppress slave rebellions. "Shall one part of the U.S. be bound to defend another part, and that other part be at liberty not only to increase its own danger, but to withhold the compensation for the burden?" King asked. "There was so much inequality & unreasonableness in all this, that the people of the Northern States could never be reconciled to it." King did not seek to throw out the Three-Fifths Compromise, but to prohibit the foreign slave trade or to enable congress to tax exports. "He could never agree to let" slaves "be imported without limitation & then be represented in the Natl. Legislature," without a concession to the North in return. "Either slaves should not be represented, or exports should be taxable."

Gouverneur Morris attacked slavery itself as an inefficient and cruel labor system. "He never would concur in upholding domestic slavery. It was a nefarious institution. It was the curse of heaven on the States where it prevailed." Whereas free labor produced "prosperity & happiness," slave labor bred "misery & poverty." Morris then exposed the theoretical hollowness of the Three-Fifths Compromise. "Upon what principle is it that the slaves shall be computed in the representation?" he asked. "Are they men? Then make them Citizens and let them vote. Are they property?

Why then is no other property included?" Morris condemned the Three-Fifths Compromise as an insult to republicanism: "The admission of slaves into the Representation when fairly explained comes to this," proclaimed Morris, "that the inhabitant of Georgia and S.C. who goes to the Coast of Africa, and in defiance of the most sacred laws of humanity tears away his fellow creatures from their dearest connections & damns them to the most cruel bondages, shall have more votes in a Govt. instituted for protection of the rights of mankind, than the Citizen of Pa. or N. Jersey who views with a laudable horror, so nefarious a practice."

Morris echoed King's point that the African slave trade would increase the nation's danger even as the prohibition of export taxes denied the means to pay for the additional protection required. When Morris moved to base representation on free people, only New Jersey supported him. The Three-Fifths Compromise was safe, but Morris and King had drawn a line in the sand against the constitution's other pro-slavery provisions similar to the one drawn by the small states with the New Jersey Plan.[40]

King had taken aim against the prohibition of federal export taxes, a feature favored by southern planters who exported cash crops like tobacco, rice, and indigo. Mason on August 15 demanded that the North not refuse the South "this security." Gouverneur Morris immediately pronounced such a "radically objectionable" provision "inadmissible" because it deprived the national government of essential revenue. He warned that congress needed the power to tax exports and even to impose an embargo on exports to punish enemy nations if necessary. Madison and Wilson chimed in that a national embargo power might be necessary to wring commercial concessions from foreign countries.[41]

Lower South delegates Williamson and Butler declared that if the export tax prohibition were removed, their region would be overtaxed. They were joined by Connecticut delegates Sherman and Ellsworth, who remained conciliatory toward the South. Gerry also favored the ban, warning that the federal government already had too much power vis-à-vis the states. Mason reminded everyone that the northern states would have a majority over the southern states in both houses of congress. Since "a majority when interested will oppress the minority," he regarded it as critical that the northern majority not be empowered to oppress the southern minority through export taxes. Madison and Wilson proposed as a compromise that a supermajority be required in congress to tax exports, but the convention reaffirmed the ban on federal export taxes.[42]

Luther Martin took aim at another pro–Lower South aspect of the Committee of Detail's draft constitution: the foreign slave trade into the United States could neither be banned nor taxed. Martin wanted to empower congress to enact "a prohibition or tax on the importation of slaves." The slave trade issue divided the Upper South states of Virginia and Maryland against the Lower South states. The opposition to the African slave trade of Upper South delegates like Martin, Mason, and Madison (who all owned slaves) did not signify growing abolitionist sentiment in that region, as some suggest. On the contrary, the Upper South remained as determined to preserve its peculiar institution as ever. So why did the slaveholding Upper South oppose the foreign slave trade? As the Upper South transitioned from highly labor-intensive crops such as tobacco to less labor-intensive produce such as corn and wheat, a surplus of slaves developed in that region. Upper South slaveholders, hoping to sell their slaves "down the river" to the Lower South, did not want competition from cheap, newly imported African slaves. In other words, banning the foreign slave trade made Upper South slaves worth more. That is why the region wanted to end the slave trade or at least to empower congress to tax it. "As to Virginia," explained Charles Cotesworth Pinckney in debate, "she will gain by stopping the importations. Her slaves will rise in value, & she has more than she wants."[43]

Luther Martin argued that the Three-Fifths Compromise would encourage the Lower South to import more slaves to gain more representation in congress. Was it fair, he reiterated, to allow that region to make the Union vulnerable to slave rebellions that the rest of the nation would be obligated to suppress? He concluded that "it was inconsistent with the principles of the revolution and dishonorable to the American character" for the constitution to protect the slave trade.[44]

Mason followed with a broadside against slavery itself. Slaves, he pronounced, "prevent the emigration" into the United States "of Whites, who really enrich & strengthen a Country." Slaves "produce the most pernicious effect on manners. Every master of slaves is born a petty tyrant." Slavery brings "the judgment of heaven on a Country. As nations can not be rewarded or punished in the next world they must be in this. By an inevitable chain of causes & effects providence punishes national sins by national calamities. . . . He held it essential in every point of view that the Genl. Govt. should have power to prevent the increase of slavery." Although Mason, the owner of dozens of slaves, attacked the institution itself, his real target was the foreign slave trade.[45]

The Lower South delegates jumped to their feet to uphold slavery and the African slave trade. "South Carolina can never receive the plan if it prohibits the slave trade," declared Charles Pinckney. "If slavery be wrong, it is justified by the example of all the world." Charles Cotesworth Pinckney asserted that "S. Carolina & Georgia cannot do without slaves." Even if he accepted a ban on the foreign slave trade, his constituents never would. "A rejection of the clause" allowing slave imports meant "an exclusion of S. Carola. from the Union." Williamson too "thought the S. States could not be members of the Union if the clause shd. be rejected." Rutledge agreed that "the true question at present is whether the Southn. States shall or shall not be parties to the Union."

Charles Pinckney maintained that the best way to end the African slave trade was for the rest of the nation to take a hands-off approach. "If the S. States were let alone they will probably of themselves stop importations," he predicted. But "an attempt to take away the right as proposed will produce serious objections to the Constitution which he wished to see adopted." Baldwin agreed that "if left to herself," Georgia "may probably put a stop to the evil."

Charles Cotesworth Pinckney argued that the entire nation, not just the Lower South, benefitted from the foreign slave trade. "The importation of slaves would be for the interest of the whole Union," he asserted. "The more slaves, the more produce to employ the carrying trade; The more consumption also, and the more of this, the more of revenue for the common treasury." Rutledge added that "if the Northern States consult their interest, they will not oppose the increase of Slaves which will increase the commodities of which they will become the carriers."

As usual, Ellsworth and Sherman sought compromise and conciliation at the expense of African Americans. Ellsworth urged his colleagues not to "be unjust towards S. Carolina & Georgia. Let us not intermeddle. As population increases poor laborers will be so plenty as to render slaves useless. Slavery in time will not be a speck in our Country." Sherman remarked that "it was better to let the S. States import slaves than to part with them, if they made that a sine qua non."[46]

Wilson and Dickinson wanted to call the Lower South's bluff on disunion. South Carolina and Georgia "would never refuse to Unite because the importation might be prohibited," pronounced Wilson, while Dickinson "could not believe that the Southn. States would refuse to confederate." King answered threat-for-threat. If the Lower South would not remain in a Union that banned slave imports, the northern states would not remain in one that allowed it.[47]

Faced with firm opposition from these northern delegates, the Lower South contingent wavered. Conceding that perhaps "slaves might be made liable to an equal tax with other imports," Charles Pinckney moved that the issue be sent to a committee. After reasserting that "N.C. S.C. & Georgia" would never "agree to the plan, unless their right to import slaves be untouched," Rutledge also advocated assignment to a committee. Sensing opportunity, Gouverneur Morris suggested submitting to a committee the slave trade issue, the matter of export taxes, and the supermajority requirement for commercial laws. "These things may form a bargain among the Northern & Southern States," he predicted. The convention then voted—with the support of every southern state—to refer these issues to a Grand Committee of Eleven, with a delegate from each state. Significantly, Charles Cotesworth Pinckney, who had already signaled the Lower South's willingness to compromise, and King, Dickinson, and Wilson, who demanded a concession to the North, all sat on the committee. So did Upper South opponents of the African slave trade, Luther Martin and Madison. The committee thus boded well for a southern concession to the North.[48]

On August 24, William Livingston of New Jersey, chair of the Committee of Eleven, reported a compromise proposal: the ban on export taxes would remain in place. Congress could prohibit the African slave trade starting in 1800 and could tax imported slaves at the same rate as other imports. The committee also recommended eliminating the requirement for a two-thirds supermajority of both houses of congress to pass commercial laws. Martin, who opposed a North-South deal that would continue the foreign slave trade, later recorded that the committee, of which he was a member, "by a great majority" quickly struck the deal. "I found the *eastern* States, notwithstanding their *aversion to slavery*, were very willing to indulge the southern States, at least with a temporary liberty to prosecute the *slave-trade*, provided the southern States would, in their turn, gratify them, by laying *no restriction on navigation acts.*" The northern states willingly conceded protections for slavery in return for commercial concessions.[49]

In debate, Charles Cotesworth Pinckney moved to push back the date when congress could shut down the foreign slave trade from 1800 to 1808. The convention accepted the change by a 7–4 vote with New Jersey, Pennsylvania, Delaware, and Virginia opposed. Madison's prediction that to leave the trade open another "twenty years will produce all the mischief that can be apprehended" fell on deaf ears.

The Livingston committee recommended that imported slaves be taxable. Sherman opposed taxing them "as acknowledging men to be property." In typical Connecticut fashion, Sherman had managed to sound antislavery while at the same time appeasing the South by opposing a tax on slave imports. King and Langdon insisted that taxing imported slaves was the price of allowing the African slave trade to continue. C. C. Pinckney conceded the point, and Mason added that the failure to tax imported slaves in effect subsidized them. The convention voted to allow a tax of up to $10 on each imported slave.[50]

During the slave trade debate, a discussion occurred as to whether to use the word "slave" or the word "persons" in the constitution. Sherman preferred the word "persons" to avoid terms "not pleasing to some people." Madison, too, "thought it wrong to admit in the Constitution the idea that there could be property in men." Years later, he added that others who opposed the foreign slave trade also "had scruples against admitting the term 'Slaves.'" Baldwin believed that the convention rejected the word "slaves" because the Confederation Congress "had hitherto avoided the use of it in their acts, and not acknowledged the existence of such a condition." Luther Martin later complained that the Livingston committee avoided "expressions which might be odious in the ears of Americans, although they were willing to admit into their system those *things* which the *expressions* signified."[51]

With the African slave trade settled, Charles Pinckney hoped to retain the supermajority requirement for commercial laws that the committee recommended eliminating. He argued that a supermajority would protect each region of the country (especially the South) from majority tyranny caused by a combination of other regions. In agreement, Mason exclaimed that "the Southern States are the *minority* in both Houses. Is it to be expected that they will deliver themselves bound hand & foot" to the northern states? Equally upset, Randolph complained that "that there were features so odious in the constitution as it now stands, that he doubted whether he should be able to agree to it."

South Carolinians C. C. Pinckney, Butler, and Rutledge all parted company with Mason and their colleague Charles Pinckney on this issue. They would allow a bare majority of congress to pass commercial laws potentially harmful to the South in return for the concession the convention had made in prohibiting congress from terminating the African slave trade before 1808. (It is worth remembering that at this time Congress could do nothing to stop individual states from prohibiting the foreign slave trade. Indeed, twelve states had already prohibited it.) Madison concurred that a supermajority requirement would make it too difficult for congress to pass the commercial legislation necessary to wring trade concessions from foreign nations. He believed, moreover, that the South need not fear the North imposing a navigation act requiring crops to be exported on northern ships. This outcome would be prevented by the fact that any bill would have to be approved by both the House and the Senate, and because the nation's geographic size and diversity would make a tyrannical national majority unlikely. Gorham rhetorically asked why the northern states would ratify a constitution that tied their hands commercially with a supermajority requirement. With South Carolina voting with the northern states, the convention rejected a two-thirds requirement for commercial laws. According to Mason, South Carolina "struck up a bargain with the 3. N. Engld. states, if they would join to admit slaves for some years," South Carolina "wd join in changing the clause which required 2/3 of the legislature" to pass commercial laws.[52]

But South Carolina wanted one more thing in return for allowing a bare majority of congress to enact commercial laws: a fugitive slave clause. Madison believed that there was a link between the Confederation Congress's passage of the Northwest Ordinance and the Constitutional Convention's adoption of the fugitive slave clause (see Chapter 3). But the delegates had not yet inserted such a provision in the constitution. On August 28, Butler and Charles Pinckney moved "to require fugitive slaves and servants be delivered up like criminals." Sherman and Wilson complained that since the government does not return runaway livestock, it should not return runaway slaves. The convention failed to act on the matter. The following day, as soon as the issue of commercial laws was settled, Butler again moved to add a fugitive slave clause to the constitution, to which the convention now agreed without dissent. This new fugitive slave measure did not associate fugitive slaves with criminals. This marked a departure from the Articles of Confederation, which had an extradition clause for criminals, but no provision for returning fugitive slaves. A final alteration in the closing days of the convention removed the word "legally" from the phrase, "No person legally held to service or labour" shall "be discharged from such service or labor." Madison explained that this change would eliminate the implication "that slavery was legal in a moral view."[53]

Upper South delegates Martin, Randolph, and especially Mason had failed to end the foreign slave trade and to retain the supermajority requirement for commercial laws. For Mason, both were non-negotiable demands. Envisioning the South as a vulnerable minority at the mercy of the North, Mason anticipated the fears of John C. Calhoun and the southern secessionists. Even though Mason had in July declared he would "bury his bones" in Philadelphia rather than to fail to agree on a constitution, he now reversed course and opposed the document. And the seeds of Randolph's refusal to sign that had been planted by the adoption of the Great Compromise now took root as well.[54]

Luther Martin later insisted that during August, he, Mason, Gerry, and other "members who considered the system, as then under consideration and likely to be adopted, extremely exceptionable, and of a tendency to destroy the rights and liberties of the United States, thought it advisable to meet together in the evenings, in order to have a communication of sentiments, and to concert a plan of conventional opposition to, and amendment of that system, so as, if possible, to render it less dangerous." Martin claimed that delegates from New Jersey, Connecticut, Delaware, South Carolina, and Georgia also attended. No concerted action emerged from such meetings. Instead, Martin went home in disgust at the beginning of September. Mason and Gerry stayed to the convention's end but refused to sign the constitution.[55]

Could the non-slaveholding delegates have forced the slaveholding delegates to accept the abolition of slavery in the new constitution? The answer is no. The southern delegations (except Delaware) would have walked out before accepting the elimination of slavery. And even if the convention had embraced emancipation, those states would then have rejected the constitution and would have formed their own confederacy. Indeed, fears of the abolition of slavery caused these five states to join six others in seceding from the Union three score and fourteen years later. Madison explained to Thomas Jefferson a month after the convention ended, "S. Carolina & Georgia were inflexible on the point of the slaves." Hamilton assured the New York ratification convention that without the Three-Fifths Compromise "no union could possibly have been formed."[56]

Could the non-slaveholding states have driven a harder bargain and forced the slaveholding states to accept a constitution less favorable to their peculiar institution? The answer is probably yes. Only North Carolina, South Carolina, and Georgia wanted to keep the foreign slave trade open. These states almost certainly would have accepted 1800 instead of 1808 as the year the slave trade could be prohibited by congress. They presumably would also have accepted a higher tax on slave imports. The alternative—to form a three-state confederacy that would have to put down its own slave rebellions, could not reclaim fugitive slaves who escaped its borders, and had little area to expand geographically—seems unthinkable. Had the convention taken this tougher stance against slavery, the institution likely would have perished much more quickly and easily than it did. But improving the lives of African Americans was not a high priority for most of the delegates, or, for that matter, for most white Americans in 1787. Their concern was establishing a strong Union and protecting their own particular interests within it, not ending the enslavement of a race of people that the overwhelming majority of whites North and South regarded as biologically inferior. Even Gouverneur Morris, the convention's most passionate and outspoken critic of slavery, engaged in sectional horse-trading on the issue. And Benjamin Franklin, president of the Pennsylvania Society for the Abolition of Slavery, declined to submit to the convention his own organization's petition against the African slave trade. Franklin explained to his abolitionist members that he "had thought it advisable to let" the petition "lie over for the present."[57]

But it is also true that the Constitution turned out just antislavery enough to enable the institution's ultimate demise. Emancipation would not happen before over 200,000 additional African slaves were imported, seventy-five more years of slavery, and 750,000 deaths in the Civil War, but the "peculiar institution" eventually perished. Had the convention given the slaveholders everything they wanted, including counting slaves as five-fifths of free people, keeping the foreign slave trade open forever, and not taxing imported slaves, it is hard to imagine slavery ending in the nineteenth century, or even in the twentieth, for that matter.[58]

By late August, the delegates had agreed upon most of the constitution. One area that had bedeviled them all summer long still remained unresolved, however: the executive branch.

NOTES

1. Adrienne Koch, ed., *Notes of Debates in the Federal Convention of 1787 Reported by James Madison* (Athens: Ohio University Press, 1966), hereafter cited as NDFC, 464; Max Farrand, ed., *The Records of the Federal Convention of 1787*. 1937 rev. ed. in four vols., reprint (New Haven, CT: Yale University Press, 1974), hereafter cited as RFC, 3:70.

2. NDFC, 304–5.

3. Ibid., 305–6, 120; Christopher Collier and James Lincoln Collier, *Decision in Philadelphia: The Constitutional Convention of 1787* (New York: Ballantine Books, 1987), 267–68.

4. NDFC, 518–19.

5. Ibid., 348–53.

6. Ibid., 354.

7. Ibid., 355, 362–63.

8. Ibid., 379–85.

9. RFC, 2:137–50.

10. NDFC, 385–96.

11. RFC, 137–50.

12. NDFC, 380.

13. Ibid., 390.

14. John P. Kaminski and Timothy D. Moore, eds., *An Assembly of Demigods: Word Portraits of the Delegates to the Constitutional Convention by Their Contemporaries* (Madison, WI: Parallel Press, 2012), hereafter cited as *Demigods*, 250–51.

15. NDFC, 390.

16. *Demigods*, 166.

17. NDFC, 385–96.

18. Donald Jackson and Dorothy Twohig, eds., *The Diaries of George Washington*, 6 vols. (Charlottesville: University of Virginia Press, 1976–1979), hereafter cited as DGW, 5:178–80; W. W. Abbot et al., eds., *The Papers of George Washington, Confederation Series*, 6 vols. (Charlottesville: University of Virginia Press, 1992–1997), hereafter cited as PGW-CS, 5:280.

19. James H. Hutson, ed., *Supplement to Max Farrand's* The Records of the Federal Convention of 1787 (New Haven, CT: Yale University Press, 1987), hereafter cited as *RFC Supplement*, 194–95, 205; Frances Leigh Williams, *A Founding Family: The Pinckneys of South Carolina* (New York: Harcourt Brace Janovich, 1978), 248–49.
20. *NDFC*, 385–96; *RFC*, 2:175.
21. *RFC*, 2:190–92, 209–12.
22. *NDFC*, 413–17.
23. Ibid., 436, 442, 448.
24. Ibid., 442–50, 454.
25. Ibid., 460–61, 580, 606–7.
26. Ibid., 401–5.
27. Ibid., 418–22, 437–42.
28. Ibid., 372–78.
29. Ibid., 425–27.
30. Ibid., 450–56.
31. Ibid., 450–59.
32. Ibid., 474–77.
33. Ibid., 477–80, 485–86, 509–10.
34. Ibid., 510–11.
35. Ibid., 541.
36. Ibid., 481–82; *RFC Supplement*, 229.
37. *NDFC*, 483–85, 494–95.
38. Ibid., 513–16.
39. *Demigods*, 50–51, 244; George William Van Cleve, *We Have Not a Government: The Articles of Confederation and the Road to the Constitutional Convention* (Chicago, IL: University of Chicago Press, 2017), 121, 215–16, 232–33, 256–58; *RFC Supplement*, 67.
40. *NDFC*, 409–13.
41. Ibid., 466–69.
42. Ibid., 498–502.
43. Ibid., 502, 505.
44. Ibid., 502.
45. Ibid., 504.
46. Ibid., 502–8.
47. Ibid., 506.
48. Ibid., 506–9.
49. Ibid., 522; *RFC*, 3:210–11.
50. *NDFC*, 530–32.
51. Ibid., 531–32; *RFC*, 3:210, 378, 436.

52. *NDFC*, 547–52; *RFC*, 3:367.
53. *NDFC*, 545–46, 552, 625, 648.
54. Ibid., 244.
55. *RFC*, 3:282.
56. Ibid., 135; John P. Kaminski et al., eds., *The Documentary History of the Ratification of the Constitution*, 29 vols. to date (Madison, WI: State Historical Society of Wisconsin, 1976–), hereafter cited as *DHRC*, 22:1728.
57. *RFC Supplement*, 44–45.
58. Richard Beeman, *Plain Honest Men: The Making of the American Constitution* (New York: Random House, 2009), 333.

CHAPTER 5

THE EXECUTIVE, THE JUDICIARY, POSTPONED PARTS, AND THE SIGNING

Designing the presidency, insisted James Wilson, was "in truth the most difficult" challenge the convention faced. Madison, too, declared that the "difficulty of finding" a method to appoint the "Executive . . . was deeply felt by the Convention." This task also proved to be one of the most time-consuming issues. Madison noted that "tedious and reiterated discussions took place over whether" the president "should consist of a single person, or a plurality of co-ordinate members, on the mode of appointment, on the duration in office, on the degree of power, [and] on the re-eligibility." Even delegates from the same state who typically voted together on other issues could not agree on the executive branch. The various positions of the individual delegates speak volumes about their worldviews and their varied personal governmental experiences.[1]

Reaching agreement on the powers of an executive who would be energetic but not tyrannical proved elusive. The dilemma, according to Abraham Baldwin, was to give "as much Power . . . as could be" while "guard[in]g against all possibility of his ascending . . . to Despotism & absolute Monarchy." Madison admitted that the convention had found it a "peculiarly embarrassing" challenge "to unite a proper energy in the Executive . . . with the essential characters of Republican Government." The debates often went in circles, with the delegates unable to settle one aspect of the presidency without having clarity on another. A change in one parameter necessitated changes in others. So, for example, the convention could not decide between a single or plural executive until they knew what powers the president would exercise. Similarly, the convention could not agree on how long the president's term would be or whether he could serve multiple terms until they decided who elected him. Election by congress required one lengthy term to avoid making the president dependent on that body for reelection. Election by the people made it safe for the president to be reelected, which in turn suggested a shorter term. For most of the summer, the agreed-upon plan called for an executive, elected by congress, who would serve one, seven-year term.[2]

Late in August, the convention handed some lingering issues, including the presidency, to a "Committee on Postponed Parts." In tying up loose ends, this committee redesigned the presidency into a truly co-equal branch, elected by the people through an electoral college for renewable four-year terms. Although it was not discussed in debate, the convention's belief that Washington would be the first president made the creation of a strong and independent executive possible. Overall, the convention strengthened the presidency over time, from the Virginia Plan to the Committee of Detail Report to the Committee on Postponed Parts Report to the final Constitution.

As for the judicial branch, the convention created a supreme court consisting of judges, appointed by the president and confirmed by the senate, who held their appointments for life. The convention originally decided that the senate alone would appoint the supreme court, but after the adoption of the Great Compromise in July, nationalist delegates, distrustful of state influence over the senate, shifted appointment of the justices to the president, with the senate confirming the nominees. Congress possessed the power to establish lower federal courts. Madison and Wilson tried time and again to get the convention to adopt an executive-judicial council of revision to review bills before passage into law. But the convention rejected such a council in favor of granting the executive a veto that could be overridden by a two-thirds vote of each house of congress. The delegates also anticipated that the supreme court would exercise judicial review but did not write this provision into the Constitution.

In September, the convention appointed a Committee of Style to prepare the last draft of the constitution. Gouverneur Morris, an elegant writer, crafted the final version. After a few more edits, the convention approved the completed document. On September 17, after three-and-one-half months of deliberations, all but three of the delegates present signed the engrossed copy of the Constitution and the convention adjourned *sine die*.

The convention first discussed the presidency on June 1, taking up Resolution 7 of the Virginia Plan: "That a national Executive be instituted, to be chosen by the national Legislature—for the term of _____ years . . . to be ineligible thereafter, to possess the executive powers of Congress." This bare-bones description suggested a fairly weak office. In composing the Virginia Plan, Madison, by his own admission, had devoted little thought to the executive branch.

When Wilson opened the debate by moving "that the Executive consist of a single person," he met with a deafening silence. The delegates faced an awkward situation. Everyone knew that if the constitution created a single executive, then the first president would likely be George Washington. No one had the courage to raise the specter of single executive becoming a tyrant right in front of the presumptive first president. Franklin, the only delegate who rivaled Washington in prestige, finally broke the silence, prodding his colleagues to speak freely. Rutledge agreed with Franklin, reminding the delegates that thanks to the secrecy rules, they need not fear the appearance of inconsistency if they changed their minds.[3]

Wilson argued that only a single president could provide the "energy dispatch and responsibility" requisite "to the office." Randolph favored instead a three-person executive because he feared that to place the office in the hands of one man would be "the foetus of monarchy." Three executives, in contrast, could check each other. Sherman, who viewed the executive as a mere agent of Congress, preferred to allow the legislature to appoint however many executives it wanted, while Gerry advocated a single executive accompanied by an advisory council.[4]

With no consensus on the matter, the delegates followed Madison's suggestion to postpone the decision over a singular or plural executive until they considered the executive's authority. Once they determined the executive's powers, they could then judge "how far they might be safely entrusted to a single officer." The convention quickly agreed that the president would have "power to carry into effect the national laws," and to make appointments "not otherwise provided for."[5]

With the convention having agreed on this rather vague definition of executive power, Rutledge and Charles Pinckney repeated Wilson's call for the executive to consist of a single person. Randolph, backed by Mason, again renewed his demand for a trio of presidents, now adding that each of the three should represent a different geographical region of the country. Randolph could have cited as a precedent the Confederation's Board of Treasury, which had commissioners from Massachusetts, New York, and Virginia. Rejecting this logic, Wilson answered that "the *tranquility* not less than the vigor of the Govt . . . would be favored by" a unitary executive. A tripartite president would lead to "uncontrouled, continued, & violent animosities" among them. The motion for a single executive carried, seven states to three, with New York, Delaware, and Maryland objecting. Prior to the Great Compromise, several small-state delegates, wary of a strong central government in which they had little voice, hesitated to support a powerful, unitary president. The decision for a single executive stood the test of time and would not be seriously questioned for the remainder of the convention, although Randolph never became reconciled to it.[6]

On June 2, John Dickinson of Delaware raised the subject of how the president might be removed in case of misbehavior. Advocating that "considerable powers be left in the hands of the States," Dickinson suggested removal by a majority vote of the state legislatures. Madison and Wilson, always seeking to deny the state legislatures a voice in what they hoped would be a strictly national government, predicted that Dickinson's resolution would establish "an equality of agency in the small with the great States; that it would enable a minority of the people to prevent the removal of an officer who had rendered himself justly criminal in the eyes of the majority." Madison and Wilson simply could not tolerate having an element of confederal government woven into the constitution. Dickinson's motion was overwhelmingly defeated with only Delaware in favor.[7]

Sherman, who viewed the president as subordinate to congress, "contended that the National Legislature should have power to remove the Executive at pleasure." Mason countered that congressional removal would make "the Executive the mere creature of the Legislature," a violation of the principle of the separation of powers. Siding with Sherman, the delegates quickly agreed that the president would be "removeable on impeachment & conviction of mal-practice or neglect of duty" by congress.

The Executive, the Judiciary, Postponed Parts, and the Signing

John Dickinson of Delaware became the first delegate to propose what eventually became the Great Compromise, which based representation in the House of Representatives on population and granted the states equal representation in the Senate. Dickinson also served on the Committee on Postponed Parts that redesigned the presidency in September. (Library of Congress)

There was no mention of criminal activity as grounds for impeachment at this stage of the discussion, only dereliction of duty.[8]

The delegates next turned to the length of the executive's term. Wilson and Sherman favored a three-year term with the option of reelection. Mason successfully countered with a seven-year term without the possibility of a second term, which the convention approved by a 5–4 vote. Since the president would, according to the Virginia Plan, be chosen by congress, he would not then be beholden to that body for reelection.[9]

At the risk of sounding "chimerical," Wilson, ever the advocate of popular sovereignty, called for the executive's direct "election by the people" instead of by congress. Allowing the people to choose both congress and the president, Wilson insisted, would ensure the independence of both branches against each other, and against the states. But the convention did not think the people capable of making a wise choice for president. Given the nation's primitive communication system, most Americans knew little about leaders in other states. Sherman, who denied that the executive should be independent of the legislature, favored appointment by congress. "An independence of the Executive on the supreme Legislature," he insisted, was "the very essence of tyranny."[10]

Finding no appetite for direct popular election, Wilson proposed instead that the executive be chosen by an electoral college. That way, people could select well-informed local citizens who possessed the requisite knowledge of national leaders, who could then make a wise choice. He "proposed that the U. States should be divided into districts, each of which should elect a certain number of persons, who should have the appointment of the Executive." Considering that an electoral college eventually prevailed in the U.S. Constitution, it is remarkable that it was defeated by an 8–2 margin with almost no debate the first time the delegates considered it. The convention once again voted by the same lopsided margin in favor of "electing the Executive by the national Legislature for the term of seven years." Pennsylvania and Maryland voted no both times. The former state preferred popular election, while the latter feared giving the executive such a lengthy term.[11]

Wilson read an address by Franklin arguing against a salary for the president. Making the office "a place of *profit*," Franklin warned, would arouse feelings of greed, leading to corruption and intrigue to obtain the office. The executive would inevitably bargain a modest salary into an excessive one, resulting in "Kingly Government." This outcome could be avoided by making the presidency "a post of *honour*" not emolument. Franklin explained that Washington's service without pay as commander in chief of the Continental Army during the Revolutionary War proved that his idea was not "Utopian." No debate ensued after Wilson finished reading Franklin's text. Madison noted that Franklin's suggestion "was treated with great respect," but only because it came from such a venerable statesman, not "from any apparent conviction of its expediency or practicability." Obviously, the absence of a presidential salary would itself promote oligarchic rule, because only the very wealthy could afford to serve.[12]

On June 9, the convention reconsidered the method of electing the president. Arguing that a president chosen by congress would be dependent upon that body, Gerry instead moved that "the National Executive should be elected by the Executives of the States" with each governor's vote weighted based on state population. Randolph strongly opposed Gerry's motion as unfair to the small states, who would never elect a president under that system. Besides, instead of being a creature of congress, the president would now become a creature of the states. "Can you suppose" that the states "will ever cordially rise the great oak, when they must sit as shrubs under its shade," he asked. Gerry's motion lost, 9–0.[13]

The convention did not return to the presidency until after the adoption of the Great Compromise over five weeks later, on July 17, when it considered the Virginia Plan as amended by the committee of the whole. After confirming that the executive would be a single person, the delegates reevaluated whether that person would be chosen by the legislature. Gouverneur Morris suggested that congressional election would make the president "the mere creature of the Legis[lature]." Indeed, "if the Executive be chosen by the Natl. Legislature, he will not be independent of it, and . . . usurpation & tyranny on the part of the Legislature will be the consequence." He preferred election by the people, who, he believed, "will never fail to prefer some man of distinguished character . . . of continental reputation." Legislative selection, in contrast, would lead not to merit, but to "intrigue . . . cabal, and . . . faction; it will be like the election of a pope by a conclave of cardinals."[14]

Mason predicted that the people could truly know the caliber of men only from their own states and would therefore be unfit to judge candidates from a continental republic. He concluded that "it would be as unnatural to refer the choice of a proper character for chief Magistrate to the people, as it would, to refer a trial of colours to a blind man." Sherman agreed that the people would "never be sufficiently informed of characters" to make a wise choice. Besides, each state would inevitably vote for a favorite son, resulting in the election of a president from the most populous state. Wilson, a perennial advocate of popular sovereignty, suggested that congress should choose the president out of the top candidates chosen by the people. He concurred with Morris that an executive chosen solely by congress would lack independence.[15]

Charles Pinckney warned that popular election would allow the large states to collude in selecting the winning candidate. Gouverneur Morris answered that the nation's enormous geographical size would protect against collusion across state lines. Here Morris applied the same reasoning that Madison used to argue that in a large republic, self-interested factions that invariably dominated small republics would cancel each other out, allowing the public good to prevail. The convention rejected presidential election by the people with only Wilson's Pennsylvania in favor.[16]

The delegates voted to allow the president to be reelected. This decision raised the question of whether a reelectable president should serve a shorter term than seven years. It also raised the question of whether a president who could serve successive terms would kowtow to congress in order to win reelection. To get around the problem of dependence on congress, Gouverneur Morris advocated that the president serve "during good behavior." Horrified, Mason warned that "an Executive during good behavior was a softer name only for an Executive for life. And that . . . would be an easy step to hereditary Monarchy." After reaffirming a seven-year presidential term, the delegates needed to revisit whether the president should be reelectable.[17]

July 19 accordingly opened with a reconsideration of the number of terms a president could serve. Defending multiple terms, Gouverneur Morris advocated a popularly elected executive powerful enough both "to pervade every part of" the continent, and to keep congress in check. The senate would check the lower house, but who besides the president could keep the entire legislature from becoming tyrannical, he asked. "The Executive therefore ought to be . . . the great protector of the Mass of the people." Morris rejected a one-term limit for three reasons. First, it would eliminate the incentive to earn reelection through meritorious service. Second, it would encourage the incumbent to engage in graft and corruption in the brief interval before leaving office. Third, it would encourage a tyrannical usurpation by the executive to remain in office. Let the people choose the president every two years, Morris argued. To objections that two years was too short a term for a president, he answered that "as long as he should behave himself well, he would be continued in his place." The geographical vastness of the country would ensure the election of a disinterested statesmen over candidates serving local interests. "The extent of the Country would secure his re-election agst. the factions & discontents of particular States," Morris assured. But if the president were elected by congress, he would have to serve for life to ensure his independence from that branch.

Randolph voiced the growing consensus that a president elected by congress must be limited to one term to ensure his independence from that body. He also worried that congressional election would inevitably lead to presidents being chosen exclusively from the large states. King revived the idea of using presidential electors chosen by the people. Wilson and Madison also both supported that concept. Gerry countered with election by electors chosen by the state governors. Gerry saw symmetry in the latter plan: "The people of the States will then choose the 1st. branch: The legislatures of the States" would choose "the 2d. branch . . . and the Executives of the States" would choose "the National Executive." The convention instead voted in favor of having electors chosen by the state legislatures elect the president for a six-year term. Gerry successfully moved that each state have between one and three electors, based on the state's population. Now, the president would be elected by the state legislatures for renewable six-year terms and removable by congress.[18]

On July 20, Charles Pinkney, Gouverneur Morris, and King, all advocates of a strong executive, opposed allowing the executive to be impeached. Pinckney feared that if congress could impeach the president, it would "hold . . . a rod over the Executive and by that means effectually destroy his independence." King added that because the president would serve for a six-year term, he could be removed if necessary on election day. Better to keep the executive independent and strong than to make him impeachable.

Most of the delegates, however, including Davie, Wilson, Madison, and Randolph, favored a congressional power to impeach the executive. "No point is of more importance that that the right of impeachment should be continued," declared Mason. "Shall any man be above Justice" especially one "who can commit the most extensive injustice?" Franklin suggested that impeachment would provide a way for the president to exonerate himself against unfounded charges. Gerry added that "a good magistrate will not fear" impeachment, while "a bad one ought to be kept in fear of" it. These pro-impeachment arguments changed Morris's mind. "He was now sensible of the necessity of impeachments" to protect against the president bribing electors or accepting bribes from foreign nations. The convention retained the provision making the executive "removeable on impeachment and conviction for mal practice or neglect of duty."[19]

Should the president have appointment power? The revised Virginia Plan called for supreme court justices to be appointed by the senate. On July 21, the convention took up Madison's motion that the judges instead be appointed by the president and confirmed by the upper house. Madison explained that the Great Compromise had changed his thinking about judicial appointments. Now that the state legislatures elected the senate, a body that he distrusted because of its confederal basis, Madison hoped to shift some of its authority to the executive branch. "The 2d. b[ranch] was very differently constituted when the appointment of the Judges was formerly referred to it, and was now to be composed of equal votes from all the States," he explained. Therefore "the principle of compromise which had prevailed in other instances required in this that their shd. be a concurrence of two" branches in making supreme court appointments, rather than allowing the upper chamber alone to make them. He feared that northerners, controlling a majority of states and therefore a majority of the senate, would appoint northern justices rather than southern justices. Backing Madison, Gouverneur Morris added that the senate should not appoint judges, because the states would often be parties to cases that came before the supreme court. "Next to the impropriety of being a Judge in one's own cause, is the appointment of the Judge," he reasoned.

Gerry, Pinckney, and Ellsworth preferred that the upper house alone appoint judges. Mason agreed. "He considered the appointment by the Executive as a dangerous prerogative" that "might even give him an influence over the Judiciary department itself." The convention rejected Madison's motion 6–3. Only the three large states supported having the executive share in supreme court appointments.[20]

On July 24, the convention reconsidered having the president chosen by electors picked by the state legislatures. Several delegates argued that the elector system was too complicated. Williamson veered off topic, calling for a trio of men—one from each region of the country—to share executive functions. "A single Magistrate," he warned, "will be an elective King. . . . He will spare no pains to keep himself in for life, and will then lay a train for the succession of his children." The discussion degenerated further when Gerry offered a hopelessly complex formula to choose the executive: the state legislatures should nominate candidates, who would be narrowed down to two finalists by the house of representatives, from which the senate would choose the president. "The *noes* were so predominant" to this quixotic proposal, wrote Madison, that there was no need to count votes. Instead, the convention restored congressional election of the executive.[21]

With congress again electing the president, Luther Martin moved to limit him once again to a single term to avoid making him dependent on that body. Gouverneur Morris did not think that any form of legislative election even for a single term could secure the independence of the president. All concurred that the longer the president's term, the less dependent upon congress he would be. But when Gerry suggested an excessively long term of fifteen years, King mocked the idea by suggesting twenty years.

Wilson observed that "the difficulties & perplexities into which the" convention "is thrown proceed from the election by the Legislature." To get around the problem, he suggested a new idea: a committee of congressmen should be drawn by lot "who should retire immediately and make the election without separating." This plan would allow election by congress but would neither involve intrigue nor rob the president of independence. Gerry responded that to allow men chosen by lot to pick the president was no better than a roll of dice. King agreed that the election "ought to be governed by reason, not chance."[22]

On July 25, Ellsworth moved that when a president was up for reelection, the governors of the states, not congress, should make the choice. It would be better, Gerry responded, to let the state governors choose the president all the time. Charles Pinckney preferred having congress choose the president but forbid him from serving consecutive terms. Morris denied that making the president step down after one term would "prevent intrigue and dependence on the Legislature" because "the man in office will look forward to the period at which he will become re-eligible."

Madison worried that the influence of foreign nations on congress could decide presidential elections. "It will be an object of great moment with the great rival powers of Europe," he predicted, "to have at the head of our Governmt. a man attached to their respective politics & interests." Instead of election by congress, the only viable alternatives were either "an appointment by Electors chosen by the people" or "an immediate appointment by the people." Madison preferred the latter option but recognized two problems with it. First, with voters supporting favorite sons, large states would have an advantage over small ones. Second, with a greater percentage of the population being able to vote in the North versus the South (because more northerners met property qualifications to vote and because of the presence of slavery in the South), more northerners would be elected president. Could these two problems be solved, wondered Williamson, by having voters choose multiple candidates, only one of whom could be from their own state?[23]

Gerry opposed any form of popular election as "radically vicious" because "of the ignorance of the people." He feared that a self-interested group that pervaded the whole Union would rig the election in favor of their candidate. As an example of such a group, he cited the Society of the Cincinnati, a fraternal and charitable organization of Continental Army officers that had become controversial because its membership passed by heredity to the oldest son of each officer. Dickinson, in contrast, "leaned towards an election by the people which he regarded as the best & purest source." He suggested letting the people of each state nominate a favorite son, out of whom congress would choose the president. On July 26, Mason reviewed the many ways of electing a president the convention had considered and the objections to them. He concluded that the original plan of having the president chosen by congress for one term had the fewest liabilities. The convention approved Mason's suggestion by a 7–3 vote.[24]

As agreed upon thus far, the executive, elected by congress for one, seven-year term, would execute the laws and exercise a limited veto. He would be impeachable for "malpractice or neglect of duty." The Committee of Detail's draft constitution, presented to the convention on August 6, fleshed out this bare-bones executive. "The President of the United States of America" would have as his title "His Excellency," the same title that had been used to address George Washington as commander in chief of the Continental Army during the Revolutionary War. The draft constitution included a presidential oath of office and called for periodic state of the union addresses. The president could be impeached for "treason, bribery, or corruption," not merely for maladministration as specified in the revised Virginia Plan. Still a fairly weak office, the executive possessed few enumerated powers. The senate alone would appoint ambassadors and justices and make treaties.[25]

The presidency did not come up again for nearly a month, as the convention busily debated the parameters of the legislative branch as outlined in the Committee of Detail Report. On August 20, Gouverneur Morris and Charles Pinckney suggested the creation of a "council of State" to oversee the president. This proposed council would include secretaries of Domestic Affairs, Commerce and Finance, Foreign Affairs, War, and the Marine, all to be appointed by the president. Rounding out this council would be a secretary of state (to prepare public messages) and the chief justice of the supreme court (to recommend updates to the laws). The convention referred the Morris-Pinckney cabinet plan to the Committee of Detail.[26]

Two days later, the committee recommended that the convention create a "privy council" to provide non-binding advice to the president. As a board whose duties were strictly advisory, this body would be very different from the executive councils created by various state constitutions, whose recommendations bound the state governors. The privy council would consist of the chief justice, the president of the senate, the speaker of the house, and the heads of the executive departments. The committee also recommended requiring that the president be at least thirty-five years old, a U.S. citizen, and an inhabitant of the nation for at least twenty-one years.[27]

On August 24, the convention debated *how* congress would elect the president. Rutledge moved that it should elect the president by a joint ballot of both houses rather than by a separate ballot in each house. Gorham liked the idea because it would prevent the two houses from clashing if each selected a different president. Sherman worried that election of the president by joint ballot would rob the states of a check on the lower house that the senate was supposed to provide. This method would deprive the states (who elected the senate) of much say in the outcome because the upper chamber, with only twenty-six seats, would cast fewer than 30 percent of the votes for president, while the lower, with sixty-five seats, would cast more than 70 percent of the votes. Dayton agreed that "a *joint* ballot would in fact give the appointment to one House."

When Wilson and Madison answered that the more populous states should have a greater say in electing the president, their argument sounded eerily similar to the one they had vainly made in opposition to the Great Compromise over representation in congress. The convention nevertheless approved the election of the president by a joint ballot of congress by a 7–4 vote, with the large states voting yes and four small states (Connecticut, New Jersey, Maryland, and Georgia) voting no.

Gouverneur Morris once again argued against allowing congress to elect the president. This mode would make the executive too dependent on the legislature, and it would limit him to one term. A much better system, Morris suggested, would be a president "chosen by Electors to be chosen by the People of the several States." Morris's motion lost, but only by a narrow 6–5 vote. Perhaps surprisingly, considering that popular election would favor the largest states, three small states (Connecticut, New Jersey, and Delaware) voted for the proposal and Massachusetts voted against it. The delegates, it seems, were more befuddled over the presidency than ever. But the electoral college concept had gained support dramatically. The presidency did not come up again until it was referred to the Committee on Postponed Parts in the convention's final days.[28]

Of the three branches of the federal government, the convention spent the least amount of time on the judicial branch. This statement is especially true of the debate over the draft constitution prepared by the Committee of Detail. One reason for the relatively brief amount of time spent on the judiciary is that it was seen as the least dangerous of the three branches. Even though the Constitution allows federal judges to sit during good behavior, the delegates rarely voiced fears of judicial domination of the government. Aside from judicial jurisdiction, moreover, the powers of that branch did not need to be enumerated the way those of the legislative and executive branches had to be.

To the Virginia Plan's call for "a National Judiciary," the committee of the whole in June added the words "to consist of One supreme tribunal, and of one or more inferior tribunals." Probably to protect the institution of slavery and to keep federal spending down, as well as to protect "the jurisdiction of the states," Rutledge questioned whether the national government needed lower courts. Madison, Wilson, and Dickinson successfully argued that there could be no independent judiciary without lower national courts distinct from the state courts. "The State and Genl. Tribunals will interfere" with one another, declared Wilson. "We want a National Judicial—let it be entire and originate from the Genl. Govt."[29]

Resolution 9 of the Virginia Plan provided for a judicial branch appointed by congress. Wilson preferred that the president appoint judges. Franklin made a humorous pitch for the Scottish mode of choosing judges, "in which the nomination proceeded from the Lawyers, who always selected the ablest of the profession in order to get rid of him, and share his practice among themselves." Madison argued for appointment by the upper house, which was "numerous eno' to be confided in" and "sufficiently stable and independent to follow their deliberate judgements." With such an array of opinions, the delegates postponed the decision until June 13, when they quickly agreed that the upper house would make supreme court appointments.[30]

When the convention revisited the appointment of the judicial branch on July 18, Gorham suggested borrowing the Massachusetts model, where the executive nominated judges and the upper house confirmed them. Luther Martin, Sherman, and Bedford argued that the senate would be better equipped to choose qualified judges from throughout the Union. Perhaps not surprisingly, these small-state delegates wanted the power to appoint judges to remain with the chamber where the small states had the most influence. It is also true that Gorham and Madison, both large-state delegates who had fought against the Great Compromise because it introduced state influence into the senate, now favored allowing the president to select judges. Once the upper house became confederal, the large-state delegates were less inclined to empower it. The convention upheld the appointment of justices by the senate, but in the convention's closing days it decided that the president would appoint and the senate would merely confirm them.[31]

According to the revised Virginia Plan, the judiciary's jurisdiction included national laws and national issues. The Committee of Detail's draft constitution further specified that the Supreme Court would try impeachments and would have original jurisdiction in cases arising on the high seas and in cases between different states or citizens of different states.[32]

The Virginia Plan called for an executive-judicial "Council of revision" that would have the power to veto bills passed by congress. Madison included a council of revision (borrowed from New York's 1777 state constitution) in the Virginia Plan because he feared that individually, neither the executive nor the judiciary could stand up to a legislature backed by a popular majority. He predicted that a republican, elected executive, lacking the power and prestige of a European monarch, would be afraid by himself to exercise a veto power against a congressional majority. The judiciary might also be too weak by itself to exercise judicial review against a law already on the books. Only by being allied in a council of revision could the executive and judicial branches keep the national legislature in check.[33]

On June 4, Gerry suggested that it would be improper for the judicial branch to share in the executive's veto power, because he envisioned that branch possessing the power to strike down laws through judicial review. He moved instead that the president alone should have a veto that could be overridden by two-thirds of each legislative house (a provision contained in Massachusetts's 1780 constitution). Wilson and Hamilton argued that for the executive to maintain its independence, it should have an absolute veto that could not be overridden by the legislature at all.

Franklin warned that if the veto power were absolute, the president could extort whatever he wanted from congress. "More power and money would be demanded, till at last eno' would be gotten to influence & bribe the Legislature into a compleat subjection to the . . . Executive." Mason agreed with Franklin that a single executive with an absolute veto was too powerful. He inquired whether "gentlemen mean to pave the way to hereditary Monarchy? Do they flatter themselves that the people will ever consent to such an innovation? If they do I venture to tell them, they are mistaken." The convention then approved by an 8–2 vote Gerry's resolution giving the executive alone the power to veto laws subject to be overridden by a two-thirds vote of each house of congress.[34]

On June 6, Wilson and Madison moved to resurrect the executive-judicial council of revision. Gerry, King, and Dickinson thought a council would interfere with the independence of the president and the separation of powers, while Pinckney believed the president could rely on his department heads for advice in exercising veto power. The council of revision was again defeated, eight states to three.[35]

On July 21, Wilson and Madison renewed their proposal for an executive-judicial council of revision. Madison again argued that neither the executive nor the judicial branch alone could resist a national legislative majority determined to enact a bad law. Only by combining those two branches could congress be held in check. "Experience in all the States had evinced a powerful tendency in the Legislature to absorb all power into its vortex," Madison warned. "This was the real source of danger to the American Constitutions; & suggested the necessity of giving every defensive authority to the other departments that was consistent with republican principles." A council of revision would also aid the legislature by lending "a consistency, conciseness, perspicuity & technical propriety"

Elbridge Gerry of Massachusetts chaired the Grand Committee of Eleven that proposed the Great Compromise. He later refused to sign the completed Constitution because he thought the federal government had been given too much power, especially to create a permanent military establishment. (Library of Congress)

to laws. Finally, the council would stop unjust bills before they became law. Judicial review, in contrast, at best provided a remedy only after unwise legislation had done damage.[36]

In support of a council of revision, Gouverneur Morris agreed that the president would be too weak vis-à-vis congress unilaterally to veto laws. Morris even worried that the president and supreme court together still might not be a match for the legislature. Mason emphasized that the council would stop the same sorts of "unjust and pernicious laws" that had so often been enacted in the states from being passed by congress. Wilson added "that the joint weight of the two departments was necessary to balance the single weight of the Legislature."[37]

Luther Martin, in contrast, preferred that the judiciary strike down bad laws through judicial review. Gerry opposed the council as "combining & mixing together" the branches of the government that must always remain separate and distinct. "No maxim was better established," agreed Caleb Strong, than that judges must expound the laws, not make them. Charles Pinckney, Dickinson, and Mercer iterated that judges, "as expositors of the Constitution," should not interfere with preparing legislation.

Madison answered that the council of revision would promote rather than undermine the separation of powers. He merely "proposed to add a defensive power to each [branch] which should maintain the Theory in practice" that "each department ought to be separate & distinct." Besides, a council of revision violated the separation of powers no more than a presidential veto. Gouverneur Morris expressed surprise "that any defensive provision for securing the effectual separation of the departments should be considered as an improper mixture of them." The convention defeated the council of revision once again in a close 4–3 vote. This decision left a qualified veto in the hands of the executive. But did it also leave the judicial branch with the power to strike down federal law through judicial review? Most delegates probably thought so, but judicial review was not written into the constitution. Chief Justice John Marshall exercised this power in the 1803 case of *Marbury vs. Madison*. Madison later worried that judicial review of federal law gave the Supreme Court an unchecked power over the legislative branch, upsetting the balance of power between them.[38]

One more time before the convention ended, on August 15, Madison sought an executive-judicial council of revision. To soften the measure a bit, he moved to allow a supermajority of congress to override a veto instead of giving the council an absolute veto. In support of Madison, Wilson placed the discussion into a larger context. In monarchies, he explained, executive tyranny of the minority needed to be guarded against. But in republics, legislative tyranny by the majority needed to be guarded against. Therefore, Wilson reasoned, the executive and judicial departments needed greater "self-defensive power" against the legislative branch. The convention once and for all rejected the council of revision so dear to Madison but did strengthen the executive vis-à-vis congress by requiring a three-fourths majority to override a veto instead of a two-thirds majority. Toward the end of the convention, the delegates reverted to the two-thirds fraction to reverse a veto.[39]

In debating an executive-judicial council to review laws passed by congress—as with Madison's call for a congressional veto of state laws—the delegates grappled with broad issues of the federal-state balance of power, and of the separation of powers among the branches of government. Men who had since 1776 viewed states as supreme now contemplated how to achieve a federal-state balance of power. Similarly, men who for a decade had favored legislative supremacy now faced the need to establish co-equal branches. The convention, after going in circles examining and adopting countless alternative concepts, achieved a true revolution in government by checking and balancing the branches and levels of government.

On August 27, Dickinson moved to allow judges to be removed by address—a procedure in which the legislature (usually by a supermajority) requests the dismissal of a judge if the executive authority chooses to do so. Such a system existed in England and in several state constitutions. Gerry and Sherman, suspicious that judicial appointments during good behavior amount to tyrannical power, supported the motion. Morris and Randolph opposed the motion because it would rob the judiciary of its independence. Wilson added that "the judges would be in a bad situation if made to depend on any gust of faction which might prevail in the two branches of our Govt." The convention stuck with tenure during good behavior for federal judges.[40]

Having worked their way through the legislative, executive, and judicial branches in the Committee of Detail's draft constitution, the delegates turned their attention to the draft's remaining provisions. They agreed that congress would admit new states to the Union on equal footing with the existing states, and that no new state would be carved out of an existing state without that state's consent. Here the delegates anticipated the admission of Vermont, an independent republic that New York claimed fell under its jurisdiction. The convention also granted congress jurisdiction over the territories but at the same time did not overturn any state's western land claims.[41]

The convention had determined that specially elected conventions in each state would consider ratifying the proposed constitution. When the delegates took up the number of states that needed to approve the constitution, suggestions ranged from seven states (a majority) to all thirteen.

Carroll and Gerry maintained that all thirteen states had to agree to terminate the Confederation. But that would allow a bare majority of a single small state, such as Rhode Island, representing less than 2 percent of the American people, to reject a constitution that everyone else favored. Madison contended that since the people of the states ("the fountain of all power"), not the state legislatures, would decide ratification, the Articles' unanimity requirement did not apply. Randolph advocated nine states to put the constitution into effect because that was the supermajority required to pass treaties and decide matters of war and peace under the Articles. Madison suggested that majorities of both states and people should be required. Gouverneur Morris favored some sort of sliding scale: if contiguous states ratified, it would necessitate the approvals of fewer states than if non-contiguous states ratified.

Allowing non-unanimous ratification raised the question of the status of non-ratifying states. Would they remain part of the Union? After the delegates agreed that the constitution would operate only on the states that ratified it, Gouverneur Morris moved to allow each state to decide for itself how it made the ratification decision. This motion led to a rehashing of all the arguments for ratification by conventions instead of by the state legislatures: First, the legislatures would not want to surrender power to a strong federal government. Second, the legislatures (except for Pennsylvania and Georgia) had two houses both of which would have to approve. Third, leading spokesmen for ratification who did not sit in a state legislature could get elected to a state convention. And fourth, the constitution, as the supreme law of the land, had to receive its authorization from the sovereign people. The delegates settled on a supermajority of nine states to achieve ratification, a requirement making it likely that a majority of people would support the Constitution.

What role would the existing Confederation Congress play in ratification? The draft constitution required the approbation of Congress as part of the ratification process. The delegates struck out this requirement but left in place the clause that the constitution would be "laid before" that body. Amid this debate, Mason, whose anger had been smoldering since his double loss in the slave trade-commercial laws debate, now erupted. He announced he "would sooner chop off his right hand than put it to the Constitution as it now stands." Unless changes were made to the document he would advocate for a second constitutional convention to make them. Randolph, whose dismay had also grown, suggested that the state ratification conventions should recommend amendments to be considered by another constitutional convention.[42]

On the last day of August, Sherman moved "to refer such parts of the Constitution as have been postponed, and such parts of Reports as have not been acted on, to a Committee of a member from each State." Despite featuring luminaries including Madison, Sherman, Dickinson, and Gouverneur Morris, the Committee on Postponed Parts was chaired by a forgotten New Jerseyian named David Brearly, chief justice of the state supreme court. It is unclear why the reticent Brearly, a forty-two-year-old former Continental Army officer, led the committee. Briefly a student at the College of New Jersey in Princeton, Brearly helped frame New Jersey's constitution. "Mr. Brearly is a Man of good, rather than brilliant parts," wrote Pierce. "As an Orator he has little to boast of, but as a Man he has every virtue to recommend him." Whatever Brearly lacked in brilliance, he clearly made up for in the respect of his fellow delegates.[43]

To congress's taxation power the Committee on Postponed Parts added the words "provide for the common defense & general welfare" of the United States. This general welfare clause, which, like the necessary and proper clause, would dramatically expand congress's implied powers, won the convention's approval without controversy, presumably because the Articles of Confederation used the same language. Madison later insisted that the convention intended the general welfare clause merely to facilitate the implementation of Congress's enumerated powers.[44]

The committee neared the end of its work without proposing any dramatic revisions in the mode of electing the president, who would still be chosen by congress for one seven-year term. John Dickinson, who had missed the committee's previous sessions because of illness, joined his committee colleagues one afternoon in September just as they rose to adjourn for the day. Dickinson declared that the American people would be unwilling to grant the president powers "so many and so great . . . unless they themselves would be more immediately concerned in his Election." So substantial would public opposition be to an energetic executive elected by congress, Dickinson continued, that it might cause the rejection of the entire constitution. "The only true and safe Principle on which these powers could be committed to an Individual," Dickinson insisted, "was—that he should be . . . *the Man of the People*." Upon hearing Dickinson's views, Gouvernuer Morris, who himself had advocated a powerful, popularly elected president, insisted, "Come, Gentlemen, let us sit down again, and converse further on this subject." After further deliberation, according to Dickinson, "James Maddison took a Pen and Paper, and sketched out a Mode for Electing the President." The committee accepted Madison's electoral procedure.[45]

On September 4, Brearly delivered the committee's report proposing sweeping changes to the presidency. For almost the entire summer, the plan had been for the president to be elected by congress to serve one, seven-year term. Now, in September, nearing the completion of its work, the convention received the committee's entirely new proposal for the executive branch. Brearly proposed that the president be elected by the people through an electoral college. With a four-year term, the president could be reelected. Each state would have as many electors as it had representatives and senators in congress. Each elector would cast two votes for president, one of which had to be for someone outside the state. Whoever received the greatest number of electoral votes, provided he had a majority, would be president. In the event of a tie, the senate would choose the victor. If no one received a majority, that body would elect the president from the top five vote getters. Whoever came in second would be vice president. The vice president would preside over the senate but would only vote to break ties.[46]

The committee report would allow the state legislatures to decide how the electors would be chosen. This method by no means guaranteed that the people would directly choose the electors. Nothing prevented the state legislatures themselves from choosing the electors. Years later, however, Rufus King claimed that the committee's intent was that "State Legislatures may by law designate those who may appoint the Electors altho' they themselves may not appoint them."[47]

The committee recommended that the president had to be at least thirty-five years old, a natural born citizen (or a citizen at the time of the adoption of the constitution), and a resident of the U.S. for fourteen years. Another significant change called for the executive to appointment ambassadors and supreme court justices "with the advice and Consent of the Senate." That body would also provide "advice and consent" to the president on foreign policy, with a two-thirds majority required to approve treaties. Previously (according to the Committee of Detail's draft constitution), the senate alone appointed ambassadors and supreme court justices and made treaties. The president would not have a council but could request advice in writing from the heads of the executive departments on matters within their purview. He could be removed from office if impeached by the house and convicted by the senate.[48]

Sherman explained that the committee made the changes to "render the Executive independent of the Legislature." A single long term had originally been given to the president to mitigate his dependence on the legislature. A popularly elected president, freed from his obligations to congress, could have a shorter term and be reelectable. Gouverneur Morris maintained that the electoral college avoided "the danger of intrigue & faction." Members of congress might collude with a presidential candidate, trading election for the spoils of office. But with relatively obscure electors meeting simultaneously in the several states, "the great evil of cabal was avoided. It would be impossible also to corrupt them." Finally, with popular election of the president, the power of impeachment and conviction could then be lodged in a congress that had not previously passed judgment on the president.

The committee having made its report, the floor opened for debate. A consensus emerged that the electoral system would eliminate potential corruption and establish the president's independence from congress. Several delegates expressed concern, however, that the absence of nationally known statesmen might continually lead to the senate's choosing the president out of the top candidates from the large states. And that meant that the upper house would both pick the president and then decide his fate in an impeachment trial. But Baldwin believed that "the increasing intercourse among the people of the States, would render important characters less & less unknown." Wilson likewise felt confident that within a short period, "Continental Characters will multiply as we more & more coalesce." He suggested, however, that the entire congress pick the president out of fewer than the five top vote getters.[49]

Several delegates again voiced concern that the senate would probably choose the president, making that body too powerful. Charles Pinckney warned that the executive would become "the mere creature of that body." Wilson agreed that "the President will not be the man of the people as he ought to be, but the Minion of the Senate." Members of the upper house would then "depress the other branch of the Legislature, and aggrandize themselves in proportion." Mason, Randolph, and even Hamilton painted a slightly different scenario. Pointing to the powers over appointments and foreign policy to be exercised jointly by the president and the senate, Mason predicted that the two would join forces to take over the government and create an aristocracy. To avoid having the upper chamber pick the president, Mason urged, just have the candidate with the most votes become president, majority or not. Advocating the same solution, Hamilton warned of "a mutual connection & influence, that will perpetuate the President, and aggrandize both him and the Senate."

Gouverneur Morris tried to allay fears that elections would end up in the hands of the senate. If each elector cast two votes for candidates in different states, the top vote getter would likely receive a majority of electoral votes. Taking a different tack, King argued that it made sense to have the large states narrow down the field of candidates in the electoral college, and then to allow the senate, where the small states had the edge, to choose the victor. Several delegates offered solutions to mitigate the senate's influence over elections in which no candidate received a majority of electoral votes. Wilson wanted the whole congress to pick the president. Gerry favored having a congressional committee chosen by lot to pick the president. Sherman advocated having congress pick the president, but that it should do so voting by state. That way, the more numerous small states would choose the president after the large states had narrowed the field in the electoral college.

The convention voted on the Brearly recommendations. It approved a four-year term, the use of electors, to require a majority of electoral votes to elect a president, and that if no one received a majority of votes, the senate would choose the victor from among the top five vote getters. Sherman modified his earlier suggestion: instead of having the entire congress, voting by state, choose the president when no one received a majority of electoral votes, have the house of representatives make the choice, voting by state. Mason supported this idea because it would weaken "the aristocratic influence of the Senate." The delegates approved this proposal and added an additional provision requiring all states to hold their presidential elections on the same day. Madison later explained that having the house elect the president voting by state in the absence of an electoral majority was "an accommodation to the anxiety of the smaller States for their sovereign equality, and to the jealousy of the larger towards the cumulative functions of the Senate." Election by the lower chamber "was thought safer also than that of the Senate, on account of the greater number of its members."[50]

The Brearly committee called for the person with the second-highest number of electoral votes to become the vice president. If there was a tie for second, the senate would choose the vice president. This position would ensure stable succession in case the chief executive died in office. The vice president would preside over the senate but would only cast a vote to break a tie. Gerry, Randolph, and Mason complained that this arrangement would give the executive branch too much influence over the upper house, and it would blend the executive and senate too much. Gouverneur Morris answered that without this duty, the vice president would have nothing to do! If that was the case, rejoined Williamson, then the vice presidency should be eliminated.[51]

Wilson wished to strike out the upper house's role in confirming nominations, leaving the appointment power entirely to the president, subject to confirmation by an executive council. Unmoved, the delegates approved senate confirmation of presidential appointments. Wilson also condemned requiring two-thirds of the senate to ratify treaties negotiated by the president. A supermajority threshold, he argued, would allow one-third of that body, potentially representing a tiny minority of the population, to block treaties. Madison and Morris wanted to retain the two-thirds requirement, except for peace treaties, which should only require a bare majority. Sherman thought that the entire legislature should approve treaties because of the high stakes involved. The delegates left the two-thirds of the senate requirement in place for all treaties.[52]

When the delegates discussed the clause enabling the president to seek written advice from the heads of the executive departments, Mason strenuously argued instead that the constitution needed to create an advisory council. He envisioned this body consisting of six members, two of whom would come from the northern states, two from the middle states, and two from the southern states. Mason hoped this distribution would restore the protection for the South that he believed disappeared when the convention failed to require a supermajority in congress to pass commercial laws.

He warned "that, in rejecting a Council to the President we were about to try an experiment on which the most despotic Governments had never ventured." Franklin, who as the president of Pennsylvania's Supreme Executive Council acted with the guidance of such a group, concurred that "a Council would not only be a check on a bad President but be a relief to a good one." Gouverneur Morris dismissed a council as accomplishing nothing more than providing a scapegoat for the president's bad decisions. The convention rejected Mason's proposed council despite the support of Wilson and Dickinson.[53]

Mason also wished to expand the circumstances under which the president could be impeached from "Treason & bribery" to include "maladministration." Otherwise "many great and dangerous offenses" will not be protected against. Madison judged the term "maladministration" to be so indeterminate that it would allow the house to impeach and the senate to convict a president almost at will. Morris answered Mason that impeachment was not the solution for misgovernance. Instead, the people would address that issue on election day. "An election . . . every four years will prevent maladministration," he declared. Mason then substituted the words "high crimes & misdemesnors," which the convention approved. The convention thus forged a majority on the standard for impeachment, but at the expense of clarity. What, exactly, did "high crimes and misdemesnors" mean? It presumably meant different things to different delegates, as it has to Americans ever since.[54]

A brief discussion ensued as to whether the senate or the supreme court should try impeachments. Each alternative had its drawbacks. A senate trial might make the president dependent on that body, while supreme court justices might refuse to convict the man who appointed them to office. Judging the former the lesser of the two evils, the delegates left impeachment trials in the upper chamber, but required the votes of two-thirds of the senators to convict.[55]

Years later, Charles Pinckney complained about the dramatic changes to the presidency that took place early in September. "The great power given to the President was never intended to have been given to him while the Convention continued in that patient & coolly deliberative situation in which they had been for nearly the whole of the preceding five months of their session," he observed. "Nor was it until within the last week or ten days that almost the whole of the Executive Department was altered." Madison conceded that "the final arrangement" of the presidency "was not exempt from a degree of the hurrying influence produced by fatigue and impatience in all such Bodies."[56]

In designing a strong, independent executive branch, the convention went against the grain of the American Revolution, which had overthrown a strong, independent executive, the king of Great Britain. The delegates overcame their fears of executive tyranny partly because they had experienced poor government without an effective executive, and partly because they anticipated that Washington would be the first president. They knew from experience that Washington would use his power carefully and then voluntarily return it to the people. Pierce Butler of South Carolina insisted that the convention invested the president with immense power because "many of the members cast their eyes towards General Washington as President; and shaped their Ideas of the Powers to be given to a President, by their opinions of his Virtue." The convention, in short, designed the presidency with Washington in mind. Remarkably, he shaped the executive office without joining the debate on the Assembly Room floor.[57]

The Committee of Detail's draft constitution provided only one procedure for amendments. Two-thirds of the state legislatures could request a constitutional convention. Hamilton wanted to add an easier way to make alterations, one that could be initiated by congress. Madison suggested also allowing two-thirds of congress to propose amendments. Three-fourths of the states would be required to ratify those proposals. Despite the high threshold for an amendment to pass, this idea made Rutledge erupt. "He never could agree to give a power by which the articles relating to slaves might be altered by the States not interested in that property and prejudiced against it." He then demanded "that no amendments which may be made prior to the year 1808, shall in any manner" end the African slave trade. In approving Madison's amendment procedure, the convention also agreed to insert Rutledge's protection of the foreign slave trade. At Mason's insistence, the delegates added language requiring congress to call a convention at the request of two-thirds of the states rather than to leave it up to legislative discretion. Mason reasoned that congress itself would never propose an amendment limiting its own power; that kind of an amendment could only be proposed by a constitutional convention.[58]

On September 8, the convention appointed a Committee of Style to "arrange the articles agreed to" into a final draft of the constitution. The delegates named were Johnson, Hamilton, Gouverneur Morris, Madison, and King. Hamilton's inclusion is a curious choice, given his self-avowed proclivity for monarchy and his spotty attendance that summer. Those liabilities were offset by Hamilton's undisputed brilliance and by his prodigious capacity for hard work. Perhaps the absolute need to keep him in town to sign the completed constitution played a role in his selection as well, since he was the lone New York delegate in Philadelphia. Antinationalists Yates and Lansing had both decamped in early July. Writing from New York on August 20, Hamilton instructed Rufus King, "Let me know when your *conclusion* is at hand; for I would choose to be present at that time." He had resumed his seat on September 6.[59]

On September 10, Gerry raised the ratification issue again. He argued that to send the finished constitution to the Confederation Congress without requiring its approval would both insult that body and would terminate the existing government with insufficient "scruple or formality." Gerry added that if nine of thirteen states could throw out the Articles so easily, then six of nine states could throw out the new constitution just as easily. Wilson answered that it would be foolhardy, "After spending four or five months in the laborious & arduous task of forming a Government for our Country," to place "insuperable obstacles in the way of its success" by requiring congressional approval. Realizing that to seek congressional endorsement might result in a protracted debate over the proposed constitution, the delegates wisely decided not to require it. The convention then instructed the Committee of Style to prepare an explanatory cover letter to accompany the completed constitution when sent to the Confederation Congress.[60]

On September 12, Johnson presented the final draft of the constitution prepared by the Committee of Style. Written by Gouverneur Morris, the document opened with a revised preamble. Instead of beginning, "We, the people of the States of" and then listing each state by name, the preamble begins, "We the people of the United States." Morris made this edit because he did not know which states would ratify and which would not, and because he wanted to emphasize that the constitution would not establish a confederation of states.

Morris reorganized and condensed the Committee of Detail's twenty-three articles down to seven. Articles I, II, and III provide the framework for the legislative, executive, and judicial branches, respectively. Article IV prescribes the relationship of the states to one another and to the federal government. Article V lays out the procedure for amendments. Article VI contains the Supremacy Clause, and Article VII describes the procedure for ratification. In preparing the final draft, Morris "rejected redundant and equivocal terms," seeking "to be as clear as our language would permit." Madison later declared that "a better choice" of draftsman than Morris "could not have been made." Although the details of the document had already been fixed, "there was sufficient room for the talents and taste stamped by the author on the face of it."[61]

Morris also drafted a cover letter to accompany the Constitution when sent to the Confederation Congress. This beautifully crafted document, signed by George Washington, explained that vesting appropriate authority in the "general government," including the power to make war and peace, to collect revenue, and to regulate commerce, necessitated a new political structure that divided power among co-equal branches. In accommodating the good of the whole, moreover, some state interests inevitably had to be sacrificed. Just as "individuals entering into society must give up a share of liberty to preserve the rest," so too must the states in order to achieve a national Union. Accordingly "the Constitution, which we now present, is the result of a spirit of amity, and of that mutual deference and concession which the peculiarity of our political situation rendered indispensable." That the constitution "is liable to as few exceptions as could reasonably have been expected, we hope and believe," concluded the letter. "That it may promote the lasting welfare of that country so dear to us all, and secure her freedom and happiness, is our most ardent wish." Carroll called for the drafting of an address to the American people to accompany the release of the proposed constitution. The convention thought it more diplomatic to address itself strictly to the Confederation Congress.

The cover letter asserted that the nation's existence depended on "the consolidation of our union." Although the word *consolidation* did not cause controversy at the convention, it quickly took on a pernicious connotation, suggesting that all political power would consolidate first in the federal government at the expense of the states, and eventually in the executive branch, at the expense of the other branches, resulting in tyranny. The convention ordered that copies of the Committee of Style's draft constitution and cover letter be printed for the delegates' perusal. Once again, Dunlap and Claypoole of the *Pennsylvania Packet* secretly prepared the required copies, as they had done with the Committee of Detail's draft constitution in early August.[62]

With one more round of edits, the constitution would be complete. Williamson successfully moved to lower the threshold to overturn a presidential veto from three-fourths of Congress to two-thirds, because the former number allowed the president and a tiny minority of Congress to thwart the popular will. Sherman, Gerry, Mason, and Charles Pinckney all agreed. Gouverneur Morris, Hamilton, and Madison argued in vain to keep the threshold to override a veto at three-fourths because they thought a lower fraction would not check misguided popular passions.[63]

On September 12, Mason urged that a full bill of rights be added to the constitution. "It would give great quiet to the people," he pleaded, "and with the aid of the State declarations, a bill might be prepared in a few hours." Sherman responded that the bill of rights in the state constitutions were "sufficient." Mason correctly answered that "the Laws of the U.S. are to be paramount to the State Bill of Rights." The state constitutions, moreover, only protected against state laws. A more compelling reason against a federal bill of rights, which none of the delegates made, was that unlike the state constitutions, which awarded blanket grants of power, the federal constitution enumerated the powers of congress. Since congress could only exercise powers listed, no federal bill of rights was necessary. The convention, presumably over-eager to wrap up its work, rejected Mason's call for a bill of rights by a whopping 10–0–1 margin with little debate. This hasty decision turned out to be a big mistake that almost led to the failure to obtain ratification. Two days later, Pinckney and Gerry tried but failed to insert the clause "that the liberty of the Press should be inviolably observed." Once again Sherman objected to the proposal. On firmer ground this time, he observed that "the power of Congress does not extend to the Press."[64]

Franklin moved to add to congress's enumerated powers the authority to build canals. Madison suggested enlarging this grant beyond canals to include all internal improvement projects. The motion failed, probably because some delegates thought congress already possessed the power by implication, while others feared making the federal government too strong vis-à-vis the states. The lack of this enumerated power would cause President Madison to veto a major internal improvements bill in 1816 on constitutional grounds. The delegates also rejected an enumerated power to build a national university.[65]

A handful of motions to give additional representatives in congress to North Carolina, Rhode Island, and Delaware failed. Granting additional congressmen to individual states, the delegates feared, would open a can of worms. The convention approved a variety of restrictions forbidding the states from collecting import duties, making treaties with other states or with foreign nations, or unilaterally going to war unless attacked. Sherman, on behalf of the small states, secured the addition of the words, "No state, without its consent, shall be deprived of its equal suffrage in the Senate."[66]

In mid-September, Randolph's smoldering discontent with the constitution burst into flames. The Virginia governor had originally presented the Virginia Plan to the convention in May and had also prepared the first draft of the Committee of Detail report in late July. But he had become disillusioned with the changes made to it. His "Republican propositions had . . . much to his regret, been widely, and, in his opinion, irreconcileably departed from." Randolph itemized his objections: the federal government in general and the president and senate in particular were too powerful, the house of representatives was too small, and the South was victimized by the lack of a supermajority requirement for commercial laws. "In this state of things it was his idea . . . that the State Conventions shd. be at liberty to offer amendments to the plan; and that these should be submitted to a second General Convention, with full power to settle the Constitution finally." Were this suggestion rejected, Randolph warned, it would "be impossible for him to put his name to the instrument."[67]

Mason, too, announced that he could not sign the constitution without provision for a second convention. As the document now stood, Mason complained, both its "power and structure" made it incompatible with liberty. As a result, "it would end either in monarchy, or a tyrannical aristocracy." Consequently, "he could neither give it his support or vote in Virginia; and he could not sign here what he could not support there." A third delegate, Blount, also announced that he opposed the constitution, but Madison did not record his reasons.[68]

Gerry, too, demanded another convention. He objected to what he regarded as the excessive powers of congress, especially the necessary and proper clause, and the power to "raise armies and money without limit," which he believed would "lay the foundation of a civil War." Gerry, who as early as August 21 had privately expressed his inclination to oppose the constitution, nevertheless soldiered on in Philadelphia so that he would not be blamed if the constitution failed. "I would not remain here two hours," he privately explained, "was I not under a necessity of staying to prevent my colleagues from saying that I broke up the representation."[69]

Charles Pinckney rejected the second convention idea as a formula for chaos. "Nothing but confusion & contrariety could spring from the experiment," he warned. "The States will never agree in their plans, and the Deputies to a second Convention coming together under the discordant impressions of their Constituents, will never agree. Conventions are serious things, and ought not to be repeated." If their experience that summer taught the delegates anything, it was that the chances of a second convention successfully rewriting the constitution were next to none. After rejecting a second convention, the delegates on Saturday, September 15, approved the final constitution and ordered the preparation of an engrossed version to be signed the following Monday. Having spent a record-tying seven hours in the Assembly Room, the delegates walked home from that penultimate session wondering what could be done to get the four holdouts to change their minds.[70]

Over the weekend, several delegates devised a strategy to unite the forty-one of them still in Philadelphia: an impassioned speech from a high-profile delegate imploring the would-be nonsigners to reverse course. Gouverneur Morris suggested the speech call for a final edit announcing that the states present unanimously approved the document. This language would enable those who personally opposed the constitution nevertheless to sign because their signatures attested not to their personal support, but to their state's support. Franklin agreed to prepare the address.[71]

On Monday morning, September 17, the convention listened to a reading of the four-page engrossed parchment copy of the constitution, which had been meticulously prepared by Jacob Shallus, the assistant clerk of the Pennsylvania Assembly. Immediately afterward, Franklin rose to speak and then handed his speech to Wilson to read. After admitting that the constitution included many things that he did not like, Franklin recounted an anecdote about "a certain french lady, who in a dispute with her sister, said 'I don't know how it happens, Sister but I meet with no body but myself, that's always in the right.'" Rather than to be guilty of that conceit, Franklin would "agree to this Constitution with all its faults, if they are such" because he doubted "whether any other Convention . . . may be able to make a better Constitution." Given the different views of fifty-odd men, "can a perfect production be expected? It therefore astonishes me, Sir, to find this system approaching so near to perfection as it does." Franklin supported the constitution "because I expect no better, and because I am not sure, that it is not the best." He begged "that every member of the Convention who may still have objections to it, would with me, on this occasion doubt a little of his own infallibility, and to make manifest our unanimity, put his name to this instrument." Franklin concluded by moving that the signing be "done in Convention by the unanimous consent of *the States* present." Since every state delegation approved the constitution, every delegate could then sign in good faith, even if some of them remained personally opposed.[72]

Gouverneur Morris and Hamilton briefly echoed Franklin. The former would accept the Constitution "with all its faults." The latter declared that "no man's ideas were more remote from the plan than his were known to be," but rhetorically asked, "is it possible to deliberate between anarchy and Convulsion on one side, and the chance of good to be expected from the plan on the other?"[73]

Expressing relief, Blount asserted that he could now sign the document despite his lingering doubts about it. But he was the only holdout to change his mind. Randolph would not budge from his opposition. He remained convinced "that the holding out this plan with a final alternative to the people, of accepting or rejecting it in toto, would really produce the anarchy & civil convulsions which were apprehended from the refusal of individuals to sign it." Gerry announced that "the proposed form" of the signing "made no difference with him." Mason sat in sullen silence. He would not sign either.[74]

At the last minute, Gorham asked for one final alteration that he believed would win much public support. Instead of having "the number of Representatives . . . not exceed one for every forty thousand," Gorham moved to substitute 30,000, thereby reducing the size of congressional districts. For only the second time all summer, and the first time since the convention began on May 25, Washington stood to speak. Overcoming the silence that he had imposed on himself as the presiding officer, Washington announced that "the smallness of the proportion of Representatives . . . had always appeared to himself among the exceptionable parts of the plan." He therefore wished to see Gorham's suggestion approved. Given Washington's prestige and moral authority, none dared dissent from his lone request.[75]

The delegates instructed Secretary Jackson to deliver the constitution and the accompanying cover letter to the Confederation Congress in New York. The convention pondered whether its journal of motions and votes kept by Jackson should be destroyed, published, or held under wraps. It would be foolish to get rid of evidence that could refute falsehoods leveled by opponents of ratification. To publish it might give ammunition to those same opponents. The delegates thought best simply to hand the journal to Washington for safekeeping until the congress under the new constitution instructed him on what to do with it. In 1796, President Washington deposited the convention journal in the State Department. In 1818, Congress directed Secretary of State John Quincy Adams to publish it.[76]

As all the delegates except Mason, Randolph, and Gerry came forward to affix their names to the engrossed parchment, Franklin made a pronouncement befitting the closing scene. Pointing to the half sun carved on the backrest of the president's chair, he observed that artists found it difficult "to distinguish in their art a rising from a setting sun. I have said he, often and often in the course of the Session, and the vicissitudes of my hopes and fears as to its issue," contemplated that carving "without being able to tell whether it was rising or setting: But now at length I have the happiness to know, that it is a rising and not a setting Sun."[77]

Forty-one of the fifty-five delegates (75 percent) attended on September 17. Thirty-eight of them signed the constitution. Read of Delaware signed for his absent colleague, Dickinson (who had gone home because of illness), making thirty-nine signatures in total. The signature of Hamilton, the lone New Yorker present, gave the illusion that the state delegation supported the constitution. In fact, Hamilton's signature represented only himself, because a minimum of two delegates were required officially to represent the state. Thus, the Constitution's statement, "Done in convention by the unanimous consent of the states present," is only true of the eleven states officially represented that day and is not true of New York. As Washington put it in his diary, "The Constitution received the Unanimous assent of 11 States and Colo. Hamilton's from New York."[78]

Its business complete, the convention lifted the "Injunction of secrecy." Now free to discuss the debates and proceedings of the convention with outsiders, many delegates forwarded the Constitution to correspondents around the country. Others shared their first-hand knowledge of the convention during the state ratification conventions. But in one regard, the pledge of secrecy still held: the delegates refrained from publishing their convention notes. Not until after Congress in 1818 instructed John Quincy Adams to publish the convention journal did any of the delegates publish their notes. And Madison, the keeper of the most comprehensive notes, decided late in life to let "the publication be a posthumous one." In 1808, however, Edmond Charles Genet, George Clinton's son-in-law, published a doctored version of some of Yates's notes in an eight-page pamphlet. Genet hoped that the pamphlet would persuade the Republican congressional caucus to nominate Clinton for president instead of Madison.[79]

After removing the secrecy rules, according to the final line of Madison's Notes, "the Convention dissolved itself by an Adjournment sine die." "The business being thus closed," Washington wrote, "the Members adjourned to the City Tavern, dined together and took a cordial leave of each other." Returning to his room, Washington "retired to meditate on the momentous w[or]k which had been executed."[80]

Three days earlier, on the afternoon of September 14, with the convention's work all but completed, the Philadelphia City Light Horse militia—many of whom had crossed the Delaware River and fought in the Battle of Trenton with Washington in 1776—held a dinner in honor of their former commander in chief at the City Tavern. The fifty-five attendees, perhaps including many convention delegates, consumed generous quantities of alcohol, as the bill for the event attests:

To 55 Gentlemans Dinners & Fruit			
— Rellishes, Olives etc.	20	12	6
— 54 Bottles of Madera.	20	5	
— 60 of Claret ditto.	21		
— 8 ditto of Old Stock.	3	6	8
— 22 Bottles of Porter ditto.	2	15	
— 8 of Cyder ditto.	16		
— 12 ditto Beer.	12		
— 7 Large Bowels of Punch.	4	4	
— Segars Spermacity candles etc.	2	5	
To Decantors Wine Glass [e]s & Tumblers Broken etc.	1	2	6
To 16 Servants and Musicians Dinners.	2		
— 16 Bottles of Claret.	5	12	
— 5 ditto Madera.	1	17	6
— 7 Bouls of Punch.	2	16	
	£89	4	2

Some of the musicians, who bore German surnames such as Schultz and Spangenberg, appear to have come to America as Hessian mercenaries. After having been captured by Washington at Trenton, they accepted amnesty and settled in the Germantown section of Philadelphia. In an ironic reversal, these recent immigrants who had crossed the Atlantic to fight against Washington now found themselves playing their instruments in his honor at the close of the convention. The 89-pound bill amounts to over $15,000 in twenty-first-century dollars. Clearly, these men knew how to reward a job well done![81]

NOTES

1. Adrienne Koch, ed., *Notes of Debates in the Federal Convention of 1787 Reported by James Madison* (Athens: Ohio University Press, 1966), hereafter cited as *NDFC*, 578; Max Farrand, ed., *The Records of the Federal Convention of 1787*. 1937 rev. ed. in four vols., reprint (New Haven, CT: Yale University Press, 1974), hereafter cited as *RFC*, 3:458; William T. Hutchinson et al., eds., *The Papers of James Madison, Congressional Series*, 17 vols. (Chicago, IL, and Charlottesville: University of Chicago Press and University of Virginia Press, 1962–1991), hereafter cited as *PJM*, 10:208.

2. *RFC*, 3:169; *PJM*, 10:207–8.
3. *NDFC*, 45–46.
4. Ibid., 46.
5. Ibid., 47.
6. Ibid., 59–60.
7. Ibid, 55–57.
8. Ibid., 57–58.
9. Ibid., 48–49.
10. Ibid.
11. Ibid., 50–51; *RFC*, 1:91.
12. *NDFC*, 51–55.
13. Ibid., 93–94; *RFC*, 1:181.
14. *NDFC*, 306–8.
15. Ibid., 306–9.
16. Ibid., 307–9.
17. Ibid., 310–13.
18. Ibid., 322–31.
19. Ibid., 331–35.
20. Ibid., 344–46.
21. Ibid., 356–57.
22. Ibid., 358–62.
23. Ibid., 363–67.
24. Ibid., 368–72.
25. Ibid., 383, 392–93.
26. Ibid., 487.
27. Ibid., 509–10.
28. Ibid., 523–27.
29. Ibid., 32, 71–73; *RFC*, 1:95, 128.
30. *NDFC*, 67–68, 112–13.
31. Ibid., 314–17.
32. Ibid., 385–96.
33. Ibid., 32; *RFC*, 1:109.
34. *NDFC*, 61–64.
35. *NDFC*, 79–81.
36. Ibid., 336–38.
37. Ibid., 338–43.
38. Ibid., 338–43, 462–63; Christopher Collier and James Lincoln Collier, *Decision in Philadelphia: The Constitutional Convention of 1787* (New York: Ballantine Books, 1987), 270–71; James H. Hutson, ed., *Supplement to Max Farrand's*

The Records of the Federal Convention of 1787 (New Haven, CT: Yale University Press, 1987), hereafter cited as *RFC Supplement*, 297.

39. NDFC, 461–65.
40. Ibid., 536–37.
41. Ibid., 556–59.
42. Ibid., 561–67.
43. Ibid., 569; John P. Kaminski and Timothy D. Moore, eds., *An Assembly of Demigods: Word Portraits of the Delegates to the Constitutional Convention by Their Contemporaries* (Madison, WI: Parallel Press, 2012), hereafter cited as *Demigods*, 60, 238.
44. NDFC, 574; RFC, 3:485, 494.
45. *RFC Supplement*, 300–301.
46. NDFC, 573–76.
47. RFC, 3:460.
48. NDFC, 573–76.
49. Ibid., 576–78.
50. Ibid., 582–94; RFC, 3:458.
51. NDFC, 574, 596–97.
52. Ibid., 598–600, 602–4.
53. Ibid., 600–602.
54. Ibid., 605.
55. Ibid., 605–7.
56. RFC, 3:427, 458.
57. Ibid., 302.
58. NDFC, 609–11, 649.
59. Ibid., 608; RFC, 3:70.
60. NDFC, 611–15.
61. Ibid., 616–26; RFC, 3:420, 499.
62. NDFC, 626–27, 642; RFC, 3:464; Richard Beeman, *Plain Honest Men: The Making of the American Constitution* (New York: Random House, 2009), 346.
63. NDFC, 628–30.
64. Ibid., 630, 640.
65. Ibid., 638–39.
66. Ibid., 642–43, 648–50.
67. Ibid., 612–14, 651.
68. Ibid., 651, 657.
69. Ibid., 652, 657; *RFC Supplement*, 234, 241, 254.
70. NDFC, 651–52; DGW, 5:185.
71. NDFC, 654.

72. Ibid., 653–54; Beeman, *Plain Honest Men*, 357–58.
73. *NDFC*, 656.
74. Ibid., 657–59.
75. Ibid., 655.
76. Ibid., 658–59; *RFC*, 3:370, 425, 431.
77. *NDFC*, 659.
78. *RFC*, 3:81; *DGW*, 5:185.
79. *RFC*, 2:650, 3:448; *RFC Supplement*, xxv–xxvi.
80. *NDFC*, 659; Donald Jackson and Dorothy Twohig, eds., *The Diaries of George Washington*, 6 vols. (Charlottesville: University of Virginia Press, 1976–1979), hereafter cited as *DGW*, 5:185; *RFC*, 3:82.
81. *DGW*, 5:185; http://teachingamericanhistory.org/convention/citytavern/.

CHAPTER 6

RATIFICATION OF THE CONSTITUTION AND THE BILL OF RIGHTS

Ratification, a sophisticated national, regional, and local debate, consisted of thirteen separate contests in thirteen separate states. In each state, the specific issues differed, but the essential question in each state remained whether the Constitution would improve or worsen the lives of its citizens. The Antifederalist opponents of the Constitution warned that eventually power would consolidate in the federal government, resulting in a tyranny. The Federalist supporters of the Constitution secured ratification not only based on the strength of their arguments, but also through skillful political maneuvering. In addition, Federalists possessed significant advantages, such as the backing of most of the country's newspapers and the support of George Washington and Benjamin Franklin, America's most influential men. Two turning-point moments in the ratification contest occurred when the Massachusetts convention agreed to unconditional ratification with recommendatory amendments, and when New York's Antifederalist leaders acquiesced upon receiving news that Virginia had become the tenth state to ratify. In 1789, James Madison proposed a bill of rights and pushed it through the First Federal Congress. Madison acted to reassure Antifederalists, to preclude structural amendments that would have weakened the powers of the federal government, to improve the Constitution by better protecting rights, and to encourage North Carolina and Rhode Island to rejoin the Union by ratifying the Constitution. The ratification of the Bill of Rights by the states in December 1791 reduced opposition to the new Constitution and solidified its political legitimacy.

"A greater Drama is now acting on this Theatre than has heretofore been brought on the American Stage, or any other in the World," observed George Washington about ratification. "We exhibit at present the novel & astonishing Spectacle of a whole People deliberating calmly on what form of government will be most conducive to their happiness." Washington did not exaggerate. The ratification of the Constitution, in which a nation of nearly three million people held state referendums on whether to adopt a new, republican form of government, marked a milestone in the rise of democracy unlike anything that had ever happened before.[1]

On September 17, 1787, as the delegates to the Constitutional Convention gathered one last time in the Assembly Room of the Pennsylvania State House to sign the completed Constitution, Benjamin Franklin confidently pronounced the carving on the back of the presiding officer's chair to be a rising and not a setting sun. But Franklin spoke prematurely. Unless the American people adopted the new form of government, the work of the convention would amount to little more than another failed attempt at political reform. It was by no means clear whether the convention's handiwork would be accepted. The ratification of the Constitution, in short, was not inevitable. On the contrary, ratification quickly became a very suspenseful drama with odds changing daily, making the result unpredictable. Decisions reached in early state conventions shaped events in other states whose conventions met later. Ratification illustrates contingency in history, where the events of today shape the events of tomorrow, which in turn shape the events of the next day.[2]

A 1788 political cartoon shows the hand of God reaching down out of the clouds to erect a pillar of the "grand federal edifice" as a state ratifies the Constitution. The notion of building this federal superstructure became a popular metaphor to describe the unfolding ratification process, and the divine inspiration that people saw behind it. Every time another state ratified the Constitution, newspapers printed an updated version of the cartoon showing another column representing the ratifying state. "I cannot avoid hoping, and believing, to use the fashionable phrase that Virginia will make the ninth column in the foederal Temple," wrote Washington.[3]

The Constitutional Convention wisely designed procedures calculated to facilitate ratification. Unlike the Articles, the Constitution would not require unanimous approval by the state legislatures. Instead, the

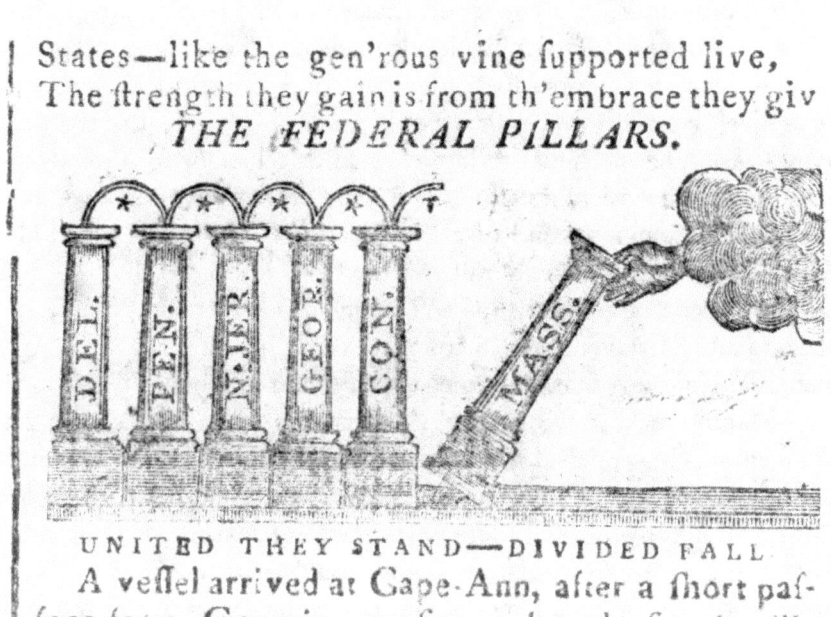

This 1788 political cartoon captures the drama of ratification by depicting the hand of God reaching out of the clouds to erect the Massachusetts pillar in the "Grand Federal Edifice." Each time another state ratified the Constitution, newspapers issued an updated version of this cartoon. (Library of Congress)

ratifications of nine state conventions would put the new framework into operation among those states. Dropping the threshold from thirteen to nine, which violated both the amendment provision of the Articles and Congress's February 1787 resolution endorsing the convention, proved key to ratification. The delegates understood that the unanimity requirement had been the stumbling block that had always thwarted amendments under the Confederation. Unanimous ratification was virtually impossible to achieve because it allowed 51 percent of the people of one small state, representing less than 2 percent of the American people, to kill a proposal desired by everyone else. The convention settled on the number nine because it was not only a supermajority of the states but would also likely represent a majority of the people. There was also a precedent behind the number, since the Articles required nine states to approve critical matters such as war and peace, borrowing money, and admitting new states.

The convention also prescribed that specially elected conventions, not the state legislatures, would decide the issue. There were both practical and theoretical reasons for using ratification conventions. On a practical level, conventions would be much more likely to ratify than the state legislatures, because the latter would be reluctant to surrender to the federal government a significant amount of their authority over matters such as commerce and taxation. The state legislatures would also pose nearly twice as many hurdles for the Constitution to clear, because all of them except Pennsylvania and Georgia had two houses that would have to ratify. Conventions, in contrast, meant securing one victory per state. Conventions that adjourned *sine die* after approving the Constitution would make ratification more permanent than a legislative act. Conventions also opened the floor debates to those who did not sit in the state legislatures, including governors, judges, and delegates to the Philadelphia convention. Federalist spokesman Alexander Hamilton did not sit in New York's legislature, but he could secure election to a state convention. In Virginia, James Madison, who had recently left the state legislature to serve in the Confederation Congress, could similarly win election to the state convention, where he could lead the fight for ratification. Furthermore, in five state constitutions religious ministers were prohibited from sitting in state legislatures, but they could be elected to state conventions.

Specially elected ratification conventions made theoretical sense as well. As the "supreme law of the land," the Constitution would take precedence over both federal and state laws. Having the state legislatures make the ratification decision suggested that state law stood higher in the constitutional hierarchy than the Constitution itself. Clearly, consent to implement the new framework had to spring directly from the sovereign people in each state acting through specially elected "constituent bodies." It is worth noting that some of the special elections for the ratification conventions had lower voting requirements than legislative elections, resulting in some districts in a 40 percent higher voter turnout. The novelty and the importance of the ratification convention balloting also contributed to the increased participation. In Pennsylvania, however, Antifederalists argued that only one-sixth of the eligible voters cast ballots for convention delegates—primarily because of the speed with which the election was held. Maryland also had a low voter turnout.

Secretary William Jackson delivered the Constitution and cover letter to the Confederation Congress in New York City on September 20. After waiting for absent delegates to arrive (including those returning from the Constitutional Convention), Congress began to consider it on the 26th. With ten of the Constitution's framers present, the document did not lack vocal advocates. But Congress also included several outspoken opponents, especially Richard Henry Lee of Virginia, and New Yorkers Melancton Smith, John Haring, and Robert Yates (who had left the Constitutional Convention disgusted with its nationalistic proceedings).[4]

Lee, who expressed shock that the convention had discarded the Articles of Confederation instead of revising them, proposed that Congress amend the Constitution to include a bill of rights. Madison warned that if Congress amended the Constitution, then two versions of the document would exist. What if some states ratified the convention's version and other states ratified Congress's version? "Confusion & disappointment," Madison believed, would "be the least evils that could ensue." Besides, if Congress tampered with the document, then, according to the Articles' amendment provision, all thirteen state legislatures would then have to ratify. Several delegates argued that for Congress to approve the proposed new government would be to commit an act of institutional suicide.

Federalists wanted to send the Constitution to the states with unanimous congressional approbation, while Antifederalists wanted to send the Constitution without congressional endorsement. Antifederalists also wanted to propose amendments or at least include a statement that the Constitutional Convention had violated the Articles. Both sides compromised. Congress would not approve the document but struck all dissent (including Lee's proposed bill of rights) from the journal. Unable to muster Congress's unanimous approbation of the Constitution, Federalists instead cleverly opted for a resolution that unanimously transmitted the Constitution "to the several Legislatures, in order to be submitted to a Convention of Delegates chosen in each State by the people thereof." Unanimous action appeared to bestow Congress's approval.[5]

Supporters of the Constitution cleverly appropriated the name *Federalists* (as opposed to nationalists) even though that title had traditionally been associated with state supremacy. Indeed, many Federalist leaders such as Madison had, in the early stages of the convention, been strict nationalists who favored a central government that operated exclusively on the people, and had vehemently opposed the part-national, part-federal hybrid that the convention eventually adopted. But during ratification, Federalists correctly claimed that they supported a federal constitution that divided power between the states and the central government.

At the same time, Federalists pinned the name *Antifederalists* on the Constitution's opponents, making them seem like mere naysayers and obstructionists who resisted needed reform. Antifederalists did not choose or embrace this name, instead calling themselves critics of the Constitution. "The term *foederalists* is . . . improperly applied to . . . the friends and supporters of the proposed constitution," wrote an opponent of the Constitution under the penname "A Farmer." But "they are *national men*, and their opponents . . . are *foederal*, in the only true and strict sense of the word." Antifederalists had always been and still were federalists in that they supported a federal system that divided power between the state and central governments. They simply wanted the balance of power to favor the states.[6]

In their speeches and writings, Federalists succeeded in getting Antifederalists to accept two ground rules that were established neither by the Constitutional Convention nor the Confederation Congress. First, the state conventions could not propose amendments to the new framework as a condition for ratification. Second, each state convention had to accept or reject the entire Constitution. It "is allowed universally to be," complained Edmund Randolph, that the Constitution must "be wholly adopted or wholly rejected."[7]

It is tempting to think of ratification as a contest between two clearly defined groups: Federalists who supported the Constitution and Antifederalists who opposed it. But that dichotomy is an oversimplification. It is more accurate to think of a spectrum of viewpoints running from hardline opponents of the Constitution at one end to firm supporters of it on the other. Everybody, including the most vehement Antifederalists, agreed that the Articles of Confederation were defective and that the central government needed additional power. According to an Antifederalist writing under the penname "Brutus" (most likely merchant and lawyer Melancton Smith of New York), "We have felt the feebleness of the ties by which these United-States are held together, and the want of sufficient energy in our present confederation."[8]

But not everybody agreed on how much more authority Congress should have. Should the existing Articles be tweaked slightly, or were they so inadequate that they had to be thrown out entirely? Some Americans wanted the proposed Constitution amended before it was ratified. Fearing that the new powers conferred on the federal government were too dangerous, they wanted to alter the Constitution before approving it. Others wanted the Constitution ratified before experience demonstrated what amendments might be necessary. Unwilling to risk a divisive or interminable debate over amendments that might lead to the Constitution's defeat, they wanted to approve it first and then alter it later. Washington warned "that an attempt to amend" prior to ratification "would be productive of more heat, & greater confusion than can well be conceived." Still others wanted the Constitution ratified as it was, without any amendments at all. Viewing the Constitution as the best possible solution to the country's political needs, they sought to approve it forthwith. In the end, the second and third groups joined forces to defeat the first group. That is, those who wanted no amendments joined forces with those who wanted amendments after ratification to defeat those who wanted amendments before ratification. In other words, Federalists ultimately allied with moderate Antifederalists to defeat hardline Antifederalists. The Constitution's supporters divided and conquered its opponents with the promise of post-ratification amendments.[9]

Like Antifederalists, Federalists could point to parts of the new framework that they did not like. But most of the Constitution's supporters suppressed their objections and united behind ratifying the Constitution because they viewed it as a vast improvement over the Articles of Confederation. Besides, to highlight faults in the document would only provide Antifederalists with ammunition to attack it. "It is a matter both of wonder and regret, that those who raise so many objections against the new constitution, should never call to mind the defects of that which is to be exchanged for it," wrote Madison in *The Federalist* 38. "It is not necessary that the former should be perfect: it is sufficient that the latter is more imperfect."[10]

After departing Philadelphia, almost all the delegates agreed that they had done the best possible job of reconciling the country's clashing interests. To a remarkable degree, they had accommodated the views of the large and small states and of the North and the South. They had also balanced the powers of the central government against those of the states, and had distributed the authority among legislative, executive, and judicial branches. "A variety of local circumstances, the inequality of states, and the dissonant interests of the different parts of the Union," wrote William Pierce, "made it impossible to give" the document "any other shape or form." Washington considered it "little short of a miracle, that the Delegates from so many different States (which States . . . are also different from each other in their manners, circumstances, and prejudices) should unite in forming a system of national Government, so little liable to well founded objections."[11]

Antifederalists, however, did not accept this logic. They judged many provisions of the new Constitution utterly unacceptable. Anonymous Antifederalist essayists included the "Federal Farmer" (possibly Elbridge Gerry) and "Brutus." Borrowing from the French political theorist Baron de Montesquieu, the Constitution's critics argued that liberty could be safe only in a geographically small country with a homogeneous population, where the government remained close to the people and uniform laws suited everyone. But "in a republic of such vast extent as the United-States," declared "Brutus," "the legislature cannot attend to the various concerns and wants of its different parts." The result is that the minority would be victimized by the majority. In a large republic, moreover, the elected officials could never truly mirror the views of the voters. Inevitably, rich and privileged men would get into office, who would pursue their own interests instead of those of the people. This concept had helped persuade states—especially Virginia—to cede their western lands to Congress.[12]

Antifederalists believed that the Constitution granted too much power to the federal government, especially the power to tax. They warned that perhaps not right away, but eventually, the federal government would turn into a consolidated tyranny. By consolidation, Antifederalists meant that power would concentrate in the federal government. Within the federal government, power would consolidate in a single branch. The president might become a monarch, or the Senate might become an aristocracy. The Supreme Court might encourage this transformation through judicial decisions that could not be overruled by any other political body.

Supreme Court justices, after all, received their offices by appointment and held them for life. Life appointments, many Antifederalists believed, were incompatible with republicanism. Although the Constitution "does not go to a perfect and entire consolidation," insisted "Brutus," "yet it approaches so near to it, that it must . . . certainly and infallibly terminate in it."[13]

Antifederalists warned that the Constitution lacked a bill of rights to protect individual liberties. The new federal government was supposed to be a government of limited and enumerated powers. But that enumeration was undermined by provisions that in effect gave Congress unlimited power, including the "necessary and proper clause," the "general welfare clause," and the "supremacy clause." Most alarming of all, the Constitution gave Congress the power to tax the people directly. Antifederalists thought the states should retain the power to tax—because the power to tax is the power to destroy. The Constitution allowed the Supreme Court to decide cases between states and the federal government. Was it not a conflict of interest to allow a branch of the federal government to settle disputes involving the federal government? Antifederalists feared that with the deck stacked against the states and the people, the Constitution would eventually lead to tyranny.

Federalists and Antifederalists gave opposite answers to three fundamental questions about government. First, how much should government do? That is, will government action achieve good or harm? Federalists trusted government to promote the public good. Washington could not "discover the propriety of preventing men from doing good, because there is a possibility of their doing evil." Similarly, James Madison wrote that "in every political institution, a power to advance the public happiness involves a discretion which may be misapplied or abused." Distrustful Antifederalists thought government should do little lest it become oppressive. An Antifederalist writing under the penname "Cato" asked, "Will not the exercise" of the powers conferred by the Constitution "tend either to the establishment of a vile and arbitrary aristocracy, or monarchy?" Second, what level of government should act? Federalists wanted the federal government to act for the public good, while Antifederalists wanted states to handle matters such as taxation. Indeed, critics of the Constitution wanted to retain a confederation of states rather than to introduce a national government acting on people. Finally, what branch of government should take action? Federalists favored the executive branch, characterized by energy and speed, whereas Antifederalists relied on legislative action by the immediate representatives of the people.[14]

In 1787 and 1788, both sides waged a tremendous political campaign. Characterized by a high level of discourse, this campaign was probably the most sophisticated political debate this country has ever seen. *The Federalist*, the most famous publication to come out of this contest, consisted of eighty-five newspaper essays that defended the Constitution topic-by-topic and section-by-section. Alexander Hamilton wrote fifty-one pieces, James Madison wrote twenty-nine, and John Jay wrote five. *The Federalist*, written under the penname "Publius," promoted ratification of the Constitution in New York. It originated as an answer to the first of sixteen essays by "Brutus," probably written by Melancton Smith.[15]

Madison's twenty-nine contributions to the series addressed some of the most fundamental Antifederalist arguments. In American Revolutionary ideology, the concept of virtue was very important. A virtuous person always put the common good ahead of personal or selfish interests. The opposite of virtue was corruption. In 1776, the colonists broke from Great Britain because they believed its rulers had become corrupt. Instead of governing for the common good, the king and Parliament seemed to be establishing a corrupt tyranny. The Revolution would thus restore virtue to politics. Americans, assuming their own inherent virtue, believed they could make republican government work. Even though past republics had failed, the Revolutionaries thought their republic would succeed because they possessed superior virtue. In the 1780s, however, Americans experienced a rude awakening, realizing that they were not as virtuous as they thought. Americans did not always put public good ahead of personal interests, as evidenced by the behavior of the state governments. Unchecked state legislatures engaged in tyranny of the majority against wealthy and religious minorities. The states also selfishly and suspiciously refused to grant Congress powers vital to the national interest, such as taxation and regulation of commerce.

These failures at the state level demonstrated the need for a political system that did not rely solely on virtue. The first state constitutions expected men to act like angels. As Madison wrote in *The Federalist* 51, "If men were angels, no government would be necessary." But humans do not behave like angels, not even Americans. Since mankind was not inherently virtuous, they required a government that thrived on self-interest. Madison's *Federalist* essays explained how the Constitutional Convention had accomplished that goal. *The Federalist* 10 turned on its head the conventional wisdom that liberty was safe only in a small republic. Madison argued that small republics led to majority tyranny, as evidenced by developments in the states. Instead, liberty is safest in a large republic, where many different self-interested factions cancel each other out, allowing the public good to emerge. Here Madison spoke in code, with small republics referring to the states and a large republic referring to the United States.[16]

In *The Federalist* 51, Madison argued that checks and balances can also substitute for virtue. First, government must divide power between three co-equal branches. The legislature, the most powerful branch, would be restrained through bicameralism, with upper and lower houses checking and balancing each other. Second, government must divide power between the federal and state levels, which would also check and balance each other. A political system so designed turned self-interest from a liability into an asset. Instead of undermining public good, selfishness would now promote it. According to *Federalist* 51, "Ambition must be made to counteract ambition." The Constitution thus used selfishness to defeat selfishness, allowing republican government to function effectively. In the words of *The Federalist* 10, the new framework provided "a republican remedy for diseases most incident to republican government."[17]

The best way to protect individual rights and liberties, according to Madison, was not with a bill of rights, a mere piece of paper. Madison in *The Federalist* 48 contemptuously referred to a bill of rights as paper walls or "parchment barriers." Several states had bills of rights, but they did not always stop popular majorities from trampling minority rights. Instead, rights could be protected only through a properly designed constitution that featured checks and balances among the branches and levels of government. Since the Constitutional Convention had written such a framework, no bill of rights was necessary.[18]

Although the different points of view of its three authors sometimes emerge, *The Federalist* remains an important document to this day because it explains the immense revolution in government the Framers achieved. We might think of *The Federalist* as the owner's manual to the Constitution. If one does not understand a clause of the Constitution, *The Federalist*

> # THE
> # FEDERALIST:
> A COLLECTION OF
> # ESSAYS,
> WRITTEN IN FAVOUR OF THE
> # NEW CONSTITUTION,
> AS AGREED UPON BY THE
> ## FEDERAL CONVENTION,
> SEPTEMBER 17, 1787.
>
> IN TWO VOLUMES.
> VOL. I.
>
> NEW-YORK:
> PRINTED AND SOLD BY JOHN TIEBOUT,
> No. 358 PEARL-STREET.
> 1799.

The title page of *The Federalist*, a series of essays written by Alexander Hamilton, James Madison, and John Jay to promote the ratification of the Constitution in New York. Prepared in response to the Antifederalist "Brutus" essays probably written by Melancton Smith, *The Federalist* is perhaps the best exposition of the Constitution ever written. (Library of Congress)

can be consulted much like an automobile owner's manual. Today, even Supreme Court justices sometimes turn to *The Federalist* to help them understand the original arguments over the Constitution.

Table 6.1 lists the thirteen state ratifications in chronological order and provides the final vote in each state. Every state held a convention, but

Table 6.1 State Votes on Ratification

1.	Delaware	December 7, 1787	30–0	100%–0%
2.	Pennsylvania	December 12, 1787	46–23	67%–33%
3.	New Jersey	December 18, 1787	38–0	100%–0%
4.	Georgia	December 31, 1787	26–0	100%–0%
5.	Connecticut	January 9, 1788	128–40	76%–24%
6.	Massachusetts	February 6, 1788	187–168	53%–47%
7.	Maryland	April 26, 1788	63–11	85%–15%
8.	South Carolina	May 23, 1788	149–73	67%–33%
9.	New Hampshire	June 21, 1788	57–47	55%–45%
10.	Virginia	June 25, 1788	89–79	53%–47%
11.	New York	July 26, 1788	30–27	53%–47%
12.	North Carolina	November 21, 1789	194–77	72%–28%
13.	Rhode Island	May 29, 1790	34–32	52%–48%

Source: Ratification at a Glance, Center for the Study of the American Constitution website, https://csac.history.wisc.edu/states-and-ratification.

every state did so its own way. The conventions met at different times and had widely varying numbers of delegates. Some small states held big conventions, while some large states held small conventions. A quick glance shows that the margins of victory became narrower over time. From being lopsided victories for the Constitution at the outset of the ratification campaign, the outcomes became cliffhangers at the end. This pattern occurred in part because Federalists in states that would ratify easily held their conventions as early as possible, while Federalists in doubtful states postponed their conventions, hoping that approvals elsewhere would generate pressure to ratify in their own states. Other factors influenced when each convention met, including the date the state legislature met and the amount of time each state allowed for public debate before the election of convention delegates occurred.

Delaware, the "First State," unanimously ratified the Constitution on December 7, 1787. Ever since 1776, the state had suffered conflict and even violence between Whigs, who supported independence, and Tories, who opposed it. Despite its internal divisions, the state demonstrated remarkable unity on external matters, supporting a stronger central government provided Delaware maintained an influential voice in it. On November 7, the state legislature voted unanimously in calling a ratification convention. A month later, the convention, led by John Dickinson and George Read, approved the Constitution without dissent after a five-day discussion. According to one report, the convention discussed the Constitution only for two hours! Delaware completed the ratification process, including calling a convention, electing delegates, and holding a convention, in eleven weeks—a remarkable achievement in an age of primitive communication, even for a small state.[19]

The Pennsylvania Assembly, sitting in the State House, immediately received the Constitution when the Constitutional Convention adjourned on September 17, but waited nearly two weeks for the go-ahead from Congress to call a convention. Several of the heavily outnumbered Antifederalists absented themselves from the legislature so that it would lack a quorum necessary to call a ratification convention. Federalists wanted to complete the call of a convention before adjourning the Assembly session. On the last day of the session, the Assembly sergeant-at-arms, assisted by a local mob of Federalist artisans, raided the lodgings of the missing Antifederalists, located two truants, and forcibly brought them to the State House. Having obtained a quorum, the legislature called a convention to meet on November 21. The election of convention delegates was to occur on November 6.

Over the next two months, the state debated the Constitution's merits. Pennsylvania's Federalists tended to be wealthy, educated, eastern opponents of the state's extremely democratic constitution of 1776. Dr. Benjamin Rush predicted that "the new federal government like a new Continental waggon will overset our State dung cart, with all its dirty contents . . . and thereby restore order and happiness to Pennsylvania." Philadelphia tradesmen seeking economic growth and urbanites from Pittsburgh also supported the new framework. Antifederalists, strong in rural central and western Pennsylvania, supported the state constitution. On October 6, in a public address in the yard outside the State House, James Wilson delivered the first explanation by a Constitutional Convention delegate. He declared that the Constitution would not threaten liberty despite the lack of a bill of rights because the powers of Congress had been carefully enumerated. Reprinted in more than forty newspapers during the ratification campaign, Wilson's speech boosted the Constitution throughout the nation. Antifederalists, led by less prominent westerners like William Findley, Robert Whitehill, and John Smilie, warned that ratification would lead to tyrannical rule by affluent elites.[20]

Federalists won more than forty of Pennsylvania's sixty-nine convention seats. The state convention gathered in the same Assembly Room of the State House where the Constitutional Convention had met. Hopelessly outnumbered, Antifederalists tried to slow down the convention's pace and to record their objections through roll-call votes whenever possible. Federalist acquiesced in allowing the Constitution to be discussed by paragraph. Antifederalists articulated their objections to the Constitution but did not change the minds of fellow delegates. After three weeks of debate, the convention ratified the Constitution on December 12 by a 46–23 vote. Pennsylvania, the geographic "keystone" of the nation and the first large state to ratify, set an important precedent for ratification: Federalists demanded an up-or-down vote on the Constitution without any opportunity for amendments. By acquiescing in this demand, Antifederalists made their task of defeating the Constitution much more difficult. But being heavily outnumbered, they had few alternatives. To have walked out of the convention would not have changed the outcome.[21]

In October, New Jersey's legislature unanimously called a convention that unanimously ratified the Constitution on December 18. Like other small states, including Delaware and Connecticut, New Jersey expressed pleasure with the Great Compromise that granted it equality with the large states in the U.S. Senate. The Constitution would also benefit the state financially and commercially. New Jersey citizens owned 10 percent of the national debt, which would likely be paid in full under the Constitution. Lacking port cities, New Jersey consumers purchased foreign goods through New York City and Philadelphia. Under the Confederation, states collected duties on imported goods. Import merchants passed along the cost to consumers in the form of higher prices, while the revenue from these duties stayed in the importing state's treasury. New Jersey consumers paid an estimated £30,000 (over $5 million today) annually into the New York treasury. James Madison fittingly described New Jersey as "a cask tapped at both ends." This situation would change under the new Constitution, which granted Congress the exclusive power to tax imports. Duties collected in New York City and Philadelphia would instead go to the federal government for the benefit of all of the states.[22]

Georgia unanimously ratified the Constitution on December 31, 1787. Along with South Carolina, Georgia had driven a hard bargain at the Constitutional Convention to protect the institution of slavery. The state had lost many slaves during the war, and Georgians wanted to replace them with African slaves. More important, the state desired the protection of the federal government not only against slave rebellions but also against the Spanish in Florida and the Creek Indians in the West.[23]

Less than two weeks after Georgia voted, Connecticut became the fifth state to ratify the Constitution. In Connecticut, as in most other states, Federalist editors operated the newspapers, preventing essays by Oliver Ellsworth, Roger Sherman, and other pro-ratification polemicists from being thoroughly answered. Only six essays against the Constitution appeared in print, five of them reprinted from other states, and only one written within the state. Most of these, in fact, were straw men set up to be answered by a subsequent Federalist newspaper essayist. Perhaps the decisive factor was that Connecticut, like New Jersey, also lacked a major port. It was reported that Connecticut consumers paid £50,000 (over $8.5 million today) annually into New York's treasury. Under the new Constitution, import duties paid at New York City would now go to the federal government instead of to a neighboring state. A few Connecticut towns instructed their delegates to vote against the Constitution, but they did not prevent a lopsided vote of 128–40 on January 9, 1788, in favor of ratification.[24]

With five states having approved by comfortable margins, the Constitution appeared well on its way to ratification. But only one of the all-important large states had held its convention. The Federalist juggernaut hit a snag in Massachusetts, the second-large state to debate the Constitution. Over 350 delegates selected by the Bay State's town meetings gathered in Boston on January 9. Preliminary headcounts conducted by leaders on both sides were indeterminate. With many of the participants expressing sympathy for the Shaysites and resentment against the eastern elites who supported the Constitution, the outcome was simply too close to call. Antifederalist strength at the Massachusetts convention can be traced in part to the state's decision to pay the delegates' expenses, ensuring heavy attendance from the poorer western and island towns.

To ensure success, Massachusetts Federalists took dramatic steps. First, they agreed to a full and open clause-by-clause debate of the document. Second, they allowed Elbridge Gerry to attend even though he had not been elected a delegate. The non-signer's presence did the Antifederalists no good, however. When Gerry tried to speak, the convention instructed him to submit his comments in writing, even in answer to questions from convention members. After an ugly verbal exchange followed by a physical scuffle with Francis Dana, Gerry left the convention never to return. Third, Federalists assured the forty-six delegates from Maine that ratification would not undermine their desire to become a separate state.

The fourth and most important move Federalists made to ensure ratification in Massachusetts was to suggest having the convention approve a list of recommendatory amendments to accompany its unconditional ratification of the Constitution. These alterations would merely be suggestions to be considered once the new government began operation. Recommendatory amendments had the potential to shift the balance of power in favor the Constitution. To increase the impact of this gambit, Federalists sought an influential individual to propose the recommendatory amendments on the convention floor.

Federalist leaders approached Governor John Hancock to see if he would make the breakthrough proposal to the convention. Hancock had won Massachusetts's governorship in 1787, defeating the unpopular James Bowdoin in the aftermath of Shays's Rebellion. Although elected president of the convention, Hancock did not attend for the first three weeks, citing an attack of gout. Rufus King and Henry Knox privately assured him that if he appeared in person and called for recommendatory amendments, it would break the deadlock and ensure the Constitution's success in the state. Taking the low road as well as the high road, King and Knox promised Federalist support for Hancock's reelection as governor if he accepted their offer. Pulling out all the stops, the two emissaries also agreed to back Hancock for vice president during the first election under the new government. They further pledged—should Virginia's failure to ratify disqualify George Washington from the presidency—that they would promote Hancock to be the first president. "We tell him that if Virginia does not unite," King explained to Knox, "that he is considered as the only fair candidate for President."[25]

The governor could not refuse the offer. King predicted that "as soon as the majority is exhibited on either side" Hancock's "health will suffer him to be abroad." In late January, he miraculously overcame his gout, was carried into the convention on a litter wearing bandages, and moved the adoption of nine recommendatory amendments to accompany the Constitution's ratification. The alterations would protect individual rights and limit Congress to its enumerated powers. Federalist leaders now dropped their next bombshell: they had recruited Samuel Adams, perhaps the second-most influential man present, to second Hancock's motion. Although Adams harbored significant reservations about the powers granted the federal government by the Constitution, he bowed to the staunch Federalism of the artisans and tradesmen who formed his base of support.

Antifederalist leaders, afraid of being outmaneuvered, tried but failed to adjourn the convention. But it was too late. The recommendatory tactic succeeded, breaking away enough Antifederalist delegates to eke out the Constitution's ratification by a narrow 187–168 margin. Rather than expressing bitterness at the outcome, Massachusetts Antifederalists, conceding that the debate had been conducted in good faith, pledged to support the new framework if ratified by nine states. "All appeared willing to bury the hatchet of animosity, and to smoke the calumet of union and love," pronounced the *Massachusetts Centinel*. Like the Pennsylvania convention, the Massachusetts convention also set a precedent for the success of the ratification campaign: if necessary, recommendatory amendments could be adopted to ensure that a closely divided state would adopt the Constitution. Six of the remaining seven conventions resorted to this tactic to achieve ratification.[26]

After surviving a close call in Massachusetts, Federalists ran into more serious trouble elsewhere in New England. At the New Hampshire convention in Exeter in February, Federalists quickly realized that their only alternative to stave off an immediate defeat in the state was to adjourn until the spring. If more states ratified in the meantime, it might improve the Constitution's chances in New Hampshire. In Rhode Island, meanwhile, the Antifederalist legislature declined to call a convention, but eventually agreed to a statewide referendum to decide the matter. The balloting, held on March 24, 1788, turned into a rout, when the Federalist towns of Newport and Providence refused to participate. With its supporters on the sidelines, the Constitution suffered a resounding defeat by an 11–1 margin. Between February 1788 and January 1790, Rhode Island's legislature voted a whopping eleven times against holding a state ratification convention! Antifederalist paper money advocates unwilling to submit to a regime that banned that form of currency clearly controlled the state. Happy that power had been decentralized to the state level, Rhode Island had, after all, boycotted the Constitutional Convention, much to the disgust of its mercantile class.[27]

In the spring of 1788, Federalists got back on track with the help of two southern states. Despite Luther Martin's vociferous opposition to the Constitution in the state assembly and in two widely circulated series of newspaper essays, Maryland's voters elected twice as many Federalists as Antifederalists to the state convention. During the gathering, held in April 1788 in Annapolis, Martin ranted to no avail that ratification would bring consolidation and tyranny. Complacent Federalists did not bother to answer the objections of Martin and other Antifederalists. The convention then easily approved the Constitution, 63–11. Maryland did not adopt recommendatory amendments because a committee appointed to consider constitutional alterations "could come to no Agreement." After the convention ended, William Paca and eleven other Antifederalist delegates published a minority address that included the recommendatory amendments rejected by the committee. This publication had so little impact that Maryland's Federalists did not respond to it. It is not clear why Maryland's Antifederalists made such an insignificant impression on the state.[28]

When South Carolina's Assembly met in January 1788, it became the only state legislature to debate the merits of the Constitution in addition to calling a ratification convention. Doing so enabled all four of the state's delegates to the Philadelphia convention, who were present, to make the Federalist case. They pointed out how well the Constitution protected slavery, citing the Three-Fifths Compromise, the ban on export taxes, the protection of the African slave trade through 1808 at least, and the fugitive slave clause. These provisions secured the support of the coastal areas, characterized by huge plantations, wealthy planters, and a significant black slave majority. In South Carolina, as in most states, the convention met in a Federalist city, in this case Charleston. Despite having a minority of the state's white, free population, the pro-Constitution lowcountry held a majority of the convention seats. The only hope for the upcountry Antifederalists—a vote to adjourn the proceedings—failed. The delegates agreed to recommendatory amendments that limited Congress's ability to tax and reserved to the state powers not expressly granted to the federal government. Then they approved the Constitution by a 149–73 vote on May 23.[29]

The New Hampshire convention, having adjourned on February 22, opened its second session on June 18 in Concord. In the meantime, Federalists had gained about half a dozen votes through the actions of local town meetings. The town of Hopkinton, which had formerly opposed ratification, now instructed its delegates to support the Constitution, while three towns that had not been represented at the February session now sent delegates. On its fourth day, the convention postponed an Antifederalist call for conditional amendments, instead approving a Federalist call for recommendatory amendments. After rejecting a motion to adjourn the convention—this time from Antifederalists—New Hampshire's delegates ratified the Constitution by a vote of 57–47 on June 21.[30]

The ratifications of eight states set the stage for a huge showdown in Virginia, which believed that the fate of the Constitution depended on it. On one hand, if the Old Dominion became the ninth state to ratify, then surely the remaining four states would fall into line as well. But on the other hand, if it rejected the Constitution, so too would the undecideds. Mighty Virginia, the most populous and prestigious state, saw itself settling the ratification contest for all Americans, producing an atmosphere of intense drama at the Richmond convention. Virginians did not learn until after their convention adjourned, however, that New Hampshire had approved the Constitution while they deliberated. New Hampshire became the critical ninth state to ratify, ahead of Virginia, the tenth state to approve.

Instead of lining up solidly behind the Constitution, Virginia's leaders divided evenly for and against the document. The Federalist lineup included Washington, Madison, George Wythe, John Marshall, Edmund Pendleton, Henry Lee, and George Nicholas. The Antifederalist forces featured Patrick Henry, George Mason, Richard Henry Lee, William Grayson, and James Monroe. All these men except Washington and Richard Henry Lee attended the state convention in Richmond. As the presumptive first president, Washington thought it best to remain above the fray. Although he followed the Constitution's fate closely and wrote many letters to prominent individuals supporting the document, Washington did not leave his Mount Vernon plantation from October 1787 through May 1788. Against his wishes, several of his letters expressing support for the Constitution found their way into newspapers throughout the country. Their publication probably assisted the Federalist cause.

George Mason drew up and began circulating his "Objections to the Constitution" even before he left Philadelphia in September 1787. Complaining that the new framework did not sufficiently restrain either the Senate or the president, Mason predicted that unconditional ratification would lead either to monarchy or to aristocracy. During the Virginia convention, Mason, who hopelessly mired himself in the details of the Constitution, proved ineffective in debate. Virginia's other non-signer, Edmund Randolph, had explained his refusal to sign a letter to the speaker of Virginia's House of Delegates dated in mid-October 1787 but not published until late December. Because the people of the states "must either adopt the constitution in the whole, or reject it in the whole," Randolph reasoned, "they would not only reject it, but bid a lasting farewell to the union." But now, eight months later, with eight states having ratified, Randolph finally decided that it was too late for amendments prior to ratification. Still believing that a rejection of the Constitution meant a dissolution of the Union, Randolph cast his lot with the Federalists.[31]

Two giants dominated the proceedings in Richmond. On the Antifederalist side stood Patrick Henry. On the Federalist side stood James Madison, diminutive in physical stature, but formidable in debate. Both men were powerful orators, but their speaking styles could not have been more different. Henry, more brilliant in the delivery than in the content, spoke like an evangelical minister preached. When Henry predicted that the Constitution would enslave the people, the audience could envision the shackles forming around their wrists. On June 24, Henry took advantage of a gathering storm. As he warned that ratification would unleash the wrath of the Almighty, a nearby thunderbolt sent jittery spectators into pandemonium.[32]

Having declined to attend the Constitutional Convention, Henry came out swinging to preserve Virginia's sovereignty against a consolidated national government. Lacking discipline, however, Henry could not stick to the clause-by-clause debate of the Constitution that Antifederalists themselves had requested. Madison, brilliant more in the content than the delivery, spoke so softly at times that the frustrated stenographer occasionally failed to record portions of speeches, noting that

"Mr. *Madison* spoke so low that he could not be distinctly heard." Instead of histrionics, Madison relied on logic, carefully building his case point by point. Madison later recalled that Henry could demolish an hour-long carefully reasoned speech with just a few sentences of impassioned oratory. But in the end, Madison answered every one of Henry's arguments. Madison spoke, noted one delegate, "with such force of reasoning, and a display of such irresistible truths, that opposition seemed to have quitted the field."[33]

The even split among Virginia's leaders foreshadowed an evenly split convention. Virginia's Tidewater and Northern Neck supported the Constitution, while the Piedmont and Southside (south of the James River) opposed it. Thirteen delegates from the region of Virginia that later became Kentucky desired above all to retain navigation rights to the Mississippi River. Madison assured them that the new federal government would possess the strength necessary to open the river to American commerce. Henry, in contrast, warned that the new regime, dominated by northerners, would sacrifice the Mississippi as John Jay had intended to do in his 1786 negotiations with Spain. Most of the Kentuckians broke Henry's way, but the Constitution prevailed nevertheless. After rejecting by a vote of 88–80 an Antifederalist proposal that amendments be circulated among the other states prior to ratification, the Virginia convention on June 25 then ratified by a narrow 89–79 margin. The convention later adopted forty recommendatory amendments to be considered by the First Federal Congress, half structural changes weakening the powers of the federal government and half protecting personal rights and liberties.[34]

That Virginia, the largest and most important state, ratified in timely fashion was critical to the ultimate success of the Constitution. Had the Old Dominion delayed its approval until after the First Federal Elections (as North Carolina and Rhode Island did), then George Washington could not have been elected president. Since the reform movement proceeded on the assumption that Washington would be the country's first chief executive, Virginia's recalcitrance would have posed a major dilemma for the new nation.

Ten states had now ratified, more than enough to set the Constitution into motion. But geographically central New York had yet to approve. When the convention met in Poughkeepsie on June 17, New Hampshire and Virginia had not yet ratified. Not surprisingly, Antifederalists outnumbered Federalists, 46–19 in the New York convention. *The Federalist* essays of Hamilton, Jay, and Madison, it seems, had little impact on the state, which did not want to lose to the new federal government the lucrative import duties it collected in New York City. Much of the New York's leadership, including Governor George Clinton, Constitutional Convention delegates Yates and Lansing, and Melancton Smith, opposed a strong national regime. These men—all of whom attended the state convention—believed that a rejection in New York, coupled with a rejection in Virginia, news of which they eagerly anticipated, would doom the Constitution. They spoke the views of almost the entire state except New York City and wealthy manor lords in the Hudson River Valley. Antifederalists determined not to approve the new framework without adding amendments in one form or another.

Federalists, including John Jay, Alexander Hamilton, and Robert R. Livingston, tirelessly championed the Constitution. For the first two weeks, the convention debated the Constitution paragraph by paragraph without changing the minds of the delegates. Hoping to turn the tide in their favor, desperate Federalists dangled the idea that ratification would keep the national capital in New York City, and threatened that the Constitution's defeat would lead the city and six lower counties to secede from the state. On June 24, the convention learned that New Hampshire had become the critical ninth state to ratify. Expected all along, this information did not have much impact in New York. Two weeks later, on July 2, however, news arrived that changed everything—Virginia had become the tenth state to ratify. With every state but Rhode Island and North Carolina now a part of the Union, New Yorkers faced an entirely new situation. Would the state remain within the Union, or would it become a separate country? Even the staunchest Antifederalists knew the answer to that question. Given the new circumstances, none other than Melancton Smith, the self-proclaimed manager of the convention, moved to the Federalist side, allowing the convention to ratify the Constitution. But considerable wrangling occurred over whether to adopt conditional or recommendatory amendments. In the end, the two sides struck a deal: the amendments would be recommendatory only, but the convention also unanimously issued a circular letter to the other states and to Congress calling for a second constitutional convention to consider the various alterations suggested by the state conventions.

The 30–27 final vote in New York on July 26 made it look as if the Constitution barely eked by. In fact, the Antifederalist leadership caucused and decided that a sufficient number of Antifederalists would either not vote or change their vote to guarantee the Constitution's ratification. The political careers of some of these "ratifying Antis" (including Melancton Smith's) suffered severely because of their actions.[35]

Although alarming to Federalists in other states, New York's circular letter did not, in the end, lead to a second constitutional convention. Instead, attention quickly shifted to the First Federal Elections, with Federalists and Antifederalists seeking to win as many seats as possible in the First Federal Congress. That body, not a second convention, could then initiate the amendment process.

North Carolina Federalists, knowing they faced an uphill battle against the provincialism of the state, scheduled the state convention in July 1788. They hoped that by then the ratifications of nine or more states would settle the matter in North Carolina as it did in New York.

A procession celebrating New York's 1788 ratification of the Constitution. The banner on the "Ship of State" float honors Alexander Hamilton's efforts in the Constitutional Convention and at the state ratification convention. (Fotosearch/Getty Images)

But even that was not enough to bring the Tar Heel state around. An acrimonious convention debate did nothing to diminish the Antifederalists' two-thirds majority, which remained unwilling to surrender state powers to a distant national government. The North Carolina convention, which particularly wanted to see the adoption of a bill of rights, voted 184–83 not to ratify the Constitution until amendments were adopted. The convention proposed a long list of both rights-related and structural amendments weakening the powers of the federal government. On November 23, 1789, after the First Federal Congress had sent twelve proposed amendments to the states for approval, a second North Carolina convention finally ratified the Constitution. The 194–77 vote was a near-reversal of the first convention's balloting.[36]

Rhode Island, the final holdout, had to be strong-armed into the Union by the federal government. In 1790, the First Federal Congress drafted bills to ban the state from trade with the rest of the nation and to collect Rhode Island's unpaid portion of the national debt. When President Washington toured the New England states in 1789, he refused to set foot in Rhode Island, viewed by some as a foreign country. Washington circumnavigated Rhode Island, making his way from Connecticut directly into Massachusetts. Not until May 29, 1790, did a state convention finally ratify by a 34–32 vote. The outcome occurred when five Antifederalists voted in favor and four others abstained. As in New York, Antifederalist leaders in Rhode Island orchestrated the ratification vote, making the outcome look closer than it really was. After Rhode Island had paid off its state debt with depreciated paper money in 1789, Antifederalists willingly joined the Union.[37]

Why did Federalists win, and Antifederalists lose, the contest over ratification? It may have had less to do with the merits of each side's arguments than with other factors. The Constitution's proponents certainly possessed some big advantages. Federalist leaders proactively devised brilliant strategies, such as requiring an up-or-down vote and conceding recommendatory amendments. Antifederalists reactively submitted to these stipulations. As New York Antifederalist Cornelius Schoonmaker put it, "Federalists have fought and beat us from our own ground with our own weapons." Federalists did not conduct a coordinated national campaign, but they did communicate across state lines better than their opponents did, in part because they knew one other from the Continental Army, from Congress, and from the Constitutional Convention. The ratification conventions met in Federalist towns with the galleries open to the public, enabling the audiences to influence the proceedings by cheering for the Constitution.[38]

The press sided with the Federalists. Of approximately ninety newspapers in the country, only half a dozen supported the Antifederalists, half a dozen remained neutral, and the rest backed ratification. In several states (particularly Connecticut and Pennsylvania), the press refused to print Antifederalist essays. When the *Pennsylvania Herald* published Antifederalist speeches, it lost subscribers and went out of business! Maryland printers did not publish the convention debates at all, while Federalists suppressed the notes taken by a stenographer because they would probably benefit the Antifederalist cause.[39]

Finally, Federalists had George Washington and Benjamin Franklin on their side. Many Americans did not know what to make of the Constitution but did know what to make of Washington and Franklin. They trusted that neither hero would support a proposal harmful to the liberty and prosperity of the American people. Many people decided that if the Constitution was good enough for Washington and Franklin, it was good enough for them. James Monroe asserted that "Washington's influence carried this government."[40]

Antifederalists predicted that over time, power would gravitate to the federal government. Within the federal government, they believed that power would concentrate in a single branch, most likely the presidency. In many ways, Antifederalists have been proven correct. They anticipated the "Imperial Presidency" of the mid-twentieth century. But Antifederalist predictions also were incorrect. Instead of trampling individual liberties, the federal government has often protected them, especially the rights of minority groups.

The Federalist-Antifederalist debate is in many ways the eternal debate in American history. How powerful should the federal government be? How powerful should the states be? Where should the line of federalism be drawn between these two levels of government? To tell the story of U.S. history is to trace this line oscillating back and forth. Anyone today who wants to shrink the size of the federal government and shift power to the states might be considered a modern-day Antifederalist.[41]

In the 1950s, historian Cecelia Kenyon famously branded Antifederalists "men of little faith" because of their distrust of governmental power. Had the Constitution's opponents truly been men of little faith, however, they would never have accepted the Federalist promise to enact amendments after ratification, nor allowed the Constitution the chance to prove itself. In truth, however, the most significant thing about the launching of the new federal government in 1789 was the rapid decline of Antifederalism. Considering how vehemently Antifederalists had opposed the Constitution, it is striking how quickly most became loyal supporters of and even participants in the new regime. For the Constitution's opponents to accept it lent political legitimacy to the new regime. The two primary reasons for the reduction of Antifederalism are the performance of George Washington as the first president and the performance of the First Federal Congress.[42]

George Washington took the oath of office as the first president of the United States on April 30, 1789, at Federal Hall in New York City. His undisputed primacy among America's Revolutionary leaders made his election a foregone conclusion. Washington received all the electoral votes cast, the only president ever to do so. Under the Constitution, each presidential electoral cast two votes for president. Thus, every elector cast one of his two votes for Washington. John Adams, the runner-up, became vice president.

Washington brought prestige to the federal government, and particularly to the presidency. Americans accepted a strong executive only because they knew that the former commander in chief of the Continental Army would be the first to hold the office. After their experience under King George III, Americans feared that executive power might lead to tyranny. But they trusted Washington because he always used power carefully, never abused it, and eventually returned it to the people. Washington made it possible for a revolution against a strong executive to end with the creation of a strong executive.

As the first president under the Constitution, Washington had no predecessors to emulate. Instead, he served as the role model, establishing precedents to be followed by his successors. "In our progress towards political happiness my situation is new," and "I walk on untrodden ground," he observed. "There is scarcely any part of my conduct wch may not hereafter be drawn into precedent." Aware that his actions would be copied by future presidents, Washington struggled to get things right the first time. Key precedents that Washington set include ensuring that he would be called simply "the president of the United States," instead of being addressed with a monarchical title, and, during the Whiskey Rebellion, demonstrating that armed rebellion against the federal government would be suppressed by force. Washington also turned his department heads into an advisory board known as the cabinet.[43]

Perhaps Washington's most famous precedent is the tradition that a chief executive retires after serving two terms. This venerated practice, which became a formal part of the Constitution with the Twenty-Second Amendment in 1951, came about more by accident than by design, however. When Washington hoped to retire after one term in office, congressional leaders and his cabinet persuaded him that the national interest required a second term. Washington's real concern was not starting a two-term tradition but making sure that he did not die in office. Had the first president died in office, it might have established a presidency for life, with the four-year elections being mere pro-forma renewals. Washington's greatest fear was dying in office. He had built his cherished reputation by walking away from power and giving it back to the American people, as he did at the end of the Revolutionary War. Had he died in office, he would have died holding power, and his reputation would have been tarnished. Washington's acceptance of the presidency, in short, was a personal sacrifice dictated by his sense of duty. Holding that office could not enhance his reputation, it could only lower it.[44]

Washington's wise policies, such as neutrality in the wars of the French Revolution in Europe, ensured that the United States enjoyed peace and prosperity during his administration (1789–1797). His leadership helped to get the new nation through an uncertain short term, so that it could enjoy a promising longer term. Washington got the United States, as historian Joseph Ellis puts it, from the improbable to the inevitable. His performance was a major reason for the evaporation of Antifederalism.[45]

Another reason for the opposition's acceptance of the Constitution was the success of the First Federal Congress (1789–1791). That body acted like a second constitutional convention in that it "breathed life into the Constitution." Just like President Washington, Congress had to figure out what that document meant and to put it into practice. Congress settled three lingering, unresolved issues of the American Revolution: paying off the national debt, finding a permanent home for the national capital, and amending the Constitution.[46]

Treasury Secretary Alexander Hamilton's financial program funded the nation's Revolutionary War debt and assumed the war debts of the states. To obtain the necessary votes to get it enacted, Hamilton, Secretary of State Thomas Jefferson, Congressman James Madison, and other leaders worked out a grand bargain known as the Compromise of 1790. This deal located the permanent national capital in Washington, D.C., after a temporary ten-year residence in Philadelphia.[47]

Throughout the ratification campaign, Antifederalists demanded amendments protecting personal rights and liberties. In 1789, James Madison prepared rights-related amendments and pushed them through Congress, so that they could be sent to the states for approval. Some historians have interpreted the passage of the Bill of Rights as an example of throwing "a tub to the whale." This phrase describes a maritime practice where sailors threw an old tub or barrel to a menacing whale to distract it from damaging or demolishing their ship. Thus, Federalists threw the Bill of Rights to the menacing Antifederalists to distract them from pursuing structural amendments that might have weakened or destroyed the powers of the federal government. Some scholars apply this thesis to the Father of the Bill of Rights, James Madison, accusing him of supporting amendments strictly to quiet the Antifederalists and to secure his election to Congress in a strongly Antifederal district in Virginia. Political factors certainly influenced Madison's thinking—no politician operates in a political vacuum. But Madison also acted to improve the Constitution.[48]

During and after the Constitutional Convention, Madison opposed a federal bill of rights for both practical and theoretical reasons. On a practical level, Madison resisted any attempt to amend the Constitution during the ratification campaign. He feared that Antifederalists would use amendments as a strategy to defeat the Constitution altogether. Madison's goal was simply to get the Constitution ratified. He was dissatisfied with parts of the new Constitution because he still thought the states were too powerful and the federal government was too weak. But he recognized that the new Constitution was a significant improvement over the Articles of Confederation. To call for amendments during ratification would only give Antifederalists ammunition with which to prevent the adoption of the new framework.[49]

Madison also opposed a bill of rights for theoretical reasons. First, he did not consider a bill of rights necessary because the Constitution specifically enumerates Congress's powers. The federal government would not have the power to violate individual rights because it would only possess the powers enumerated in Article 1, Section 8. Indeed, the addition of a bill of rights would be dangerous because it would imply that Congress could exceed its enumerated powers. Second, a bill of rights was unnecessary because the Constitution was itself already a bill of rights. For example, Article 1, Section 9 protected against ex post facto laws (retroactive punishment for offenses that were not crimes at the time committed), bills of attainder (legislative charges and punishment for crimes without judicial due process of law or a conviction), and against violations of the writ of habeas corpus (failing to provide judicial due process to those arrested and to bring them to a speedy trial). Third, it is very difficult and dangerous to start listing rights, because anything that is omitted has in effect been surrendered.[50]

The fourth reason against a bill of rights was for Madison the most compelling of all. Mere words on a sheet of paper, what Madison in *The Federalist* 48 sarcastically called "parchment barriers," were powerless to protect rights. Words on a piece of paper simply could not stop a tyrannical majority from violating the rights of the minority. For Madison, the way to protect the minority was not a bill of rights, but in the design and structure of the government. Checks and balances among the branches and levels of government, not a piece of paper, would protect personal rights. The Constitutional Convention had already built those safeguards into the Constitution.[51]

But Madison conceded that there were powerful arguments in favor of a bill of rights. The Constitution protected some rights, like the writ of habeas corpus, but not others like freedom of speech and of the press. If the Constitution needed to protect some rights explicitly, it also needed to protect other rights explicitly as well. Besides, the Constitution contains blanket grants of power, including the general welfare clause, the necessary and proper clause, and the supremacy clause. These blank checks undermined the argument that Congress is limited to enumerated powers. And if the federal government could exceed its enumerated powers, then personal rights would be in jeopardy without a bill of rights.

To these standard Antifederalist arguments in favor of a bill of rights, Madison added a few of his own, which turned conventional wisdom on its head. Antifederalists envisioned a bill of rights protecting the majority from a tyrannical minority such as a king. Madison envisioned the opposite. He saw rights-related amendments protecting the minority from a tyrannical majority. While Madison clearly believed that parchment barriers by themselves cannot safeguard rights, he did realize that they could help. He recognized that a federal bill of rights could help educate the public about its rights, making it less likely that an ignorant majority would trample the rights of the minority. Madison also understood that a bill of rights would provide a weapon with which victims of oppression could seek redress in court. A bill of rights would be necessary for the Supreme Court to overturn an unjust law through judicial review. Most appealing of all to Madison, a bill of rights could enable the federal government to strike down unjust state laws. He had long theorized about using a congressional veto of state legislation to protect minority rights. A bill of rights that applied not only to the federal government, but to the states as well, would achieve a similar result as the congressional veto.[52]

Even after the Constitution's ratification, Antifederalists remained a powerful threat. Opponents of the Constitution now tried to get themselves elected to Congress, where they could weaken the powers of the federal government through both legislation and amendments. To cut the ground from under Antifederalists, Madison also began to advocate amendments. He now favored alterations because for the first time they would help the new Constitution rather than to undermine it. But Madison's conversion to a bill of rights was not a simple case of political opportunism.[53]

The principled nature of Madison's conversion is illustrated by the private correspondence over a bill of rights that he carried on with his friend Thomas Jefferson. As soon as Jefferson, serving in Paris as U.S. minister to France, read the Constitution, he wrote Madison arguing against "the omission of a bill of rights." In a breakthrough letter to Jefferson of October 17, 1788, Madison himself finally came out for rights-related amendments. Madison's letter to Jefferson reviewed the objections to a bill of rights. But then it countered those objections, building a theoretical case in favor of a bill of rights. "My own opinion has always been in favor of a bill of rights," he wrote his friend. "At the same time I have never thought the omission a material defect, nor been anxious to supply it even by *subsequent* amendment, for any other reason than it is anxiously desired by others. I have favored it because I supposed it might be of use, and if properly executed could not be of disservice." The timing of Madison's change of heart was caused by the need to elect Federalists to office under the new Constitution. He was also motivated by his own personal desire for a seat in Congress. But there was also conviction behind Madison's new position, as his private letter to Jefferson demonstrates.[54]

In 1788, Virginia's Federalists ran Madison for the U.S. Senate. The state legislature, which elected senators, was dominated by Antifederalists led by Patrick Henry. When the legislature voted, Madison came in third behind two Antifederalists who won Virginia's two Senate seats. Attention then shifted to the race for the House of Representatives. Henry's forces hoped to finish Madison off once and for all politically by handing him another defeat. The legislature accordingly gerrymandered Madison into a strongly Antifederal congressional district and required candidates to run in their home districts. Henry even persuaded James Monroe, a war hero, to stand against Madison. Facing this serious challenge, Madison engaged in hard campaigning, including an open-air debate with Monroe in December 1788 from which he suffered frostbite. Madison did not change his position on amendments because he had done that already. Instead, he clarified his new position to his constituents by writing letters to prominent citizens. To George Eve, pastor of the Blue Run Baptist Church in Madison's home town of Orange, he wrote, "amendments, if pursued with a proper moderation and in a proper mode, will be not only safe, but may serve the double purpose of satisfying the minds of well meaning opponents, and of providing additional guards in favour of liberty." Madison's campaigning succeeded, helping him win the congressional seat with 57 percent of the vote.[55]

Madison took the lead on amendments in the House of Representatives. When President Washington asked him to ghostwrite his inaugural address, Madison inserted a recommendation for a bill of rights. After sifting through the two hundred changes proposed by the state ratifying conventions, Madison drafted amendments protecting freedom of religion, speech, the press, assembly, and the right to bear arms. He included protections for those criminally accused or convicted, safeguards for due process of law, and a prohibition of unreasonable searches and seizures. One of the most powerful arguments against a bill of rights was that any rights inadvertently omitted could be considered as surrendered. Madison's solution was to assert that there were more rights than those explicitly protected in the Constitution and in the amendments, and that powers not delegated to Congress were reserved to the states or to the people. These concepts eventually became the Ninth and Tenth Amendments.

One of Madison's proposals read, "No state shall violate the equal rights of conscience, or the freedom of the press, or the trial by jury in criminal cases." Madison here sought to safeguard the rights of individuals against tyrannical legislation passed by the state legislatures. This provision attempted to add to the prohibitions on the states listed in Article I, Section 10, as well as to serve as a substitute measure for a congressional veto of state laws. This proposal, not recommended by any Antifederalists, was Madison's own original contribution. He considered it "the most valuable amendment on the whole list," a clear indication that he aimed at protecting rights, not merely placating Antifederalists.[56]

In debate, Madison defended his proposals against Antifederalists who argued that they did not go far enough and against Federalists who argued that other matters deserved higher priority and that the proposed amendments went too far in altering the Constitution. In promoting amendments, he rehearsed the theoretical arguments that he had already made privately to Jefferson. By educating the public, a bill of rights "may be one mean to controul the majority from those acts to which they might be otherwise inclined." Rights-related amendments would also enable "independent tribunals of justice" to "consider themselves in a peculiar manner the guardians of those rights." Madison argued, in short, that "the abuse of the powers of the general government may be guarded against in a more secure manner than is now done," by a bill of rights "while no one advantage . . . shall be damaged or endangered."[57]

Madison originally wanted to incorporate his amendments directly into the text of the Constitution, and he specified where in the document each provision would be inserted. He feared that simply to tack the amendments onto the end of the document would set up a conflict between the amendments and the original Constitution. Roger Sherman successfully countered that the Constitution had already become a sacred text not to be tampered with. Congress opted instead to appended Madison's amendments to the document as a numbered list. After a long fight, Madison secured passage of twelve amendments to be sent to the states for approval.[58]

Before passage, the Senate deleted Madison's favorite amendment, the proposal that protected personal rights from state infringement. Madison's attempt to provide federal protection against majority tyranny in the states thus failed. His goal of having the federal government guard individuals from state encroachments would not be achieved until the twentieth century. Beginning in the 1920s, a series of Supreme Court cases extended most of the Bill of Rights to apply to the states as well as to the federal government.[59]

By the end of 1791, ten of Madison's twelve amendments won ratification by three-fourths of the states. The first two amendments approved by Congress failed to win the support of three-fourths of the states. When proposals one and two failed, the other amendments moved up two places in number. The current First Amendment was originally Madison's third amendment, the current Second Amendment was originally Madison's fourth, and so on. The claim that Madison put freedom of speech and religion in the First Amendment because he considered them the most important rights is false. The order of the amendments has nothing to do with their importance. Rather, Madison's plan to insert the amendments into the text of the Constitution explains their order. Madison placed the alterations from first to last based on the order in which they would be inserted into the document.[60]

Which two proposals failed? The first would have kept congressional districts at 30,000 people per representative until Congress reached one hundred members. This amendment called for the enlargement of the House of Representatives eventually to 200 at which time Congress could change the ratio of representation and the size of the House. Madison's other amendment provided that congressional compensation could not be altered until after Congress faced the voters in an election. In the eighteenth century, this amendment came close to passing, but did not achieve the necessary ratification in three-fourths of the states. Unlike modern amendment proposals like the Equal Rights Amendment, no time limit for passage was placed on the amendments. Madison's compensation proposal languished for over two hundred years, a few states short of ratification. In the early 1990s, states began passing it again. When Michigan approved in 1992, the requisite threshold had finally been reached. Madison's 1789 proposal thus became the Twenty-Seventh Amendment, limiting alterations in congressional compensation.[61]

Madison has become known as the Father of the Constitution and as the Father of the Bill of Rights. Some historians have joked that Madison's paternity of rights-related amendments was a reluctant one, since he aimed at nothing more than to toss a tub to the Antifederalist whale. Madison's private correspondence with Jefferson, his passionate congressional crusade for amendments, and his inclusion of provisions that Antifederalists had not sought, however, show that he also supported a bill of rights to improve the Constitution. Madison, in short, earned and deserves the title Father of the Bill of Rights. Those amendments convinced most Antifederalists to give up their opposition to the Constitution. Even before its final approval in December 1791, Madison assured Washington that "the great bulk of the late opponents are entirely at rest." In addition to legitimizing the Constitution, the Bill of Rights has become one of the most important parts of the document. The debate over how the Constitution and its amendments should be interpreted by Congress, the President, the courts, and the American people, however, has continued.[62]

NOTES

1. W. W. Abbot et al., eds., *The Papers of George Washington, Confederation Series*, 6 vols. (Charlottesville: University of Virginia Press, 1992–1997), hereafter cited as *PGW-CS*, 6:488.

2. Adrienne Koch, ed., *Notes of Debates in the Federal Convention of 1787 Reported by James Madison* (Athens: Ohio University Press, 1966), hereafter cited as *NDFC*, 659. See Pauline Maier, *Ratification: The People Debate the Constitution, 1787–1788* (New York: Simon & Schuster, 2010).

3. Maier, *Ratification*, Illustration 20; *PGW-CS*, 6:325.

4. *Journals of the Continental Congress, 1774–1789*, 34 vols. (Washington: Government Printing Office, 1904–1937), 33:488, 540–44.

5. Ibid.; Robert A. Rutland, ed., *The Papers of George Mason*, 3 vols. (Chapel Hill: University of North Carolina Press, 1970), hereafter cited as *PJM*, 10:178–81.

6. Herbert Storing, *What the Antifederalists Were For* (Chicago, IL: University of Chicago Press, 1981), 9–10; Baltimore *Maryland Gazette*, March 7, 1788.

7. Max Farrand, ed., *The Records of the Federal Convention of 1787*. 1937 rev. ed. in four vols., reprint (New Haven, CT: Yale University Press, 1974), hereafter cited as *RFC*, 3:125–26.

8. Michael P. Zuckert and Derek A. Webb, eds., *The Anti-Federalist Writings of the Melancton Smith Circle* (Indianapolis, IN: Liberty Fund, 2009), 168.

9. RFC, 3:242.

10. George W. Carey and James McClellan, eds., *The Federalist* (Indianapolis, IN: Liberty Fund, 2001), 191.

11. RFC, 3:101, 270.

12. Zuckert and Webb, eds., *Anti-Federalist Writings of the Smith Circle*, 177.

13. Ibid., 169.

14. PGW-CS, 5:423; PJM, 10:391; Bruce Frohnen, ed., *The Anti-Federalists: Selected Writings and Speeches* (Washington: Regnery Publishing, 1999), 18.

15. Carey and McClellan, *The Federalist*, xxxix–xlvi.

16. Ibid., 42–49, 269.

17. Ibid., 48, 267–72.

18. Ibid., 256.

19. John P. Kaminski et al., eds, *The Documentary History of the Ratification of the Constitution*, 29 vols. to date (Madison, WI: State Historical Society of Wisconsin, 1976–), hereafter cited as DHRC, 3:37–41.

20. Ibid., 2:167–72; RFC Supplement, 250.

21. DHRC, 30–35.

22. Ibid., 3:119–25; NDFC, 7.

23. Richard Beeman, *Plain Honest Men: The Making of the American Constitution* (New York: Random House, 2009), 383–84; Maier, *Ratification*, 123–24.

24. DHRC, 3:328–32; Christopher Collier, *All Politics Is Local: Family, Friends, and Provincial Interests in the Creation of the Constitution* (Hanover, NH: University Press of New England, 2003), 79–131.

25. DHRC, 6:1107–23; Robert Ernst, *Rufus King: American Federalist* (Chapel Hill: University of North Caronia Press, 1968), 132.

26. DHRC, 6:1107–23; Ernst, *Rufus King*, 133.

27. John P. Kaminski et al., eds., "Introduction to the Ratification of the Constitution in Rhode Island," in *Documentary History of the Ratification of the Constitution Digital Edition* (Charlottesville: University of Virginia Press, 2009), hereafter cited as DHRCDE, 9–14.

28. DHRC, 7:618–20.

29. Ibid., 3:72–76, 300–306.

30. Maier, *Ratification*, 314–16.

31. RFC, 3:123–27.

32. DHRC, 10:1506, 1511–12.

33. Ibid., 1203; PGW-CS, 6:316.

34. DHRC, 9:897–900.

35. Ibid., 22:1669–74.

36. Beeman, *Plain, Honest Men*, 403–5; Maier, *Ratification*, 400–421.

37. Kaminski et al., eds., "Introduction to the Ratification of the Constitution in Rhode Island," in *DHRCDE*; Jack D. Warren, *The Presidency of George Washington* (Mount Vernon, VA: Mount Vernon Ladies Association, 2000), 12.

38. *DHRC*, 22:1674.

39. John K. Alexander, *The Selling of the Constitutional Convention: A History of News Coverage* (Madison, WI: Madison House, 1990).

40. Stanislaus Murray Hamilton, ed., *The Writings of James Monroe . . .*, 7 vols. (New York: G.P. Putnam's Sons, 1898–1903), 1:186.

41. Joseph Ellis, *Founding Brothers: The Revolutionary Generation* (New York: Vintage Books, 2002), 14–16.

42. Cecelia Kenyon, "Men of Little Faith: The Antifederalists on the Nature of Representative Government," *William and Mary Quarterly*, 3rd ser., 12 (1955) 3–43; David J. Siemers, *Ratifying the Republic: Antifederalists and Federalists in Constitutional Time* (Stanford, CA: Stanford University Press, 2002), 1–46.

43. W. W. Abbot et al., eds., *The Papers of George Washington, Presidential Series*, 19 vols. to date (Charlottesville: University Press of Virginia, 1987–), 4:552; Stuart Leibiger, *Founding Friendship: George Washington, James Madison, and the Creation of the American Republic* (Charlottesville: University of Virginia Press, 1999), 97–123.

44. Leibiger, *Founding Friendship*, 153–68.

45. Ellis, *Founding Brothers*, 3.

46. Charlene Bangs Bickford and Kenneth R. Bowling, *The Birth of the Nation: The First Federal Congress, 1789–1791* (Madison, WI: Madison House, 1989), 1–7.

47. Kenneth R. Bowling, *The Creation of Washington, D.C.: The Idea and Location of the American Capital* (Fairfax, VA: George Mason University Press, 1991), 182–207.

48. Kenneth R. Bowling, "The Founding Fathers and the Adoption of the Federal Bill of Rights," *Journal of the Early Republic*, 8 (1988), 223–51.

49. Stuart Leibiger, "James Madison and Amendments to the Constitution: 'Parchment Barriers,'" *Journal of Southern History*, 59 (1993), 441–46.

50. Ibid., 446–48, 452–53.

51. Ibid., 447.

52. Ibid., 457, 461.

53. Ibid., 454.

54. *PJM*, 10:336–37, 11:295–300. See also Lance Banning, *Jefferson & Madison: Three Conversations from the Founding* (Madison, WI: Madison House, 1995), 1–26, 125–58.

55. *PJM*, 11:404–5; Ralph Ketcham, *James Madison: A Biography* (New York: Macmillan, 1971), 277.

56. Leibiger, "James Madison and Amendments," 460–61, Helen E. Veit et al., eds., *Creating the Bill of Rights: The Documentary Record from the First Federal Congress* (Baltimore, MD: Johns Hopkins University Press, 1991), 11–14; *PJM*, 12:196–210, 344.

57. *PJM*, 12:196–210.

58. Leibiger, "James Madison and Amendments," 462–65; Veit et al., eds., *Creating the Bill of Rights*, 3–4, 66–95.

59. Leibiger, "James Madison and Amendments," 466.

60. Ibid., 462, 467.

61. Ibid., 467.

62. Ibid., 442, 467–68; *PJM*, 12:453.

CONCLUSION

Shortly after the close of the convention, Elizabeth Powell, wife of former Philadelphia mayor Samuel Powell, asked Benjamin Franklin, "Well Doctor what have we got a republic or a monarchy[?]" Franklin's answer sheds light on the purpose of the delegates. "A republic replied the Doctor if you can keep it." The Framers designed a novel republican form of government to replace the failing Confederation. James Madison wrote in *The Federalist* 51 that the new Constitution established a "compound republic" that was partly national and partly federal. The document, which divides power between the federal government and the states, launched a new phase of the American "experiment" in representative democracy. Now it was up to the American people to prove whether this new framework—unlike any other government in the world at the time—could last. Not until the end of the American Civil War nearly a century later would it become clear, as Abraham Lincoln put it in his Gettysburg Address, "that government of the people, by the people, for the people shall not perish from the earth." Today the U.S. Constitution is the world's oldest written national constitution still in use. It has shaped U.S. history and influenced world history for over 225 years. "The system" has indeed lasted "for ages."[1]

NOTE

1. RFC, 3:85. Samuel Powell served as mayor of Philadelphia from 1775–1776 and 1789–1790. www.phila.gov/phils/Mayorlst.htm; Carey and McClellan, eds., *The Federalist*, 270.

BIOGRAPHICAL ESSAYS

JOHN DICKINSON (1732–1808)

Dickinson became a Philadelphia lawyer after studying in Middle Temple, London. In 1767 and 1768, his *Letters from a Farmer in Pennsylvania* eloquently defended colonial rights. He represented Pennsylvania in the First and Second Continental Congresses, where he wrote the 1775 Olive Branch Petition seeking redress of colonial grievances from King George III. An opponent of independence, Dickinson absented himself from the Continental Congress rather than to vote against it. Then he enlisted in the army. Although he faithfully supported the Revolutionary cause, his reluctance to break from Great Britain nevertheless caused accusations of timidity and of harboring monarchical or aristocratic sympathies.

In 1776, Dickinson prepared a first draft of the Articles of Confederation that gave more power to the national government than the final version. Simultaneously a citizen of two states, he became president of Delaware in 1781 and president of Pennsylvania's Supreme Executive Council in 1782. After permanently settling in Delaware, he became chair of the 1786 Annapolis convention.

A small-state nationalist at the Constitutional Convention, Dickinson favored a strong central government provided Delaware retained a powerful voice in it. At the beginning of June, he became the first delegate to suggest what eventually became the Great Compromise between the large and small states: representation in the lower house should be based on state population, while each state should have an equal number of senators in the upper house. Dickinson served on the Committee on Postponed Parts that redesigned the presidency in the convention's final days. Fellow Delaware delegate George Read signed the Constitution for Dickinson when illness forced him to leave Philadelphia early. During the ratification campaign, Dickinson wrote the "Fabius" essay in support of the Constitution.

Source: William Murchison, *The Cost of Liberty: The Life of John Dickinson* (2013).

BENJAMIN FRANKLIN (1706–1790)

Born and raised in Boston, Franklin arrived in Philadelphia as a teenager after fleeing an apprenticeship to his abusive brother. Probably the most famous colonial American, Franklin acquired wealth and prominence as a printer. His publications included the *Pennsylvania Gazette* newspaper, and *Poor Richard's Almanac*, an annual book with farming tips, clever proverbs, and other useful information. Having made his fortune in printing, Franklin turned to science and philanthropy, emerging as a leading figure of the Enlightenment. He invented the Franklin Stove, the lightning rod, and bifocal glasses, and charted the Gulf Stream in the Atlantic Ocean. His famous experiment flying a kite in a thunderstorm proved that lightning is electricity. His scientific journal articles established him as a world authority on electricity and won him honorary doctorate degrees from Oxford and St. Andrews universities in England and Scotland. To make Philadelphia a better place to live, he started a fire company, a library, and a hospital.

Franklin spent years in England before the Revolution as a lobbyist for various colonies. Appointed to the Continental Congress, he helped Thomas Jefferson draft the Declaration of Independence. With international name recognition for his scientific achievements, he became, at age seventy, the U.S. first ambassador to France, with whom he negotiated the French Alliance so indispensable to American independence. Viewed in Europe as a rustic philosopher from the American wilderness, Franklin played the part by giving himself a "Noble Savage" makeover, dressing like an American frontiersman in the streets of Paris. Fellow diplomat John Adams complained that Franklin spent too much time dining out and socializing instead of looking after his official duties, and that he became too accommodating to the French at the expense of America's national interest.

The oldest delegate to the Constitutional Convention, the eighty-one-year old suffered chronic pain from gout and kidney stones, for which he took opium. Although Franklin offered undistinguished policy proposals at the convention, he played a key role as an advocate of compromise and unity. He frequently entertained groups of delegates at his nearby home, often under the mulberry tree in his yard. On the convention's last day, he implored the delegates to put aside their doubts and to add their names to the document.

Source: Walter Isaacson, *Benjamin Franklin: An American Life* (2003).

ELBRIDGE GERRY (1744–1814)

A Marblehead, Massachusetts, merchant and Harvard College graduate, Gerry served in Massachusetts's colonial legislature from 1772 to 1774, and then in the colony's provincial congress from 1774 to 1775. A delegate to the Continental Congress from 1776 to 1780, Gerry, along with John Adams, became an early advocate of independence. He signed both the Declaration of Independence and the Articles of Confederation. He served in the Confederation Congress from 1783 to 1785.

At the Constitutional Convention, Gerry chaired the Grand Committee of Eleven that suggested the Great Compromise between the large and small states. Gerry ultimately refused to sign the Constitution, however, because he feared that it did not sufficiently limit the powers of the federal government. A so-called Old Republican, he especially dreaded that a permanent peacetime military establishment, known in the eighteenth century as a "standing army," would lead to tyranny. Invited to attend the Massachusetts ratification convention, Gerry left in disgust after failing to receive permission to speak there.

Gerry represented Massachusetts from 1789 to 1793 in the U.S. Congress. President John Adams appointed him a special envoy to France in 1797 along with Charles Cotesworth Pinckney and John Marshall. In an incident known as the XYZ Affair, French agents demanded a bribe from the American diplomats in return for an appointment with

Foreign Minister Marquis de Talleyrand. This insulting treatment led to the Quasi-War with France, an undeclared naval conflict on the Atlantic Ocean in 1798. Gerry served as governor of Massachusetts from 1810 to 1812. He became vice president in 1813 under James Madison and died in office.

Source: George Athan Billias, *Elbridge Gerry: Founding Father and Republican Statesman* (1976).

ALEXANDER HAMILTON (1757–1804)

Born to unmarried parents on the West Indian island of Nevis in 1757, Hamilton soon became an orphan. Local merchants taught him their profession and then sent him to America in 1772 to attend King's College (later Columbia University) in New York. When the Revolution broke out, Hamilton joined the Continental Army. After leading an artillery company, he became an aide to General Washington. Having acquired a field command, Colonel Hamilton led a successful attack on British fortifications during the 1781 Yorktown campaign. Quitting the army for politics, Hamilton entered the New York legislature and then the Confederation Congress. He became a lawyer and "married up" to Elizabeth Schuyler, the daughter of New York patrician Philip Schuyler.

A brilliant and prolific thinker and writer, Hamilton emerged as an outspoken nationalist thanks to his wartime frustration with Congress's inability adequately to man and supply the Continental Army. In 1782, he backed a successful resolution in the New York legislature for Congress to call a constitutional convention. As a delegate to the Annapolis convention, he authored the report calling the 1787 Philadelphia convention.

At the Constitutional Convention Hamilton expressed skepticism about the viability of republicanism and unabashedly defended the British monarchical system as the ideal form of government. He advocated the establishment of a powerful national government with a president and senate serving during good behavior, and a drastic reduction in the powers of the states. Hamilton became the lone signer from New York. Hamilton authored fifty-one of *The Federalist* essays and served in New York's ratification convention.

As the first Treasury secretary from 1789 to 1795 under President Washington, he backed the funding of the national debt, the assumption of the state debts by the federal government, and the creation of a national bank. He was killed in a duel by Vice President Aaron Burr in 1804.

Source: Ron Chernow, *Alexander Hamilton* (2004).

RUFUS KING (1755–1827)

A native of Maine and a graduate of Harvard College, King studied law and became an attorney and an opponent of slavery. A Massachusetts delegate to the Confederation Congress from 1784 to 1787, he helped to draft the Northwest Ordinance ending slavery in the Northwest Territory. During John Jay's 1786 negotiations with Spanish envoy Don Diego de Gardoqui, King temporarily favored the establishment of a separate northern confederacy that could sign a trade agreement with Spain. Until late 1786, he believed Congress capable of enacting political reform. Only in February 1787, amid Shays's Rebellion and the collapse of the Confederation, did he finally support a constitutional convention.

King, who privately deplored the "madness of Democracy" that prevailed in his state, emerged as a strong nationalist at the Constitutional Convention. He took aim at the pro-South and proslavery features that emerged in the draft constitution prepared by the Committee of Detail. These provisions allowed the international slave trade to remain open indefinitely, prohibited slave imports or exports of any kind from being taxed, and required a two-thirds supermajority of each house of Congress to pass commercial acts. King led a successful effort to allow Congress to tax slave imports, to close the African slave trade beginning in 1808, and to eliminate the supermajority requirement to pass commercial laws. He defended the Constitution at the Massachusetts ratification convention. King moved to New York and represented that state in the U.S. Senate from 1789 to 1796 and from 1813 to 1825, where he condemned the admission of Missouri to the Union as a slave state. He served as minister to Great Britain from 1796 to 1803 and from 1825 to 1826. The Federalists ran him for vice president in 1804 and 1808, and for president in 1816.

Source: Robert Ernst, *Rufus King: American Federalist* (1968).

JAMES MADISON (1751–1836)

Born into the Virginia gentry, Madison grew up at Montpelier, the family plantation located in the piedmont region of the state. After being privately tutored and attending local academies, he entered the College of New Jersey (which later became Princeton University). A participant in the 1776 Virginia convention, Madison in 1777 accepted appointment to Virginia's executive council and served under wartime governors Patrick Henry and Thomas Jefferson. From 1780 to 1783, as a delegate to the Continental and Confederation congresses, he tried but failed to obtain for the national government the power to collect revenue through an impost.

Entering the Virginia General Assembly in 1784, Madison became disturbed by the "injustice" of state laws, as he witnessed an overly powerful legislature engaging in what he saw as majority tyranny. He attended the 1786 Annapolis convention and the 1787 Constitutional Convention. Madison's "Virginia Plan," the starting point for the Constitutional Convention, aimed to replace the Confederation with a strong national government that operated directly on the people and that based representation on population or taxes paid. Madison's twenty-nine essays in *The Federalist* argued that the Constitution's checks and balances would prevent majority tyranny and that the republic's large geographical size would ensure that self-interested factions canceled one another out. He led the pro-Constitution forces to victory in Virginia's ratification convention.

Serving in the U.S. House of Representatives from 1789 to 1797, Madison authored the Bill of Rights and became a leader of the Jeffersonian Republican Party. Returning to the state legislature, he wrote the Virginia Resolutions of 1798, declaring the Alien and Sedition Acts unconstitutional. Madison served as secretary of state under Thomas Jefferson from 1801 to 1809. As president from 1809 to 1817, he led the nation through the War of 1812. In retirement, Madison prepared his *Notes of Debates in the Federal Convention of 1787* for posthumous publication.

Source: Stuart Leibiger, "James Madison," in Stephen L. Schechter et al., eds., *American Governance* (2016), 3:225–29.

GEORGE MASON (1725–1792)

George Mason IV received private tutoring before the premature death of his father forced him to rely on self-education. Mason, who established Gunston Hall plantation located on the Potomac River in Virginia, lived a sedentary life because he suffered from gout. Regularly turning down public service appointments because of poor health, Mason bitterly described public service as "an oppressive & unjust Invasion of my personal Liberty." He dropped out of Virginia's colonial legislature, the House of Burgesses, after only one year, fed up with logrolling, pork-barrel projects, and long-winded speeches.

In July 1774 Fairfax County adopted the Fairfax Resolves, authored by Mason, which declared that the rights of Englishmen applied to the colonists and requested a Continental Congress to defend colonial liberties. As a delegate to the Virginia convention in 1776, he prepared Virginia's Declaration of Rights, the first Bill of Rights of the American Revolution. Mason also drafted the state's first constitution, adopted on June 29, 1776.

During the 1785 Mount Vernon Conference, Mason authored the Mount Vernon Compact, which led to the calling of the Annapolis convention. At the Constitutional Convention he sat on the Grand Committee of Eleven that proposed the Great Compromise over legislative representation. He refused to sign the final document, angry that it left the international slave trade open, that it allowed a bare majority of each house of congress to pass commercial laws, and that it lacked a bill of rights. His "Objections to this Constitution" warned that the new framework would lead to a monarchy or aristocracy. Mason argued in vain against the Constitution at the Virginia ratification convention.

Source: Jeff Broadwater, *George Mason: Forgotten Founder* (2006), quoted at 136.

GOUVERNEUR MORRIS (1752–1816)

Born to an affluent New York family, Morris attended King's College (later Columbia University), and then became an attorney. After helping to write New York's 1777 constitution as a member of the state's provincial congress, Morris entered the Continental Congress. The following year, political enemies in New York led by Governor George Clinton successfully opposed his reelection.

Settling in Philadelphia, Morris became a resident of Pennsylvania and served in the Confederation's finance department under Superintendent of Finance Robert Morris (no relation). With no strong state allegiance and a clear understanding of the economic weaknesses of the Confederation, Morris emerged as a powerful nationalist. At the Constitutional Convention, Gouverneur Morris gave more speeches than any other participant except James Wilson. He advocated representation based on population, a strong executive, and property qualifications to vote and hold office. His eloquent attacks on the institution of slavery helped to reduce several provisions favoring that institution. As a member of the Committee on Postponed Parts, he helped to redesign the presidency into a coequal branch. As a member of the Committee of Style, he drafted the final version of the Constitution. Returning to New York, he resided at Morrisania, his family's estate. He served as a special envoy to Great Britain in 1791, as U.S. minster to France from 1792 to 1794, and as a U.S. senator from New York from 1800 to 1803.

Source: James Kirschke, *Gouverneur Morris: Author, Statesman and Man of the World* (2005).

EDMUND RANDOLPH (1753–1813)

Born into a prominent Virginia family, Randolph attended the College of William & Mary and then became an attorney. Unlike his Loyalist father, Randolph pledged allegiance to the Revolution and served as an aide to General Washington during the war. By age twenty-seven, Randolph had already served as a delegate to the 1776 Virginia convention, as mayor of Williamsburg, as Virginia's attorney general, and as a member of the Continental and Confederation congresses. Perhaps the experience of being the son of a Loyalist and having had to prove his patriotism to his fellow Virginians caused Randolph to be obsessed with maintaining public approval in his state.

While serving as governor of Virginia, Randolph also attended the 1786 Annapolis convention. At the Constitutional Convention, he presented the Virginia Plan, calling for the Confederation to be replaced with a strong national government with representation based on population or taxes paid. As a member of the Committee of Detail, he prepared the first draft of the U.S. Constitution. Randolph refused, however, to sign the Constitution because he wished to see a second convention propose amendments to it. Randolph publicly warned that if the people of the states "must either adopt the constitution in the whole, or reject it in the whole," they would "not only reject it, but bid a lasting farewell to the union." At the Virginia ratification convention, he reversed course and supported adoption of the new framework because he believed that only remaining alternatives were ratification or disunion.

President George Washington appointed Randolph the first attorney general of the United States in 1789, and then named him secretary of state in 1793. In 1795, Randolph resigned amid allegations—probably false—that he had accepted a bribe from the French in return for urging the president to reject the Jay Treaty.

Source: John J. Reardon, Edmund Randolph: A Biography (1974).

ROGER SHERMAN (1721–1793)

Self-made and self-educated, Sherman worked his way up from being a shoemaker and almanac printer to become a lawyer and businessman. Entering politics, he held local offices such as justice of the peace before winning election to Connecticut's General Assembly in 1755. He then advanced to the state's upper chamber before being appointed to the Superior Court. A member of the Congregationalist church, Sherman often cited Reformed Protestant theology in his speeches and writings, including those against slavery, which he helped to abolish in Connecticut. Like many New England men, Sherman believed that church and state should support one another, and that while dissenters should worship freely, the state government must encourage Christianity to promote the public good.

Beginning with the 1765 Stamp Act, Sherman rejected Parliament's right to legislate for the colonies. Serving in Congress from 1774 through 1784, he helped draft the Declaration of Independence and the Articles of Confederation. In the floor debate over the Articles, he anticipated the 1787 Connecticut Compromise by advocating that legislation should obtain the support of both a majority of delegates and of states. By 1787 Sherman agreed that Congress needed the power to tax and regulate commerce.

At age sixty-seven Sherman was the second-oldest delegate to the Constitutional Convention. He firmly believed that the legislative branch should dominate the federal government's other branches. He sat on the Grand Committee of Eleven that proposed the Great Compromise over legislative representation. His advocacy of this compromise resulted more from his desire to defend the states-qua-states than to defend the small states. After the convention, he wrote essays supporting the Constitution and attended Connecticut's ratification convention. He served in the U.S. House of Representatives from 1789 to 1791, and the U.S. Senate from 1791 to 1793.

Source: Mark David Hall, *Roger Sherman and the Creation of the American Republic* (2013).

GEORGE WASHINGTON (1732–1799)

George Washington, born at Pope's Creek plantation in Westmoreland County, Virginia, became a frontier surveyor after his father's death forced him to fend for himself. He started the Seven Year's War (known in America as the French and Indian War) in 1754 with an ill-advised assault on a detachment of French troops. The following year, Washington demonstrated tremendous bravery in the Battle of the Monongahela, where the French and their Indian allies routed British forces and killed British general Edward Braddock. Despite making his Virginia regiment as effective as Redcoats, he failed to obtain a British officer's commission.

Washington became prosperous through innovative farming on his Mount Vernon estate on the Potomac River. His marriage to wealthy widow Martha Dandridge Custis elevated him to the top of Virginia's gentry. During the 1770s, Washington increasingly saw British colonial policy as a conspiracy to enslave him and his countrymen. He represented Virginia in the First and Second Continental Congresses in Philadelphia in 1774 and 1775. After the battles of Lexington and Concord, the delegates unanimously named him commander in chief of the Continental

Army. Making sure his army never got destroyed in battle by the stronger British forces, he nevertheless seized favorable opportunities to win victories at Trenton, Princeton, and Yorktown. Refusing to become a dictator as previous military leaders had done, he established military subordination to the democratically elected civilian government as a cornerstone of American constitutionalism. At the war's end, he became heralded as the American Cincinnatus for setting aside his sword and returning to his plow like his ancient Roman counterpart.

After serving as president of the 1787 Constitutional Convention, Washington was unanimously elected the first president under the U.S. Constitution. He brought prestige to the presidential office and established numerous executive precedents. In 1797 he retired after two terms in office and died two years later.

Source: Stuart Leibiger, "George Washington," in Stephen L. Schechter et al., eds., *American Governance* (2016), 5:288–90.

JAMES WILSON (1742–1798)

Arriving in Philadelphia from Scotland at the age of twenty-three, Wilson studied law under John Dickinson, became an attorney, and joined the upper class. He unwisely sought riches through questionable land speculations that eventually ruined him.

As a Continental congressman, Wilson voted in favor of independence after having argued against it. During the Revolutionary War, he gained a reputation as an elitist who sympathized with the British during the occupation of Philadelphia. In 1779, he fled the city after enraged local militiamen attacked his home, dubbed "Fort Wilson." He helped to write the Articles of Confederation and the Pennsylvania Constitution.

The Constitutional Convention's most outspoken proponent of popular election of federal officeholders, Wilson advocated "raising the federal pyramid to a considerable altitude, and for that reason wished to give it as broad a basis as possible." A true nationalist, Wilson also advocated the concept of dual citizenship. As citizens of a state, people interacted with the state government. But instead of state governments interacting with the central government, Wilson favored having citizens also interact directly with the national government.

Wilson supported the Three-Fifths Compromise in return for the support of South Carolina and Georgia for basing representation in congress on population. He served on the Committee of Detail that prepared a first draft of the Constitution. Wilson defended the Constitution in a speech in the yard outside the Pennsylvania State House and at the Pennsylvania ratification convention. Appointed as an associate justice of the Supreme Court by President Washington in 1789, he served until his death nine years later.

Source: Page Smith, *James Wilson: Founding Father* (1956).

PRIMARY DOCUMENTS

1. Annapolis Convention Report, September 14, 1786

Pronouncing the condition of the United States under the Confederation as "critical," this report, authored by Alexander Hamilton, called upon the states to send delegates to the Constitutional Convention to meet in Philadelphia in May 1787. It instructed the Philadelphia convention "to take into consideration the situation of the United States, and to devise such further provisions as shall appear to them necessary to render the constitution of the Federal Government adequate to the exigencies of the Union."

Proceedings of the Commissioners to Remedy Defects of the Federal Government, Annapolis in the State of Maryland. September 14, 1786.

To the Honorable, The Legislatures of Virginia, Delaware, Pennsylvania, New Jersey, and New York—assembled at Annapolis, humbly beg leave to report.

That, pursuant to their several appointments, they met, at Annapolis in the State of Maryland on the eleventh day of September Instant, and having proceeded to a Communication of their Powers; they found that the States of New York, Pennsylvania, and Virginia, had, in substance, and nearly in the same terms, authorized their respective Commissions "to meet such other Commissioners as were, or might be, appointed by the other States in the Union, at such time and place as should be agreed upon by the said Commissions to take into consideration the trade and commerce of the United States, to consider how far a uniform system in their commercial intercourse and regulations might be necessary to their common interest and permanent harmony, and to report to the several

States such an Act, relative to this great object, as when unanimously ratified by them would enable the United States in Congress assembled effectually to provide for the same."

That the State of New Jersey had enlarged the object of their appointment, empowering their Commissioners, "to consider how far a uniform system in their commercial regulations and other important matters, mighty be necessary to the common interest and permanent harmony of the several States," and to report such an Act on the subject, as when ratified by them, "would enable the United States in Congress assembled, effectually to provide for the exigencies of the Union."

That appointments of Commissioners have also been made by the States of New Hampshire, Massachusetts, Rhode Island, and North Carolina, none of whom, however, have attended; but that no information has been received by your Commissioners, of any appointment having been made by the States of Connecticut, Maryland, South Carolina or Georgia.

That the express terms of the powers of your Commissioners supposing a deputation from all the States, and having for object the Trade and Commerce of the United States, Your Commissioners did not conceive it advisable to proceed on the business of their mission, under the Circumstances of so partial and defective a representation.

Deeply impressed, however, with the magnitude and importance of the object confided to them on this occasion, your Commissioners cannot forbear to indulge an expression of their earnest and unanimous wish, that speedy measures be taken, to effect a general meeting, of the States, in a future Convention, for the same, and such other purposes, as the situation of public affairs may be found to require.

If in expressing this wish, or in intimating any other sentiment, your Commissioners should seem to exceed the strict bounds of their appointment, they entertain a full confidence, that a conduct, dictated by an anxiety for the welfare of the United States, will not fail to receive an indulgent construction.

In this persuasion, your Commissioners submit an opinion, that the Idea of extending the powers of their Deputies, to other objects, than those of Commerce, which has been adopted by the State of New Jersey, was an improvement on the original plan, and will deserve to be incorporated into that of a future Convention; they are the more naturally led to this conclusion, as in the course of their reflections on the subject, they

Primary Documents

have been induced to think, that the power of regulating trade is of such comprehensive extent, and will enter so far into the general System of the federal government, that to give it efficacy, and to obviate questions and doubts concerning its precise nature and limits, may require a correspondent adjustment of other parts of the Federal System.

That there are important defects in the system of the Federal Government is acknowledged by the Acts of all those States, which have concurred in the present Meeting; That the defects, upon a closer examination, may be found greater and more numerous, than even these acts imply, is at least so far probably, from the embarrassments which characterize the present State of our national affairs, foreign and domestic, as may reasonably be supposed to merit a deliberate and candid discussion, in some mode, which will unite the Sentiments and Councils of all the States. In the choice of the mode, your Commissioners are of opinion, that a Convention of Deputies from the different States, for the special and sole purpose of entering into this investigation, and digesting a plan for supplying such defects as may be discovered to exist, will be entitled to a preference from considerations, which will occur without being particularized.

Your Commissioners decline an enumeration of those national circumstances on which their opinion respecting the propriety of a future Convention, with more enlarged powers, is founded; as it would be a useless intrusion of facts and observations, most of which have been frequently the subject of public discussion, and none of which can have escaped the penetration of those to whom they would in this instance be addressed. They are, however, of a nature so serious, as, in the view of your Commissioners, to render the situation of the United States delicate and critical, calling for an exertion of the united virtue and wisdom of all the members of the Confederacy.

Under this impression, Your Commissioners, with the most respectful deference, beg leave to suggest their unanimous conviction that it may essentially tend to advance the interests of the union if the States, by whom they have been respectively delegated, would themselves concur, and use their endeavors to procure the concurrence of the other States, in the appointment of Commissioners, to meet at Philadelphia on the second Monday in May next, to take into consideration the situation of the United States, to devise such further provisions as shall appear to them necessary to render the constitution of the Federal Government adequate to the exigencies of the Union; and to report such an Act for that purpose to the United States in Congress assembled, as when agreed to, by them, and afterwards confirmed by the Legislatures of every State, will effectually provide for the same.

Though your Commissioners could not with propriety address these observations and sentiments to any but the States they have the honor to represent, they have nevertheless concluded from motives of respect, to transmit copies of the Report to the United States in Congress assembled, and to the executives of the other States.

Source: Charles C. Tansill, comp. *Documents Illustrative of the Formation of the Union of the American States.* Washington, D.C.: Government Printing Office, 1927, House Document No. 398.

2. Virginia Appoints Delegates to the Constitutional Convention, November–December 1786

Virginia, the first state to appoint delegates to the Constitutional Convention, chose prestigious delegates and circulated its resolutions to the other states to encourage them to attend as well. The following is the act appointing delegates to the convention, followed by an extract from the Journal of the House of Delegates of Virginia on the election of convention delegates.

An act for appointing deputies from this commonwealth to a convention proposed to be held in the city of Philadelphia in May next, for the purpose of revising the federal constitution. [Passed the Virginia House of Delegates on November 9, 1786 and in the Virginia Senate on November 23, 1786.]

WHEREAS the Commissioners who assembled at Annapolis, on the fourteenth of September last, for the purpose of devising and reporting the means of enabling Congress to provide effectually for the Commercial Interest of the United States, have represented the necessity of extending the revision of the federal system to all its defects; and have recommended, that Deputies for that purpose be appointed by the several Legislatures to meet in convention in the city of Philadelphia, on the second Monday of May next; a provision which seems preferable to a discussion of the subject in Congress, where it might be too much interrupted by the ordinary business before them; and where it would besides, be deprived of

Primary Documents

the valuable councils of sundry individuals, who are disqualified by the constitution or laws of particular states, or restrained by peculiar circumstances from a seat in that Assembly: And whereas the General Assembly of this Commonwealth, taking into view the actual situation of the Confederacy, as well as reflecting on the alarming representations made from time to time, by the United States in Congress, particularly in their act of the fifteenth day of February last, can no longer doubt that the crisis is arrived at which the good people of America are to decide the solemn question, whether they will by wise and magnanimous efforts reap the just fruits of that independence which they have so gloriously acquired, and of that Union which they have cemented with so much of their common blood; or whether, by giving way to unmanly jealousies and prejudices, or to partial and transitory interests, they will renounce the auspicious blessings prepared for them by the Revolution, and furnish to its enemies an eventual triumph over those, by whole virtue and valour, it has been accomplished: And whereas the same noble and extended Policy, and the same fraternal and affectionate sentiments, which originally determined the Citizens of this Commonwealth, to unite with their Brethren of the other States, in establishing a fœderal Government, cannot but be felt with equal force now as the motives to lay aside every inferior consideration, and to concur in such farther concessions and provisions, as may be necessary to secure the great objects for which that Government was instituted, and to render the United States as happy in Peace, as they have been glorious in war.

Be it therefore enacted, by the General Assembly of the Commonwealth of Virginia, That seven Commissioners be appointed by joint ballot of both Houses of Assembly, who, or any three of them, are hereby authorized as Deputies from this Commonwealth to meet such Deputies as may be appointed and authorized by other states, to assemble in Convention at Philadelphia, as above recommended, and to join with them in devising and discussing all such alterations and farther provisions, as may be necessary to render the fœderal Constitution, adequate to the exigencies of the Union, and in reporting such an act for that purpose, to the United States in Congress, as when agreed to by them, and duly confirmed by the several states, will effectually provide for the same.

And be it further enacted, That in case of the death of any of the said Deputies, or of their declining their appointments, the Executive are hereby authorized to supply such vacancies; and the Governor is requested to transmit forthwith a copy of this Act, to the United States in Congress, and to the Executives of each of the states in the Union.

Source: William Waller Henig, ed. *The Statues at Large; Being a Collection of All the Laws of Virginia* . . ., 13 vols. Richmond and Philadelphia, 1819–1823, 12:256–57. Available at the Library of Congress.

In the House of Delegates

Monday the 4th of December 1786.

The House according to the Order of the Day proceeded by joint Ballot with the Senate to the appointment of Seven Deputies from this Commonwealth to a Convention proposed to be held in the City of Philadelphia in May next for the purpose of revising the Fœderal Constitution, and the Members having prepared Tickets with the names of the Persons to be appointed, and deposited the same in the Ballot-boxes, Mr. Corbin, Mr. Matthews, Mr. David Stuart, Mr. George Nicholas, Mr. Richard Lee, Mr. Wills, Mr. Thomas Smith, Mr. Goodall and Mr. Turberville were nominated a Committee to meet a Committee from the Senate in the Conference-Chamber and jointly with them to examine the Ballot-boxes and report to the House on whom the Majority of Votes should fall. The Committee then withdrew and after some time returned into the House and reported that the Committee had, according to order, met a Committee from the Senate in the Conference-Chamber, and jointly with them examined the Ballot-boxes and found a majority of Votes in favor of George Washington, Patrick Henry, Edmund Randolph, John Blair, James Madison, George Mason and George Wythe Esquires.

Source: Journal of the House of Delegates of Virginia, October 1786, Sess., 85–86.

3. The Confederation Congress's Resolution Approving the Constitutional Convention, February 21, 1787

Congress's resolution helped provide political legitimacy to the Constitutional Convention. Congress endorsed the Constitutional Convention "for the sole and express purpose of revising the Articles of Confederation." Congress's charge to the convention to revise the Articles of Confederation was more modest than the Annapolis convention report, which called on the convention to render the Constitution "adequate to the exigencies of the Union."

Whereas there is provision in the articles of Confederation & perpetual Union for making alterations therein by the assent of a Congress of the United States and of the legislatures of the several States; And whereas experience hath evinced that there are defects in the present Confederation, as a mean to remedy which several of the States and particularly the State of New York by express instructions to their delegates in Congress have suggested a convention for the purposes expressed in the following resolution and such convention appearing to be the most probable mean of establishing in these states a firm national government.

Resolved that in the opinion of Congress it is expedient that on the second Monday in May next a Convention of delegates who shall have been appointed by the several states be held at Philadelphia for the sole and express purpose of revising the Articles of Confederation and reporting to Congress and the several legislatures such alterations and provisions therein as shall when agreed to in Congress and confirmed by the states render the federal constitution adequate to the exigencies of Government & the preservation of the Union.

Source: Journals of the Continental Congress, manuscript vol. 38, Library of Congress.

4. James Madison to George Washington, April 16, 1787

James Madison shared with his friend and collaborator, George Washington, his thoughts on the political reforms that ought to take place. He called for the establishment of a national government with executive, legislative, and judicial branches, in which representation would no longer be based on state equality. Congress would have the power to tax, to regulate commerce, to legislate in all matters that "require uniformity" among the states, and to veto state laws.

DEAR SIR

I have been honoured with your letter of the 31 of March, and find with much pleasure that your views of the reform which ought to be pursued by the Convention, give a sanction to those which I have entertained. Temporising applications will dishonor the Councils which propose them, and may foment the internal malignity of the disease, at the same time that they produce an ostensible palliation of it. Radical attempts, although unsuccessful, will at least justify the authors of them.

Having been lately led to revolve the subject which is to undergo the discussion of the Convention, and formed in my mind *some* outlines of a new system, I take the liberty of submitting them without apology, to your eye.

Conceiving that an individual independence of the States is utterly irreconcileable with their aggregate sovereignty; and that a consolidation of the whole into one simple republic would be as inexpedient as it is unattainable, I have sought for some middle ground, which may at once support a due supremacy of the national authority, and not exclude the local authorities wherever they can be subordinately useful.

I would propose as the ground-work that a change be made in the principle of representation. According to the present form of the Union in which the intervention of the States is in all great cases necessary to effectuate the measures of Congress, an equality of suffrage, does not destroy the inequality of importance, in the several members. No one will deny that Virginia and Massts. have more weight and influence both within & without Congress than Delaware or Rho. Island. Under a system which would operate in many essential points without the intervention of the State legislatures, the case would be materially altered. A vote in the national Councils from Delaware, would then have the same effect and value as one from the largest State in the Union. I am ready to believe that such a change would not be attended with much difficulty. A majority of the States, and those of greatest influence, will regard it as favorable to them. To the Northern States it will be recommended by their present populousness; to the Southern by their expected advantage in this respect. The lesser States must in every event yield to the predominant will. But the consideration which particularly urges a change in the representation is that it will obviate the principal objections of the larger States to the necessary concessions of power.

I would propose next that in addition to the present federal powers, the national Government should be armed with positive and compleat authority in all cases which require uniformity; such as the regulation of trade, including the right of taxing both exports & imports, the fixing the terms and forms of naturalization, &c &c.

Over and above this positive power, a negative *in all cases whatsoever* on the legislative acts of the States, as heretofore exercised by the Kingly prerogative, appears to me to be absolutely necessary, and to be the least possible encroachment on the State jurisdictions. Without this defensive power, every positive power that can be given on paper will be evaded & defeated. The States will continue to invade the national jurisdiction, to violate treaties and the law of nations & to harrass each other with rival and spiteful measures dictated by mistaken views of interest. Another happy effect of this prerogative would be its controul on the internal vicisitudes of State policy; and the aggressions of interested majorities on the rights of minorities and of individuals. The great desideratum which has not yet been found for Republican Governments, seems to be some disinterested & dispassionate umpire in disputes between different passions & interests in the State. The majority who alone have the right of decision, have frequently an interest real or supposed in abusing it. In Monarchies the sovereign is more neutral to the interests and views of different parties; but unfortunately he too often forms interests of his own repugnant to those of the whole. Might not the national prerogative here suggested be found sufficiently disinterested for the decision of local questions of policy, whilst it would itself be sufficiently restrained from the pursuit of interests adverse to those of the whole Society? There has not been any moment since the peace at which the representatives of the union would have given an assent to paper money or any other measure of a kindred nature.

The national supremacy ought also to be extended as I conceive to the Judiciary departments. If those who are to expound & apply the laws, are connected by their interests & their oaths with the particular States wholly, and not with the Union, the participation of the Union in the making of the laws may be possibly rendered unavailing. It seems at least necessary that the oaths of the Judges should include a fidelity to the general as well as local constitution, and that an appeal should lie to some national tribunals in all cases to which foreigners or inhabitants of other States may be parties. The admiralty jurisdiction seems to fall entirely within the purview of the national Government.

The national supremacy in the Executive departments is liable to some difficulty, unless the officers administering them could be made appointable by the supreme Government. The Militia ought certainly to be placed in some form or other under the authority which is entrusted with the general protection and defence.

A Government composed of such extensive powers should be well organized and balanced. The Legislative department might be divided into two branches; one of them chosen every _____ years by the people at large, or by the legislatures; the other to consist of fewer members, to hold their places for a longer term, and to go out in such a rotation as always to leave in office a large majority of old members. Perhaps the negative on the laws might be most conveniently exercised by this branch. As a further check, a council of revision including the great ministerial officers might be superadded.

A national Executive must also be provided. I have scarcely ventured as yet to form my own opinion either of the manner in which it ought to be constituted or of the authorities with which it ought to be cloathed.

An article should be inserted expressly guarantying the tranquillity of the States against internal as well as external dangers.

In like manner the right of coercion should be expressly declared. With the resources of Commerce in hand, the national administration might always find means of exerting it either by sea or land; But the difficulty & awkwardness of operating by force on the collective will of a State, render it particularly desirable that the necessity of it might be precluded. Perhaps the negative on the laws might create such a mutuality of dependence between the General and particular authorities, as to answer this purpose. Or perhaps some defined objects of taxation might be submitted along with commerce, to the general authority.

To give a new System its proper validity and energy, a ratification must be obtained from the people, and not merely from the ordinary authority of the Legislatures. This will be the more essential as inroads on the *existing Constitutions* of the States will be unavoidable...

JS. MADISON JR.

Source: Jared Sparks, ed. *The Writings of George Washington, Volume IX.* Boston: Russell, Odiorne, and Metcalf, 1835, 516–20.

5. The Virginia Plan, May 29, 1787

Virginia's governor, Edmund Randolph, proposed these resolutions to the convention. Drawn up by Madison and discussed by the delegates from Virginia in the days before the convention began, this plan became the starting point for the convention. The Virginia Plan proposed not a modest revision of the Articles of Confederation, but an entirely new national government with executive, legislative, and judicial branches that operated on the people directly without the states as intermediaries. Representation in both legislative houses would be based on each state's "number of free inhabitants" or taxes paid.

1. Resolved, that the Articles of Confederation ought to be so corrected and enlarged as to accomplish the objects proposed by their institution; namely, "common defence, security of liberty, and general welfare."
2. Resolved, therefore, that the rights of suffrage in the National Legislature ought to be proportioned to the quotas of contribution, or to the number of free inhabitants, as the one or the other rule may seem best in different cases.
3. Resolved, that the National Legislature ought to consist of two branches.
4. Resolved, that the members of the first branch of the National Legislature ought to be elected by the people of the several States every _____ for the term of _____; to be of the age of _____ years at least; to receive liberal stipends by which they may be compensated for the devotion of their time to the public service; to be ineligible to any office established by a particular State, or under the authority of the United States, except those peculiarly belonging to the functions of the first branch, during the term of service, and for the space of _____ after its expiration to be incapable of reelection for the space of _____ after the expiration; of their term of service, and to be subject to recall.
5. Resolved, that the members of the second branch of the National Legislature ought to be elected by those of the first, out of a proper number of persons nominated by the individual Legislatures, to be of the age of _____ years at least; to hold their offices for a term sufficient to insure their independency; to receive liberal stipends, by which they may be compensated for the devotion of their time to the public service; and

to be ineligible to any office established by a particular State, or under the authority of the United States, except those peculiarly belonging to the functions of the second branch, during the term of service; and for the space of _____ after the expiration thereof.

6. Resolved, that each branch ought to possess the right of originating acts; that the National Legislature ought to be empowered to enjoy the legislative rights vested in Congress by the Confederation, and moreover to legislate in all cases to which the separate States are incompetent, or in which the harmony of the United States may be interrupted by the exercise of individual legislation; to negative all laws passed by the several States contravening, in the opinion of the National Legislature, the Articles of Union, or any treaty subsisting under the authority of the Union; and to call forth the force of the Union against any member of the Union failing to fulfil its duty under the Articles thereof.

7. Resolved, that a National Executive be instituted; to be chosen by the National Legislature for the term of _____; to receive punctually, at stated times, a fixed compensation for the services rendered, in which no increase nor diminution shall be made, so as to affect the magistracy existing at the time of increase or diminution; and to be ineligible a second time; and that, besides a general authority to execute the national laws, it ought to enjoy the executive rights vested in Congress by the Confederation.

8. Resolved, that the Executive, and a convenient number of the national Judiciary, ought to compose a Council of Revision, with authority to examine every act of the National Legislature, before it shall operate, and every act of a particular Legislature before a negative thereon shall be final; and that the dissent of the said council shall amount to a rejection, unless the act of the National Legislature be again passed, or that of a particular Legislature be again negatived by _____ of the members of each branch.

9. Resolved, that a National Judiciary be established; to consist of one or more supreme tribunals, and of inferior tribunals to be chosen by the National Legislature; to hold their offices during good behavior, and to receive punctually, at stated times, fixed compensation for their services, in which no increase or diminution shall be made, so as to affect

the persons actually in office at the time of such increase or diminution. That the jurisdiction of the inferior tribunals shall be to hear and determine, in the first instance, and of the supreme tribunal to hear and determine, in the dernier resort, all piracies and felonies on the high seas; captures from an enemy; cases in which foreigners, or citizens of other States, applying to such jurisdictions, may be interested; or which respect the collection of the national revenue; impeachments of any national officers, and questions which may involve the national peace and harmony.

10. Resolved, that provision ought to be made for the admission of States lawfully arising within the limits of the United States, whether from a voluntary junction of government and territory, or otherwise, with the consent of a number of voices in the National Legislature less than the whole.
11. Resolved, that a republican government, and the territory of each State, except in the instance of a voluntary junction of government and territory, ought to be guaranteed by the United States to each State.
12. Resolved, that provision ought to be made for the continuance of Congress and their authorities and privileges, until a given day after the reform of the Articles of Union shall be adopted, and for the completion of all their engagements.
13. Resolved, that provision ought to be made for the amendment of the Articles of Union, whensoever it shall seem necessary; and that the assent of the National Legislature ought not to be required thereto.
14. Resolved, that the legislative, executive, and judiciary powers, within the several States ought to be bound by oath to support the Articles of Union.
15. Resolved, that the amendments which shall be offered to the Confederation, by the Convention, ought, at a proper time or times, after the approbation of Congress, to be submitted to an assembly or assemblies of representatives, recommended by the several Legislatures, to be expressly chosen by the people to consider and decide thereon.

Source: Records of the Federal Convention of 1787, The Papers of James Madison, Library of Congress.

6. The New Jersey Plan, June 15, 1787

The small states disapproved of the Virginia Plan because it would allow the large states to dominate the government through a bicameral congress in which representation in both houses would be based on the state's free population or taxes paid. William Paterson proposed the New Jersey Plan, a set of amendments to the Articles of Confederation, as an alternative. Each state would continue to have a single vote in the existing unicameral Confederation Congress. The New Jersey Plan would add executive and judicial branches to the Confederation and give it the power to tax imports and to regulate commerce.

1. Resolved, that the Articles of Confederation ought to be so revised, corrected, and enlarged, as to render the Federal Constitution adequate to the exigencies of government, and the preservation of the Union.
2. Resolved, that, in addition to the powers vested in the United States in Congress, by the present existing Articles of Confederation, they be authorized to pass acts for raising a revenue, by levying a duty or duties on all goods or merchandizes of foreign growth or manufacture, imported into any part of the United States; by stamps on paper, vellum or parchment; and by a postage on all letters or packages passing through the general post-office; to be applied to such Federal purposes as they shall deem proper and expedient; to make rules and regulations for the collection thereof; and the same, from time to time, to alter and amend in such manner as they shall think proper; to pass acts for the regulation of trade and commerce, as well with foreign nations as with each other; provided that all punishments, fines, forfeitures and penalties, to be incurred for contravening such acts, rules and regulations, shall be adjudged by the common law Judiciaries of the State in which any offence contrary to the true intent and meaning of such acts, rules, and regulations, shall have been committed or perpetrated, with liberty of commencing in the first instance all suits and prosecutions for that purpose in the Superior common law Judiciary in such State; subject, nevertheless, for the correction of all errors, both in law and fact, in rendering judgment, to an appeal to the Judiciary of the United States.
3. Resolved, that whenever requisitions shall be necessary, instead of the rule for making requisitions mentioned in the Articles of Confederation, the United States in Congress be authorized to make such requisitions in proportion to the whole number of white and other free

citizens and inhabitants, of every age, sex, and condition, including those bound to servitude for a term of years, and three-fifths of all other persons not comprehended in the foregoing description, except Indians not paying taxes; that, if such requisitions be not complied with, in the time specified therein, to direct the collection thereof in the non-complying States; and for that purpose to devise and pass acts directing and authorizing the same; provided, that none of the powers hereby vested in the United States in Congress, shall be exercised without the consent of at least _____ States; and in that proportion, if the number of confederated States should hereafter be increased or diminished.

4. Resolved, that the United States in Congress be authorized to elect a Federal Executive, to consist of _____ persons, to continue in office for the term of _____ years; to receive punctually, at stated times, a fixed compensation for their services, in which no increase nor diminution shall be made so as to affect the persons composing the Executive at the time of such increase or diminution; to be paid out of the Federal treasury; to be incapable of holding any other office or appointment during their time of service, and for _____ years thereafter: to be ineligible a second time, and removable by Congress, on application by a majority of the Executives of the several States; that the Executive, besides their general authority to execute the Federal acts, ought to appoint all Federal officers not otherwise provided for, and to direct all military operations; provided, that none of the persons composing the Federal Executive shall, on any occasion, take command of any troops, so as personally to conduct any military enterprise, as General, or in any other capacity.

5. Resolved, that a Federal Judiciary be established, to consist of a supreme tribunal, the Judges of which to be appointed by the Executive, and to hold their offices during good behaviour; to receive punctually, at stated times, a fixed compensation for their services, in which no increase nor diminution shall be made so as to affect the persons actually in office at the time of such increase or diminution. That the Judiciary so established shall have authority to hear and determine, in the first instance, on all impeachments of Federal officers; and, by way of appeal, in the dernier resort, in all cases touching the rights of ambassadors; in all cases of captures from an enemy; in all cases of piracies and felonies on the high seas; in all cases in which foreigners may be interested; in the

construction of any treaty or treaties, or which may arise on any of the acts for the regulation of trade, or the collection of the Federal revenue: that none of the Judiciary shall, during the time they remain in office, be capable of receiving or holding any other office or appointment during their term of service, or for _____ thereafter.

6. Resolved, that all acts of the United States in Congress, made by virtue and in pursuance of the powers hereby, and by the Articles of Confederation, vested in them, and all treaties made and ratified under the authority of the United States, shall be the supreme law of the respective States, so far forth as those acts or treaties shall relate to the said States or their citizens; and that the Judiciary of the several States shall be bound thereby in their decisions, any thing in the respective laws of the individual States to the contrary notwithstanding: and that if any State, or any body of men in any State, shall oppose or prevent the carrying into execution such acts or treaties, the Federal Executive shall be authorized to call forth the power of the confederated States, or so much thereof as may be necessary, to enforce and compel an obedience to such acts, or an observance of such treaties.
7. Resolved, that provision be made for the admission of new States into the Union.
8. Resolved, that the rule for naturalization ought to be the same in every State.
9. Resolved, that a citizen of one State committing an offence in another State of the Union, shall be deemed guilty of the same offence as if it had been committed by a citizen of the State in which the offence was committed.

Source: Records of the Federal Convention of 1787, The Papers of James Madison, Library of Congress.

7. Alexander Hamilton's Plan of Government, June 18, 1787

Hamilton disliked both the Virginia and New Jersey plans because they did not sufficiently strengthen the federal government. He doubted the viability of republicanism and admired the British monarchical form of government. In the

Primary Documents

document that follows, he described his preferred form of government, which included a president and senate to sit during good behavior and a drastic reduction in the powers of the states.

I. The supreme Legislative power of the United States of America to be vested in two different bodies of men; the one to be called the Assembly, the other the Senate; who together shall form the Legislature of the United States, with power to pass all laws whatsoever, subject to the negative hereafter mentioned.

II. The Assembly to consist of persons elected by the people to serve for three years.

III. The Senate to consist of persons elected to serve during good behaviour; their election to be made by electors chosen for that purpose by the people. In order to this, the States to be divided into election districts. On the death, removal or resignation of any Senator, his place to be filled out of the district from which he came.

IV. The supreme Executive authority of the United States to be vested in a Governor, to be elected to serve during good behaviour; the election to be made by Electors chosen by the people in the Election Districts aforesaid. The authorities and functions of the Executive to be as follows: to have a negative on all laws about to be passed, and the execution of all laws passed; to have the direction of war when authorized or begun; to have, with the advice and approbation of the Senate, the power of making all treaties; to have the sole appointment of the heads or chief officers of the Departments of Finance, War, and Foreign Affairs; to have the nomination of all other officers, (ambassadors to foreign nations included,) subject to the approbation or rejection of the Senate; to have the power of pardoning all offences except treason, which he shall not pardon without the approbation of the Senate.

V. On the death, resignation, or removal of the Governor, his authorities to be exercised by the President of the Senate till a successor be appointed.

VI. The Senate to have the sole power of declaring war; the power of advising and approving all treaties; the power of approving or rejecting all appointments of officers, except the heads or chiefs of the Departments of Finance, War, and Foreign Affairs.

VII. The supreme Judicial authority to be vested in Judges, to hold their offices during good behaviour, with adequate and permanent salaries. This court to have original jurisdiction in all causes of capture, and an appellative jurisdiction in all causes in which the revenues of the General Government, or the citizens of foreign nations, are concerned.

VIII. The Legislature of the United States to have power to institute courts in each State for the determination of all matters of general concern.

IX. The Governor, Senators, and all officers of the United States, to be liable to impeachment for mal- and corrupt conduct; and upon conviction to be removed from office, and disqualified for holding any place of trust or profit: all impeachments to be tried by a Court to consist of the Chief —, or Judge of the Superior Court of Law of each State, provided such Judge shall hold his place during good behavior and have a permanent salary.

X. All laws of the particular States contrary to the Constitution or laws of the United States to be utterly void; and the better to prevent such laws being passed, the Governor or President of each State shall be appointed by the General Government, and shall have a negative upon the laws about to be passed in the State of which he is the Governor or President.

XI. No State to have any forces land or naval; and the militia of all the States to be under the sole and exclusive direction of the United States, the officers of which to be appointed and commissioned by them.

Source: Records of the Federal Convention of 1787, The Papers of James Madison, Library of Congress.

8. Benjamin Franklin's Speech, September 17, 1787

Benjamin Franklin prepared and James Wilson read this speech on the convention's last day. It aimed to persuade the delegates to put aside their doubts and unanimously sign the Constitution. Franklin suggested that the signing be "done in Convention by the unanimous consent of the States present." Since a majority of the delegates present from every state delegation approved the Constitution, every delegate could then sign in good faith, even those who remained personally opposed. All but three of the delegates present signed the document.

Doctor FRANKLIN rose with a speech in his hand, which he had reduced to writing for his own convenience, and which Mr. WILSON read in the words following: —

MR. PRESIDENT:

I confess that there are several parts of this Constitution which I do not at present approve, but I am not sure I shall never approve them. For having lived long, I have experienced many instances of being obliged by better information, or fuller consideration, to change opinions even on important subjects, which I once thought right, but found to be otherwise. It is therefore that, the older I grow, the more apt I am to doubt my own judgment, and to pay more respect to the judgment of others. Most men, indeed, as well as most sects in religion, think themselves in possession of all truth, and that wherever others differ from them, it is so far error. Steele, a Protestant, in a dedication, tells the Pope, that the only difference between our churches, in their opinions of the certainty of their doctrines, is, "the Church of Rome is infallible, and the Church of England is never in the wrong." But though many private persons think almost as highly of their own infallibility as of that of their sect, few express it so naturally as a certain French lady, who, in a dispute with her sister, said, "I don't know how it happens, sister, but I meet with nobody but myself that is always in the right — *il n'y a que moi qui a toujours raison.*"

In these sentiments, Sir, I agree to this Constitution, with all its faults, if they are such; because I think a General Government necessary for us, and there is no form of government, but what may be a blessing to the people if well administered; and believe further, that this is likely to be well administered for a course of years, and can only end in despotism, as other forms have done before it, when the people shall become so corrupted as to need despotic government, being incapable of any other. I doubt, too, whether any other Convention we can obtain may be able to make a better Constitution. For, when you assemble a number of men to have the advantage of their joint wisdom, you inevitably assemble with those men all their prejudices, their passions, their errors of opinion, their local interests, and their selfish views. From such an assembly can a perfect production be expected? It therefore astonishes me, sir, to find this system approaching so near to perfection as it does; and I think it will astonish our enemies, who are waiting with confidence to hear that our councils are confounded, like those of the builders of Babel; and that our states are on the point of separation, only to meet hereafter for the purpose of cutting one another's throats. Thus I consent, Sir, to this Constitution, because I expect no better, and because I am not sure, that it is not the best. The opinions I have had of its errors I sacrifice to the public good. I have never whispered a syllable of them abroad. Within these walls they were born, and here they shall die. If every one of us, in returning to our constituents, were to report the objections he has had to it, and endeavor to gain partisans in support of them, we might prevent its being generally received, and thereby lose all the salutary effects and great advantages resulting naturally in our favor among foreign nations as well as among ourselves, from our real or apparent unanimity. Much of the strength and efficiency of any government, in procuring and securing happiness to the people, depends on opinion,—on the general opinion of the goodness of the government, as well as of the wisdom and integrity of its governors. I hope, therefore, that for our own sakes, as a part of the people, and for the sake of posterity, we shall act heartily and unanimously in recommending this Constitution (if approved by Congress and confirmed by the Conventions) wherever our influence may extend, and turn our future thoughts and endeavors to the means of having it well administered.

On the whole, Sir, I cannot help expressing a wish that every member of the Convention, who may still have objections to it, would with me, on this occasion, doubt a little of his own infallibility, and to make manifest our unanimity, put his name to this instrument. He then moved, that the Constitution be signed by the members, and offered the following as a convenient form, viz: "Done in Convention by the unanimous consent of the States present, the seventeenth of September, &c. In witness whereof, we have hereunto subscribed our names."

Source: Records of the Federal Convention of 1787, The Papers of James Madison, Library of Congress.

9. Cover Letter Transmitting the Constitution to the Confederation Congress, September 17, 1787

In addition to drafting the final version of the Constitution, Gouverneur Morris of the Committee of Style prepared this cover letter to the Confederation Congress in New York. The letter explained that vesting appropriate authority in the "general government," including the power to make war and peace, to collect revenue, and to regulate commerce, necessitated a new political structure that balanced power among the three branches of government.

We have now the honor to submit to the consideration of the United States, in Congress assembled, that Constitution which has appeared to us the most advisable.

The friends of our country have long seen and desired, that the power of making war, peace, and treaties; that of levying money and regulating commerce, and the correspondent executive and judicial authorities, should be fully and effectually vested in the general government of the Union. But the impropriety of delegating such extensive trust to one body of men is evident. Thence results the necessity of a different organization. It is obviously impracticable, in the federal government of these States, to secure all rights of independent sovereignty to each, and yet provide for the interest and safety of all. Individuals entering into society must give up a share of liberty, to preserve the rest. The magnitude of the sacrifice must depend as well on situation and circumstances, as on the object to be obtained. It is at all times difficult to draw with precision the line between those rights which must be surrendered, and those which may be reserved. And on the present occasion this difficulty was increased by a difference among the several States, as to their situation, extent, habits, and particular interests.

In all our deliberations on this subject, we kept steadily in our view that which appeared to us the greatest interest of every true American, the consolidation of our union, in which is involved our prosperity, felicity, safety, perhaps our national existence. This important consideration, seriously and deeply impressed on our minds, led each State in the Convention to be less rigid in points of inferior magnitude, than might have been otherwise expected. And thus the Constitution, which we now present, is the result of a spirit of amity, and of that mutual deference and concession, which the peculiarity of our political situation rendered indispensable.

That it will meet the full and entire approbation of every State is not, perhaps, to be expected. But each will doubtless consider, that had her interest alone been consulted, the consequences might have been particularly disagreeable and injurious to others. That it is liable to as few exceptions as could reasonably have been expected, we hope and believe; that it may promote the lasting welfare of that country so dear to us all; and secure her freedom and happiness, is our most ardent wish.

Source: Records of the Federal Convention of 1787, The Papers of James Madison, Library of Congress.

10. The Confederation Congress's Resolution Transmitting the Constitution to the State Legislatures, September 28, 1787

Federalists in Congress wanted to send the Constitution to the states with congressional approbation. Antifederalists instead wanted to propose amendments to the document. Unable to muster Congress's endorsement of the Constitution, Federalists secured this unanimous resolution that simply transmitted the Constitution to the state legislatures, so that they could call state ratification conventions.

The United States In CONGRESS Assembled, FRIDAY, September 28, 1787.

PRESENT—New-Hampshire, Massachusetts, Connecticut, New-York, New-Jersey, Pennsylvania, Delaware, Virginia, North-Carolina, South-Carolina, and Georgia, and from Maryland Mr. Ross.

Congress having received the Report of the Convention lately assembled in Philadelphia,

Resolved Unanimously, THAT the said Report, with the Resolutions and Letter accompanying the same, be transmitted to the several Legislatures, in order to be submitted to a Convention of Delegates, chosen in each State by the People thereof, in Conformity to the Resolves of the Convention, made and provided in that Case. Charles Thomson, Secretary.

Philadelphia, Printed by Dunlap & Claypoole.

Source: Continental Congress Broadside Collection, Library of Congress. Available at: www.loc.gov/resource/bdsdcc.22801/?sp=1&st=text.

11. James Wilson's State House Yard Speech, October 6, 1787

In this public address, delivered in the yard outside the Pennsylvania State House, James Wilson gave the first explanation of the Constitution by a former delegate to the Constitutional Convention. He declared that the new framework would not threaten liberty despite the lack of a bill of rights because the powers of Congress had been carefully enumerated. Reprinted in more than forty newspapers during the ratification campaign, Wilson's speech boosted the Constitution throughout the nation.

Mr. Chairman and Fellow Citizens:

Having received the honor of an appointment to represent you in the late convention, it is perhaps my duty to comply with the request of many gentlemen whose characters and judgements I sincerely respect, and who have urged that this would be a proper occasion to lay before you any information which will serve to explain and elucidate the principles and arrangements of the constitution that has been submitted to the consideration of the United States. . . .

It will be proper . . . to mark the leading discrimination between the State constitutions and the constitution of the United States. When the people established the powers of legislation under their separate governments, they invested their representatives with every right and authority which they did not in explicit terms reserve; and therefore upon every question respecting the jurisdiction of the House of Assembly, if the frame of government is silent, the jurisdiction is efficient and complete. But in delegating federal powers, another criterion was necessarily introduced, and the congressional power is to be collected, not from tacit implication, but from the positive grant expressed in the instrument of the union.

Hence, it is evident, that in the former case everything which is not reserved is given; but in the latter the reverse of the proposition prevails, and everything which is not given is reserved.

This distinction being recognized, will furnish an answer to those who think the omission of a bill of rights a defect in the proposed constitution; for it would have been superfluous and absurd to have stipulated with a federal body of our own creation, that we should enjoy those privileges of which we are not divested, either by the intention or the act that has brought the body into existence. For instance, the liberty of the press, which has been a copious source of declamation and opposition—what control can proceed from the Federal government to shackle or destroy that sacred palladium of national freedom? If, indeed, a power similar to that which has been granted for the regulation of commerce had been granted to regulate literary publications, it would have been as necessary to stipulate that the liberty of the press should be preserved inviolate, as that the impost should be general in its operation. With respect likewise to the particular district of ten miles, which is to be made the seat of federal government, it will undoubtedly be proper to observe this salutary precaution, as there the legislative power will be exclusively lodged in the President, Senate, and House of Representatives of the United States. But this could not be an object with the Convention, for it must naturally depend upon a future compact to which the citizens immediately interested will, and ought to be, parties; and there is no reason to suspect that so popular a privilege will in that case be neglected. In truth, then, the proposed system possesses no influence whatever upon the press, and it would have been merely nugatory to have introduced a formal declaration upon the subject—nay, that very declaration might have been construed to imply that some degree of power was given, since we undertook to define its extent.

Another objection that has been fabricated against the new constitution, is expressed in this disingenious form—"The trial by jury is abolished in civil cases." I must be excused, my fellow citizens, if upon this point I take advantage of my professional experience to detect the futility of the assertion. Let it be remembered then, that the business of the Federal Convention was not local, but general—not limited to the views and establishments of a single State, but co-extensive with the continent, and comprehending the views and establishments of thirteen independent sovereignties. When, therefore, this subject was in discussion, we were involved in difficulties which pressed on all sides, and no precedent could be discovered to direct our course. The cases open to a trial by jury differed in the different States. It was therefore impracticable, on that ground, to have made a general rule. The want of uniformity would have rendered any reference to the practice of the States idle and useless; and it could not with any propriety be said that, "The trial by jury shall be as heretofore," since there has never existed any federal system of jurisprudence, to which the declaration could relate. Besides, it is not in all cases that the trial by jury is adopted in civil questions; for cases depending in courts of admiralty, such as relate to maritime captures, and such as are agitated in courts of equity, do not require the intervention of that tribunal. How, then was the line of discrimination to be drawn? The Convention found the task too difficult for them, and they left the business as it stands, in the fullest confidence that no danger could possibly ensue, since the proceedings of the Supreme Court are to be regulated by the Congress, which is a faithful representation of the people; and the oppression of government is effectually barred, by declaring that in all criminal cases the trial by jury shall be preserved.

This constitution, it has been further urged, is of a pernicious tendency, because it tolerates a standing army in the time of peace. This has always been a topic of popular declamation; and yet I do not know a nation in the world which has not found it necessary and useful to maintain the appearance of strength in a season of the most profound tranquility. Nor is it a novelty with us; for under the present articles of confederation, Congress certainly possesses this reprobated power, and the exercise of that power is proved at this moment by her cantonments along the banks of the Ohio. But what would be our national situation were it otherwise? Every principle of policy must be subverted, and the government must declare war, before they are prepared to carry it on. Whatever may be the provocation, however important the object in view, and however necessary dispatch and secrecy may be, still the declaration must precede the preparation, and the enemy will be informed of your intention, not only before you are equipped for an attack, but even before you are fortified for a defence. The consequence is too obvious to require any further delineation, and no man who regards the dignity and safety of his country can deny the necessity of a military force, under the control and with the restrictions which the new constitution provides.

Perhaps there never was a charge made with less reasons than that which predicts the institution of a baneful aristocracy in the federal Senate. This body branches into two characters, the one legislative and the other executive. In its legislative character it can effect no purpose, without me co-operation of the House of Representatives, and in its executive character it can accomplish no object without the concurrence of the President. Thus fettered I do not know any act which the Senate can of itself perform, and such dependence necessarily precludes every idea of influence and superiority. But I will confess that in the organization of this body a compromise between contending interests is descernible; and when we reflect how various are the laws commerce, habits, population and extent of the confederated States, this evidence of mutual concession and accommodation ought rather to command a generous applause, than to excite jealousy and reproach. For my part, my admiration can only be equalled by my astonishment in beholding so perfect a system formed from such heterogeneous materials.

The next accusation I shall consider is that which represents the federal constitution, as not only calculated, but designedly framed, to reduce the State governments to mere corporations and eventually to annihilate them. Those who have employed the term corporation upon this occasion are not perhaps aware of its extent. In common parlance, indeed, it is generally applied to petty associations for the ease and convenience of a few individuals; but in its enlarged sense, it will comprehend the government of Pennsylvania, the existing union of the States, and even this projected system is nothing more than a formal act of incorporation. But upon what presence can it be alleged that it was designed to annihilate the State governments? For I will undertake to prove that upon their existence depends the existence of the Federal plan. For this purpose, permit me to call your attention to the manner in which the President, Senate and House of Representatives are proposed to be appointed. The President is to be chosen by electors, nominated in such manner as the legislature of each State may direct; so that if there is no legislature there can be no electors, and consequently the office of President cannot be supplied.

The Senate is to be composed of two Senators from each State, chosen by the Legislature; and, therefore, if there is no Legislature, there can be no Senate. The House of Representatives is to be composed of members chosen every second year by the people of the several States, and the electors in each State shall have the qualifications requisite for electors of the most numerous branch of the State Legislature; unless, therefore, there is a State Legislature, that qualification cannot be ascertained, and the popular branch of the federal constitution must be extinct. From this view, then, it is evidently absurd to suppose that the annihilation of the separate governments will result from their union; or, that having that intention, the authors of the new system would have bound their connection with such indissoluble ties. Let me here advert to an arrangement highly advantageous, for you will perceive, without prejudice to the powers of the Legislature in the election of Senators, the people at large will acquire an additional privilege in returning members to the House of Representatives; whereas, by the present confederation, it is the Legislature alone that appoints the delegates to Congress.

The power of direct taxation has likewise been treated as an improper delegation to the federal government; but when we consider it as the duty of that body to provide for the national safety, to support the dignity of the union, and to discharge the debts contracted upon the collected faith of the States for their common benefit, it must be acknowledged that those upon whom such important obligations are imposed, ought in justice and in policy to possess every means requisite for a faithful performance of their trust. But why should we be alarmed with visionary evils? I will venture to predict that the great revenue of the United States must, and always will, be raised by impost, for, being at once less obnoxious and more productive, the interest of the government will be best promoted by the accommodation of the people. Still, however, the objects of direct taxation should be within reach in all cases of emergency; and there is no more reason to apprehend oppression in the mode of collecting a revenue from this resource, than in the form of an impost, which by universal assent, is left to the authority of the federal government. In either case, the force of civil institutions will be adequate to the purpose; and the dread of military violence, which has been assiduously disseminated, must eventually prove the mere effusion of a wild imagination or a factious spirit. But the salutary consequences that must flow from thus enabling the government to receive and support the credit of the union, will afford another answer to the objections upon this ground. The State of Pennsylvania particularly, which has encumbered itself with the assumption of a great proportion of the public debt, will derive considerable relief and advantage, for, as it was the imbecility of the present confederation which gave rise to the funding law, that law must naturally expire, when a competent and energetic federal system shall be substituted—the State will then be discharged from an extraordinary burthen, and the national creditor will find it to be his interest to return to his original security.

After all, my fellow-citizens, it is neither extraordinary or unexpected that the constitution offered to your consideration should meet with opposition. It is the nature of man to pursue his own interest in preference to the public good, and I do not mean to make any personal reflection when I add that it is the interest of a very numerous, powerful and respectable body to counteract and destroy the excellent work produced by the late convention. All the officers of government and all the appointments for the administration of justice and the collection of the public revenue which are transferred from the individual to the aggregate sovereignty of the States, will necessarily turn the stream of influence and emolument into a new channel. Every person, therefore, who enjoys or expects to enjoy a place of profit under the present establishment, will object to the proposed innovation; not, in truth, because it is injurious to the liberties of his country, but because it affects his schemes of wealth and consequence. I will confess, indeed, that I am not a blind admirer of this plan of government, and that there are some parts of it which, if my wish had prevailed, would certainly have been altered. But when I reflect how widely men differ in their opinions, and that every man (and the observation applies likewise to every State) has an equal pretension to assert his own, I am satisfied that anything nearer to perfection could not have been accomplished. If there are errors, it should be remembered that the seeds of reformation are sown in the work itself and the concurrence of two-thirds of the Congress may at any time introduce alterations and amendments. Regarding it, then, in every point of view, with a candid and disinterested mind, I am bold to assert that it is the best form of government which has ever been offered to the world.

Source: Pennsylvania Packet, October 10, 1787.

12. George Mason's Objections to This Constitution of Government, October 7, 1787

James Madison wrote that Virginia delegate George Mason left Philadelphia "in an exceeding ill humour indeed." Even before departing the city, Mason prepared and began circulating his reasons for refusing to sign the Constitution. Complaining that the new framework did not sufficiently restrain either the Senate or the president, Mason predicted that unconditional ratification would lead either to monarchy or to aristocracy.

There is no Declaration of Rights, and the laws of the general government being paramount to the laws and constitution of the several States, the Declarations of Rights in the separate States are no security. Nor are the people secured even in the enjoyment of the benefit of the common law.

In the House of Representatives there is not the substance but the shadow only of representation; which can never produce proper information in the legislature, or inspire confidence in the people; the laws will therefore be generally made by men little concerned in, and unacquainted with their effects and consequences.

The Senate have the power of altering all money bills, and of originating appropriations of money, and the salaries of the officers of their own appointment, in conjunction with the president of the United States, although they are not the representatives of the people or amenable to them.

These with their other great powers, viz.: their power in the appointment of ambassadors and all public officers, in making treaties, and in trying all impeachments, their influence upon and connection with the supreme Executive from these causes, their duration of office and their being a constantly existing body, almost continually sitting, joined with their being one complete branch of the legislature, will destroy any balance in the government, and enable them to accomplish what usurpations they please upon the rights and liberties of the people.

The Judiciary of the United States is so constructed and extended, as to absorb and destroy the judiciaries of the several States; thereby rendering law as tedious, intricate and expensive, and justice as unattainable, by a great part of the community, as in England, and enabling the rich to oppress and ruin the poor.

The President of the United States has no Constitutional Council, a thing unknown in any safe and regular government. He will therefore be unsupported by proper information and advice, and will generally be directed by minions and favorites; or he will become a tool to the Senate—or a Council of State will grow out of the principal officers of the great departments; the worst and most dangerous of all ingredients for such a Council in a free country; From this fatal defect has arisen the improper power of the Senate in the appointment of public officers, and the alarming dependence and connection between that branch of the legislature and the supreme Executive.

Hence also sprung that unnecessary officer the Vice-President, who for want of other employment is made president of the Senate, thereby dangerously blending the executive and legislative powers, besides always giving to some one of the States an unnecessary and unjust pre-eminence over the others.

The President of the United States has the unrestrained power of granting pardons for treason, which may be sometimes exercised to screen from punishment those whom he had secretly instigated to commit the crime, and thereby prevent a discovery of his own guilt.

By declaring all treaties supreme laws of the land, the Executive and the Senate have, in many cases, an exclusive power of legislation; which might have been avoided by proper distinctions with respect to treaties, and requiring the assent of the House of Representatives, where it could be done with safety.

By requiring only a majority to make all commercial and navigation laws, the five Southern States, whose produce and circumstances are totally different from that of the eight Northern and Eastern States, may be ruined, for such rigid and premature regulations may be made as will enable the merchants of the Northern and Eastern States not only to demand an exhorbitant freight, but to monopolize the purchase of the commodities at their own price, for many years, to the great injury of the landed interest, and impoverishment of the people; and the danger is the greater as the gain on one side will be in proportion to the loss on the other. Whereas requiring two-thirds of the members present in both Houses would have produced mutual moderation, promoted the general interest, and removed an insuperable objection to the adoption of this government.

Under their own construction of the general clause, at the end of the enumerated powers, the Congress may grant monopolies in trade and commerce, constitute new crimes, inflict unusual and severe punishments, and extend their powers as far as they shall think proper; so that the State legislatures have no security for the powers now presumed to remain to them, or the people for their rights.

There is no declaration of any kind, for preserving the liberty of the press, or the trial by jury in civil causes; nor against the danger of standing armies in time of peace.

The State legislatures are restrained from laying export duties on their own produce.

Both the general legislature and the State legislature are expressly prohibited making ex post facto laws; though there never was nor can be a legislature but must and will make such laws, when necessity and the public safety require them; which will hereafter be a breach of all the constitutions in the Union, and afford precedents for other innovations.

This government will set out a moderate aristocracy: it is at present impossible to foresee whether it will, in its operation, produce a monarchy, or a corrupt, tyrannical aristocracy; it will most probably vibrate some years between the two, and then terminate in the one or the other.

The general legislature is restrained from prohibiting the further importation of slaves for twenty odd years; though such importations render the United States weaker, more vulnerable, and less capable of defence.

Source: Jared Sparks, ed. *The Writings of George Washington, Volume IX.* Boston: Russell, Odiorne, and Metcalf, 1835, 544–47.

13. Brutus I, October 18, 1787

This Antifederalist essay is the first of sixteen written under the penname "Brutus" (probably by Melancton Smith) to oppose the ratification of the Constitution in New York. Here Brutus argues that liberty is safe only in a small republic with a homogeneous population, and that the Constitution will cause political power to consolidate in the federal government, leading to tyranny.

To the Citizens of the State of New-York.

When the public is called to investigate and decide upon a question in which not only the present members of the community are deeply interested, but upon which the happiness and misery of generations yet unborn is in great measure suspended, the benevolent mind cannot help feeling itself peculiarly interested in the result.

In this situation, I trust the feeble efforts of an individual, to lead the minds of the people to a wise and prudent determination, cannot fail of being acceptable to the candid and dispassionate part of the community. Encouraged by this consideration, I have been induced to offer my thoughts upon the present important crisis of our public affairs.

Perhaps this country never saw so critical a period in their political concerns. We have felt the feebleness of the ties by which these United-States are held together, and the want of sufficient energy in our present confederation, to manage, in some instances, our general concerns. Various expedients have been proposed to remedy these evils, but none have succeeded. At length a Convention of the states has been assembled, they have formed a constitution which will now, probably, be submitted to the people to ratify or reject, who are the fountain of all power, to whom alone it of right belongs to make or unmake constitutions, or forms of government, at their pleasure. The most important question that was ever proposed to your decision, or to the decision of any people under heaven, is before you, and you are to decide upon it by men of your own election, chosen specially for this purpose. If the constitution, offered to [your acceptance], be a wise one, calculated to preserve the invaluable blessings of liberty, to secure the inestimable rights of mankind, and promote human happiness, then, if you accept it, you will lay a lasting foundation of happiness for millions yet unborn; generations to come will rise up and call you blessed. You may rejoice in the prospects of this vast extended continent becoming filled with freemen, who will assert the dignity of human nature. You may solace yourselves with the idea, that society, in this favoured land, will fast advance to the highest point of perfection; the human mind will expand in knowledge and virtue, and the golden age be, in some measure, realised. But if, on the other hand, this form of government contains principles that will lead to the subversion of liberty—if it tends to establish a despotism, or, what is worse, a tyrannic aristocracy; then, if you adopt it, this only remaining assylum for liberty will be [shut] up, and posterity will execrate your memory.

Momentous then is the question you have to determine, and you are called upon by every motive which should influence a noble and virtuous mind, to examine it well, and to make up a wise judgment. It is insisted, indeed, that this constitution must be received, be it ever so imperfect. If it has its defects, it is said, they can be best amended when they are experienced. But remember, when the people once part with power, they can seldom or never resume it again but by force. Many instances can be produced in which the people have voluntarily increased the powers of their rulers; but few, if any, in which rulers have willingly abridged their authority. This is a sufficient reason to induce you to be careful, in the first instance, how you deposit the powers of government.

With these few introductory remarks I shall proceed to a consideration of this constitution:

The first question that presents itself on the subject is, whether a confederated government be the best for the United States or not? Or in other words, whether the thirteen United States should be reduced to one great republic, governed by one legislature, and under the direction of one executive and judicial; or whether they should continue thirteen confederated republics, under the direction and controul of a supreme federal head for certain defined national purposes only?

This enquiry is important, because, although the government reported by the convention does not go to a perfect and entire consolidation, yet it approaches so near to it, that it must, if executed, certainly and infallibly terminate in it.

This government is to possess absolute and uncontroulable power, legislative, executive and judicial, with respect to every object to which it extends, for by the last clause of section 8th, article Ist, it is declared "that the Congress shall have power to make all laws which shall be necessary and proper for carrying into execution the foregoing powers, and all other powers vested by this constitution, in the government of the United States; or in any department or office thereof." And by the 6th article, it is declared "that this constitution, and the laws of the United States, which shall be made in pursuance thereof, and the treaties made, or which shall be made, under the authority of the United States, shall be the supreme law of the land; and the judges in every state shall be bound thereby, any thing in the constitution, or law of any state to the contrary notwithstanding."

It appears from these articles that there is no need of any intervention of the state governments, between the Congress and the people, to execute any one power vested in the general government, and that the constitution and laws of every state are nullified and declared void, so far as they are or shall be inconsistent with this constitution, or the laws made in pursuance of it, or with treaties made under the authority of the United States.—The government then, so far as it extends, is a complete one, and not a confederation. It is as much one complete government as that of New-York or Massachusetts, has as absolute and perfect powers to make and execute all laws, to appoint officers, institute courts, declare offences, and annex penalties, with respect to every object to which it extends, as any other in the world. So far therefore as its powers reach, all ideas of confederation are given up and lost.

It is true this government is limited to certain objects, or to speak more properly, some small degree of power is still left to the states, but a little attention to the powers vested in the general government, will convince every candid man, that if it is capable of being executed, all that is reserved for the individual states must very soon be annihilated, except so far as they are barely necessary to the organization of the general government. The powers of the general legislature extend to every case that is of the least importance—there is nothing valuable to human nature, nothing dear to freemen, but what is within its power. It has authority to make laws which will affect the lives, the liberty, and property of every man in the United States; nor can the constitution or laws of any state, in any way prevent or impede the full and complete execution of every power given. The legislative power is competent to lay taxes, duties, imposts, and excises;—there is no limitation to this power, unless it be said that the clause which directs the use to which those taxes, and duties shall be applied, may be said to be a limitation; but this is no restriction of the power at all, for by this clause they are to be applied to pay the debts and provide for the common defence and general welfare of the United States; but the legislature have authority to contract debts at their discretion; they are the sole judges of what is necessary to provide for the common defence, and they only are to determine what is for the general welfare: this power therefore is neither more nor less, than a power to lay and collect taxes, imposts, and excises, at their pleasure; not only the power to lay taxes unlimited, as to the amount they may require, but it is perfect and absolute to raise them in any mode they please. No state legislature, or any power in the state governments, have any more to do in carrying this into effect, than the authority of one state has to do with that of another.

In the business therefore of laying and collecting taxes, the idea of confederation is totally lost, and that of one entire republic is embraced.

It is proper here to remark, that the authority to lay and collect taxes is the most important of any power that can be granted; it connects with it almost all other powers, or at least will in process of time draw all other after it; it is the great mean of protection, security, and defence, in a good government, and the great engine of oppression and tyranny in a bad one. This cannot fail of being the case, if we consider the contracted limits which are set by this constitution, to the late governments, on this article of raising money. No state can emit paper money—lay any duties, or imposts, on imports, or exports, but by consent of the Congress; and then the net produce shall be for the benefit of the United States. The only mean therefore left, for any state to support its government and discharge its debts, is by direct taxation; and the United States have also power to lay and collect taxes, in any way they please. Every one who has thought on the subject, must be convinced that but small sums of money can be collected in any country, by direct taxe[s], when the foederal government begins to exercise the right of taxation in all its parts, the legislatures of the several states will find it impossible to raise monies to support their governments. Without money they cannot be supported, and they must dwindle away, and, as before observed, their powers absorbed in that of the general government.

It might be here shewn, that the power in the federal legislative, to raise and support armies at pleasure, as well in peace as in war, and their controul over the militia, tend, not only to a consolidation of the government, but the destruction of liberty.—I shall not, however, dwell upon these, as a few observations upon the judicial power of this government, in addition to the preceding, will fully evince the truth of the position.

The judicial power of the United States is to be vested in a supreme court, and in such inferior courts as Congress may from time to time ordain and establish. The powers of these courts are very extensive; their jurisdiction comprehends all civil causes, except such as arise between citizens of the same state; and it extends to all cases in law and equity arising under the constitution. One inferior court must be established, I presume, in each state at least, with the necessary executive officers appendant thereto. It is easy to see, that in the common course of things, these courts will eclipse the dignity, and take away from the respectability, of the state courts. These courts will be, in themselves, totally independent of the states, deriving their authority from the United States, and receiving from them fixed salaries; and in the course of human events it is to be expected, that they will swallow up all the powers of the courts in the respective states.

How far the clause in the 8th section of the 1st article may operate to do away all idea of confederated states, and to effect an entire consolidation of the whole into one general government, it is impossible to say. The powers given by this article are very general and comprehensive, and it may receive a construction to justify the passing almost any law. A power to make all laws, which shall be necessary and proper, for carrying into execution, all powers vested by the constitution in the government of the United States, or any department or officer thereof, is a power very comprehensive and definite, and may, for ought I know, be exercised in a such manner as entirely to abolish the state legislatures. Suppose the legislature of a state should pass a law to raise money to support their government and pay the state debt, may the Congress repeal this law, because it may prevent the collection of a tax which they may think proper and necessary to lay, to provide for the general welfare of the United States? For all laws made, in pursuance of this constitution, are the supreme law of the land, and the judges in every state shall be bound thereby, any thing in the constitution or laws of the different states to the contrary notwithstanding.— By such a law, the government of a particular state might be overturned at one stroke, and thereby be deprived of every means of its support.

It is not meant, by stating this case, to insinuate that the constitution would warrant a law of this kind; or unnecessarily to alarm the fears of the people, by suggesting, that the federal legislature would be more likely to pass the limits assigned them by the constitution, than that of an individual state, further than they are less responsible to the people. But what is meant is, that the legislature of the United States are vested with the great and uncontroulable powers, of laying and collecting taxes, duties, imposts, and excises; of regulating trade, raising and supporting armies, organizing, arming, and disciplining the militia, instituting courts, and other general powers. And are by this clause invested with the power of making all laws, proper and necessary, for carrying all these into execution; and they may so exercise this power as entirely to annihilate all the state governments, and reduce this country to one single government.

And if they may do it, it is pretty certain they will; for it will be found that the power retained by individual states, small as it is, will be a clog upon the wheels of the government of the United States; the latter therefore will be naturally inclined to remove it out of the way. Besides, it is a truth confirmed by the unerring experience of ages, that every man, and every body of men, invested with power, are ever disposed to increase it, and to acquire a superiority over every thing that stands in their way. This disposition, which is implanted in human nature, will operate in the federal legislature to lessen and ultimately to subvert the state authority, and having such advantages, will most certainly succeed, if the federal government succeeds at all. It must be very evident then, that what this constitution wants of being a complete consolidation of the several parts of the union into one complete government, possessed of perfect legislative, judicial, and executive powers, to all intents and purposes, it will necessarily acquire in its exercise and operation.

Let us now proceed to enquire, as I at first proposed, whether it be best the thirteen United States should be reduced to one great republic, or not? It is here taken for granted, that all agree in this, that whatever government we adopt, it ought to be a free one; that it should be so framed as to secure the liberty of the citizens of America, and such an one as to admit of a full, fair, and equal representation of the people. The question then will be, whether a government thus constituted, and founded on such principles, is practicable, and can be exercised over the whole United States, reduced into one state?

If respect is to be paid to the opinion of the greatest and wisest men who have ever thought or wrote on the science of government, we shall be constrained to conclude, that a free republic cannot succeed over a country of such immense extent, containing such a number of inhabitants, and these encreasing in such rapid progression as that of the whole United States. Among the many illustrious authorities which might be produced to this point, I shall content myself with quoting only two. The one is the baron de Montesquieu, spirit of laws, chap. xvi. vol. I [book VIII]. "It is natural to a republic to have only a small territory, otherwise it cannot long subsist. In a large republic there are men of large fortunes, and consequently of less moderation; there are trusts too great to be placed in any single subject; he has interest of his own; he soon begins to think that he may be happy, great and glorious, by oppressing his fellow citizens; and that he may raise himself to grandeur on the ruins of his country. In a large republic, the public good is sacrificed to a thousand views; it is subordinate to exceptions, and depends on accidents. In a small one, the interest of the public is easier perceived, better understood, and more within the reach of every citizen; abuses are of less extent, and of course are less protected." Of the same opinion is the marquis Beccarari.

History furnishes no example of a free republic, any thing like the extent of the United States. The Grecian republics were of small extent; so also was that of the Romans. Both of these, it is true, in process of time, extended their conquests over large territories of country; and the consequence was, that their governments were changed from that of free governments to those of the most tyrannical that ever existed in the world.

Not only the opinion of the greatest men, and the experience of mankind, are against the idea of an extensive republic, but a variety of reasons may be drawn from the reason and nature of things, against it. In every government, the will of the sovereign is the law. In despotic governments, the supreme authority being lodged in one, his will is law, and can be as easily expressed to a large extensive territory as to a small one. In a pure democracy the people are the sovereign, and their will is declared by themselves; for this purpose they must all come together to deliberate, and decide. This kind of government cannot be exercised, therefore, over a country of any considerable extent; it must be confined to a single city, or at least limited to such bounds as that the people can conveniently assemble, be able to debate, understand the subject submitted to them, and declare their opinion concerning it.

In a free republic, although all laws are derived from the consent of the people, yet the people do not declare their consent by themselves in person, but by representatives, chosen by them, who are supposed to know the minds of their constituents, and to be possessed of integrity to declare this mind.

In every free government, the people must give their assent to the laws by which they are governed. This is the true criterion between a free government and an arbitrary one. The former are ruled by the will of the whole, expressed in any manner they may agree upon; the latter by the will of one, or a few. If the people are to give their assent to the laws, by persons chosen and appointed by them, the manner of the choice and the number chosen, must be such, as to possess, be disposed, and consequently qualified to declare the sentiments of the people; for if they do not know, or are not disposed to speak the sentiments of the people, the people do not govern, but the sovereignty is in a few. Now, in a large extended country, it is impossible to have a representation, possessing the sentiments, and of integrity, to declare the minds of the people, without having it so numerous and unwieldly, as to be subject in great measure to the inconveniency of a democratic government.

The territory of the United States is of vast extent; it now contains near three millions of souls, and is capable of containing much more than ten times that number. Is it practicable for a country, so large and so numerous as they will soon become, to elect a representation, that will speak their sentiments, without their becoming so numerous as to be incapable of transacting public business? It certainly is not.

In a republic, the manners, sentiments, and interests of the people should be similar. If this be not the case, there will be a constant clashing of opinions; and the representatives of one part will be continually striving against those of the other. This will retard the operations of government, and prevent such conclusions as will promote the public good. If we apply this remark to the condition of the United States, we shall be convinced that it forbids that we should be one government. The United States includes a variety of climates. The productions of the different parts of the union are very variant, and their interests, of consequence, diverse. Their manners and habits differ as much as their climates and productions; and their sentiments are by no means coincident. The laws and customs of the several states are, in many respects, very diverse, and in some opposite; each would be in favor of its own interests and customs, and, of consequence, a legislature, formed of representatives from the respective parts, would not only be too numerous to act with any care or decision, but would be composed of such heterogenous and discordant principles, as would constantly be contending with each other.

The laws cannot be executed in a republic, of an extent equal to that of the United States, with promptitude.

The magistrates in every government must be supported in the execution of the laws, either by an armed force, maintained at the public expence for that purpose; or by the people turning out to aid the magistrate upon his command, in case of resistance.

In despotic governments, as well as in all the monarchies of Europe, standing armies are kept up to execute the commands of the prince or the magistrate, and are employed for this purpose when occasion requires: But they have always proved the destruction of liberty, and [are] abhorrent to the spirit of a free republic. In England, where they depend upon the parliament for their annual support, they have always been complained of as oppressive and unconstitutional, and are seldom employed in executing of the laws; never except on extraordinary occasions, and then under the direction of a civil magistrate.

A free republic will never keep a standing army to execute its laws. It must depend upon the support of its citizens. But when a government is to receive its support from the aid of the citizens, it must be so constructed as to have the confidence, respect, and affection of the people. Men who, upon the call of the magistrate, offer themselves to execute the laws, are influenced to do it either by affection to the government, or from fear; where a standing army is at hand to punish offenders, every man is actuated by the latter principle, and therefore, when the magistrate calls, will obey: but, where this is not the case, the government must rest for its support upon the confidence and respect which the people have for their government and laws. The body of the people being attached, the government will always be sufficient to support and execute its laws, and to operate upon the fears of any faction which may be opposed to it, not only to prevent an opposition to the execution of the laws themselves, but also to compel the most of them to aid the magistrate; but the people will not be likely to have such confidence in their rulers, in a republic so extensive as the United States, as necessary for these purposes. The confidence which the people have in their rulers, in a free republic, arises from their knowing them, from their being responsible to them for their conduct, and from the power they have of displacing them when they misbehave: but in a republic of the extent of this continent, the people in general would be acquainted with very few of their rulers: the people at large would know little of their proceedings, and it would be extremely difficult to change them. The people in Georgia and New-Hampshire would not know one another's mind, and therefore could not act in concert to enable them to effect a general change of representatives. The different parts of so extensive a country could not possibly be made acquainted with the conduct of their representatives, nor be informed of the reasons upon which measures were founded. The consequence will be, they will have no confidence in their legislature, suspect them of ambitious views, be jealous of every measure they adopt, and will not support the laws they pass. Hence the government will be nerveless and inefficient, and no way will be left to render it otherwise, but by establishing an armed force to execute the laws at the point of the bayonet—a government of all others the most to be dreaded.

In a republic of such vast extent as the United-States, the legislature cannot attend to the various concerns and wants of its different parts. It cannot be sufficiently numerous to be acquainted with the local condition and wants of the different districts, and if it could, it is impossible it should have sufficient time to attend to and provide for all the variety of cases of this nature, that would be continually arising.

In so extensive a republic, the great officers of government would soon become above the controul of the people, and abuse their power to the purpose of aggrandizing themselves, and oppressing them. The trust committed to the executive offices, in a country of the extent of the United-States, must be various and of magnitude. The command of all the troops and navy of the republic, the appointment of officers, the power of pardoning offences, the collecting of all the public revenues, and the power of expending them, with a number of other powers, must be lodged and exercised in every state, in the hands of a few. When these are attended with great honor and emolument, as they always will be in large states, so as greatly to interest men to pursue them, and to be proper objects for ambitious and designing men, such men will be ever restless in their pursuit after them. They will use the power, when they have acquired it, to the purposes of gratifying their own interest and ambition, and it is scarcely possible, in a very large republic, to call them to account for their misconduct, or to prevent their abuse of power.

These are some of the reasons by which it appears, that a free republic cannot long subsist over a country of the great extent of these states. If then this new constitution is calculated to consolidate the thirteen states into one, as it evidently is, it ought not to be adopted.

Though I am of opinion, that it is a sufficient objection to this government, to reject it, that it creates the whole union into one government, under the form of a republic, yet if this objection was obviated, there are exceptions to it, which are so material and fundamental, that they ought to determine every man, who is a friend to the liberty and happiness of mankind, not to adopt it. I beg the candid and dispassionate attention of my countrymen while I state these objections—they are such as have obtruded themselves upon my mind upon a careful attention to the matter, and such as I sincerely believe are well founded. There are many objections, of small moment, of which I shall take no notice—perfection is not to be expected in any thing that is the production of man—and if I did not in my conscience believe that this scheme was defective in the fundamental principles—in the foundation upon which a free and equal government must rest—I would hold my peace.

Source: New York Journal, October 18, 1787.

14. Amendments Recommended by the Massachusetts Ratification Convention, February 6, 1788

To get the Constitution approved in Massachusetts, Federalists resorted to having the state convention approve a list of recommendatory amendments to accompany its unconditional ratification of the Constitution. These alterations would merely be suggestions to be considered once the new government began operation. Six of the remaining seven state conventions followed this recommendatory amendment precedent to achieve ratification.

In Convention of the delegates of the People of the Commonwealth of Massachusetts February 6th 1788.

The Convention have impartially discussed, & fully considered the Constitution for the United States of America, reported to Congress by the Convention of Delegates from the United States of America, & submitted to us by a resolution of the General Court of the said Commonwealth, passed the twenty fifth day of October last past, & acknowledging with grateful hearts, the goodness of the Supreme Ruler of the Universe in affording the People of the United States in the course of his providence an opportunity deliberately & peaceably without fraud or surprize of entering into an explicit & solemn Compact with each other by assenting to & ratifying a New Constitution in order to form a more perfect Union, establish Justice, insure Domestic tranquillity, provide for the common defence, promote the general welfare & secure the blessings

Primary Documents

of Liberty to themselves & their posterity; Do in the name & in behalf of the People of the Commonwealth of Massachusetts assent to & ratify the said Constitution for the United States of America.

And, as it is the opinion of this Convention that certain amendments & alterations in the said Constitution would remove the fears & quiet the apprehensions of many of the good people of this Commonwealth & more effectually guard against an undue administration of the Federal Government, The Convention do therefore recommend that the following alterations & provisions be introduced into the said Constitution: —

> *First,* That it be explicitly declared that all Powers not expressly delegated by the aforesaid Constitution are reserved to the several States to be by them exercised.
>
> *Secondly,* That there shall be one representative to every thirty thousand persons according to the Census mentioned in the Constitution until the whole number of the Representatives amounts to Two hundred.
>
> *Thirdly,* That Congress do not exercise the powers vested in them by the fourth Section of the first article, but in cases when a State shall neglect or refuse to make the regulations therein mentioned or shall make regulations subversive of the rights of the People to a free & equal representation in Congress agreeably to the Constitution.
>
> *Fourthly,* That Congress do not lay direct Taxes but when the Monies arising from the Impost & Excise are insufficient for the publick exigencies nor then until Congress shall have first made a requisition upon the States to assess levy & pay their respective proportions of such Requisition agreeably to the Census fixed in the said Constitution; in such way & manner as the Legislature of the States shall think best, & in such case if any State shall neglect or refuse to pay its proportion pursuant to such requisition then Congress may assess & levy such State's proportion together with interest thereon at the rate of Six per cent per annum from the time of payment prescribed in such requisition
>
> *Fifthly,* That Congress erect no Company of Merchants with exclusive advantages of commerce.

Sixthly, That no person shall be tried for any Crime by which he may incur an infamous punishment or loss of life until he be first indicted by a Grand Jury, except in such cases as may arise in the Government & regulation of the Land & Naval forces.

Seventhly, The Supreme Judicial Federal Court shall have no jurisdiction of Causes between Citizens of different States unless the matter in dispute whether it concerns the realty or personally be of the value of three thousand dollars at the least, nor shall the Federal Judicial Powers extend to any actions between Citizens of different States where the matter in dispute whether it concerns the Realty or personally is not of the value of Fifteen hundred dollars at the least.

Eighthly, In civil actions between Citizens of different States every issue of fact arising in Actions at common law shall be tried by a Jury if the parties or either of them request it.

Ninthly, Congress shall at no time consent that any person holding an office of trust or profit under the United States shall accept of a title of Nobility or any other title or office from any King, prince or Foreign State.

And the Convention do in the name & in behalf of the People of this Commonwealth enjoin it upon their Representatives in Congress at all times until the alterations & provisions aforesaid have been considered agreeably to the Fifth article of the said Constitution to exert all their influence & use all reasonable & legal methods to obtain a ratification of the said alterations & provisions in such manner as is provided in the said Article.

And that the United States in Congress Assembled may have due notice of the Assent & Ratification of the said Constitution by this Convention it is, Resolved, that the Assent & Ratification aforesaid be engrossed on Parchment together with the recommendation & injunction aforesaid & with this resolution & that His Excellency John Hancock Esqr President & the Hong William Cushing Esqr Vice President, of this Convention transmit the same, counter-signed by the Secretary of the Convention under their hands & seals to the United States in Congress Assembled

 JOHN HANCOCK President
 WM CUSHING Vice President

GEORGE RICHARDS MINOT, Secretary.

Pursuant to the Resolution aforesaid WE the President & Vice President abovenamed Do hereby transmit to the United States in Congress Assembled, the same Resolution with the above Assent and Ratification of the Constitution aforesaid for the United States, And the recommendation & injunction above specified.

In Witness whereof We have hereunto set our hands & Seals at Boston in the Commonwealth aforesaid this Seventh day of February Anno Domini, one thousand Seven Hundred & Eighty eight, and in the Twelfth year of the Independence of the United States of America.

JOHN HANCOCK President [SEAL.]
Wm CUSHING Vice President [SEAL.]

Source: Jonathan Elliot, ed. *The Debates in the Several State Conventions on the Adoption of the Federal Constitution*, 2nd ed., 4 vols. Washington, D.C.: Government Printing Office, 1836, 2:176–78.

15. *The Federalist,* Number 51, February 8, 1788

Alexander Hamilton, James Madison, and John Jay wrote The Federalist *to answer* Brutus. *In this essay, one of his twenty-nine contributions to the series, James Madison argued that the Constitution's checks and balances among the branches and levels of government will protect the rights and liberties of the people. He further claimed that in a large republic the size of the United States, self-interested factions will cancel one another out, preventing majority tyranny.*

To the People of the State of New York:

TO WHAT expedient, then, shall we finally resort, for maintaining in practice the necessary partition of power among the several departments, as laid down in the Constitution? The only answer that can be given is, that as all these exterior provisions are found to be inadequate, the defect must be supplied, by so contriving the interior structure of the government as that its several constituent parts may, by their mutual relations, be the means of keeping each other in their proper places. Without presuming to undertake a full development of this important idea, I will hazard a few general observations, which may perhaps place it in a clearer light, and enable us to form a more correct judgment of the principles and structure of the government planned by the convention.

In order to lay a due foundation for that separate and distinct exercise of the different powers of government, which to a certain extent is admitted on all hands to be essential to the preservation of liberty, it is evident that each department should have a will of its own; and consequently should be so constituted that the members of each should have as little agency as possible in the appointment of the members of the others. Were this principle rigorously adhered to, it would require that all the appointments for the supreme executive, legislative, and judiciary magistracies should be drawn from the same fountain of authority, the people, through channels having no communication whatever with one another. Perhaps such a plan of constructing the several departments would be less difficult in practice than it may in contemplation appear. Some difficulties, however, and some additional expense would attend the execution of it. Some deviations, therefore, from the principle must be admitted. In the constitution of the judiciary department in particular, it might be inexpedient to insist rigorously on the principle: first, because peculiar qualifications being essential in the members, the primary consideration ought to be to select that mode of choice which best secures these qualifications; secondly, because the permanent tenure by which the appointments are held in that department, must soon destroy all sense of dependence on the authority conferring them.

It is equally evident, that the members of each department should be as little dependent as possible on those of the others, for the emoluments annexed to their offices. Were the executive magistrate, or the judges, not independent of the legislature in this particular, their independence in every other would be merely nominal. But the great security against a gradual concentration of the several powers in the same department, consists in giving to those who administer each department the necessary constitutional means and personal motives to resist encroachments of the others. The provision for defense must in this, as in all other cases, be made commensurate to the danger of attack. Ambition must be made to counteract ambition. The interest of the man must be connected with the constitutional rights of the place. It may be a reflection on human nature, that such devices should be necessary to control the abuses of government. But what is government itself, but the greatest of all reflections on human nature? If men were angels, no government would be necessary. If angels were to govern men, neither external nor internal controls on government would be necessary. In framing a government which is to be administered by men over men, the great difficulty lies in this: you must first enable the government to control the governed; and in the next place oblige it to control itself.

A dependence on the people is, no doubt, the primary control on the government; but experience has taught mankind the necessity of auxiliary precautions. This policy of supplying, by opposite and rival interests, the defect of better motives, might be traced through the whole system of human affairs, private as well as public. We see it particularly displayed in all the subordinate distributions of power, where the constant aim is to divide and arrange the several offices in such a manner as that each may be a check on the other that the private interest of every individual may be a sentinel over the public rights. These inventions of prudence cannot be less requisite in the distribution of the supreme powers of the State. But it is not possible to give to each department an equal power of self-defense. In republican government, the legislative authority necessarily predominates. The remedy for this inconveniency is to divide the legislature into different branches; and to render them, by different modes of election and different principles of action, as little connected with each other as the nature of their common functions and their common dependence on the society will admit. It may even be necessary to guard against dangerous encroachments by still further precautions. As the weight of the legislative authority requires that it should be thus divided, the weakness of the executive may require, on the other hand, that it should be fortified.

An absolute negative on the legislature appears, at first view, to be the natural defense with which the executive magistrate should be armed. But perhaps it would be neither altogether safe nor alone sufficient. On ordinary occasions it might not be exerted with the requisite firmness, and on extraordinary occasions it might be perfidiously abused. May not this defect of an absolute negative be supplied by some qualified connection between this weaker department and the weaker branch of the stronger department, by which the latter may be led to support the constitutional rights of the former, without being too much detached from the rights of its own department? If the principles on which these observations are founded be just, as I persuade myself they are, and they be applied as a criterion to the several State constitutions, and to the federal Constitution it will be found that if the latter does not perfectly correspond with them, the former are infinitely less able to bear such a test.

There are, moreover, two considerations particularly applicable to the federal system of America, which place that system in a very interesting point of view. First. In a single republic, all the power surrendered by the people is submitted to the administration of a single government; and the usurpations are guarded against by a division of the government into distinct and separate departments. In the compound republic of America, the power surrendered by the people is first divided between two distinct governments, and then the portion allotted to each subdivided among distinct and separate departments. Hence a double security arises to the rights of the people. The different governments will control each other, at the same time that each will be controlled by itself. Second. It is of great importance in a republic not only to guard the society against the oppression of its rulers, but to guard one part of the society against the injustice of the other part. Different interests necessarily exist in different classes of citizens. If a majority be united by a common interest, the rights of the minority will be insecure.

There are but two methods of providing against this evil: the one by creating a will in the community independent of the majority that is, of the society itself; the other, by comprehending in the society so many separate descriptions of citizens as will render an unjust combination of a majority of the whole very improbable, if not impracticable. The first method prevails in all governments possessing an hereditary or self-appointed authority. This, at best, is but a precarious security; because a power independent of the society may as well espouse the unjust views of the major, as the rightful interests of the minor party, and may possibly be turned against both parties. The second method will be exemplified in the federal republic of the United States. Whilst all authority in it will be derived from and dependent on the society, the society itself will be broken into so many parts, interests, and classes of citizens, that the rights of individuals, or of the minority, will be in little danger from interested combinations of the majority.

In a free government the security for civil rights must be the same as that for religious rights. It consists in the one case in the multiplicity of interests, and in the other in the multiplicity of sects. The degree of security in both cases will depend on the number of interests and sects; and this may be presumed to depend on the extent of country and number of people comprehended under the same government. This view of the subject must particularly recommend a proper federal system to all the sincere and considerate friends of republican government, since it shows that in exact proportion as the territory of the Union may be formed into more circumscribed Confederacies, or States oppressive combinations of a majority will be facilitated: the best security, under the republican forms, for the rights of every class of citizens, will be diminished: and consequently the stability and independence of some member of the government, the only other security, must be proportionately increased. Justice is the end of government. It is the end of civil society. It ever has been and ever will be pursued until it be obtained, or until liberty be lost in the pursuit. In a society under the forms of which the stronger faction can readily unite and oppress the weaker, anarchy may as truly be said to reign as in a state of nature, where the weaker individual is not secured against the violence of the stronger; and as, in the latter state, even the stronger individuals are prompted, by the uncertainty of their condition, to submit to a government which may protect the weak as well as themselves; so, in the former state, will the more powerful factions or parties be gradually induced, by a like motive, to wish for a government which will protect all parties, the weaker as well as the more powerful.

It can be little doubted that if the State of Rhode Island was separated from the Confederacy and left to itself, the insecurity of rights under the popular form of government within such narrow limits would be displayed by such reiterated oppressions of factious majorities that some power altogether independent of the people would soon be called for by the voice of the very factions whose misrule had proved the necessity of it. In the extended republic of the United States, and among the great variety of interests, parties, and sects which it embraces, a coalition of a majority of the whole society could seldom take place on any other principles than those of justice and the general good; whilst there being thus less danger to a minor from the will of a major party, there must be less pretext, also, to provide for the security of the former, by introducing into the government a will not dependent on the latter, or, in other words, a will independent of the society itself. It is no less certain than it is important, notwithstanding the contrary opinions which have been entertained, that the larger the society, provided it lie within a practical sphere, the more duly capable it will be of self-government. And happily for the REPUBLICAN CAUSE, the practicable sphere may be carried to a very great extent, by a judicious modification and mixture of the FEDERAL PRINCIPLE.

PUBLIUS.

Source: New York Packet, February 8, 1788.

BIBLIOGRAPHICAL ESSAY

PRINTED PRIMARY SOURCES

The most valuable printed primary source on the Constitutional Convention is Max Farrand, ed., *The Records of the Federal Convention of 1787*. 1937 rev. ed. in four vols., reprint (New Haven, CT, 1974). Volumes one and two contain the convention notes taken by Madison and the nine other note-takers, including Robert Yates, Rufus King, and James McHenry. It also has the Convention Journal kept by convention secretary William Jackson. Volume three (*Supplementary Records of Proceedings in Convention*) contains the delegates' comments on the convention from 1787 through 1836, when James Madison, the last surviving delegate, died. Volume four is the index to the set. James H. Hutson edited a *Supplement to Max Farrand's* The Records of the Federal Convention of 1787 (New Haven, CT, 1987). Adrienne Koch, ed., *Notes of Debates in the Federal Convention of 1787 Reported by James Madison* (Athens, OH, 1966), a useful one-volume edition of Madison's notes, is cited in this book. *Journals of the Continental Congress, 1774–1789*, 34 vols. (Washington, 1904–1937) includes the Confederation Congress's actions pertaining to the Constitutional Convention.

John P. Kaminski and Timothy D. Moore, eds., *An Assembly of Demigods: Word Portraits of the Delegates to the Constitutional Convention by Their Contemporaries* (Madison, WI, 2012) includes firsthand descriptions of the convention delegates. Richard Leffler et al., eds., *William Pierce on the Constitutional Convention and the Constitution* (Dallas, TX, 2011) includes the convention notes and character sketches of the convention members by Georgia delegate William Pierce.

Modern, scholarly letterpress editions of the papers of the convention delegates include Harold C. Syrett et al., eds., *The Papers of Alexander Hamilton*, 27 vols. (New York, 1961–1987); William T. Hutchinson et al., eds., *The Papers of James Madison, Congressional Series*, 17 vols. (Chicago, IL, and Charlottesville, VA, 1962–1991); Robert A. Rutland, ed., *The Papers of George Mason*, 3 vols. (Chapel Hill, NC, 1970); W. W. Abbot et al., eds., *The Papers of George Washington, Confederation Series*, 6 vols. (Charlottesville, VA, 1992–1997); Donald Jackson and Dorothy Twohig, eds., *The Diaries of George Washington*, 6 vols. (Charlottesville, VA, 1976–1979); and Kermit L. Hall and Mark David Hall., eds., *The Collected Works of James Wilson*, 2 vols. (Indianapolis, IN, 2007). Paul H. Smith et al., eds. *Letters of Delegates to Congress, 1774–1789*, 25 vols. (Washington, 1976–2000) includes the letters of those Constitutional Convention delegates who were also members of the Confederation Congress.

The definitive printed primary source on the ratification of the Constitution is John P. Kaminski et al., eds., *The Documentary History of the Ratification of the Constitution*, 29 vols. to date (Madison, WI, 1976–), which includes the debates and proceedings of the state ratification conventions, as well as Federalist and Antifederalist writings. Other valuable printed primary sources on ratification include George W. Carey and James McClellan, eds., *The Federalist* (Indianapolis, IN, 2001); Bruce Frohnen, ed., *The Anti-Federalists: Selected Writings and Speeches* (Washington, 1999); and Michael P. Zuckert and Derek A. Webb, eds., *The Anti-Federalist Writings of the Melancton Smith Circle* (Indianapolis, IN, 2009).

The definitive printed primary source on the birth of the Bill of Rights is Helen E. Veit et al., eds., *Creating the Bill of Rights: The Documentary Record from the First Federal Congress* (Baltimore, MD, 1991).

SECONDARY SOURCES

Monographs on the Confederation period include Sean Condon, *Shays's Rebellion: Authority and Distress in Post-Revolutionary America* (Baltimore, MD, 2015); Merrill Jensen, *The New Nation: A History of the United States during the Confederation, 1774–1781* (New York, 1950); Jack N. Rakove, *The Beginnings of National Politics: An Interpretive History of the Continental Congress* (New York, 1979); Leonard L. Richards, *Shays's Rebellion: The American Revolution's Final Battle* (Philadelphia, 2002); Richard B. Morris,

The Forging of the Union, 1781–1789 (New York, 1987); and George William Van Cleve, *We Have Not a Government: The Articles of Confederation and the Road to the Constitutional Convention* (Chicago, IL, 2017).

Monographs on the Constitutional Convention include Charles Beard, *An Economic Interpretation of the Constitution of the United States* (New York, 1913); Richard Beeman, *Plain Honest Men: The Making of the American Constitution* (New York, 2009); Christopher Collier, *All Politics Is Local: Family, Friends, and Provincial Interests in the Creation of the Constitution* (Hanover, NH, 2003); Christopher Collier and James Lincoln Collier, *Decision in Philadelphia: The Constitutional Convention of 1787* (New York, 1987); Paul Finkelman, *Slavery and the Founders: Race and Liberty in the Age of Jefferson*, 3rd ed. (New York, 2014); John P. Kaminski, *Secrecy and the Constitutional Convention* (Madison, WI, 2005); Michael Klarman, *The Framers' Coup: The Making of the United States Constitution* (New York, 2016); Staughton Lynd, "The Compromise of 1787," *Political Science Quarterly*, 81 (1966), 225–50; Staughton Lynd, *Class Conflict, Slavery, and the United States Constitution* (Indianapolis, IN, 1967); Richard B. Morris, *The Framing of the Federal Constitution* (Washington, 1986); David O. Stewart, *The Summer of 1787: The Men Who Wrote the Constitution* (New York, 2007); David Waldstreicher, *Slavery's Constitution: From Revolution to Ratification* (New York, 2010); and Sean Wilentz, *No Property in Man: Slavery and Antislavery at the Nation's Founding* (Cambridge, MA, 2018).

Biographical and other works on the delegates to the Constitutional Convention include William Murchison, *The Cost of Liberty: The Life of John Dickinson* (Wilmington, DE, 2013); George Athan Billias, *Elbridge Gerry: Founding Father and Republican Statesman* (New York, 1976); Walter Isaacson, *Benjamin Franklin: An American Life* (New York, 2003); Lance Banning, *Jefferson & Madison: Three Conversations from the Founding* (Madison, WI, 1995); Mary Sarah Bilder, *Madison's Hand: Revising the Constitutional Convention* (Cambridge, MA, 2015); Irving Brant, *James Madison*, 6 vols. (Indianapolis, IN, 1941–1961); Ralph Ketcham, *James Madison: A Biography* (New York, 1971); Stuart Leibiger, "James Madison and Amendments to the Constitution: 'Parchment Barriers,'" *Journal of Southern History*, 59 (1993), 441–46; Drew R. McCoy, *The Last of the Fathers: James Madison and the Republican Legacy* (Cambridge, MA, 1989); Jack N. Rakove, *A Politician Thinking: The Creative Mind of James Madison*

(Norman, OK, 2017); Jack N. Rakove, *James Madison and the Creation of the American Republic* (Glenview, IL, 1990); Jeff Broadwater, *George Mason: Forgotten Founder* (Chapel Hill, NC, 2006); James Kirschke, *Gouverneur Morris: Author, Statesman and Man of the World* (New York, 2005); Marty D. Matthews, *Forgotten Founder: The Life and Times of Charles Pinckney* (Columbia, SC, 2004); John J. Reardon, *Edmund Randolph: A Biography* (New York, 1974); Mark David Hall, *Roger Sherman and the Creation of the American Republic* (New York, 2013); James Thomas Flexner, *Washington: The Indispensable Man* (New York, 1974); Edward L. Larson, *The Return of George Washington* (New York, 2014); Stuart Leibiger, *Founding Friendship: George Washington, James Madison, and the Creation of the American Republic* (Charlottesville, VA, 1999); and Page Smith, *James Wilson: Founding Father* (Chapel Hill, NC, 1956).

Monographs and articles on ratification include John K. Alexander, *The Selling of the Constitutional Convention: A History of News Coverage* (Madison, WI, 1990); Cecelia Kenyon, "Men of Little Faith: The Antifederalists on the Nature of Representative Government," *William and Mary Quarterly*, 3rd ser., 12 (1955) 3–43; Pauline Maier, *Ratification: The People Debate the Constitution, 1787–1788* (New York, 2010); David J. Siemers, *Ratifying the Republic: Antifederalists and Federalists in Constitutional Time* (Stanford, CA, 2002); and Herbert Storing, *What the Antifederalists Were For* (Chicago, IL, 1981).

Monographs and articles on the launching of the federal government include Charlene Bangs Bickford and Kenneth R. Bowling, *The Birth of the Nation: The First Federal Congress, 1789–1791* (Madison, WI, 1989); Kenneth R. Bowling, "The Founding Fathers and the Adoption of the Federal Bill of Rights," *Journal of the Early Republic*, 8 (1988), 223–51; Joseph Ellis, *Founding Brothers: The Revolutionary Generation* (New York, 2002); and Jack D. Warren, *The Presidency of George Washington* (Mount Vernon, VA, 2000).

Other useful monographs include Willi Paul Adams, *The First American Constitutions: Republican Ideology and the Making of the State Constitutions in the Revolutionary Era* (Chapel Hill, NC, 1980); Danielle Allen, *Our Declaration: A Reading of the Declaration of Independence in Defense of Equality* (New York, 2014); Kenneth R. Bowling, *The Creation of Washington, D.C.: The Idea and Location of the American Capital* (Fairfax, VA, 1991); Forrest McDonald, *E Pluribis Unum: The Formation of the American*

Republic, 1776–1790, 2nd ed. (Indianapolis, IN, 1979), 236; Norman J. Risjord, *Chesapeake Politics, 1781–1800* (New York, 1978); Garry Wills, *Negro President: Jefferson and the Slave Power* (Boston, MA, 2003); and Gordon Wood, *The Creation of the American Republic, 1776–1787* (Chapel Hill, NC, 1969).

ONLINE SOURCES

The Library of Congress (DLC) website (www.loc.gov/) features digital versions of both manuscript and printed sources on the Constitutional Convention. The Papers of James Madison collection includes electronic manuscript scans of Madison's papers, including manuscript scans of *Notes of Debates in the Federal Convention of 1787*. The Library of Congress website also offers electronic scans of the papers of other convention delegates, including George Washington. The printed version of Farrand's *The Records of the Federal Convention of 1787* may also be accessed online at the DLC website.

The papers of Benjamin Franklin, Alexander Hamilton, James Madison, and George Washington can be searched through the Founders Online page of the National Archives website (https://founders.archives.gov/about).

The Constitutional Convention and Ratification pages of the Teaching American History website (www.teachingamericanhistory.org) provide a plethora of material, including Madison's *Notes of Debates in the Federal Convention of 1787*, brief biographies of the delegates, an interactive map of eighteenth-century Philadelphia, a collection of paintings of the convention, and a record of the delegates' attendance at the convention.

The letterpress edition of *The Documentary History of the Ratification of the Constitution* may be accessed online through the website of the Wisconsin Historical Society (https://uwdc.library.wisc.edu/collections/history/constitution/). The University of Wisconsin's Center for the Study of the Constitution (CSAC) website (https://csac.history.wisc.edu/) features excellent state-by-state essays and maps on ratification, and collections of primary source documents on the framing and ratification of the Constitution. See also *The Documentary History of the Ratification of the Constitution Digital Edition* (Charlottesville, VA, 2009).

INDEX

Abbot, W. W., 14
Act for Securing the Rights of
    Conscience (CT), 10
Adams, Abigail, 13–14
Adams, John, xviii, 3, 5, 7, 27, 75,
    80, 98, 99, 225, 240, 241
Adams, John Quincy, 52, 54, 67–68,
    192, 193
Adams, Samuel, 3, 216
African slave trade, xxi, xxxii, 127,
    134, 147–150, 152–153,
    155–156, 186, 217, 243, 245
Albany, New York, 92
Albany Plan, 2
Alexandria, Virginia, 17–19
Alien Acts, 244
American Revolution, 135, 142,
    185, 208, 226
Annapolis, Maryland, 5, 26, 217
Annapolis convention, xx, xxxi, 2,
    22, 23–28, 32, 35, 36, 42n49,
    48, 50, 239, 242, 244, 245,
    246, 251–254, 257
Antifederalists, xxi–xxii, 199–225,
    227–229, 231, 233, 272
    acceptance of Federalist ground
        rules by, 204
    decline of, 225, 233
    labeled by Federalists, 204–205
    lack of newspaper support for,
        214, 224
    See also "Brutus" essays;
        "Objections to This
        Constitution of
        Government"
Articles of Confederation, xix, xxxi,
    2, 4, 6, 9, 10, 16, 22–23, 25–26,
    35, 45, 48, 64, 66, 69, 71, 72,
    82, 90, 98, 99, 154, 179, 186,
    200–205, 227, 239, 241, 247,
    249, 257, 261–262, 264–266.
    See also United States,
    Confederation period in

Baldwin, Abraham, xxv, xxviii,
    107–109, 116, 150, 152, 159, 181
Bancroft, George, 121
Baptist Church, 38
Bassett, Richard, xxv, xxix
Bayard, John, 146
Beard, Charles, xviii, 37
Beccarari, Marquis de, 288
Beckley, John, 52
Bedford, Gunning, xxv, xxviii, 78,
    106–118, 108–110, 173
Beeman, Richard, 107, 116

Bethlehem, Pennsylvania, 136
Bilder, Mary Sarah, 54–55,
    85–86n19
Bingham, Anne, 61
Bingham, William, 61
Birch, W., xii, 47
Blair, John, xxvi, xxix, 256
Blount, William, xxv, xxix, 57–58,
    63, 117, 118, 136, 189,
    191
Blue Run Baptist Church, 230
Board of Treasury, 162
Boston, Massachusetts, 30–31,
    214, 240
Bowdoin, James, 31–32, 215
Braddock, Edward, 248
Brearly, David, xxviii, 63, 79, 105,
    179–180, 182
Broom, Jacob, xxv, xxviii, 37
"Brutus" essays, xiv, 204–208, 210,
    281–292, 295
Burr, Aaron, 243
Butler, Pierce, xxvi, xxviii, 74–75,
    111, 114, 136, 140, 142, 144,
    148, 153–154, 185

Caesar, Julius, 34
Calhoun, John C., 154
Carroll, Daniel, xxv, xxviii, 131,
    137–139, 144, 178, 187
Caswell, Richard, 57, 58, 118
"Cato," essays, 207
Charles I, King of Great Britain, 16
Charleston, South Carolina, 217
Chase, Samuel, 16, 17
Chesapeake Bay, 16, 21–22
Cicero, 73
Cincinnati, Society of the, 38, 170
Cincinnatus, 34, 249
"Circular to the States," 14, 34

City Tavern, 38, 60, 193
Civil War, 155, 237
Clark, Abraham, 27
Claypoole, David, 137, 188, 273
Clinton, George, xviii, 58, 66,
    86n19, 92, 193, 221, 246
Clymer, George, xxv, xxviii
Coles, Edward, 25, 119
College of New Jersey. See Princeton
    University
Collier, Christopher, 101, 107
Columbia University (King's
    College), 242, 245
Committees at Constitutional
    Convention. See
    Constitutional Convention,
    Committees at
Common Sense Philosophy. See
    Scottish Common Sense
    Philosophy
Compromise of 1790, 227
Concord, Massachusetts, 31
Concord, New Hampshire, 218
Congregationalist church, 247
Connecticut, 3, 5, 7, 10, 26, 35,
    45, 93, 99, 107, 213,
    223, 252
  delegation to Constitutional
    Convention of, 49, 71, 77,
    83, 84, 90, 92, 98, 100, 114,
    117, 136, 152, 155, 172
  population of, 70
  ratification by, xxxiii, 214, 224
Connecticut Compromise. See
    Constitutional Convention,
    Great Compromise
consolidation, 188, 206, 207, 217,
    258, 271, 283, 285–287
Constitutional Convention, 47, 209,
    223–224, 228, 258

bill of rights and, 145–146,
    188–189
calling of, 22, 35–37
chronology of, xxxi
Committees at, 56, 109
    of Detail, xiii, xxi, xxxii, 51, 67,
        127, 131–138, 140, 145, 147,
        149, 160, 170–173, 178, 181,
        185, 243, 247, 250
    election of, 109
    Grand Committee of Eleven (on
        representation), xi, xiii, xxxii,
        19, 89, 108–112, 115–117,
        138, 175, 241, 245, 248
    Livingston Committee (on
        militias), 146–147, 151–153
    on Postponed Parts (Brearly
        committee), xiii, xxxii, 160,
        163, 172, 179–180, 239, 246
    on Rules, 55–59
    of Style, xiii, xxi, xxxii, 138,
        141, 160, 186–188, 246, 271
compensation of congressmen,
    144–145
compromises at
    African slave trade compromise,
        153–154
    Great Compromise (Connecticut
        Compromise), xi, xii, xiii,
        xxi, xxxii, 19, 53, 75, 91,
        98, 101, 115–122, 127–128,
        138, 154, 160–163, 165, 168,
        172–173, 175, 213, 239, 241,
        245, 248
    Three-Fifths Compromise, 45, 68,
        82–84, 110, 114–115, 117,
        119, 131–132, 136, 147, 148,
        150, 155, 217, 250
council of revision and, 66, 160,
    173–177

cover letter to Confederation
    Congress of, xiii, 141,
    187–188, 192, 203, 271–272
delegates to praised, xvii–xviii
executive branch and, 66
    advisory council for, 171, 184
    compensation for, 164–165
    design of, xii, xiii, xxi, xxxii,
        50, 84, 122, 132, 136,
        159–172, 180–185, 262
    election of, 164–167, 168–169,
        170–172, 180–183
    length of term of, 163–164
    plural or unitary executive,
        161–162
    removal of executive and,
        162–163, 167–168, 184–185
    veto of, 174, 176–177
export tax and, 148–149
federal officeholding requirements
    and, 140–144
hotchpot at, 79, 82, 98
hours of, 60
journal of, xiii, 52, 54, 121,
    192–193
judicial branch and, 66
    appointment of, 84, 168
    design of, xxi, 132, 136, 160,
        172–173, 177, 262–263
    judicial review by, 128, 160,
        174, 176–177
legislative branch and
    design of House of
        Representatives by, 74,
        76–77
    design of Senate by, 74, 77–78,
        100–112, 122, 131–132,
        138–140, 262–263
    money bills and, 110–111, 115,
        132, 139–140

powers of, 74–75, 133–135, 145, 189
regulation of state militias by, 146–147
representation in, 71, 75–78, 82–84, 98, 100–106, 110–111, 113, 116, 132
veto of state laws by, xxxii, 66, 75, 127–129, 132–133, 177, 231, 262
voting requirements under, 140
New Jersey Plan and, xii, xxxi, 69, 89–98, 100, 123n3, 128, 148, 264–266
notes taken during, 24, 45, 52–56, 67, 85–86n19, 102, 190, 244
rules of, 45, 55–57, 109, 118, 193
secrecy and, 55–59
signing of constitution by, xxxii, 161, 191–193, 200
slavery and, xxi, 82–84, 105–106, 110, 112–115, 119, 127, 130, 134–136, 147–156, 172, 186, 214, 243, 246 (*see also* African slave trade)
Speeches, Motions, and Committee Assignments in, xxvii
Virginia Plan and, xi, xii, xx, 12–13, 48, 50, 56, 63–67, 69–71, 74–75, 77, 79, 83, 89, 91–100, 107, 119, 127–128, 130, 131, 136, 160–161, 164–165, 168, 170–174, 189, 244, 247, 261–263, 266
introduced, xii, xxxi, 45–46, 63–67
Washington-elected president of, 45, 50

Continental Army, 28, 46, 50, 136, 143, 164, 170, 223, 225, 242, 248–249
Corbin, Francis, 64
Country party (RI), 36
Coxe, Tench, 27
Creek Indians, 214
Crèvecoeur, Hector St. Jean de, xv
Crosskey, William, W., 54
Cushing, William, 294–295
Cutler, Manasseh, 46, 58, 80, 118

Dana, Francis, 215
Dane, Nathan, 58
Davie, William R, xxv, 122, 167
Great Compromise and, 108, 117–118
slavery and, 114
Speeches, Motions, and Committee Assignments of, xxviii
Dayton, Jonathan, xxv, xxviii, 51, 63, 68, 79, 103, 146, 171
Declaration of Independence, 3, 7, 17, 46, 48, 49, 71, 109, 133, 240, 241, 247
Delaware, 22, 24, 26, 35, 45, 48, 74, 75, 112–113, 189, 213, 251, 258
delegation to Constitutional Convention of, 49, 71, 76, 83, 84, 90, 92, 98, 115, 117, 140, 155, 162, 172
population of, 70
ratification by, xxxii, 211, 212
Delaware River, 193
Demosthenes, 73
Dickinson, John, xxv, 3, 26, 48, 78, 92, 121, 140, 144, 151–152,

Index 311

172, 176–177, 179–180, 192,
212, 249
biographical sketch of, 239–240
description of, 75
executive branch and, xiii, 162,
170, 174, 180, 184
Great Compromise and, 75–77,
100, 138, 239
illustration of, 163
Speeches, Motions, and Committee
Assignments of, xxviii
Dunlap, John, 137, 188, 273

Edinburgh, University of, 72
Ellis, Joseph, 226
Ellsworth, Oliver, xxv, 62, 72, 90,
100, 102, 104, 121, 130, 131,
135, 140, 142–144, 148,
168–169, 214
description of, 98–99
Great Compromise and, 98–99,
108–109, 116
slavery and, 150
Speeches, Motions, and
Committee Assignments of,
xxvii
Eve, George, 230
Exeter, New Hampshire, 216

"Fabius" essays, 240
Fairfax County Resolves, 245
"Farmer, A," essays, 204
Fayette, Marquis de, xi, 28–29
"Federal Farmer" essays, 206
Federal Hall, 225
Federalist, The, xiv, 208–211, 221,
242, 244
The Federalist 10, 76, 85n19,
209, 210

The Federalist 38, 205
The Federalist 48, 209, 228
The Federalist 51, 208–209, 237,
295–300
illustration of title page of, 210
Federalists, 199–225, 230–231, 272
advantages enjoyed by, 223–224
Antifederalists labeled by,
204–205
ground rules of accepted,
204, 213
newspaper support of, 214, 224
See also *Federalist, The*, *Federalist*
51; Wilson, James,
Statehouse Yard Speech of
Few, William, xxv, xxix, 106, 118,
136
Fife, Scotland, 72
Findley, William, 213
First Federal Elections. See U.S.
Congress, First Federal
Elections for
Fitch, John, 62
Fitzsimons, Thomas, xxv, xxviii
Fleming, William, 4
Florida, 214
foreign slave trade. See African slave
trade
"Fort Wilson," 249
France, 6, 240, 246, 247
Franklin, Benjamin, xxv, 3, 38, 46,
50, 52, 53, 58, 75, 105, 122,
141, 142, 155, 161, 172, 184,
188, 190–191
biographical sketch of, 240–241
calls for prayer, 103
description of, 80–82
Elizabeth Powell anecdote
and, 237

executive branch and, 164,
    167–168, 174
Great Compromise and, 108–111
illustration of, 81
praises delegates, xvii–xviii
ratification and, xxii, 199, 224
rising sun chair anecdote and,
    192, 200
Speeches, Motions, and
    Committee Assignments of,
    xxviii
urges delegates to sign
    constitution, xii, 81,
    191–193, 241, 268–270
Franklin, William Temple, 52
French Alliance, 240
French and Indian War, 248
French Revolution, 226
fugitive slave clause. *See* U.S.
    Constitution, fugitive slave
    clause

Gardoqui, Don Diego de, 25, 243
general welfare clause. *See* U.S.
    Constitution, general welfare
    clause
Genet, Edmond Charles, 86n19, 193
George III, King of Great Britain, 1,
    7, 9, 48, 209, 225, 239
George Mason Memorial, xi, 19
Georgia, 8, 26, 35, 45, 113, 148, 178,
    202, 252, 290, 250
    delegation to Constitutional
        Convention of, 49, 70, 83,
        84, 92, 107, 113–114, 117,
        155, 172
    population of, 70
    ratification by, xxxiii, 214
    slavery and, 150–151
Germantown, Philadelphia, 194

Gerry, Elbridge, xix, xxv, 32, 59, 62,
    70, 71–72, 75, 78, 83, 104,
    130, 136, 138, 142, 143, 148,
    154, 177, 178, 186
biographical sketch of, 241–242
description of, 71–72
executive branch and, 161, 165, 167,
    168, 170, 174, 182–183, 188
Great Compromise and, xiii,
    108–110, 111, 116–117, 120,
    175, 241
illustration of, 175
objections against constitution of,
    175, 190, 241
ratification and, 206, 214
refusal to sign constitution of, xiii,
    154, 175, 191, 241
regulation of state militias and,
    145–146, 175
Speeches, Motions, and Committee
    Assignments of, xxvii
Gettysburg Address, 237
Gillman, Nicholas, xxvi, xxix, 49,
    58, 144
Glasgow University, 72
Gorham, Nathaniel, xxv, xxvii,
    32, 36, 69, 111, 113, 116,
    127–128, 130–131, 136, 139,
    153–154, 171, 173, 191–192
Grand Federal Edifice cartoon, 200
    illustration, 201
Grayson, William, 119, 218
Great Britain, 6, 7, 15, 31, 33, 50, 177,
    185, 209, 240, 243, 246, 290
    Constitution of, 8, 95
    Parliament of, 7, 8, 9, 103, 106,
        140, 144, 209, 247
Great Compromise. *See*
    Constitutional Convention,
    Great Compromise

Great Lakes, 1
Greece, Ancient, 288
Griffin, Cyrus, 4, 64
Gulf Stream, 240
Gunston Hall, 245

Habeas Corpus, 145, 228
Hamilton, Alexander, xix, xxv, 1,
    53, 55, 56, 83, 94, 104, 105,
    111, 185, 227
  Annapolis Convention and,
    26–27, 251–254
  biographical sketch of, 242–243
  Committee of Style and, 186
  convention speech of, xii, 94–98
  description of, 26–27
  executive branch and, 95–96, 174,
    183, 188
  The Federalist and, xiv, 208, 210,
    221–222, 242, 295
  illustration of, 96
  monarchism of, 95–97, 242
  plan of government of, 95–96,
    242, 266–268
  ratification and, xiv, 155, 202, 221
  signs constitution, xii, 191,
    192–193, 242
  Speeches, Motions, and
    Committee Assignments of,
    xxviii
Hancock, John, 32, 215–216,
    294–295
Haring, John, 203
Harvard College, 104, 241, 243
Henderson, Alexander, 16, 18,
    19–20, 21–22
Henry, Patrick, xviii, 3, 4, 35, 37,
    230, 244, 256
  Mount Vernon Conference and,
    16–17

  ratification and, 218–220
Henry, Prince of Prussia, 32
Hessians, 193–194
Hiltzheimer, Jacob, 38
Hopkinson, Francis, 73
Hopkinton, New Hampshire, 218
hotchpot. *See* Constitutional
    Convention, hotchpot at
House, Mary, 38
Houston, William Churchill, xxv,
    xxix, 63
Houstoun, William, xxv, xxviii, 107
Hudson River Valley, 221
Hutson, James, 55

Imperial Presidency, 224
Independence Hall. *See*
    Pennsylvania State House
Indian Queen Tavern, 38, 52
Ingersoll, Jared, xxv, xxix
Ireland, 140

Jackson, William, xiii, 12, 52, 54,
    121, 203
Jay, John, xiv, xviii, 25–26, 80, 208,
    210, 220, 221, 243, 295
Jay Treaty, 247
James I, King of Great Britain, 16
James River, 220
Jefferson, Thomas, xviii, 3, 4, 10,
    53, 57, 85n19, 155, 227,
    229–231, 233, 240, 244
  descriptions by, xvii, 13, 18, 64, 99
Jenifer, Daniel of St. Thomas, xxv,
    xxviii, 16–18, 20, 107,
    137–138
Jensen, Merrill, 37
Johnson, William Samuel, xxv, xvii,
    xxviii, 62, 97, 100, 103–104,
    116, 136, 186–187

Jones, Walter, 24
judicial review, 128, 160, 174, 176–177

Kentucky, 220
Kenyon, Cecelia, 224
King, Rufus, xxv, 32, 49, 58, 59, 63, 68, 74, 82, 105, 106, 108, 111, 113, 115, 116, 130, 186, 215–216
  biographical sketch of, 243
  description of, 147
  executive branch and, 167, 169, 174, 180–181
  slavery and, 146–147, 151–153, 242
  Speeches, Motions, and Committee Assignments of, xxvii
King's College. *See* Columbia University
Klarman, Michael, 91, 123n3
Knox, Henry, 32, 37, 215–216

Langdon, John, xxvi, xxvii, 49, 60, 62, 144, 152
Lansing, John, xxv, 58, 66, 86n19, 90, 94, 97, 116, 186, 221
  description of, 92–93
  Speeches, Motions, and Committee Assignments of, xxviii
Lee, Henry, 218
Lee, Richard Henry, xviii, 203, 218–219
Letters from a Farmer in Pennsylvania, 239
Lincoln, Abraham, 145, 237
Lincoln, Benjamin, 32
Livingston, William, xxv, xxix, 146, 152–153, 221

Lloyd, Gordon, 55, 63
London, 31, 103
Loyalists, 10, 28, 246
Ludlum, David, 59
Lynd, Staughton, 118

McClurg, James, xxvi, xxviii, 58, 136
McHenry, James, xxv, xxviii, 67, 137–139
Madison, James, xxvi, 8, 38–39, 50, 51, 67, 69, 102, 103, 105, 120, 144, 148, 166, 185–186, 189, 242, 256
  Annapolis Convention and, 23–27, 42n49, 244
  Bill of Rights and, xxii, xxxiii, 199, 227–233
  biographical sketch of, 244–245
  Committee on Postponed Parts and, 179, 180
  Confederation Congress and, 4–5
  Constitutional Convention notes of, 24, 45, 52–56, 67, 85–86n19, 102, 190, 244
  council of revision and, 13, 160, 173–177
  description of, 11–12
  executive branch and, 122, 159–162, 164, 167–169, 171, 180, 182–183, 188, 260
  The Federalist and, xiv, 209–210, 221, 244
    The Federalist 10, 76, 85n19, 209
    The Federalist 38, 205
    The Federalist 48, 209, 228
    The Federalist 51, 208–209, 237, 295–300

Index

Great Compromise and, 108–111, 120–122, 137, 168, 171
illustration of, 12
judicial branch and, 172–174, 259
legislative branch and, 259–260
  regulation of commerce and, 153, 259–260
  representation and, 71, 74, 76–77, 98, 103, 105, 112, 115, 139, 258
  veto of state laws and, 1, 13, 55, 75, 78–79, 127–128, 177, 231, 260
letter to George Washington of, 257–260
majority tyranny and, xix, 10–11, 13, 78, 259, 298–300
Mount Vernon Conference and, 16–18, 22, 25, 244
praises delegates, xvii–xviii
quoted, xvii, 6, 14, 18, 24–25, 36–37, 45, 56, 57–58, 70, 72, 74, 77, 80, 92, 97, 102, 103, 110, 111, 113, 116, 122, 141, 142, 146, 152, 153, 155, 165, 169, 175, 178, 183, 185, 187, 207, 279
ratification and, 130, 204, 207, 218–220, 260
Shays's Rebellion and, 33–34
slavery and, 55, 82, 152–155
Speeches, Motions, and Committee Assignments of, xxvii
Virginia General Assembly and, 23–24, 34, 202, 244
Virginia Plan and, xi, 12–13, 46, 56, 63–64, 74–75, 77, 132, 161, 244, 261
Madison's Hand, 54–55, 85n19
Maine, 215, 243

Mann's Tavern, 26
Marblehead, Massachusetts, 241
Marbury vs. Madison, 176
Marshall, John, 176, 218, 241
Martin, Alexander, xxv, xxix, 56
Martin, Luther, xxv, 57, 63, 90, 107–109, 114, 128, 137, 144, 146, 173, 176
  African slave trade and, 149–150, 151–155
  description of, 101
  executive branch and, 169
  ratification and, 217
  Speeches, Motions, and Committee Assignments of, xxviii, 102–103
Maryland, 2, 16, 26, 35–36, 45, 141, 149, 252
  delegation to Constitutional Convention of, 49, 83, 90, 92, 107, 114, 116, 137–139, 162, 164, 172
  Mount Vernon Conference and, 20–22, 24
  population of, 70
  Potomac Company and, 15–16, 20–22
  ratification by, xxxiii, 203, 217
Mason, George, xxvi, 24, 38, 46, 56, 62, 67, 70–71, 75, 100, 103, 113, 140, 142, 143, 145, 148, 256
  African slave trade and, 149–150, 152–154
  Bill of Rights and, 188
  biographical sketch of, 245
  congressional regulation of commerce and, 153–155
  congressional representation and, 73, 76–77

description of, 18
executive branch and, 162, 164,
    170, 174, 175, 178, 182–184
Grand Committee of Eleven and,
    xi, 109–111, 138, 245
illustration of, 19
money bills and, 138–139
Mount Vernon Conference and,
    16–19, 21–22, 245
"Objections to This Constitution
    of Government" of, 245,
    279–281
praises delegates, xvii
ratification and, 130, 218–219,
    245
refuses to sign constitution, xi, 19,
    155, 179, 190, 192, 245, 279
Speeches, Motions, and
    Committee Assignments of,
    xxvii
Massachusetts, 5, 26, 35–36, 45, 76,
    102, 162, 173, 223, 252, 258,
    284
constitution of (1780), 8, 30–31,
    36, 174
delegation to Constitutional
    Convention of, 49, 69, 79,
    83, 84, 89, 92, 111, 115, 117,
    172
population of, 70
ratification by, xxii, xxxiii, 117,
    199, 201, 214–216, 241, 243
recommendatory amendments of,
    292–295
Shays's Rebellion in, 28–33, 72
Massachusetts Centinel, 216
Mercer, John Francis, xxv, xxviii, 63,
    137–138, 143–144, 176
Michigan, 232

Middle Temple, 134, 239
Mifflin, Thomas, xxv, xxix, 51
Minot, George Richards, 28, 295
Mississippi River, 1, 7, 25–26,
    125n71, 220
Missouri, 243
Monongahela, Battle of, 248
Monroe, James, 119, 218, 224, 230
Montesquieu, Baron de, 2, 206, 287
Montpelier, 244
Moravians, 136
Morris, Gouverneur, xxv, 37, 69–70,
    105–106, 110–111, 113, 122,
    128, 130, 131, 136–139,
    143–146, 177, 178, 179, 190
biographical sketch of, 245–246
cover letter to confederation
    congress of, 141, 271–272
description of, 46–48
drafts final version of constitution,
    xiii, 141, 160, 186–187, 246
executive branch and, 165–169,
    171–172, 175, 180–181, 183,
    188, 246
illustration of, 141
slavery and, xiii, 141, 147, 151,
    155, 246
Speeches, Motions, and
    Committee Assignments of,
    xxvii, 53
voting requirements for congress
    and, 140–142
Morris, Mary, 60, 137
Morris, Robert, xxv, xxix, 38–39, 48,
    49–50, 60, 136, 246
Morrisania estate, 246
Mount Vernon, xi, 14–15, 17, 20,
    25, 33, 39, 60, 219, 248
Compact, 21–25

Conference, xi, xx, xxxi, 1, 16–25, 41n41, 245
   illustration of, 17

Navigation Acts, 134
Nevis, 242
New England, 49, 72, 100, 119, 131, 154, 216, 223, 247
New Hampshire, 7, 26, 33, 35, 83, 105, 113, 144, 252, 290
   delegation to Constitutional Convention of, 49
   population of, 70
   ratification by, xxxiii, 216, 221
New Jersey, 7, 26–27, 35, 45, 79, 93, 148, 251–252
   delegation to Constitutional Convention of, 49, 70, 74, 75, 77, 83, 84, 90, 92, 98, 115, 117, 152, 155, 172, 193
   population of, 70
   ratification by, xxxiii, 213–214
New Jersey Plan. *See* Constitutional Convention, New Jersey Plan and
New York, xi, xiv, 27, 29, 35, 45, 93, 99, 162, 178, 213, 242, 243, 251, 257, 281, 284, 295
   constitution of (1777), 173, 245
   delegation to Constitutional Convention of, 49, 71, 74, 83, 84, 92, 96, 98, 117
   ratification by, xiv, xxii, xxxiii, 155, 199, 208, 220–223, 242
   illustration of, 221
New York, 5, 90, 213–214, 221, 225
New York Journal, 292
New York Packet, 300
Newport, Rhode Island, 216

Nicholas, George, 218
North, xi, 19, 83, 110, 114, 118–119, 151–154, 156, 170, 206, 258, 280
North Carolina, 10, 26, 35, 45, 151, 189, 252
   delegation to Constitutional Convention of, 69, 83, 84, 89, 92, 114, 116, 138
   population of, 69, 70
   ratification by, xxxiii, 199, 220, 221, 222–223
Northwest Ordinance, xxxii, 38, 119–120, 125n71, 154, 243
Northwest Territory, 1, 7, 243
Notes of Debates in the Federal Convention of 1787, 24, 45, 52–56, 67, 85–86n19, 102, 190, 244

"Objections to This Constitution of Government," 219, 279–281
Observations on the Plan of Government Submitted to the Federal Convention, 68
Ohio Company, 119
Ohio River, 15, 22, 120, 275
Old Republican, 72
Olive Branch Petition, 239
Orange, Virginia, 230
Otto, Louis-Guillaume, 135
Oxford University, 104, 240

Paca, William, 217
Paterson, William, xxv, 59, 67, 79, 93, 108, 112–113, 120, 121, 130
   description of, 90
   illustration of, 91

New Jersey Plan and, xii, xxxii, 89–91, 264
Speeches, Motions, and Committee Assignments of, xxviii
Patriot, The, 10
Paris, 240
Peale, Charles Willson, xii, 60–61
Pendleton, Edmund, 56, 218
Pennsylvania, 5, 22, 24, 26, 36, 45, 102, 148, 178, 184, 202, 239, 251, 276, 278
assembly of, 5, 46, 212
constitution of (1776), 7–8, 73, 249
delegation to Constitutional Convention of, 38–39, 46–50, 69, 79, 82, 83, 84, 92, 111, 114–115, 117, 139, 152, 164, 166
population of, 70
ratification by, xii, xxxiii, 47, 211, 212–214, 216, 224
Pennsylvania Gazette, 240
Pennsylvania Herald, 224
Pennsylvania Journal, 57
Pennsylvania Packet, 137, 188, 278
Pennsylvania Society for the Abolition of Slavery, 155
Pennsylvania State House (Independence Hall), xii, 5, 46, 47, 51, 59, 200, 212–213, 273
Perkins, Enoch, 104
Petersham, Battle of, 32
Philadelphia, Pennsylvania, 38, 59, 61–62, 137, 213, 227, 240, 246, 249, 253–257
Philadelphia City Light Horse, 193

Pierce, William, xxv, 48, 51–52, 57–59, 77, 106, 107, 118, 136, 206
descriptions by, 12, 27, 47, 64–66, 69, 72, 73, 75, 80, 82, 90, 93, 99, 102–103, 107, 108, 147, 179
Speeches, Motions, and Committee Assignments of, xxviii
Pinckney, Charles, xxvi, 70, 74–75, 77–79, 103, 108, 116, 128, 137, 144–145, 146, 153, 176, 190
executive branch and, 162, 166, 167, 171, 174, 182, 184, 188
federal officeholding requirements and, 142–143
plan of government of, 67–69, 78, 82–83, 131, 133
slavery and, 150, 151, 152
Speeches, Motions, and Committee Assignments of, xxvii
Pine, Robert Edge, 60
Pinkney, Charles Cotesworth, xxvi, 71, 76–77, 108, 136, 153, 241
slavery and, 131, 135, 149–152, 154
Speeches, Motions, and Committee Assignments of, xxviii, 55
Pittsburgh, Philadelphia, 212
Pocomoke River, 16, 21
Poor Richard's Almanac, 240
Popes' Creek Plantation, 248
Potomac River, 17, 20, 21, 22, 245, 248
Great Falls of, 15
Potomac Company and, 15–16, 20
Powell, Elizabeth, 61, 136, 237
Powell, Samuel, 61, 87n35, 237
Presbyterian Church, 38

Index

Princeton, Battle of, 249
Princeton, New Jersey, 5, 90
Princeton University (The College of New Jersey), 90, 99, 102, 106, 179, 244
Providence, Rhode Island, 217

Quasi War, 242

Randolph, Edmund, xxvi, 24, 52, 58–59, 70, 94, 135, 153, 178, 256
  biographical sketch of, 246–247
  calls for second constitutional convention, 65, 179, 189, 191, 247
  Committee of Detail and, 127, 134, 247
  description of, 64
  executive branch and, 161–162, 165, 167, 182–183
  Great Compromise and, 111, 120, 122
  illustration of, 65
  money bills and, 138
  Mount Vernon Conference and, 16–18
  ratification and, 204, 219, 247
  refuses to sign constitution, xii, 65, 154, 247
  Speeches, Motions, and Committee Assignments of, xxvii, 53
  Virginia Plan and, xii, xxxi, 45, 63–67, 261
  ratification. *See* U.S. Constitution, ratification of
Read, George, xxv, xxviii, 48–49, 71, 193, 212, 240
Redman, John, 60

regulators, 31
Republican Party, 244
Revolutionary War, 38, 50, 72, 92, 104, 226
Rhode Island, 3, 6, 7, 10, 26, 58, 83, 178, 189, 252, 258, 299
  absence from Constitutional Convention of, 2, 35–36, 49, 105, 217
  population of, 70
  ratification by, xxxiii, 199, 216–217, 220–221, 223
Richards, Leonard L., 28
rising-sun chair, 50, 192–193, 200
Risjord, Norman, 16
Rome, Ancient, 288
Ross, David, 24
Rush, Benjamin, 72, 73, 80, 212
Rutledge, John, xxvi, 50, 60, 74–75, 108, 111, 120, 129, 139, 142, 145, 153, 161–162, 172
  Committee of Detail and, 127, 134–137
  executive branch and, 171
  illustration of, 135
  slavery and, 150, 185
  Speeches, Motions, and Committee Assignments of, xxvii

St. Andrews University, 72, 240
School for Scandal, The, 136
Schoonmaker, Cornelius, 223
Schuyler, Elizabeth, 242
Schuyler, Philip, 92, 242
Scotland, 72, 240, 249
Scottish Common Sense Philosophy, xix, 72
Sedition Act, 244
Seven Year's War, 248
Shallus, Jacob, 190

Shays, Daniel, xi, 28–32
Shays's Rebellion, xi, xix, xx,
    2, 28–34, 36, 72,
    214–215, 243
Shepard, William, 31
Sheridan, Richard, 136
Sherman, Roger, xxv, 71–72, 76, 77,
    103, 129, 136, 144, 148, 173,
    177, 179, 214
  Bill of Rights and, 188,
    231–232
  biographical sketch of, 247–248
  description of, 99–100
  executive branch and, 161–165,
    171, 182–183, 188
  Great Compromise and, xiii,
    99–101, 108, 110, 111,
    115–116, 248
  illustration of, 101
  slavery and, 151, 153
  Speeches, Motions, and
    Committee Assignments of,
    xxvii
Shippen, William, 52, 59
slave trade. See African slave trade
slavery. See Constitutional
    Convention, slavery and
Smilie, John, 213
Smith, Melancton, xiv, 203–205,
    208, 210, 221–222, 281
Smith, Meriwether, 4, 24
South, xi, 19, 26, 45, 69, 83, 92, 109,
    110, 114, 117–119, 125n71,
    127, 130, 134, 136, 147,
    149–154, 156, 170, 184, 206,
    258, 280
South Carolina, 7, 26, 35, 45, 148,
    252, 250
  delegation to Constitutional
    Convention of, 49, 69–70, 77,
    82, 83, 84, 92, 113–114, 116,
    134, 139, 153–155, 214, 217
  population of, 69, 70
  ratification by, xxxiii, 217–218
  slavery and, 150–151
Spaight, Richard Dobbs, xxv, xxviii,
    57, 62–63, 117
Spain, 125n71, 6, 7, 15, 26, 214,
    220, 243
Springfield, Massachusetts, 31
Springsbury, 60
Stamp Act, 247
State House Yard Speech. See
    Wilson, James, Statehouse
    Yard Speech of
Stewart, David, 107, 109
Stiles, Ezra, xvii
Stone, Thomas, 16, 17, 20
Strong, Caleb, xxv, xxviii, 63,
    116–117, 139, 176

Talleyrand, Marquis de, 242
Taney, Roger B., 101
Tennessee, 118
Thomson, Charles, 72, 273
Three-Fifths Compromise. See
    Constitutional Convention,
    Three-Fifths Compromise
Trenton, Battle of, 193, 249
Trenton, New Jersey, 137
Tucker, St. George, 24, 57
Tyler, John, 23

United States, 54, 192, 209
  Confederation period in, 27–28,
    32, 37, 56, 65–66, 75, 89, 91,
    94, 105, 107, 115, 116, 133,
    178, 201, 213, 225, 253, 255,
    257, 262 (see also Articles of
    Confederation)

population of, 70
U.S. Confederation Congress, xx,
    xxxii, xxxiii, 1, 6, 10–11,
    22, 23, 25, 37, 57, 63, 66,
    74, 82–83, 89–91, 94, 99,
    102, 104, 106, 116, 117, 119,
    125n71, 134, 153–154, 192,
    204, 206, 212, 221, 224, 251,
    254, 255–258, 262–265, 270,
    271–272, 280–281
  ratification and, 179, 203
  resolution endorsing
      Constitutional Convention,
      xxxi, 35–36, 201, 256–257
  structure of, 3–5
  transmits constitution to states,
      272–273
U.S. Congress, xxii, 192
  Bill of Rights and, xxxiii,
      227–233
  First Federal Congress, 199, 220,
      223, 225–227
  First Federal Elections for, xxxiii,
      220–221
  U.S. House of Representatives,
      230, 232, 277, 279–280
  U.S. Senate, 230, 232, 276–277,
      279–280
U.S. Constitution, 23, 68, 69, 120,
    237
  amendments to, 185, 227
    Bill of Rights, xxi, xxii, xxxiii,
        199, 227–233
    Equal Rights Amendment, 232
    First, 232
    Ninth, 231
    Second, 232
    Tenth, 231
    Twenty-Second, 226
    Twenty-Seventh, 233

  clauses
    fugitive slave, xxxii, 120, 154,
        217
    general welfare, 179, 207, 228,
        284
    necessary and proper, 127, 134,
        145, 179, 190, 207, 228, 283,
        286
    supremacy, 128, 133, 187, 207,
        228, 283, 286
    Three-Fifths (see Constitutional
        Convention, Three-Fifths
        Compromise)
  ratification of, xxi–xxii, 130–132,
      178–179, 186–187
    amendments and, 205,
        215–216, 218, 221, 223
    Connecticut and, xxxiii, 211,
        214, 224, 248
    Delaware and, xxxii, 211–212
    Georgia and, xxxiii, 211, 214
    Maryland and, xxxiii, 211, 217
    Massachusetts and, xxii, xxxiii,
        211, 214–216
    Massachusetts recommendatory
        amendments and, 292–295
    New Hampshire and, xxxiii,
        211, 216, 221
    New Jersey and, xxxiii, 211
    New York and, xiv, xxii, xxxiii,
        211, 221–223
    newspapers and, 214, 224
    North Carolina and, xxxiii,
        211, 220–221, 223
    Pennsylvania and, xxxiii,
        211–213, 224, 250
    Rhode Island and, xxxiii, 211,
        216–217, 220, 221, 223
    South Carolina and, xxxiii,
        211, 217–218

state votes on, 211
Virginia and, xxxiii, 211, 218–221
U.S. Continental Congress, 2, 3, 5, 9, 10, 57, 134
U.S. Supreme Court, 23, 136, 206–207, 211, 229, 232

Valley Forge, Pennsylvania, 136
Van Cleve, George William, 125n71
Vaughn, Samuel, 41n41
Vermont, xi, 29, 32, 178
"Vices of the Political System of the U.S.," 23, 85n19
Virginia, 2, 6, 26, 32, 38, 102, 112–113, 149, 162, 206, 227, 246, 251, 258
  constitution of (1776), 7, 8, 9, 16, 245
  delegation to Constitutional Convention of, 39, 46, 48, 49, 51, 62, 64, 66, 69, 79, 83, 84, 92, 111, 114, 117, 139, 152
  General Assembly of, 4, 10–11, 22, 23, 34, 42n49, 219, 254–256
  House of Burgesses of, 245
  Mount Vernon Conference and, 20–22, 25
  population of, 70
  Potomac Company and, 15–16, 20–22
  ratification by, xxxiii, 199, 218–222, 247
  Resolutions of 1798 of, 244
Virginia Plan. *See* Constitutional Convention, Virginia Plan and
virtue, 208–209

Wadsworth, Jeremiah, 99
Walnut Street Prison, 80
Washington, D.C., 237
Washington, George, xix, xxvi, 1, 3, 4, 13–15, 27, 37, 38–39, 46, 47, 52, 54, 67, 97, 111, 128, 136, 143, 146, 170, 192, 206, 242, 246, 256
  biographical sketch of, 248–249
  Constitutional Convention president, xii, xxxi, 45, 50, 53, 60, 61, 69, 103, 108, 187, 248
  decision to attend Constitutional Convention of, 34–35
  description of, 13–14, 18
  design of presidency and, xii, 51, 61, 160–161, 185
  diary of, 20, 57, 193
  illustration of, 61
  letter from Madison to, 257–260
  Mount Vernon and, 17–20
  Mount Vernon Conference and, xi, 16–22, 24–25, 41n41
  Potomac Company and, 15
  presidential election of, 61
  presidency of, xxxiii, 192, 223, 225–226, 230, 233, 242, 247, 248, 250
  ratification and, xxii, 199, 200, 205, 207, 215, 218–221, 225
  Shays's Rebellion and, 33–34
  silence during Constitutional Convention of, 50–51, 61
  social activities of, 60–62, 136–137, 193
  Speeches, Motions, and Committee Assignments of, xxviii
  two-term tradition and, 226

Washington, Martha Dandridge
    Custis, 38, 248
Watson, Elkanah, 80
Webster, Noah, 23, 42n49
West, 6, 7, 15, 20
West Indies, 5
Wharton vs. Wise, 23
Whiskey Rebellion, 226
Whitehill, Robert, 213
William and Mary, College of, 246
Williamsburg, Virginia, 246
Williamson, Hugh, xxv, xxvii, 63,
    100, 117–119, 138–139, 144,
    148, 150, 170, 183, 188
Wilson, James, 78, 79, 80, 82–83,
    102, 105, 111, 113–115, 128,
    137, 141, 142–143, 145, 148,
    151–152, 153, 163–164, 186,
    191, 246, 268–269
  biographical sketch of, 249–250
  Committee of Detail and, xiii, 68,
    127, 129, 131, 133–134, 250
  council of revision and, 160, 176
  description of, 72–73
  dual citizenship and, 73, 93–94,
    100–101, 249
  executive branch and, 122,
    159–167, 184
  election of, 169, 171,
    181–182
  unitary executive and, 161
  Great Compromise and, 108–109,
    120, 138, 171
  illustration of, 129
  judicial branch and, 172–175
  money bills and, 139
  popular sovereignty and, xiii, xix,
    73, 76–78, 129, 164, 165,
    249
  Speeches, Motions, and
    Committee Assignments of,
    xxvii
  State House Yard Speech of,
    212–213, 250, 273–278
Wolcott, Erastus, 99
Wythe, George, xxvi, xxviii, 3, 4,
    55, 63, 218, 256

XYZ Affair, 241

Yale College, 99, 103, 107
Yates, Robert, xxv, xxix, 54, 58, 66,
    86n19, 90, 94, 97, 102,
    108–109, 116, 186, 193, 203,
    221
Yorktown, Virginia, 242, 249

About the Author

Stuart Leibiger, PhD, is professor of history at La Salle University. He is author of *Founding Friendship: George Washington, James Madison, and the Creation of the American Republic*, and editor of *A Companion to James Madison and James Monroe*. In 2015, he won the George Washington Memorial Award, a lifetime achievement award for the study of George Washington given annually by the George Washington Masonic Memorial Association in Alexandria, Virginia. In 2016, he received La Salle University's Lindback Distinguished Teaching Award.

www.ingramcontent.com/pod-product-compliance
Lightning Source LLC
Chambersburg PA
CBHW070228230426
43664CB00014B/2238